The Cambridge Companion to
Comparative Law

We can only claim to understand another legal system when we know the cultural and social context that surrounds the positive law in which lawyers are trained. To avoid ethnocentricity and superficiality, we must go beyond judicial decisions, doctrinal writings, and the black-letter law of codes and statutes, and probe the 'deeper structures' where law meets cultural, political and socio-economic factors. It is only when we acquire such awareness and knowledge of the critical factors affecting both the backgrounds and implications of rules that it becomes possible to control the present and possibly future developments in the world's legal institutions. This collection of essays aims to provide the reader with a fundamental understanding of the dynamic relationship between the law and its cultural, political, and socio-economic context.

Mauro Bussani is Professor of Comparative Law at the University of Trieste and Scientific Director of the International Association of Legal Sciences (IALS-Unesco). He is co-editor of a Cambridge University Press series, and a member of numerous international scientific institutions. He has been Visiting Professor in Brazil, France, Hungary, China, Portugal, Serbia, Switzerland, the United Kingdom, and the United States. His principal publications include twenty-one books (of five of which he was the editor) and more than one hundred essays, in Italian, English, French, Spanish, Portuguese and Chinese.

Ugo Mattei is Professor of Civil Law at the University of Turin, Alfred and Hanna Fromm Distinguished Professor of International and Comparative Law at University of California Hastings College of the Law, and Academic Co-ordinator of the International University College of Turin. He is co-editor of a Cambridge University Press series and of *Global Jurist*. He holds positions on the scientific council of many international institutions and law reviews. His work is highly interdisciplinary and has been published and translated widely in books and journals.

Cambridge Companions to Law

Cambridge Companions to Law offers thought-provoking introductions to different legal disciplines, invaluable to both the student and the scholar. Edited by world-leading academics, each offers a collection of essays which both map out the subject and allow the reader to delve deeper. Critical and enlightening, the *Companions* library represents legal scholarship at its best.

The Cambridge Companion to European Private Law
Edited by Christian Twigg-Flesner

The Cambridge Companion to International Law
Edited by James Crawford and Martti Koskenniemi

The Cambridge Companion to Comparative Law
Edited by Mauro Bussani and Ugo Mattei

The Cambridge Companion to
Comparative Law

Edited By

Mauro Bussani

and

Ugo Mattei

CAMBRIDGE UNIVERSITY PRESS
Cambridge, New York, Melbourne, Madrid, Cape Town,
Singapore, São Paulo, Delhi, Mexico City

Cambridge University Press
The Edinburgh Building, Cambridge CB2 8RU, UK

Published in the United States of America by Cambridge University Press, New York

www.cambridge.org
Information on this title: www.cambridge.org/9780521895705

© Cambridge University Press 2012

First published 2012

Printed and bound in the United Kingdom by the MPG Books Group

A catalogue record for this publication is available from the British Library

Library of Congress Cataloguing in Publication data
The Cambridge companion to comparative law / edited by Mauro Bussani and Ugo Mattei.
    p. cm.
Includes index.
ISBN 978-0-521-89570-5
1. Comparative law. 2. Legal polycentricity. 3. Civil law. I. Bussani,
Mauro. II. Mattei, Ugo. III. Title: Companion to comparative law.
K559.C36   2012
340′.2–dc23   2012013419

ISBN 978-0-521-89570-5 Hardback
ISBN 978-0-521-72005-2 Paperback

Contents

Contributors

Khaled Abou El Fadl is the Omar and Azmeralda Alfi Distinguished Professor in Islamic Law at the UCLA School of Law and Chair of the Islamic Studies Interdepartmental Program at UCLA. His books include *The Great Theft, Rebellion and Violence in Islamic Law, Speaking in God's Name: Islamic Law, Authority and Women*, and *The Search for Beauty in Islam: A Conference of the Books*.

George A. Bermann is Jean Monnet Professor of European Union Law and Walter Gellhorn Professor of Law at the Columbia University School of Law and Director of the European Legal Studies Center, professeur affilié of the Ecole de Droit de Sciences Po, faculty member of the Collège d'Europe (Bruges), and current president of the International Academy of Comparative Law.

Francesca Bignami is Professor of Law at the George Washington University. She has published widely in the field of comparative administrative law, and is currently working on a monograph on fundamental rights and policy rationality in Europe and the United States.

J. David Bleich is a professor of Talmud and Director of the Postgraduate Institute for Jurisprudence and Family Law at the Rabbi Isaac Elchanan Theological Seminary, Professor of Law at the Benjamin N. Cardozo School of Law, and Herbert and Florence Tenzer Professor of Jewish Law and Ethics at Yeshiva University.

Mauro Bussani is Professor of Comparative Law at the University of Trieste and Scientific Director of the International Association of Legal Sciences (IALS-Unesco). He is co-editor of a Cambridge University Press series, and a member of numerous international scientific institutions. His principal publications include twenty-one books (of five of which he was the editor) and more than one hundred essays, in Italian, English, French, Spanish, Portuguese and Chinese.

Oscar G. Chase is the Russell D. Niles Professor of Law at the New York University School of Law, Co-Director of the Institute of Judicial Administration, and vice-president of the International Association of Procedural Law. His books include *Law, Culture, and Ritual: Disputing*

Processes in Cross-Cultural Context, Civil Litigation in New York, and *Common Law, Civil Law and the Future of Categories* (editor with Janet Walker).

Günter Frankenberg is Professor of Public Law, Philosophy of Law and Comparative Law at the Goethe University in Frankfurt. He has participated as legal consultant in law- and constitution-making projects in central and eastern European countries. His publications include *Autorität und Integration. Zur Grammatik von Recht und Verfassung* and *Staatstechnik: Perspektiven auf Rechtsstaat und Ausnahmezustand.*

Nuno Garoupa is Professor of Law, the H. Ross and Helen Workman Research Scholar and Co-Director of the Illinois Program on Law, Behavior & Social Science at the University of Illinois College of Law. He was awarded the Spanish Julian Marias Research Prize 2010 in social sciences and humanities.

Tom Ginsburg is Leo Spitz Professor of International Law at the University of Chicago, where he also holds an appointment in the Political Science Department. He holds BA, JD and Ph.D. degrees from University of California Berkeley.

Elisabetta Grande is Professor of Comparative Law at the Università del Piemonte Orientale. She is a member of the International Academy of Comparative Law. She has published extensively in Italian, English, and French on comparative criminal law, comparative criminal procedure, African law, and legal anthropology.

Arthur Jacobson is Max Freund Professor of Litigation and Advocacy at the Benjamin N. Cardozo School of Law, Yeshiva University. He is writing, with Professor J. David Bleich, a book on contemporary issues in Jewish law.

Duncan Kennedy is Carter Professor of General Jurisprudence at Harvard Law School, where since 1971 he has taught private law theory, housing law and policy, and globalization of law. He is the author of, among other pieces, *Legal Education and the Reproduction of Hierarchy* and *A Critique of Adjudication: fin de siècle.*

Diego López-Medina is Professor of Law at the Universidad de los Andes in Bogotá. He has written extensively on issues of comparative law, constitutional law, and legal theory. He has served as judge ad hoc for the Constitutional Court of Colombia and the Inter-American Court of Human Rights.

Ugo Mattei is Professor of Civil Law at the University of Turin, Alfred and Hanna Fromm Distinguished Professor of International and Comparative Law at University of California Hastings College of the Law, and Academic

Co-ordinator of the International University College of Turin. His work is highly interdisciplinary and has been published widely in books and journals.

Vernon Valentine Palmer is Thomas Pickles Professor of Law and Co-director of the Eason Weinmann Center for Comparative Law at Tulane University, and president of the World Society of Mixed Jurisdiction Jurists. His books include *Mixed Jurisdictions Worldwide: The Third Legal Family* and *Pure Economic Loss* (with Mauro Bussani).

Barbara Pozzo is Professor of Comparative Law, University of Insubria (Como), Co-ordinator of the Ph.D. Programme in Comparative Law, Faculty of Law, University of Milan, and a Member of the International Academy of Comparative Law. She is editor of the series *Le lingue del diritto* (Milan: Giuffrè).

Mathias Reimann is Hessel E. Yntema Professor of Law at the University of Michigan, and a Titular Member of the International Academy of Comparative Law. He is editor-in-chief of the *American Journal of Comparative Law*. His main areas of interest include comparative law, conflict of laws, and legal history.

Lawrence Rosen is William N. Cromwell Professor of Anthropology at Princeton University and Adjunct Professor of Law at Columbia University Law School. His books include *Bargaining for Reality*, *Law as Culture*, *The Culture of Islam*, *The Justice of Islam*, *Varieties of Muslim Experience*, and *The Anthropology of Justice*.

Teemu Ruskola is Professor of Law at Emory University. He has been a visiting professor at Cornell and Georgetown universities and at the Woodrow Wilson School at Princeton University. He is the recipient of several fellowships, and author of a forthcoming book entitled *Legal Orientalism: China, the United States, and Modern Law*.

Rodolfo Sacco is Professor Emeritus of Civil Law at the University of Turin, and holds honorary doctorates from the universities of Paris II and Geneva. He is a Member of the Accademia dei Lincei, of the Academia Europaea, and of the International Academy of Comparative Law. His books include *Il contratto*, *Introduzione al diritto comparato*, *Sistemi giuridici comparati*, *Droit africain*, and *Anthropologie juridique*.

Vincenzo Varano is Professor of Comparative Law at the University of Florence, where he served as Dean of the Law Faculty; he is a Member of the Global Faculty at New York University and a Titular Member of the International Academy of Comparative Law. He has written extensively on comparative law, civil procedure, and judicial organization, and is co-author of *Civil Litigation in Comparative Context.*

Franz Werro is Professor of Law at the University of Fribourg and at Georgetown Law, Georgetown University. He teaches and researches in the law of obligations, European private law, and comparative law. He has written extensively on European private law, product liability, and privacy law.

Abbreviations

ADR	Alternative Dispute Resolution
ALI	American Law Institute
BCE	before Common Era
BGB	Bürgerliches Gezetzbuch
BVG	Bundesverfassungsgericht
CARICOM	Caribbean Community
CE	Common Era
CEELI	Central and East European Law Initiative
DCFR	Draft Common Frame of Reference
EC	European Communities
ECHR	European Convention for the Protection of Human Rights and Fundamental Freedoms (European Convention on Human Rights)
ECJ	European Court of Justice
ECR	European Court Report
ECtHR	European Court of Human Rights
EEC	European Economic Community
EMRK	Europaïsche Menschenrechtskonvention
EU	European Union
EUA	Estados Unidos da América
FAO	Food and Agriculture Organization (of UN)
FED. R. CIV. PROC.	Federal Rules of Civil Procedure
ICAO	International Civil Aviation Organization
ICC	International Criminal Court
ILC	International Law Commission
NBC	National Broadcasting Company
NCPC	Nouveau code de procedure civile
NOU	Norges offentlige utredninger
OHADA	Organisation pour l'harmonisation en Afrique du droit des affaires
OJ	*Official Journal of the European Union*

OPEC	Organization of the Petroleum Exporting Countries
StGB	Strafgesetzbuch
TEC	Treaty Establishing the European Community
TFEU	Treaty on the Functioning of the European Union
UN	United Nations
UNCITRAL	United Nations Commission on International Trade Law
UNIDROIT	Institut International pour l'Unification du Droit Privé/International Institute for the Unification of Private Law
USAID	United States Agency for International Development
WIPO	World Intellectual Property Organization
WTO	World Trade Organization

Preface

Diapositives versus movies – the inner dynamics of the law and its comparative account

Comparative law means different things to different people, and each of these meanings can, in and of itself, be scientifically acceptable. Comparative law may be seen as the macro-comparison of the world's legal systems; as the study of legal transplants – that is, of the borrowing of ideas between legal cultures and/or systems; as the most fruitful way of exploring the relationship between law and society, and the underlying perceptions of law; as well as the magnifying glass through which one best observes how state law lives side by side with other (supranational and domestic) sources of law and, thereby, how relative the notion of state power (as spread by mainstream political analysis) can be. This *Companion* goes through these and other possible meanings of comparative law, trying to show how the diverse working methods entailed by each of them can all be useful tools for the understanding of legal phenomena, as long as they stay close to what the law is and to how the law lives in the different settings – regardless of what one might like (and regardless of what any kind of personal and cultural bias may expect) the law to be.

This very approach also helps one realize how our discipline should, and this *Companion* does, take up the challenge launched by the fast evolving fields of international law and 'global' law. The latter areas are crowded – with some prominent exceptions – with experts whose cultural toolkits make the analysis focus largely on positive, or would-be positive (as is the case for most soft-law initiatives), legal rules. Comparative law, by contrast, looks at the law taking into consideration all the possible interactions between the primary sources, be they official or unofficial, dictating the rules and the activities necessary to apply the rules. Therefore, for any comparatist, there is no serious chance of leaving aside any unofficial factor, including those of a geopolitical nature, able to affect the convictions and the legal culture of the rule-setters, the decision-makers, and the law-users.

Nowadays, much literature is produced by scholars who take a quick look at non-domestic legal systems, and thereby present their studies as comparative, while their analysis remains embedded in the positive law paradigm. This scholarship – it is a point the present editors want to emphasize – betrays both the cognitive and the critical vocations of our discipline.

Starting with the latter vocation, it is very hard to believe that a field of study can be of any value, not to mention of any use, when its working method simply aims to pile up notions and details that are available to any law school student provided with a decent access to social sciences databases. Further, one should be aware that this method makes the legal scholar look like someone who can extend at will the scope of her research, being a neutral investigator for whom the crucial questions invariably come out of the data she finds and never vice versa. As is well known, this is often the case in comparative law scholarship too. But this does not come for free. In reality, such a neutrality claim serves to cover up a hidden agenda and/or to make the 'neutral' scholar plainly side with the mainstream narrative affecting a given area of the law.

In this *Companion* the reader finds some contributions that directly point to this risk. To begin with, Duncan Kennedy's chapter (Ch. 2) sets out with candour what the overall critical function of our discipline could be, and analyses the covert ideology underpinning the historically dominant rhetoric of the Western jurist. The self-congratulatory tone of most Western constitutional law scholarship (even when self-portrayed as critical), and its often parochial co-ordinates are challenged by the insightful analysis of Günter Frankenberg (Ch. 8). In the same vein, a sort of counter-test is offered by the brilliant contribution of Nuno Garoupa and Tom Ginsburg (Ch. 3) on comparative law and economics. The reader can realize therein how even the most advanced scholarship in this field may choose to keep itself away from the inextricable connection of comparative law with history and society. But the intertwining between history, law, and economics are worth a further remark.

While the need for historical awareness has not been seriously challenged by anyone in the field of comparative law for quite a long time, in the last decades many economics departments have churned out a large amount of literature using stylized comparative data (we might say comparative caricatures) from a very large number of countries (almost one hundred in certain papers). The most famous of these studies, dubbed 'legal origins', have been sponsored by the World Bank and their uncritical goal was to prove, after having drawn a few regressions, the superiority of Western 'developed' legal systems, mostly belonging to the common law tradition, in producing 'market-friendly environments'. One should perhaps not devote too much attention to these ideological fabrications, if it were not that this kind of study has been quite influential in advising on legal reforms in many countries, and has attracted a degree of attention in the international policy-making community unprecedented for anything claiming to be a comparative law study. While the scholarly credibility of these analyses has been easily challenged and undermined, their policy impact seems to have resisted even the crisis of 2008 – to nobody's surprise, as the still dominant rhetoric is pushing for global and national reforms to be nothing but market-friendly and financial-markets-prone. This phenomenon, however, does nothing but harm to the reputation of such an old and very serious domain of research as comparative law. Across the broad spectrum of social sciences, comparison is one of the few historically tested scientific instruments for developing reliable theories, and in our discipline no one would have dared (perhaps since Wigmore's *Panorama*) to venture a comparison of so many legal systems in so little space knowing so little about any one of them. The very fact that studies of this kind were able, in some prestigious quarters, to claim representation of our field, shows a serious shortcoming in the way in which the comparative law community is able to communicate beyond its professional members.[1] This is one of the shortcomings that the present *Companion* tries to address.

Outside the relatively small number of insiders, there is indeed a sense that comparison is not a professional endeavour per se but just a method or an 'approach' that, no matter how superficially, any legal scholar can introduce as a footnote to her work. Years ago, Mathias Reimann lamented that the comparative law scholarly community had been unable to agree on a canon, and that this lack of a standard, and of a minimum core of agreement on what is the subject matter of comparative law, has produced the sense that an academically acceptable comparison can be performed by anybody, sometimes not even a lawyer, just because, one might say, 'it is better than nothing'.[2]

---

[1] A noteworthy exception may be the passionate lecture, 'Civil and Religious Law in England: A Religious Perspective', given by the archbishop of Canterbury, Dr Rowan Williams, at the Royal Courts of Justice on 7 February 2008, in which, among many other insightful remarks, the archbishop stressed that 'if the reality of society is plural ... this means that we have to think a little harder about the role and rule of law in a plural society of overlapping identities'. The whole text is available at archbishopofcanterbury.org.

[2] M. Reimann, 'The Progress and Failure of Comparative Law in the Second Half of the Twentieth Century', (2002) 50 *American Journal of Comparative Law* 671, 689.

This 'better than nothing' attitude betrays the above-mentioned cognitive vocation of our discipline. This orientation is scientifically noxious and culturally naive, if not dangerous, and it may be all the more so when mixed with the usual degree of arrogance that is typical of leading academic environments. Is it 'better than nothing' that some highly intelligent and well-recognized law professors, who know nothing of the history and social traditions of a given country, might dare to spend time in an academic conference preaching on what that country 'should have done' in order to be more successful in its transition towards capitalism? Is the current dismissive or condescending attitude of many Western constitutional law experts towards the Ecuadorian or Bolivian constitutions that, with an innovation of high theoretical and political significance, have endowed Mother Nature with inalienable rights 'better than nothing'? Is the widespread inclination of many European private law scholars (as pointed out by Franz Werro, in Ch. 6) to venture into harmonization debates without any serious analytical background other than a black-letter rules comparison of three or four 'paradigmatic' legal systems 'better than nothing'? Unfortunately, as Diego López-Medina points out in Chapter 16, superficial analyses only feed stereotypes. In public debates, however, these stereotypes become powerful drivers of meaning that, while useful to some, neglect the reality to which they should apply. This is one of the reasons why the 'better than nothing' scholarship had better pay due respect to the concluding canon of Wittgenstein's *Tractatus Logico-Philosophicus*.

To be sure, we cannot expect each and every scholar to be a fully fledged comparatist in order to venture into some comparison, given the language and cultural barriers that make good comparative law a highly demanding endeavour. However, the least demand that comparative law should be able to make is to be treated by mainstream positivistic scholars like any other discipline endowed with its own canons (perhaps reaching just one canon is not even advisable), its own subject matter, and its own recurrent debates, and that anyone embarking on using it should at least familiarize herself with this basic landscape.

No one should pretend to be a legal anthropologist without having patiently gone through the 'homework' necessary to become one (which includes perhaps a long period of fieldwork), or to be a legal economist without having become familiar with basic micro-economics and with the body of literature that since the 1960s has been produced in the shadow of

Ronald Coase, Guido Calabresi, or Richard Posner. Similarly, no one should claim to be a comparatist without having gone through the painstaking effort of actual in-depth comparison (which includes long periods of exposure to different legal settings) and having spent or spending most of his or her intellectual energy asking questions as to how to do it better, hopefully continuing to dig in the mine of data and problems that have to be understood in order to make relevant and significant comparative statements about the law of two or more systems. The lack of such a scientific approach straightforwardly entails the risk of amateurism (and of being academically marginalized as an amateur) in any domain, from sociology to anthropology to economics. By contrast, no such risks are perceived when a lawyer (or even a non-lawyer!) ventures to write about comparative law. Blatant ignorance of the tradition of our discipline seems completely accepted. To give but one example, the issue of exporting law has been discussed by comparative law scholars for more than forty years. Yet no traces of this debate, and of the critical knowledge it has produced, can be found in the very abundant scholarship focused on the comparative efficiency of legal systems, as currently benchmarked by the above-mentioned 'legal origins' literature, or in the equally lavish literature devoted to the exportation of democracy (see, instead, Ch. 18 of this *Companion*).

Like any other *Companion*, this one had to square size constraints with the need for as comprehensive a survey as possible. We have attempted a selection of fundamental comparative law contributions according to two criteria.

To begin with, we consider this *Companion* to be a 'third generation' contribution. We do not present entries such as 'legal transplants', or on the Western classical 'common law/civil law' divide, simply because these are lenses through which one is currently bound to look at any legal experience, (i) 'legal transplants' being a dimension that is ineradicable anywhere from the dynamism of the law; and (ii) the Western 'divide' being the usual yardstick (too often the only one) for any comparative debate. By contrast, we have included contributions by some of the scholars best equipped to show that in-depth comparative knowledge of how the Western legal traditions work and the legal transplants are discussed, can actually improve our understanding of a variety of subject matters. Beyond Chapter 18, authored by one of the present editors, an example would be the criminal justice chapter (Ch. 9), which we have assigned to a scholar (Elisabetta Grande) whose work on legal transplants in this domain has been seminal and much imitated. In the same vein, the chapter on the East Asian legal tradition (Ch. 12) is authored by Teemu Ruskola, a scholar whose work on 'legal orientalism' is becoming a landmark of our discipline, while the chapter on comparative private law (Ch. 6) is written by a *juriste-savant*, Franz Werro, whose analysis is evidence of the fertility of the 'common core' approach,[3] within and beyond the boundaries of the Euro-academic private law debate.

The second criterion has been that of seeking scholars capable of building on the foundational toolkits of comparative law either because they are among those whose names are closely related to a classic topic of our discipline (Vernon Palmer's chapter on mixed legal systems, Ch. 17, is an example) or because their in-depth knowledge of comparative law can shed a bright light on a particular area. Paradigmatic in this respect are Rodolfo Sacco's chapter on African law (Ch. 15), as well as the chapters by Barbara Pozzo on language (Ch. 5), by George Bermann on international organizations (Ch. 11), and by Francesca Bignami on administrative law (Ch. 7). Further, we have selected leading international experts who over the years have consistently contributed to, and broadened, the core business of comparative law. An example is the entry on comparative civil justice by Oscar Chase and Vincenzo Varano (Ch. 10), which not only is the joint product of a common lawyer and a civilian, but is enlightened by the awareness of both these renowned scholars that the law never is merely a professional business. The same awareness underpins the chapters on the Jewish and the Islamic legal traditions, written by Arthur Jacobson and David Bleich, and Khaled Abou El Fadl, respectively (Chs. 13 and 14). These entries not only are masterful explanations of legal dimensions beyond the stereotypes to which we are used, but show once more the necessity of making Western ethnocentrism that pervades our discipline a cognitive tool the better to understand the poor quality of most of our historical analysis, rather than an excuse for cultural blindness. Also, this *Companion* could not but acknowledge the tremendous strain that economic globalization has produced on the structures of the modern sovereign state. This is a tension that makes it increasingly difficult to stick to the tradition of positivism that has determined the traditional distinctions between comparative law, foreign law, and international law. Chapter 1, the entry by Mathias

[3] See, e.g., R. B. Schlesinger, 'The Past and Future of Comparative Law', (1995) 43 *American Journal of Comparative Law* 477.

Reimann, and the aforementioned ones by Bermann and Bignami, witness and highlight how today one should be equipped to compare an array of law-producing entities – among themselves or with the structures of domestic law – that often defy being squeezed into the mainstream positivistic account of the sources of law, both because of the supra-national nature of these entities, and because they produce thriving legality at levels different from those controlled by the state.

No scholarly discipline ever transforms its intellectual posture in a short time. We believe that, since the fall of the Berlin Wall, comparative law, by going through a genuine phase of foundational critique, has been successful in this necessary endeavour. This is why our aim here was to overcome the traditional way of shooting diapositives of the different fields, and to provide the reader with an account showing the inner dynamics of the law. We are confident that, thanks to the efforts and the patience of our authors, we are offering an honest, and hopefully a challenging, (motion) picture of our discipline in this age of transformation.

Mauro Bussani and Ugo Mattei

Part I

Knowing comparative law

Comparative law and neighbouring disciplines 1

Mathias Reimann

Looking at comparative law in the broader context of other disciplines helps us to understand the field mainly for two reasons: *distinguishing it* from other disciplines shows more clearly what comparative law is; and *relating it* to cognate subjects shows how it interacts with neighbouring fields, especially how it contributes to, benefits from, or overlaps with them.

As a result, contrasting comparative law and its neighbouring disciplines has long been a standard exercise performed in many introductions (treatises and casebooks) to the field; these exercises are usually brief and necessarily superficial (see 'Further reading', section 1).[1] Today, there is also a plethora of essays which explore the relationship between comparative law and a particular neighbouring discipline in greater depth; these essays are often extensive and sophisticated ('Further reading', section 2).

There is a traditional list of disciplines to which comparative law has routinely been related: the study of foreign law, private and public international law, legal history, the sociology of law, and, sometimes, legal philosophy. Today, one should add at least transnational law, legal anthropology, and the economic analysis of law. To be sure, any such list is somewhat arbitrary, in particular because it could plausibly be extended, for example by including linguistic studies. Even further extension, however, would make the list unmanageable in the context of this survey.

The standard introductory accounts usually fail to recognize (or at least to articulate) that, due to its dual nature, comparative law relates to its neighbouring disciplines in two fundamentally different ways. One feature that defines comparative law is its object: it deals with other legal systems. It is therefore among the *international subjects* on the law curriculum (*infra*, section 1.1). This it shares with the study of foreign law (as such), private international law (conflict of laws), public international law (the law of nations), and transnational law (as a peculiar blend). The discipline's other

---

[1] Some have bravely resisted the temptation to wade into these murky waters; see, e.g., A. Gambaro and R. Sacco, *Sistemi Giuridici Comparati*, 2nd edn (Turin: Utet, 2004).

defining feature is its approach: it compares legal systems, rules, and so on. It is therefore one of many possible *perspectives on law* (*infra*, section 1.2). This it shares with legal history, legal sociology, legal philosophy, and several other disciplines approaching the study of law from a particular angle.

Like comparative law itself, all the neighbouring disciplines discussed below are highly heterogeneous. In the interest of conciseness, a general overview like this essay must simplify to a degree that will make specialists in these disciplines cringe. I ask their indulgence.

1.1 Comparative law and the international curriculum

Probably the most defining feature of comparative law is that it makes domestic lawyers look beyond their own system to others. In this regard, comparative law is closely related to four other fields: the study of foreign law (subsection 1.1.1), private international law (1.1.2), public international law (1.1.3), and, today, transnational law (1.1.4). Together, these fields (and their many subcategories) constitute the international curriculum. As a result, they are often lumped together rather indiscriminately – witness the many 'Centres', 'Institutes', and 'Journals' of 'International and Comparative Law'. In fact, most domestic lawyers have at best a vague sense of the differences between, say, 'comparative' and 'international' law, fundamental though these differences are. It is therefore understandable that comparatists feel the need clearly to distinguish their discipline from its 'international' neighbours.

The most fundamental difference is one that separates comparative law on the one hand from all the rest on the other: comparative law is a *method* of studying law and a stock of *academic knowledge*, while the other 'international' disciplines consist (at least largely) of positive legal rules. In other words, there is no comparative *law* (only the comparative study and knowledge of it), but there *is* foreign, private and public international, and transnational *law*.[2]

---

[2] As is generally acknowledged, 'comparative law' is thus a badly misleading term which is in part responsible for the confusion often prevailing among non-specialists about the nature of the game. Foreign terms, such as *droit comparé*, *Rechtsvergleichung*, and *diritto comparato* are much more apt since they show that the discipline is about the comparison of law(s).

Beyond that, the differences, and the various relationships, between comparative law and the other elements of the international curriculum depend on which of these other elements we consider.

1.1.1 The study of foreign law

How the study of foreign law relates to comparative law has often been debated. There are two main views; one may call them 'idealist' and 'realist'.

The idealist view is that the study of foreign law in and of itself is not comparative law. This view defines the discipline by its core method: comparison. As a result, studying foreign law is not part of it because it does not compare anything. Of course, even this view recognizes the study of foreign law as a first step towards comparison, but it regards this step merely as necessary, not as sufficient. It is also widely acknowledged that the study of foreign law can be (more or less) implicitly comparative. This may be the case, for example, where foreign law is explained to a domestic audience because such an explanation requires 'translating' it into domestic terms.

The realist view conceives of comparative law as a field defined by actual activity. From this perspective, it does comprise the study of foreign law because that is what most comparatists do in fact most of the time. As is widely admitted, most classroom teaching, conference discussions, and scholarly publications sailing under the flag of 'comparative law' really describe, critique, or draw lessons from, foreign law without much, if any, real comparison. Thus, if the study of foreign law does not count as comparative law, much of the work comparatists produce and consume lies outside the field proper – which, as a result, becomes small indeed.

Which of these views one prefers depends largely on how strictly one wants to set comparative law apart from other endeavours which are regarded as less challenging as well as less rewarding. Shutting the mere study of foreign law out of the field means insisting that comparative law fulfil its methodological ambition – which is laudable. Yet it does so at the cost of describing the field in a manner not reflecting reality – which is misleading.

1.1.2 Private international law

Private international law (in the Anglo-American orbit more often called 'conflict of laws') consists of the doctrines, principles, and rules governing transboundary private law disputes. Its core are the rules determining which of several (national or state) laws is chosen to apply (choice of law). It also deals with procedural matters, in particular jurisdiction in transboundary cases, the recognition of foreign judgments, and various more technical issues such as service of process or the taking of evidence abroad.

This shows that private international law is, as mentioned before, a system of legal doctrines and positive rules which makes it fundamentally different from comparative law as a method of study and a body of academic knowledge. As a result, private international law is strongly practice-oriented (albeit based on much academic theory), while comparative law is at its core 'a science'[3] (notwithstanding its important practical uses). Yet, despite their different characters, the interaction between the two fields is so close that one can almost speak of a symbiotic relationship.

At bottom, their close relationship is rooted in the fact that they both constantly deal with foreign law. Comparative law studies it for a variety of purposes, while private international law considers it to resolve cases. The result is that both disciplines require similar skills and toolkits – an interest in, and understanding of, other legal systems; foreign-language capabilities; access to foreign legal sources; and so on. Small wonder that both disciplines are often pursued by the same scholars or in the same departments and institutions (such as the Max Planck Institute for Foreign and International Private Law in Hamburg). This makes sense because the two disciplines closely interact in theory and in practice. Their interaction has two main dimensions.

One dimension is that comparatists study private international law. Of course, they study a myriad of other legal subjects as well, but it is fair to say that private international law is a somewhat special case. Since both comparatists and private international lawyers are already constantly looking beyond the domestic order, a comparison of rules governing choice of law, jurisdiction, and judgments recognition comes more naturally than a comparison of, say, contracts, civil procedure, or constitutions. To be sure, more serious comparative work on conflicts rules is needed, but there is a long and live tradition of looking at conflicts rules from a broad, often worldwide, perspective.[4]

---

[3] K. Zweigert and H. Kötz, *An Introduction to Comparative Law*, trans. T. Weir, 3rd rev. edn (Oxford: Clarendon; New York: Oxford University Press, 1998), even speak of a 'pure science' (6).

[4] The classic (and monumental) work is E. Rabel, *The Conflict of Laws – A Comparative Study*, 4 vols. (Ann Arbor: University of Michigan Press, 1945–58); a more recent example is S. Symeonides, *Private International Law at the End of the 20th Century – Progress or Regress* (The Hague: Kluwer, 2000).

The other dimension is that private international lawyers use comparative law. They do so all the time and in three principal ways. First, where conflicts rules call for the application of foreign law, comparative law helps to provide judges with the foreign laws called into question – that is, to make them accessible, intelligible, and thus practically applicable. Second, where private international lawyers (or legislators) make conflicts rules, they routinely employ comparative material. This is true on the domestic level (e.g., in drafting national conflicts codifications or statutes). It is even more true on the international level – that is, in the drafting of conflicts conventions (especially by the Hague Conference on Private International Law). And it is true as well for the more recent process of Europeanization of private international law in the form of EU regulations. This pervasiveness of comparative law in the legislative process has entailed a high degree of international uniformity in private international law, at least with regard to the basic principles and general rules. Third, private international law frequently needs comparative law in order actually to apply existing conflicts rules. For example, conflicts rules often employ terms the proper construction of which requires an understanding of their respective meanings in all the legal orders involved in a case.[5] Also, many conflicts conventions explicitly command that courts interpreting their terms consider what other jurisdictions have done, so that uniformity of meaning is maintained. Thus, even in its practical, day-to-day operations, 'no system of private international law can escape involvement with the discipline of comparative law'.[6]

It is perhaps somewhat ironic that despite this very close relationship, the disciplines are, in one sense, enemies: much of comparative law aims at the international unification of law (a trend especially pronounced in Europe today). Where such unification succeeds, conflicts disappear, and without them private international law becomes superfluous. In this regard, one discipline can undermine the very existence of the other. There is, however, no reason to believe that international legal unification

---

[5] This is the famous problem of 'qualification' (or, in US English, 'characterization'); the classic work is E. Rabel, 'Das Problem der Qualifikation', (1931) 5 *Rabels Zeitschrift* 241; for a mercifully brief explanation see M. Reimann, 'Comparative Law and Private International Law', in M. Reimann and R. Zimmermann (eds.), *The Oxford Handbook of Comparative Law* (Oxford University Press, 2006), 1384–7.

[6] A. von Mehren, 'The Contribution of Comparative Law to the Theory and Practice of Private International Law', (1977–8) 26 *American Journal of Comparative Law* 32, 33.

will be so successful that it will put private international lawyers out of work any time soon.

1.1.3 Public international law

It is difficult and dangerous to generalize about the relationship between comparative law and public international law, because the latter field has become so diversified. One should at least, however, distinguish between its classic core and its more recent subcategories.

The classic core of public international law consists of the general principles and positive rules that govern the relationship between sovereign (nation) states on the world scene (as the law *inter nationes*). This already shows that lumping it together with comparative law is a highly questionable business. In fact, it is but a slight exaggeration to say that the only commonality between the two fields is that they are not about domestic law (at least not primarily). And, indeed, in contrast to private international law, the classic law of nations has relatively little to do with comparative law.

To begin with, comparative lawyers normally do not study classic international law. This is mainly because the traditional law of nations is perceived as a fairly uniform (international) system which provides little, if any, opportunity to compare anything (like the different national versions of private international law). Of course, the public international law system could itself be compared with other regimes, including domestic ones. Such a comparison could be highly informative,[7] but there is almost no work of this sort. Comparatists are focused on national systems and have by and large ignored international law as an object of study.

Furthermore, comparative law is of modest practical use to classic public international law. While comparatists routinely insist that their discipline serves public international law in various ways, they are often deluding themselves. Most commonly, they invoke Article 38(1)(c) of the Statute of the International Court of Justice, which lists 'general principles of law recognized by civilized nations' as one of the sources of international law. Comparatists like to claim that 'l'interprétation de cette formule ne peut être qu'à base de droit comparé'.[8] That sounds plausible in theory, but

[7] M. Reimann, 'Beyond National Systems: A Comparative Law for the International Age', (2001) 75 *Tulane Law Review* 1103.

[8] R. David and C. Jauffret-Spinosi, *Les grands systèmes de droit contemporains*, 11th edn (Paris: Dalloz, 2002), 7.

comparative law is so rarely employed in practice here that it plays no significant role.[9] This is for good reason: serious comparative study to ascertain such general principles on a worldwide scale would be an almost impossible task and may not even be necessary.[10] Another area in which comparative law sometimes claims to be useful is treaty interpretation. Yet, again, its role in this context is in practice very small. It is true that courts struggling with a treaty provision sometimes consider how other courts have applied it,[11] and that involves looking at various solutions. Rarely, however, does this involve any real comparison, because the goal is usually not the search for the best solution but, rather, the determination of the parties' intention when making the treaty or the maintenance of uniformity of interpretation. There is an area, however, which is rarely mentioned by comparatists and in which their discipline is actually more commonly utilized – that is, the drafting of treaties (and of Principles and other projects, e.g. by the International Law Commission). Here, publicists often draw on the law and experience of several systems in order to find the best rule or at least to facilitate consensus. Still, on the whole, the use of comparative law in traditional public international law remains very limited.

Matters are different with regard to some of the more specialized sub-categories of international law that have developed over the past few decades. For example, the interpretation of international human rights treaties, especially the European Convention on Human Rights by the European Court of Human Rights, has frequently employed comparison among member state laws to ascertain the meaning and scope of treaty provisions.[12] The same is true for the European Court of Justice, especially

---

[9] B. Cheng, *General Principles of Law as Applied by International Courts and Tribunals* (London: Grotius Publications, 1953, repr. 2006), 392; A. Zimmermann, C. Tomuschat, and K. Oellers-Frahm (eds.), *The Statute of the International Court of Justice, A Commentary* (New York: Oxford University Press, 2006) marginal notes 259–261. An interesting exception is the separate opinion by Judge Bruno Simma in *Case Concerning Oil Platforms (Iran v. United States)*, [2003] ICJ Rep. 161. Even Simma's comparative survey, however, does not approach (or purport to be) a comparative ascertainment of general principles by considering all 'civilized nations'.

[10] Cheng, *General Principles*, 376; Zimmermann et al., *Statute of the International Court of Justice*, marginal note 258.

[11] See Vienna Convention on the Law of Treaties, Art. 31(3)(b) (treaty interpretation should take into account 'any subsequent practice in the application of the treaty').

[12] P. Mahoney, 'The Comparative Method in Judgments of the European Court of Human Rights: Reference Back to National Law', in G. Canivet, M. Andenas, and D. Fairgrieve (eds.), *Comparative Law Before the Courts* (London: BIICL, 2004), 135.

in developing 'general principles of European Law'[13] but also in the interpretation of various EC or EU treaties. Unfortunately, the respective comparative exercises are often so superficial and methodologically dubious that they amount to little more than result-driven cherry-picking.

In addition, there is a more basic, but also more vaguely defined, contribution comparatists can make to international law: the comparative study of laws can elucidate, and sometimes even explain, the differences between the legal cultures in the world. It can thus help us to understand the various techniques, predilections, and sensitivities that determine how people in different parts of the globe think about, what they expect from, and how they react to law, including international law. An understanding of, and tolerance for, these differences is essential to the larger international law projects of maintaining peace, promoting international co-operation, and effectively protecting human rights. This aspect 'est peut-être devenu, à notre époque, le principal [intérêt]'[14] of comparative law writ large.

1.1.4 Transnational law

In the last two decades the term 'transnational law' has become common usage. The relationship of this field to comparative law is difficult to analyse because the field itself is not clearly defined. Half a century ago, 'transnational law' was invented as an umbrella concept covering 'all law which regulates actions or events that transcend national frontiers'.[15] Thus understood, it encompasses not only public and private international law but also all domestic and foreign law dealing with transboundary issues. Today, the term is mainly used to indicate that these traditional categories have blended to a point where the distinctions between them are artificial as well as potentially dysfunctional. Transnational law has thus become a somewhat amorphous term denoting the multi-faceted and multi-layered international legal order that has emerged from the phenomenon known as globalization.

Transnational law presents at least three new challenges to comparative law. First, comparative law must look beyond the traditional (Westphalian) system of coexisting nation states, and come to grips with much more complex and fluid relationships between a multiplicity of overlapping and

---

[13] T. Tridimas, *The General Principles of EU Law*, 2nd edn (New York: Oxford University Press, 2006).

[14] David and Jauffret-Spinosi, *Grands systèmes*, 6.

[15] P. Jessup, *Transnational Law* (New Haven: Yale University Press, 1956), 2.

intersecting legal orders. Second, comparatists must include the study of inter-, trans-, and supranational regimes (both global and regional), such as international trade, human rights, and the European Union.[16] And, third, in order to create a realistic picture of the global legal order, comparative law must look beyond state law and include the non-state norms which play an enormous role in the world today.[17]

Comparative studies are thus a necessary part of transnational law. They are needed to describe, explain, and help to co-ordinate the multiple legal orders we face in the early twenty-first century. Yet, in order to do so, comparative law must rethink many of the traditional dichotomies on which it has long rested, such as the divide between international and national or between private and public law, because these dichotomies no longer capture what is essential in this new environment.

1.2 Comparative law as a perspective on law

Comparative law looks at legal material from an outside perspective, so to speak. It shares this feature with fields such as legal history, sociology of law, or legal philosophy. How does comparative law relate to these other 'perspective' disciplines?

The answer to that question depends largely on what comparative law is ultimately all about – that is, on its principal goals and methods. Unfortunately, there is no consensus in this regard.[18] Comparatists have debated these fundamentals for many decades, the avowed goals and methods have constantly changed, and, today, there is a veritable panoply of both.[19] As a result, comparative law means different things to different people. For the mainstream, the discipline consists of the comparison of the

---

[16] M. Reimann, 'Beyond National Systems: A Comparative Law for the International Age', (2001) 75 *Tulane Law Review* 1103.

[17] G. Teubner (ed.), *Global Law without a State* (Aldershot: Dartmouth, 1997).

[18] There is not even agreement whether comparative law is merely a method or rather an academic discipline and perhaps even a field of knowledge in its own right; see M. Reimann, 'The Progress and Failure of Comparative Law in the Second Half of the Twentieth Century', (2002) 50 *American Journal of Comparative Law* 672, 684–5.

[19] This may sound appealing but there are serious downsides. The prevailing epistemological and methodological disagreements have entailed not only an *embarras de richesse* but also a high degree of confusion in fundamental questions. This confusion leaves the discipline without an overall sense of direction.

world's present legal systems or particular elements thereof in pursuit of a variety of academic and practical objectives.[20] Many comparatists, however, take a more specific approach. For some, comparative law is mainly the study of legal transplants – that is, of the borrowing of ideas between legal cultures over time; this turns it into a form of legal history. For others, the discipline is primarily about exploring the relationship between law and society which tends to merge it with the sociology of law. Yet others have focused on underlying mentalities, perceptions of law, or the law of pre-modern societies, which links comparative law closely to cultural studies, legal philosophy, and legal anthropology, respectively. These are just examples of particular directions, to which many others could be added. In what follows, we shall explore the relationship between comparative law and neighbouring perspectives essentially from the mainstream point of view, although we shall also mention areas of overlap between more idiosyncratic versions and particular neighbouring fields.

With regard to 'outside' perspectives on law, legal history and legal sociology are the most commonly discussed neighbouring disciplines, mainly because comparative law has interacted with them for more than a century. We shall consider them in some detail and then briefly glance at legal philosophy as well. Beyond these three lie a variety of other fields, such as legal anthropology and the economic analysis of law, which have traditionally been less routinely considered by comparatists.

1.2.1 Legal history

It is by now a banality that comparative law and legal history are closely related, in that both look at law beyond the present domestic legal order, the former in space, the latter in time. This kinship has inspired Hein Kötz to call the disciplines 'twin sisters' (leaving it open which 'is the more comely').[21]

It is also beyond cavil that both disciplines can greatly benefit from each other. Comparative law often needs a historical dimension in order fully to understand the laws, processes, and institutions it considers – modern similarities and differences in judicial decision-making, for example, are fully intelligible only against the background of their historical

---

[20] Zweigert and Kötz, *Introduction to Comparative Law*, 15–47. For a critique, see Reimann, 'Progress and Failure of Comparative Law', 685–90.
[21] Zweigert and Kötz, *Introduction to Comparative Law*, 8.

development.[22] Similarly, legal history often needs a comparative dimension in order to show which phenomena or developments were peculiar to a place or region and which were broadly common – the impact of the reception of Roman law, for example, can be properly understood only in an all-European context.[23] As Jim Gordley explained, each discipline has often made the 'common mistake' of ignoring the other – and promptly run into easily avoidable errors.[24] Fortunately, at least since the middle of the twentieth century, most of the good comparative work has been historically informed, just as much top-notch historical work has been comparative.

There are several instances in which the relationship between these two disciplines has been so close that they have virtually amalgamated. An example from the late nineteenth century are the studies of Henry Sumner Maine, Joseph Kohler, Hermann Post, and others, in what has often been labelled 'legal ethnology'. Inspired by Bachofen and Darwin, these authors sought to determine how civilizations and legal institutions develop from primitive to modern stages. Today, this scholarship is largely (although in part unjustly) discredited for its crude methodology and its false belief in a common path of all mankind.[25] In the last third of the twentieth century, the disciplines have been joined by Alan Watson, for whom comparative law is mainly the study of legal transplants over time and thus an exercise in legal history.[26] Around the same time, the concept of a 'legal tradition' was born when scholars combined comparative and historical perspectives by looking at the great legal cultures of the world as they are shaped by their development.[27] Still more recently, the efforts of Reinhard Zimmermann and others to utilize the medieval and early modern *ius commune*[28] as a source for a common (private) law

---

[22] J. Dawson, *The Oracles of the Law* (Ann Arbor: University of Michigan Press, 1968).

[23] P. Koschaker, *Europa und das römische Recht*, 4th edn (Munich: Beck, 1966 [1947]).

[24] J. Gordley, 'Comparative Law and Legal History', in M. Reimann and R. Zimmermann (eds.), *The Oxford Handbook of Comparative Law* (Oxford University Press, 2006), 753, 763–8.

[25] E.g., in Maine's famous phrase, '*from Status to Contract*'. H. Sumner Maine, *Ancient Law* (London: J. Murray, 1861), 100. For a concise and informative summary of the nineteenth century legal ethnology, see Zweigert and Kötz, *Introduction to Comparative Law*, 8–9.

[26] A. Watson, *Legal Transplants* (Athens, GA: University of Georgia Press, 1974).

[27] The classic work is J. H. Merryman, *The Civil Tradition*, 3rd edn (Palo Alto: Stanford University Press, 2007 [1969]); see also H. P. Glenn, *Legal Traditions of the World*, 3rd edn (New York: Oxford University Press, 2007 [2000]).

[28] I.e., the body of civil and canon law as taught and expounded by academic scholars throughout most of western and central Europe.

of Europe have merged both dimensions in comparative histories of core legal doctrines and rules.[29]

Yet, in spite of these commonalities and combinations, the relationship between the two fields is also marked by differences and difficulties. It must suffice here to mention two of each.

The most important differences pertain to methodology and objectives. With regard to methodology, legal historiography today shows a fairly high degree of rigour and agreement, while comparative law is plagued by laissez-faire and confusion. The reason is mainly that legal historiography is primarily pursued by historians who have extensive graduate training and serious professional standards, while comparative law is mostly left to lawyers, who often have no graduate training in comparative law and thus work amateurishly. With regard to objectives, legal history is overwhelmingly pursued simply the better to understand the past (and, by reflection, the present); it rarely claims or has much utility for current legal practice. Comparative law, by contrast, is pursued not only for knowledge's sake but in large part also for its practical utility, for example in private international law (*supra*, subsection 1.1.2). It is thus but a slight caricature to say that legal history is methodologically sophisticated but practically useless while comparative law is methodologically underdeveloped but practically important.

These differences have led to difficulties. One such difficulty surfaced in the project of a common private law for Europe. When certain scholars sought to employ legal history (especially the *ius commune*) for purposes of contemporary legal unification, a bitter dispute ensued between two camps. On the one side were the comparatists who emphasized current practical needs and who had no methodological problems with using historical research for modern law-making. On the other side were the (purist) legal historians who cared little about present-day needs but regarded an instrumentalization of their discipline as methodologically corrupting and epistemologically fatal.[30] Another difficulty is that the differences regarding methodology and objectives are major obstacles for a true integration of the two disciplines. While there is a considerable number of works that may justly be called 'comparative legal history', they do not constitute a coherent field. They

---

[29] R. Zimmermann, *The Law of Obligations* (Oxford University Press, 1990).

[30] The discussion resulted in a symposium; see G. Dilcher and P. Caroni (eds.), *Norm und Tradition/Fra norma e tradizione* (Cologne: Böhlau Köln, 1998).

also often remain on the descriptive level, stop short of actual comparison, and thus produce few or no explicit conclusions. A more pervasively comparative legal history would be highly desirable, especially for Europe. But it would also be difficult to pursue – in no small part because the requisite co-operation between historians and comparatists would constantly be hindered by their methodological and epistemological differences.

1.2.2 Legal sociology

At first glance, comparative law and legal sociology are rather different enterprises: one compares legal systems (and their components), the other studies the relationship between law and society. For the former, law is primarily part of an aspirational order, for the latter it is primarily a fact of social life. Thus the former usually contains strong normative elements, the latter is essentially a descriptive social science.[31] Indeed, these disciplines have often led entirely separate lives. They may even get along pretty well without each other: there is good legal sociology that is not comparative[32] as well as good comparative law that is not sociological.[33] Claims of an intimate relationship are based on, and true only for, specific branches of these disciplines.[34]

Nonetheless, co-operation between comparative law and legal sociology is often extremely desirable. If legal sociology seeks to describe and explain the interaction between law and society, looking beyond just one legal system helps in at least two ways: it expands the database and thus the testing ground for hypotheses, and it introduces additional variables that can be used to control results. The hypothesis that legal systems usually make 'the haves come out ahead', for example, gains much weight if it is verifiable not in one legal system but in several.[35] In a similar vein, if comparative law seeks to understand the similarities and differences between legal systems (and their components), a sociological perspective

---

[31] The epistemological value of these distinctions has recently, and justly, been questioned; see, e.g., A. Riles, 'Comparative Law and Socio-legal Studies', in M. Reimann and R. Zimmermann (eds.), *The Oxford Handbook of Comparative Law* (Oxford University Press, 2006), 775, 801–2.

[32] A well-known book that provides an example is M. Galanter and T. Palay, *Tournament of Lawyers* (University of Chicago Press, 1991).

[33] See, e.g., T. Kadner Graziano, *Comparative Contract Law* (Basingstoke: Palgrave Macmillan, 2009).

[34] See *infra*, notes 38–47 and accompanying text.

[35] M. Galanter, 'Why the "Haves" Come Out Ahead', (1974–5) 9 *Law and Society Review* 95.

can add crucial descriptive depth and enormous explanatory potential. Such a perspective shows, for example, that law is only one among many mechanisms of social control, so that one society may invoke law where another relies on customary or religious norms. Also, a sociological perspective forces an observer to look not only at the law in the books but also at the law in action, which can completely change the picture. Finally, sociology helps to explain legal rules, processes, and institutions as results of living conditions, political structures, or market realities. In short, it opens the comparatist's eyes to the social contingency of law.

Ultimately, the degree to which comparative law benefits from legal sociology depends on which concept of law comparatists embrace. Where this concept is essentially positivist and doctrinal so that law is conceived as a system of principles and rules, the gulf between the disciplines is fairly wide and legal sociology is rarely consulted. This has been the mainstream tradition in continental Europe, where, even today, prestigious comparative law projects can remain remarkably uninterested in the sociological dimension of law. The current efforts to unify European private law on the (quasi-) legislative level provide the perhaps most striking, as well as disconcerting, example.[36] Where the comparatists' concept of law is pragmatic and sociological, the gulf between the disciplines is narrow, and comparative law without a sociological perspective becomes nearly unthinkable. As a result of legal realism, this is especially true of the United States,[37] where legal scholarship has generally taken an interdisciplinary turn. Over the last few decades, comparative legal studies in much of the world have often veered in the American direction, looking beyond law as a mere system of rules and considering its social embeddedness. This has entailed an increasing overlap of comparative law and legal sociology.

Indeed, there are many specific contexts in which the relationship between comparative law and legal sociology is so intimate that they become well-nigh indistinguishable. This is perhaps most obvious at the dawn of modern sociology – that is, in the work of Max Weber.[38] Weber has,

---

[36] Study Group on European Private Law, *Principles, Definitions and Model Rules of European Private Law, Draft Common Frame of Reference* (Munich: Sellier, 2009).

[37] M. Rheinstein, *Einführung in die Rechtsvergleichung*, 2nd edn (Munich: Beck, 1987), 63–8.

[38] M. Weber, *Economy and Society*, ed. G. Roth and C. Wittich, vol. II (Berkeley: University of California Press, 1978), 641–900. One can make similar claims with regard to the (much earlier) work of Montesquieu or even Rousseau.

of course, cast a long shadow.[39] His approach has shaped, for example, the work of his erstwhile student Max Rheinstein, who famously postulated that wherever comparative law seeks to explore the social function of law, it 'is legal sociology'.[40] Weber has also inspired the scholarship of Mirjan Damaška, whose descriptions of authority structures as hierarchical or co-ordinate have been highly influential in the last quarter century.[41] Especially in recent years, a sociological approach has informed compara-tive law in a broad variety of contexts: the study of non-Western legal systems[42] and the comparative analysis of legal cultures;[43] the role of custom, especially in former colonies; the debates about law and develop-ment projects, in particular about efforts to export Western notions of the rule of law to developing countries; the scholarship on legal actors and institutions;[44] the debate about the relative autonomy of law in the context of legal transplants; the legal formants approach;[45] and, most recently, the scholarship on global legal pluralism[46] and on the role of non-state law.[47]

1.2.3 Legal philosophy

Legal philosophy is not as routinely discussed in its relationship to com-parative law as are legal history and sociology.[48] Yet it is worth at least brief consideration. This is not because there is so much interaction between these two disciplines but because there is so little, and because there should be more.

---

[39] Riles, 'Comparative Law and Socio-legal Studies', 778.
[40] Rheinstein, *Einführung in die Rechtsvergleichung*, 28.
[41] M. Damaška, *The Faces of Justice and State Authority* (New Haven: Yale University Press, 1986).
[42] This includes socialist law; see, e.g., I. Markovits, *Justice in Lüritz* (Princeton University Press, 2010).
[43] See, e.g., the work of Erhard Blankenburg, Roger Cotterell, Patrick Glenn, Werner Menski, and David Nelken; cultural perspectives are also prominent in the work of Vivian Curran and Annelise Riles.
[44] See, e.g., A. Garapon and I. Papadopoulos, *Juger en Amérique et en France* (Paris: Odile Jacob, 2003).
[45] R. Sacco, 'Legal Formants', (1991) 39 *American Journal of Comparative Law* 1 and 343.
[46] See, e.g., the work of Bonaventura de Sousa Santos, Gunther Teubner, and William Twining.
[47] See, e.g., the symposium 'Beyond the State: Rethinking Private Law', (2008) 56 *American Journal of Comparative Law* 527.
[48] But see Rheinstein, *Einführung in die Rechtsvergleichung*, 18–20.

In a sense, comparative law and legal philosophy are almost opposites. Speaking very generally, the former focuses on the multitude of legal systems, the latter on law as a general phenomenon; the former seeks to understand similarities and differences, the latter the deeper meaning and ramifications of an idea; the former is essentially empirical (although not necessarily in a social-science sense), the latter is interested in values and moral judgments (although not necessarily in a metaphysical sense). As a result, the disciplines do not easily connect.

And yet there is considerable potential for (at least some) co-operation. Legal philosophy is enriched by an understanding of what unites the laws of the world and what divides them; after all, deriving philosophical insight from looking at one system only makes any general claims about law inherently questionable. Comparative law, in turn, cannot fully understand legal systems unless it understands their underlying values, notions of justice, and general mentalities. One should therefore expect comparatists to pay considerable attention to the legal philosophy undergirding the law(s) they consider.[49] By rarely doing so, comparatists miss considerable epistemological opportunities.

Comparative law and philosophy have connected, however, in the field of jurisprudence – that is, the general theory of law (*théorie générale de droit, Rechtstheorie*).[50] Unfortunately, this field has long lost what prominence it once had in the nineteenth and earlier twentieth centuries. Today it is largely out of fashion and few comparatists have paid serious attention to it.

1.2.4 Other disciplines (legal anthropology and economic analysis of law)

In recent years, two other disciplines – legal anthropology and the economic analysis of law – have interacted with comparative law. These interactions have a somewhat longer tradition with respect to legal anthropology, and are of more recent vintage with regard to law and economics. Both are covered here only briefly, because their relationship with comparative law is the topic of separate chapters.

---

[49] W. Ewald, 'What Was It Like to Try a Rat?', (1995) 143 *Pennsylvania Law Review* 1889.
[50] See, e.g., R. Pound, *Jurisprudence*, 5 vols. (St. Paul: West, 1959).

Comparative law and legal anthropology are kindred fields.[51] This is true not only because legal systems are constitutive elements of legal cultures[52] but also because both disciplines compare legal rules, institutions, and practices in order to draw conclusions from the similarities and differences they observe.[53] The disciplines differ in focus, however: comparatists look primarily at the technical and normative side of law, while anthropologists are more interested in its cultural origins and functions.

This divergence in focus entails significant differences regarding objects and methods. Comparative law usually studies modern legal systems – that is, those of highly developed societies – while legal anthropology focuses mostly on traditional laws and customs – that is, those of indigenous groups – although some anthropologists have looked beyond the traditional terrain at modern societies and their professional norms.[54] Comparatists deal almost exclusively with official law – that is, state-sanctioned rules, while anthropologists are often concerned with laws, customs, or practices that may not be backed by state authority. Comparatists mostly work from desks with books (and nowadays computers), while anthropologists go into 'the field' in order to gather ethnographic data; as a result, comparative law does not necessarily involve empirical work, while legal anthropology is unimaginable without it. Despite these differences, however, where scholars compare legal cultures and their elements, comparative law can virtually become a form of legal anthropology and vice versa. Several legal anthropologists have done important comparative work,[55] and some comparative law scholars have successfully ventured into legal anthropology.[56]

[51] For a brief introduction to the latter see J. Donovan, *Legal Anthropology* (Lanham: AltaMira, 2008).

[52] Both can easily overlap with legal sociology because legal systems are important elements of both human cultures and human societies. Thus it is often hard to tell (and perhaps pointless to ask) where legal anthropology ends and legal sociology begins.

[53] It is a different issue that the stage of actual comparison (not to mention the drawing of meaningful conclusions from it) is often not reached in either discipline.

[54] See, e.g., A. Riles, 'The Anti-Network: Private Global Governance, Legal Knowledge, and the Legitimacy of the State', (2008) 56 *American Journal of Comparative Law* 605.

[55] In the last few decades, the leading figure has been Laura Nader; see, e.g., L. Nader, *The Life of the Law* (Berkeley: University of California Press, 2002).

[56] A classic is K. N. Llewellyn and E. Adamson Hoebel, *The Cheyenne Way* (Norman: University of Oklahoma Press, 1941). A more recent example is W. Fikentscher, *Law and Anthropology* (Munich: Bayerische Akademie der Wissenschaften, 2009). See also R. Cooter and W. Fikentscher, 'Indian Common Law', (1998) 46 *American Journal of Comparative Law* 287 and 509; 'American Indian Law Codes', (2008) 56 *American Journal of Comparative Law* 29.

Once again, both disciplines can learn from each other, and their co-operation can have a significant synergetic effect. At a minimum, legal anthropology can benefit from the comparatists' more precise knowledge of legal rules and more technical understanding of how legal institutions and processes work. Thus comparative lawyers can open anthropologists' eyes to the conceptual underpinnings, peculiar mechanics, and policy goals of law. Conversely, anthropologists can teach comparative lawyers how deeply legal systems are embedded in their respective cultural contexts, and how these contexts often entail different perceptions of social realities and problems. Thus a cultural perspective can provide an important corrective for the facile functionalism that has been so prevalent in comparative law for much of the mid- and late twentieth century.

An anthropological approach to comparative law becomes outright essential when the discipline turns to legal systems with strong indigenous elements, because here the cultural aspects of law quickly become more important than the technical ones. So far, many of these systems, especially in Africa, have received little attention from comparative lawyers even though the effects of globalization have made it increasingly impossible (or at least costly) to ignore them. Thus the recent calls for comparative law to include more non-Western systems imply a call to adopt (at least in part) a more anthropological perspective.

Economic analysis of law and comparative law have consciously interacted for only about two decades. In part this is because law and economics as a distinct field is barely half a century old. In part it is also because, for the first twenty years or so, this field rose to prominence in the United States, where comparative law was in decline in the 1960s to the 1980s. Also, the highly abstract approach and narrow theoretical focus of the original, Chicago approach to law and economics was essentially closed to comparative perspectives. Over the last twenty years, however, several legal scholars have brought the two disciplines together. As a result, 'comparative law and economics' has established itself as a small but thriving speciality with its own aficionados, workshops (especially the Comparative Law and Economics Forum under the guidance of Robert Cooter), and its own, rapidly growing, literature.[57]

---

[57] It is questionable whether 'comparative law and economics' should be labelled a 'discipline' in its own right; see F. Faust, 'Comparative Law and Economic Analysis of Law', in M. Reimann and R. Zimmermann (eds.), *The Oxford Handbook of Comparative Law* (Oxford University Press, 2006), 837, 863–4.

As is now widely recognized, the blending of comparative and economic analysis can create huge benefits. The comparative study of law can profit greatly from economic perspectives, especially from thinking in terms of efficiency, transactions costs, and consumer preference. In particular, looking at law as a market in which solutions compete[58] can help comparatists understand the phenomenon of legal transplants (especially why they occur) and trends towards convergence of rules or results (perhaps towards the most efficient solutions), as well as the limits of borrowing and legal unification (because the efficiency of legal rules often depends on how they fit into the respective cultural and institutional environments). Thus economic analyses can explain why government actors have chosen, or should choose, one solution over another when making law or deciding disputes, and why private parties select certain laws over others when incorporating businesses or drafting contracts.

Conversely, comparative perspectives can enrich the economic analysis of law in various ways. Perhaps most importantly, comparative law is a powerful antidote to the original parochialism of law and economics. This parochialism created a glaring discrepancy between theory and evidence, in that it derived generalized causal claims about substantive law solely from observations of the common law tradition, mainly as manifested in the United States. Testing these theories usually ignored the fact that the same rules can have very different effects in different environments – that is, depending on differences regarding institutions and procedures, as well as social and cultural conditions. This tunnel-vision problem can be overcome, or at least alleviated, by looking beyond the domestic legal order to other systems. Thus comparative law proffers a much broader data base and a more solid grounding for claims about the economic implications and functions of law. In addition, comparative law can provide law and economics theory with a reality check because it supplies, in Ugo Mattei's words, 'a reservoir of institutional alternatives, which are not merely theoretical but actually tested by legal history'.[59]

The combination of comparative and economic analyses has not only developed into a special sub-discipline, it has also been used by scholars of business law and market regulation for quite some time. In particular, scholarship on the economics of corporate governance, but also of foreign

[58] See E. O'Hara and L. Ribstein, *The Law Market* (New York: Oxford University Press, 2009).
[59] U. Mattei, *Comparative Law and Economics* (Ann Arbor: University of Michigan Press, 1997), 28.

investment, securities laws, and antitrust regimes, has frequently looked at rules and institutions beyond the domestic orbit. The traditional reference points have been western Europe (including the United Kingdom), the United States, and Japan, although the focus has recently shifted to the emerging economies of China, India, and other non-Western countries. While this scholarship rarely employs that label, it is, so to speak, comparative law and economics in action.

More recently there has been considerable trouble in paradise when claims made by economists clashed with objections from comparative lawyers in the debate about the 'legal origins' thesis. In 1997 a group of economists began to allege that the origin of a legal system determines its predisposition towards economic development; in particular, they claimed that legal systems originating in the common law tradition provide a better environment for economic growth than legal systems shaped by civil law.[60] When this view was adopted by the World Bank in its *Doing Business* report in 2002 and subsequent years, it triggered vociferous protest by comparative lawyers. They denounced the legal origins thesis (in large measure correctly) as ill-founded, naive, and yet another manifestation of a US-centric view of the world. In the meantime, economists have modified and fine-tuned their position, and comparative lawyers reflect more soberly on the relationship between their discipline and issues of economic development.[61]

1.3 In conclusion: comparative law between independence and interdisciplinarity

Comparative law has long aspired to be both practically useful and academically sophisticated. The desire to be practically useful drives its interaction with other subjects in the international curriculum, especially the study of foreign law and private international law (*supra*, section 1.1). In this regard, comparative law is pretty much at ease because its practical utility is beyond doubt. The desire to be academically sophisticated underlies its relationship with other fields presenting broader perspectives on law (*supra*, section 1.2). In this context, comparative law is uneasy because it is

---

[60] The, by now classic, article is R. La Porta, F. Lopez de Silanes, A. Shleifer, and R. Vishy, 'Legal Determinants of External Finance', (1997) 52 *Journal of Finance* 1131.

[61] See 'Symposium on Legal Origins', (2009) 57 *American Journal of Comparative Law* 765.

torn between two conflicting needs: to define itself as a subject in its own right and to draw on its neighbouring disciplines.

There are essentially two ways to react to this tension. The more traditional reaction, which appears to be still prevalent in Europe, is to emphasize the discipline's independent status. In order to understand 'what comparative law really is', this view seeks 'to distinguish it from other areas of legal science' so that one also recognizes 'what comparative law is *not*'.[62] The problem with this approach is that many of the distinctions it draws are artificial; as even mainstream European comparatists admit, a meaningful comparison of legal systems must include perspectives from other fields. The other reaction, more prevalent in the United States today, is to foreground the interdisciplinary element in comparative law.[63] This view regards distinctions between comparative law and neighbouring disciplines merely as a matter of emphasis, if not outright pointless. The problem here is that comparative law tends to blend into its neighbouring disciplines, leading to the question what, if anything, is distinctive about it.

Beyond all that lies a further, and rather practical, dilemma. On the one hand, comparative law must embrace the historical, sociological, anthropological, philosophical, economic, etc. dimensions of law, at least if it wants to proceed beyond sterile rules comparison on the merely technical level. On the other hand, this demands professional skills in other disciplines that few comparatists can be expected to command; after all, it is difficult enough to be conversant with several *legal* systems. As a result, comparative law can interact with its neighbouring disciplines only if the discipline either accepts more or less amateurish work by comparatists going solo or if it pursues teamwork with specialists in other fields more much seriously than is currently common.

Further reading

Overview works on comparative law and neighbouring disciplines in general

P. de Cruz, *Comparative Law in a Changing World*, 3rd edn (New York: Routledge, 2007), 8–10

---

[62] Zweigert and Kötz, *Introduction to Comparative Law*, 6 (emphasis in original).
[63] See, e.g., U. Mattei, 'An Opportunity Not to Be Missed: The Future of Comparative Law in the United States', (1998) 46 *American Journal of Comparative Law* 709.

R. David and C. Jauffret-Spinosi, *Les grands systèmes de droit contemporains*, 11th edn (Paris: Dalloz, 2002), 3–13

U. Mattei, T. Ruskola, and A. Gidi, *Schlesinger's Comparative Law*, 7th edn (New York: Foundation Press, 2009), 7–30

M. Rheinstein, *Einführung in die Rechtsvergleichung*, 2nd edn (Munich: Beck, 1987), 16–31

K. Zweigert and H. Kötz, *An Introduction to Comparative Law*, trans. T. Weir, 3rd rev. edn (Oxford: Clarendon; New York: Oxford University Press, 1998), 6–12

In-depth analyses of comparative law and specific neighbouring disciplines

'Beiträge zum 32. Deutschen Rechtshistorikertag in Regensburg (Symposium on Comparative Law and Legal History)', (1999) 7 *Zeitschrift für Europäisches Privatrecht* 494

R. Caterina, 'Comparative Law and Economics', in J. Smits (ed.), *Elgar Encyclopedia of Comparative Law* (Cheltenham: Edward Elgar, 2006), 161

R. Cotterell, 'Comparative Law and Legal Culture', in M. Reimann and R. Zimmermann (eds.), *The Oxford Handbook of Comparative Law* (Oxford University Press, 2006), 709

G. de Geest and R. van den Bergh (eds.), *Comparative Law and Economics*, 3 vols. (Cheltenham: Edward Elgar, 2004)

F. Faust, 'Comparative Law and Economic Analysis of Law', in M. Reimann and R. Zimmermann (eds.), *The Oxford Handbook of Comparative Law* (Oxford University Press, 2006), 837

J. Gordley, 'Comparative Law and Legal History', in M. Reimann and R. Zimmermann (eds.), *The Oxford Handbook of Comparative Law* (Oxford University Press, 2006), 753

U. Mattei, *Comparative Law and Economics* (Ann Arbor: University of Michigan Press, 1997)

U. Mattei and F. Cafaggi, 'Comparative Law and Economics', in *New Palgrave Dictionary of Economics and the Law* (London: Macmillan, 1998), vol. I, 346

H. Muir-Watt, 'Private International Law', in J. Smits (ed.), *Elgar Encyclopedia of Comparative Law* (Cheltenham: Edward Elgar, 2006), 566

M. Reimann, 'Rechtsvergleichung und Rechtsgeschichte im Dialog', (1999) 7 *Zeitschrift für Europäisches Privatrecht* 497

M. Reimann, 'Comparative Law and Private International Law', in M. Reimann and R. Zimmermann (eds.), *The Oxford Handbook of Comparative Law* (Oxford University Press, 2006), 1363

A. Riles, 'Comparative Law and Socio-legal Studies', in M. Reimann and R. Zimmermann (eds.), *The Oxford Handbook of Comparative Law* (Oxford University Press, 2006), 775

Political ideology and comparative law 2

Duncan Kennedy

2.1 Introduction

In the first half of the nineteenth century, the historical school usefully and
also abusively derived legal difference from differences in national culture
and national history. Towards the end of the century, it was common to
understand systems as flowing in their details from a large conceptual
characteristic (for example, codified versus common law; place on the evolutionary spectrum running from status to contract; formal rationality versus
qadi justice). In the next period, the dominant mode was to understand
systems as having adopted varied solutions to common functional problems.

These methodologies of comparison are related to the juristic methodologies of their times. Weber's typology of modes of legal rationality, with
German pandectism at the top, was a manifestation of the classical legal
thought that was declining as he wrote.[1] The functionalist method is patently
consonant with the emergence of social legal thought, whose slogan was that
law is a means to social ends and whose juristic method was teleological.[2]

In contemporary legal thought, 'balancing' or 'proportionality' is a prevalent legal methodology. Is there an equivalent comparative methodology?
A preliminary answer would be that one way to understand any particular
difference between two contemporary legal systems is as the product of
different balances between conflicting considerations, be they principles or
policies, rights, powers, or whatever.

Traditionally, common lawyers have understood legislative law-making as
reflecting the situational balance of political power, and sharply contrasted
it with judicial and scholarly legal interpretation, understood as scientific, as
technical, or, at the very least, as non-political. Civilians have had much the

---

[1] Max Weber, *Max Weber on Law in Economy and Society*, ed. M. Rheinstein, trans.
E. Shils (Cambridge, MA: Harvard University Press, 1954).
[2] K. Zweigert and H. Kötz, *An Introduction to Comparative Law* , trans. T. Weir, 2nd rev.
edn (Oxford: Clarendon, 1987).

same notion, once exception is made for the epochal legislative moments of codification, heavily influenced by the scholars. Over the course of the twentieth century, critiques of the varieties of 'formalism', meaning jurid-ical techniques that isolated legal interpretation from 'extra-juristic' con-siderations, brought gaps, conflicts, and ambiguities to the centre of legal consciousness. Balancing conflicting considerations is the standard contemporary method for choosing an interpretation when traditional methods – precedential, conceptual, or teleological – are, for some reason, not operative.

The rise of balancing as a juristic method, rather than a method restricted to legislation, threatens the sharp distinction between legislation and legal interpretation across the whole domain of Western-influenced legal sys-tems. Ideal typical balancing firmly rejects ideological considerations, requiring that factors be 'universalizable'. This is supposed to guarantee the non-political character of the technique. Nonetheless, the relatively low level of constraint imposed on the jurist by this methodology makes inevi-table a 'hermeneutic of suspicion' that outcomes either follow from partic-ular ideologies or represent compromises of conflicting ideologies rather than of conflicting universal principles and values.[3]

This might not be so bad if it were possible to understand balancing as nothing more than a disfavoured method of last resort. But it is also common to see rules justified in precedential or conceptual or teleological terms as the product of *covert* balancing, disguised by the abuse of deduction, or of teleology, or of precedent. Systems that present themselves as flowing coher-ently from values or principles may 'actually' be compromises or hotch-potches of *conflicting* values and principles. If the norm is the product of covert balancing, it is, even more than in the case of overt balancing, subject to the suspicion that it is politically rather than 'technically' determined.

In other words, a first operation critiques legal solutions that present themselves as precedentially or conceptually or teleologically required, showing that the solution represents in fact a balance of conflicting con-siderations. The second operation indicates the ideological orientation or orientations that plausibly motivated a solution that was formally pre-sented as a balance of universalizable considerations.

---

[3] D. Kennedy, *A Critique of Adjudication: fin de siècle* (Cambridge, MA: Harvard University Press, 1997).

In the contemporary period it would seem that a plausible account of legal differences would have to take into account the influence of ideological conflict in the production of law, including legal interpretation. This is true because 'we' practise the double hermeneutic of suspicion described above, wanting first to understand the purportedly legally necessary as the product of balancing, and then to understand balancing as involving conflicting ideologies.

It is striking that this approach is sufficiently unfamiliar that we have no canonical list of ideologies at play, and no list of domains of legal comparison where the ideological interpretation of difference is already well established. But there are also plenty of promising starting points, as I shall try to show.

To avoid any misunderstanding, ideological differences, producing varying legal compromises behind the screen of overt or covert balancing, will not explain anything like the total range of legal difference. Each of the earlier approaches retains its usefulness. It is still useful to attend to national and international history (for example, colonial and post-colonial history) and to systemic/conceptual differences, such as common versus civil law or logically formal method versus teleology, and to identify typical functional problems of modern social organization to which legal systems offer a variety of solutions. What is open to criticism is the categorical exclusion of the ideological factor in constructing explanatory schemas.

Further, this exclusion seems to me open to the same kind of ideology critique that we now habitually direct at the law itself, that is, open to an ideological critique of the academic discipline of comparative law. The categorical exclusion of ideological analysis (with the interesting exception of the category 'socialist law' in René David's families typology) is a residue of that very self-conception of the non-political jurist that balancing has called into question.

2.2 The analytic scheme

2.2.1 What is balancing/proportionality?

The rise since 1945 of balancing/proportionality (hereinafter simply 'balancing') is a striking aspect of law as practised around the world. It has attracted a great deal of attention from comparative lawyers, legal theorists, and sociologists of law. This section briefly lays out what I take to be its various characteristics in both private and public law.

In balancing, we understand ourselves to be choosing a norm (not choosing a winning party) among a number of permissible alternatives, on the ground that it best combines conflicting normative considerations. The considerations vary in strength or 'weight' across an imagined spectrum of fact situations. They include moral considerations often called 'principles', but also values, policies, precedents, rights, and powers. Considerations of administrability (or legal certainty) and of institutional competence (appropriate role for the judge, subsidiarity, etc.) are part of the calculus. It is common to balance a consideration from one category (say, a right) against a consideration from another category (say, the value of legal certainty).

Balancing is often called a technique of 'last resort'. This approach is unsophisticated, since it leaves out of account the legal 'work' by which lawyers often strive to turn a question that seems at first susceptible of a coherence-based solution into a question that requires balancing.[4]

It is a condition of legitimate balancing that the considerations must be derivable from the body of legal materials, either as enacted or as inferable (this is the survival of the classical 'method of construction' within the balancing enterprise). And they must also be 'universalizable', meaning that they must be at least formally in the interests of 'everyone', in contrast to interests understood to be 'ideological', or 'partisan', or 'sectarian'. It is worth noting that, in secular systems, religious reasons are not considered universalizable. In religiously based systems, those of the established faith are highly pertinent, and, moreover, can be balanced.

2.2.2 The shadow of ideology

The conflicting considerations model operates in 'the shadow of ideology'. Participants in the discourse know that there is always a possibility that a given balancing analysis will seem to be ad hoc in its definition of the situation to be dealt with, and merely post hoc in its deployment of conflicting considerations reduced to easily manipulable argument-bites.

The shadow of ideology is not a 'fact'. In characterizing contemporary legal consciousness, the point is not that all attempts at deduction or teleology must fail, so that the 'truth' is the ineluctability of balancing and

---

[4] Ibid.

ideological contamination. The point is to convey the overall situation in which the reduction of doctrine to balancing, and of balancing to ideology, is an ever present possibility.

2.2.3 Commonplace ideological analysis

For the purpose of making sense of legal difference through a notion of ideology, we do not need a strict definition. What seems to me a plausible approach is to offer a list of 'isms' that seem to motivate legislative activity, but that also can be the ideological 'shadow' that those who practise the double hermeneutic of suspicion of juristic activity discern in juristic balancing.

In my own work, I have spent considerable effort on giving definitions of American conservatism and liberalism, understood as ideologies.[5] In the kind of analysis we are discussing, nationalism, black nationalism, Arab nationalism, feminism, radical feminism, liberal feminism, libertarianism, anarchism, fascism, communism, and socialism can all play the same role. Neo-liberalism of the type propagated by the international financial institutions, and advocacy of the 'European social model' are ideological in a similar way. For these purposes, I would not characterize present-day Catholicism, or Christianity, or Islam, or Protestantism or Methodism or Hinduism as ideologies. But it seems to me that 'Islamism', American Christian conservatism, Social Catholicism, liberal and conservative Catholicism, and Hindu nationalism, do fit into the list.

To begin with a very simple example: it is common to analyse national legislation that regulates immigration from the global south to the global north as reflecting conflicts between 'nativism' and what? The alternative to nativism is likely to be called a 'liberal' orientation. Observers might link nativism loosely to nationalism (or in a denunciatory mode to fascism or racism) while linking liberalism to humanitarianism (or in a denunciatory mode to the capitalist interest in driving down wages and weakening organized labour).

Now, if we are interested in contrasting Italian and US immigration law, we might stop at the level of legislation. But it might well be the case that very important questions of law had been settled not by statute but by judicial interpretation, including, of course, constitutional interpretation imposing restraints on permissible legislative activity.

---

[5] Ibid.

When analysing the case law interpreting immigration statutes, or assessing their constitutionality, or the legal academic literature that analyses and propounds alternative interpretations, it is intuitive to engage in the double hermeneutic of suspicion. This means that even though the judgment of the court claims that it is implementing the 'plain meaning' of the statute or constitution, we may well decide that there was no plain meaning, and that the court engaged in covert balancing.

In the second step, we might decide that the best way to make sense of any particular difference between the judicial decisions in the two legal systems would be to place the contrasting norms at different points along an ideological spectrum running from nativism to liberalism. Then we might, or might not, attempt the further step of accounting causally for the differences in outcome by reference to the relative strength of 'nativist' versus 'liberal' ideological tendencies in the views of the particular decision-makers, or, more ambitiously, in the views of what we took to be the relevant strata of Italian and American society.

I do not see what I have just written as very controversial. The difficulties arise when we try to establish the truth of some concrete instance of this kind of analysis, when we try to figure out the parameters of its appropriate application, and particularly to reason causally. For this purpose, it may be useful to try a loose but not completely vague definition of an ideology and of an ideological conflict, as these notions might come into play in interpreting a legal difference.

2.2.4 A tentative definition of 'ideology'

Ideologies are the theory part of political projects, in the very broad sense of projects that aim to change or to preserve some controversial dimension of social life. We call the theory an ideology only if it combines claims of particular groups or interests with the universalizing claim that people who do not share the interest, or will be hurt by its success, should nonetheless agree to that success. The 'nativist' has a theory of who is entitled and who is not to enter the country, and understands his or her claim to be an appeal to the moral values and good sense of the person who will be excluded by his programme, even if s/he has no expectation that the prospective immigrant will in fact agree that s/he should be excluded.

In this conception, the ideology is operated by an 'ideological intelligentsia' that does the theory work. It has its own interests distinct from those of the represented group, and is at least somewhat independent of that group, although not so independent as to be altogether distinct. In other words, an ideology is not 'just a superstructure'.

Ideological conflict often has a symmetrical character, but an ideology can confront something as vague as 'the status quo' or an entrenched interest with no universalizing apparatus to back it up. Ideology is a critical word. It is typically used by a critic charging that the universalizing of the advocate is mere window dressing for the selfish pursuit of an interest. In other words, that the fragile equilibrium between the 'selfish' dimension of group commitment and the universalizing dimension of 'principle' has tilted towards the interest.

There is a striking homology between the critique of an ideology and the critique of balancing. Ideologies make universalizing claims in favour of the outcomes they aim at; in balancing, the considerations to be balanced must be stated in universal terms. Their opponents criticize ideologues for manipulating a universalizing discourse for particularist ends, just as those suspicious of balancing criticize the balancer as a covert ideologist.

When the critic accuses the balancing judge of covertly importing his ideology rather than applying or interpreting the law, he takes it for granted that suspicion has already discredited the universalizing claims of the ideology whose presence he senses. It is just because it has been identified as particular rather than universal that it has been excluded from the set of legitimate considerations for legal balancing. It is therefore enough, in order to undermine the claim that the judge is acting as a judge (and not as an unelected legislator), to show that the ideology in question is plausibly the 'true' motive.

This definition of ideology is supposed to correspond to a common current usage, and it seems important to distinguish it quite sharply from an earlier usage. Contrary to the orthodox Marxist idea, but corresponding to the early Marx and the Gramscian mode, there are diverse ideological projects at work in a given society, rather than a single one corresponding to the 'mode of production'. An ideology, as noted already, is not a 'superstructure'. And there is no presumption that an ideology flows in a coherent way from a central premise – as, for example, the 'law of the commodity' in Pashukanis. Rather, my presumption is that ideologies are incoherent, ambiguous, full of gaps, just as is the body of legal materials. An ideologist will have to engage in the same kind of interpretive work as the jurist when trying to decide what 'his' ideology requires in a given circumstance.

2.3 Splendours and miseries of ideological analysis

Here I begin with examples that are supposed to be easy, and then move on to instances that illustrate what is problematic about this type of analysis.

2.3.1 Some easy(?) examples

Suppose that we are interested in comparing the rules that in different countries govern an employer's attempt to discharge a worker. We know from the outset that there is a spectrum running from the extreme of 'employment at will', with virtually no restrictions on discharge, to the highly protective regime of discharge only for 'good cause', with elaborate procedural protections. There is a familiar transnational debate between advocates of 'flexibility' and advocates of 'protection'. This debate seems to fit easily into the definition of ideological conflict I gave above. Observers of juristic activity interpret decisions interpreting national laws through the double hermeneutic of suspicion, discerning ideological orientations behind balancing decisions and also behind decisions that claim a more formal basis in precedent, concepts, or teleology.

In the current debate about the harmonization of European private law, there is an evident tension on the subject of duties of good faith between England, Scotland, and Ireland, and to some extent Spain, on the one hand, and the civil law countries of the Continent on the other. In a comparative study, Zimmermann insists that we understand the difference neither as intrinsic to common versus civil law, nor as an index of enlightenment, but as reflecting different balances between the interests in legal certainty and ethical content. This is not in any overt way a left/right debate, but rather one internal to law. Nonetheless, the participants often seem acutely aware that in the background is the general political question of the extent to which classical private law rules should be 'shanghaied', according to one side, or just developed, according to the other side, to protect weak parties against strong parties. It is therefore analogous to the flexibilization debate.

If we want to understand the legal regimes governing foreign exchange, foreign trade, parastatal organizations, banking, agricultural pricing, education, and health, of countries across the global south, it is obvious that they vary to the extent to which they have adopted the policies of openness to the world market, privatization, and deregulation advocated by the

World Bank since about 1980. These policies in turn are comprehensible only against the background of 'import substitution industrialization', with its host of legal institutions, that global southern countries adopted between 1945 and 1980. Differences here flow quite directly from the ideological battle, and from the intervention of the international financial institutions and the aid agencies of developed countries. The constitutional courts of countries in this category (for example Colombia, Egypt, Ghana, India, Mexico) are well understood as engaged in a complex mediation of the contending ideological camps.[6]

The criminal law rules governing crimes of honour in the countries of the Middle East have been interestingly arrayed on a spectrum according to the extent to which they embody classic crime of honour versus classic crime of passion rules. For example, in the honour paradigm male brothers and fathers are authorized to kill, immediacy is not an important requirement, and illegitimate pregnancy is a valid trigger. For passion, only the husband can kill, immediately, if he catches his wife in flagrante. Abu-Odeh argues that while we need this spectrum to understand what is at stake in defining the crime, variations are probably caused not by different ideological forces at the societal level, but by the accident of the codifier's preference. On the other hand, judicial interpretation, which moves along the same spectrum, generally in the honour direction, may be well interpreted as caused by shifts in the balance between traditionalist and modernist factions in the judiciary and in the society at large.[7]

These cases, to my mind, illustrate the plausibility of ideological analysis. Those that follow illustrate the ambiguities, not to speak of the sometimes severe difficulties, that arise as we try to test the outer limits of application of the general scheme.

2.3.2 Conceptual difficulties

Here I briefly describe three sources of perplexity, ambiguity, and doubt in the enterprise of ascribing country differences to differences in the balance of ideological forces.

---

[6] R. Hirchl, *Toward Juristocracy: The Origins and Consequences of the New Constitutionalism* (Cambridge, MA: Harvard University Press, 2004).
[7] L. Abu-Odeh, 'Honor Killings and the Construction of Gender in Arab Societies', (2010) 58 *American Journal of Comparative Law* 911.

2.3.2.1 Mediation of ideological conflict versus mere law application

Current work in comparative constitutional law has paid surprisingly little attention to the ideological conflict between what we might loosely call authoritarian and republican orientations *within* a regime of constitutional democracy. In a system of separation of powers, an entrenched bill of rights, and judicial review, authoritarians tend to favour the presidency over parliament and the judiciary, plebiscites, emergency powers, domestic 'order', national security, patriotism, the armed forces, an official role for organized religion, and family values. On the other side, republicans favour the legislature over the president, interest group pluralism rather than corporatism, a secular state, civil liberties defended by a strong independent judiciary. This dimension of conflict is independent of that, say, between left and right on economic issues, populism versus elitism, and so forth.

The contrast may well be invisible to the reader of the constitutional text in isolation, but easy to discern in legal argumentation, including not only judicial decisions but also legal scholarship and the arguments of politicians. The analyst, however, will have to deal with the delicate question of how much of this juristic activity is 'just' derivation of outcomes from written constitutional norms according to non-political juristic methods, and how much should be interpreted as the mediation of ideological conflict. In other words, the analyst will have to engage in the double hermeneutic of suspicion, interrogating first the formal techniques adopted by the jurist and then searching for traces of the authoritarian or republican orientation where it appears that there was interpretive choice.

The plausibility of the first move, to establish that there was choice, is crucial to the whole project. Within a legal culture, some lawyers seem to be instinctive critics, quick to discern balancing behind a necessitarian screen, while others are notably legalist. Between legal cultures, the same distinction reproduces itself: in some the reduction of doctrine to balancing is commonplace, in others practically unknown.

In southern Europe and in Latin America today, it is quite common for a civilian lawyer to refer to more or less 'positivist' approaches, contrasting them with a reasoning style that resorts frequently to balancing or proportionality. Positivists in this sense are those who insist that the legal reasoning methods of literalism, originalism, induction/deduction ('construction'), and precedent, based on the presupposed coherence of the law as a whole, will in all, or in most, or in many more cases than the balancers admit, produce legally 'true' answers, if only the interpreter takes them seriously.

It seems clear (at least to me) that depending on where one places oneself on the scale between positivism and critique, one is more or less likely to practise the first hermeneutic of suspicion. And this difference between positivists and critics is an ideological one, in the sense I developed above. It is a division internal to the legal profession, and the interests represented do not correspond to the left/right division of the broader society. It is striking that Latin positivists include a 'Jacobin' left strand, committed in the mode of the French Revolution to the empowerment of popular assemblies at the expense of judges. In the common law countries, 'positivism' is much more English than it is American, with Canadians and Australians situating themselves in between.

Ideological analysis of legal texts has the built-in controversial element that the analyst is necessarily ideologically embedded in one or another attitude on this spectrum. Before we can attribute a difference to juristic ideology, we shall have to convince the reader that the difference in question was not explained much more simply by differences in the legal texts, as opposed to the exercise of choice by the jurist.

2.3.2.2 Difference along a spectrum without ideological conflict

According to Abu-Odeh, we can analyse the family law rules of the classical Sunni schools using the contract/status dichotomy, but we shall not find the schools aligned along the spectrum: the rules of each school seem more or less randomly to incorporate elements from each paradigm. On the other hand, in analysing the modernization of Egyptian family law over the last century, it is clear to Abu-Odeh that elite male legislators and jurists develop the law by 'splitting the difference' (her phrase) between the models, mediating between feminists and religious traditionalists.[8]

My conclusion here is that it is a question for inquiry in each case whether what seem to the observer to be crucial distinctions along a gradient are part of the self-conscious and therefore plausibly ideological motivations for particular actors or groups. As in Abu-Odeh's example, a given spectrum can be present for observation without having any 'operative' importance. And it can change its role over time, as it apparently did here.

---

[8] L. Abu-Odeh, 'Modernizing Muslim Family Law: The Case of Egypt', (2004) 37 *Vanderbilt Journal of Transnational Law* 1043.

2.3.2.3 What 'causes' a mediation of ideological conflict?

Suppose that we can array a set of possible rule-choices along a spectrum that runs from one ideological alternative to another, and that judges in different countries have chosen different points on the spectrum. Suppose that we can plausibly argue that the judges and their audience interpreted choice as having, as a matter of fact but not necessarily of motive, disposed of the ideological stakes in play. Have we 'explained' the difference between countries?

Exposing the ideological context is likely to make the difference between countries a good deal more intelligible than it would be if we had nothing but a 'merely legal' explanation of what happened. But from a sociological or historical point of view, we are still far from a full account. Most obviously, we need to be able to affirm that there was enough in the way of a gap, conflict, or ambiguity in the pre-existing law so that we can deploy the double hermeneutic of suspicion, and interpret what the judges did as choice along the spectrum, rather than as a 'merely legal' act of interpretation or of balancing.

Supposing choice, and that we think ideological conflict was a factor, we would like to know what caused the difference between the ideological mediations in the two countries. The ideological preference that influenced the outcome might be located in an individual judge or judges, or in the judiciary at large, or in the stratum of society from which the judiciary is drawn, or in the society as a whole. As soon as we start down this road, we shall have to ask to what extent ideological differences at the societal level are consequences as well as causes of juristic choice. In other words, judicial choices may have decisively influenced the ideological tendencies that they seem merely to reflect. Ideological analysis of the type I have been describing is nothing more than a starting point.

2.4 The conundrum of the varieties of capitalism

In recent years a fascinating literature largely outside the academic discipline of comparative law has grown up, contrasting, in a general way, two modes of capitalism in highly developed Western countries (Japan is sometimes included and sometimes not). The axes of comparison are corporate law, labour law, social welfare law, and civil procedure. As far as I know, there is as yet no attempt to synthesize the work in these four areas, and I have no intention of trying anything so ambitious here.

2.4.1 The varieties

2.4.1.1 Corporate law

The central contrast in the varieties literature is between two regimes defined in economic terms with only minimal reference to law. 'Competitive capitalism' operates through companies with diffuse stock ownership that is heavily traded, with short-term financing and a vigorous market for corporate control. The 'co-operative capitalist' economies are dominated by (equally large and powerful) companies controlled by a small number of large-blocholding long-term stockholders, operating through the board of directors, with long-term financing.

There are nonetheless a number of clear legal correlatives for the competitive model: derivative suits, regulation of insider trading, antitrust prohibitions on inter-firm co-operation, limited disclosure and good faith duties to creditors and workers, permissive rules on hostile takeovers, and government regulation through bright-line rules administered by courts. On the other side: the opposite regulatory strategy, designed to force good faith co-operation among stakeholders, all under the supervision of administrative agencies using broad standards, with limited small shareholder protection and considerable restrictions on hostile takeovers.[9]

2.4.1.2 Labour law

In labour law, on one side: collective bargaining based on exclusive, compulsory union representation of a bargaining unit, which may be a fraction of the workforce of a firm or a whole firm, with the union chosen in an election with one option being no union at all, leading to a party-specific collective bargaining agreement, against the background of limited government regulation of individual employment contracts. On the other side: many unions operating in a given unit, sectoral rather than unit-specific bargaining, with result imposed by government on all employers and employees in the sector, combined with some form of compulsory worker representation at the plant level and sometimes worker representation on the enterprise board of directors.

---

[9] P. Hall and D. Soskice (eds.), *Varieties of Capitalism: The Institutional Foundations of Comparative Advantage* (Oxford University Press, 2001).

2.4.1.3 Welfare law

The liberal regime here involves as key traits time-limited unemployment benefits, along with means-tested and time-limited welfare benefits, uniform but set at a sub-poverty level, stigma for recipients, and benefits directed to single mothers more easily than to two-parent families. The principal alternative 'corporatist' regime involves universal, not means-tested, state provision of benefits to those unable to work, with variable benefit levels depending on prior employment experience, from ample to modest, without stigma, with incentives designed to keep families together rather than breaking them up.[10]

2.4.1.4 Civil procedure

Ugo Mattei has sharply contrasted the US regime, which he sees as government by strong judges, with the European regime characterized by strong legislative and administrative institutions. The US regime is powered by privately initiated litigation, through which judges engage in continuous economic and social regulatory rule-making (Mattei is far along towards the 'critical' end of the positivism spectrum). Some key characteristics of the US model are class actions, extensive discovery, no shifting of lawyers' fees to losing parties, contingency fees for plaintiff's lawyers, punitive damages, and long-arm jurisdiction. All these are absent or weak or merely emergent in Europe.[11]

2.4.2 A puzzle: 'organic' versus 'semiotic'

In interpreting these differences, we mix and match what I shall call an 'organicist' and a 'semiotic' approach.[12] As organicists, we account for the multitude of legal details by explaining how they are derived from or 'fit with' or are 'syntonic with' the 'natures' of the 'varieties' in question. We account for the difference between the systems taken as wholes in terms of their autonomous internal development, perhaps calling it 'evolution', or in other words, historically. On this account, the varieties are 'wholes'.

---

[10] G. Esping-Andersen, *The Three Worlds of Welfare Capitalism* (Cambridge: Polity Press, 1990).

[11] U. Mattei, 'A Theory of Imperial Law: A Study on U.S. Hegemony and the Latin Resistance', (2003) 10 *Indiana Journal of Global Legal Studies* 383.

[12] D. Kennedy, 'Thoughts on Coherence, Social Values and National Tradition in Private Law', in M. Hesselink (ed.), *The Politics of a European Civil Code* (Amsterdam: Kluwer Law International, 2006), 9.

Within the organic approach, we may attribute more or less importance to law. At one extreme, Hall and Soskice, in their (brilliant) initial elaboration, grant it none at all as a causal factor in the constitution of their varieties. They describe corporate institutions and market configurations as though they arose and now perpetuate themselves without any need for a legal structure. They seem to have adopted, implicitly, something like the model of Eugen Ehrlich (derived from Savigny). A given economic formation has a set of norms of behaviour that emerge over time from the practical experiences of life, and they 'fit' the life form in which they arise. These social norms are sometimes then turned into positive law and systematized by some combination of scholars and judges and legislators. In this model, the legal systems that seem to 'govern' liberal and co-operative capitalisms are in actuality simply reflections of the strong underlying norms of proper behaviour peculiar to each socio-economic system, and their role is the marginal one of sanctioning cheaters and backsliders.[13]

The main alternative is the 'mutually constitutive' theory: the legal 'rules of the game' are formative of economic practices rather than merely reflective, but always in a dialectical, synergistic relation to those same practices and to social norms that are not legalized. The rules function 'externally' to the economy, in the sense that actors often, although not always, take them as given, and pursue their interests within the system they provide. When those with legal power change the legal regime, they may (depending on the circumstances) induce quite basic changes in the actors' strategies and even in their conceptions of their interests.

At the same time, economic actors are constantly trying to change legal rules to suit their projects, and they often succeed. They generally aim at short-term opportunistic modifications that will increase their profits, rather than at systemic change. But these can have large cumulative effects, when they are not opposed by opposite opportunistic pressures. For example, in the United States the procedural rules (concerning derivative actions, insider trading, class actions, punitive damages, contingency fees, and no-penalty-for-losing) create large incentives for the kinds of shareholder behaviour that Hall and Soskice identify with competitive capitalism. For years, the quite different European rules have seemed to be drifting slowly

---

[13] E. Ehrlich, *Fundamental Principles of the Sociology of Law*, trans. W. Moll (Cambridge, MA: Harvard University Press, 1936).

in the US direction. It is hard to avoid the thought that there may be significant consequences for the 'co-operative' model.

We understand the differences 'semiotically' when we treat each of the multitude of legal details as a distinct policy choice between alternatives available in all systems. The choice is intelligible not as flowing from a larger systemic whole, but as choice along a spectrum, motivated by arguments or interests or conditions that are similar, but vary in force across systems. In the semiotic account, the overall difference between systems is simply the sum of the individual differences, with no attribution of unity or coherence or wholeness to either system, or to its sub-domains.

In practice, we use both modes of explanation. On the one hand, it seems clear that there is something 'coherent' about combining high levels of small-shareholder protection with tight control of insider trading and vigorous antitrust enforcement and, more broadly, with the pro-plaintiff procedural regime. Indeed, there are many plausible connections between corporate, labour, welfare, and procedural law. Mark Roe argues that a strong labour movement incentivizes a closely held, bank-dominated corporate structure. The insiders will be capable of adopting long-term strategies in business downturns, when workers cannot be fired, unlike diffuse shareholders with a short-term orientation to stock values.[14]

Esping-Andersen attributes the more generous, less stigmatizing European corporatist welfare regime partly to the strength of the labour movement. Within the organicist approach, there is circular or mutual causation among elements: it seems plausible that the relatively pro-union regime of the European model is in part the consequence of the corporate and welfare and procedural regimes, as well as vice versa.

In the examples of ideological analysis I have given so far, particular rules are presented as compromises of conflicting transnational ideological forces, in other words according to what I am calling the semiotic approach. A strong argument for this way of proceeding is that, in comparing, for example, the competitive with the co-operative corporate law model, we can put protection of small shareholders on a spectrum from less to more; neither model requires a particular point on that spectrum; and there is a great deal of variation in fact. It is striking that the supposedly purer US regime is more open to good-faith requirements, supposedly emblematic of the continental

---

[14] M. Roe, 'Political Preconditions to Separating Ownership from Corporate Control', (2000) 53 *Stanford Law Review* 539.

and civilian European co-operative model (Teubner), than the supposedly somewhat less competitive British regime. Moreover, while the polar models correspond quite closely to the German and US systems, most developed industrial countries fall in between, tilting one way or another on different legal dimensions.

But there is no necessity to bring ideology to bear only through the semiotic approach. Organicist ideological analysis could, for example, treat the polar types as instantiating coherent polar ideologies, and the intermediate forms as compromises between them. In that case, we should explain the differences between the polar regimes organically, as all flowing from the choice of an overarching ideology. For the intermediate compromise regimes, we would return to the semiotic approach, mapping the way the particular rules of intermediate regimes respond to the conflicting ideological forces. Something like this seems to be happening in the current 'varieties' debate.

2.4.3 Varieties of ideological analysis

The 'legal origins' school accounts for many corporate and labour law systemic differences organically. The competitive model of corporate law and the contractarian labour bargaining model are characteristic of the common law universe that includes Britain, Canada, Australia, New Zealand, and the United States. The co-operative corporate regime and the more state-regulated labour regime are typical of civil law countries around the world (ignoring the fact that the co-operative model characterizes the core continental European countries, not Scandinavia or southern Europe or Latin America, which are mixed). 'Legal origins' ties many aspects of each complex to these common law versus civil law origins. It then argues that the data shows unequivocally that growth is better in the Anglo countries.[15]

The 'legal origins' thesis was congruent with the US legal academic theory that Anglo corporate law was destined to become universal because of its greater efficiency in a globalized world economy. Many of the characteristics that legal origins attributed to the common law corresponded to what law and economics scholars had identified as efficient arrangements.[16]

---

[15] E. Glaeser and A. Schleifer, 'Legal Origins', (2002) 117 *Quarterly Journal of Economics* 1193.

[16] H. Hansman and R. Kraakman, 'The End of History for Corporate Law', in J. Gordon and M. Roe (eds.), *Convergence and Persistence in Corporate Governance* (Cambridge University Press, 2004), 33.

It is interesting that the place of ideology in an organicist explanation can vary over time. The 'legal origins' theory was introduced fifteen years ago in a context where the common law versus civil law distinction had come to seem, first, not very great, and, second, not tied to any significant larger ideological interests. In this respect the situation was quite different in 1900, when many jurists believed in a profound organic difference between the systems, and the world was divided between a dominant British common law empire and rival French, Dutch, and nascent German civil law empires. The consuls of the imperial rivals did classic ideological battle in Ottoman, Persian, Japanese, and Chinese courts.

The attribution of economic growth and efficiency to the common law has retriggered the antique common law versus civil law conflict, and added a centre-left/centre-right dimension. At a first level of critique, it is implausible, to say the least, that common law origins explain high growth rates, or that there is an efficiency-driven tendency for developed systems to converge on the Anglo system.[17]

According to the hermeneutic of suspicion, we move towards understanding juristic elaboration of the various statutory, administrative, and constitutional rules that compose the corporate, labour, welfare, and procedural regimes as reflections of the battle between neoliberal-common-law and European-social-model-civil-law approaches. According to matching negative stereotypes, the cultural individualism of the first generates skewed income distribution and rule by business lobbies, while the other trumpets solidarity and co-operation in the covert interest of the self-dealing large corporate institutions of a stagnant European status quo.

It might be better to treat the polar types not as instantiating coherent polar ideologies, but as themselves contradictory amalgams of competing elements. To call the Anglo model 'free market' (Teubner) or the European model 'social' ignores the 'ordo-liberal' character of both. The Anglo model is based on very elaborate regulation through antitrust and small-shareholder protective legal rules, and the European social model leaves wide scope for private ordering by dominant corporate interests. Within both the German and the US systems, the combination of the long boom and the global financial crisis has produced numerous proposals on each side to move it

---

[17] M. Roe, 'Legal Origins, Politics and Modern Stock Markets', (2006) 120 *Harvard Law Review* 460; L. Bebchuk and M. Roe, 'A Theory of Path Dependence in Corporate Ownership and Governance', in J. Gordon and M. Roe (eds.), *Convergence and Persistence in Corporate Governance* (Cambridge University Press, 2004), 69.

towards the other. In this perspective, the ideological battle is within the poles as much as between them, and the semiotic trumps the organic.

2.5 Tentative ideology critique of the discipline of comparative law

The examples above suggest (no more than that) a large potentially fertile field of inquiry into the functioning of ideology as a cause of non-legislative legal differences, that is, of differences in case law and in legal academic writing. The mainstream of comparative law has not been particularly focused in this direction. Indeed, it seems to me that it is likely that such a focus would be painful or awkward. Why?

The distinction between the legal and the political, understood as between science and ethics, fact and norm, logical judgment and value judgment, is what Rodolfo Sacco might call a 'cryptotype' in comparative law: a distinction from the past which continues to influence analysis without being theorized as orienting the activity in question.

A comparative lawyer is likely to take as the model of inquiry the comparison of civil codes, or of common law private law systems, or of a code with a common law system. Beyond that, it seems easy enough to compare civil or criminal procedural rules, or the institutional structure of administrative agencies and courts. The types of comparison that I proposed above seem to belong to a somewhat different domain, because judges and academics seem to be operating as lawmakers motivated in the way legislators are motivated, in the way we commonly designate as 'political'.

Balancing as a juristic technique puts the jurist in the position of the legislator. In the contemporary period, the legislator is understood as representative of the people, legitimated procedurally, that is, by election, rather than substantively – not by the ethical correctness of his choices but by his status as representative of the views of his constituents, who have the power to dismiss him if he fails in that mission. Comparative law in the age of balancing has to be about the various different ways in which balancing, and the problematic of juristic activity in its presence, play out across the world's legal systems, and that means that it has to be about, at least in part, ideological conflict as it translates into the activities of jurists.

At that point the comparative lawyer is likely to ask a question along the lines, 'What do I have to contribute, as a legally trained researcher, to an inquiry that is really about comparative politics?'[18] The comparative lawyer's understanding extends beyond the complex discursive particularities of juristic activity to the sociology of law, to the investigation of effects of legal difference. He is equally at home with causal statements in the organicist mode about national cultural or functional characteristics that help to explain the content of national legal regimes.

But here we are speaking of the cause of legal difference when that difference cannot be understood as generated 'intra-juristically' or in terms of a larger national particularity. When we understand judicial or doctrinal writing as ideologically driven, we are, precisely, *not* understanding it as legally or culturally or functionally driven.

The obvious answer would appear to be that legally trained scholars are uniquely qualified to disentangle the elements that propel the law-making or law-influencing activities that jurists virtually always represent as non-political. In other words, legal scholars, by contrast with political scientists and sociologists, are the masters of the double hermeneutic of suspicion. By contrast, 'straight' social scientists tend either to reify law in what contemporary jurists see as a formalist mode, or to dereify it in a cynical mode. Each mode denies the important ways in which politics pursued through law differs from politics pursued through diplomatic or military or electoral or legislative or administrative agency activity.

Which brings me to the suspicion that what is at stake in keeping ideology out of comparative law analysis is not the appropriate division of academic labour, but the preservation of the jurist's sense that s/he is operating at a remove from politics. In short, the comparatist who unhesitatingly claims to be far beyond any simple-minded law/politics dichotomy, to have lived the double hermeneutic of suspicion to the maximum, reinstates that dichotomy by his choice of topics to address. And it is hard not to suspect in the comparatist's choice of topic a residual attachment to the prestige, or at least to the security, that the jurist has derived from his firm placement on the scientific side of the dichotomy.

---

[18] M. Tushnet, 'Comparative Constitutional Law', in M. Reimann and R. Zimmermann (eds.), *The Oxford Handbook of Comparative Law* (Oxford University Press, 2006), 1225.

Further reading

L. Abu-Odeh, 'Honor Killings and the Construction of Gender in Arab Societies',
(2010) 58 *American Journal of Comparative Law* 911

'Modernizing Muslim Family Law: The Case of Egypt', (2004) 37 *Vanderbilt Journal of Transnational Law* 1043

R. Alexy, *A Theory of Constitutional Rights*, trans. J. Rivers (Oxford University Press, 1984)

L. Althussscr, 'Ideology and Ideological State Apparatuses', in Althusser, *Lenin and Philosophy and Other Essays* (New York: Monthly Review Press, 1971)

L. Bebchuk and M. Roe, 'A Theory of Path Dependence in Corporate Ownership and Governance', in J. Gordon and M. Roe (eds.), *Convergence and Persistence in Corporate Governance* (Cambridge University Press, 2004), 69

E. Ehrlich, *Fundamental Principles of the Sociology of Law*, trans. W. Moll (Cambridge, MA: Harvard University Press, 1936)

G. Esping-Andersen, *The Three Worlds of Welfare Capitalism* (Cambridge: Polity Press, 1990)

E. Glaeser and A. Schleifer, 'Legal Origins', (2002) 117 *Quarterly Journal of Economics* 1193

A. Gramsci, *Selections from the Prison Notebooks*, trans. Q. Hoare and G. Nowell Smith (New York: International Publishers, 1971)

J. Habermas, *The Theory of Communicative Action: Reason and the Rationalization of Society* (Boston, MA: Beacon Press, 1985)

P. Hall and D. Soskice (eds.), *Varieties of Capitalism: The Institutional Foundations of Comparative Advantage* (Oxford University Press, 2001)

H. Hansman and R. Kraakman, 'The End of History for Corporate Law', in J. Gordon and M. Roe (eds.), *Convergence and Persistence in Corporate Governance* (Cambridge University Press, 2004), 33

R. Hirchl, *Toward Juristocracy: The Origins and Consequences of the New Constitutionalism* (Cambridge, MA: Harvard University Press, 2004)

O. W. Holmes, 'Privilege, Malice and Intent', (1894) 8 *Harvard Law Review* 1

D. Kennedy, *A Critique of Adjudication: fin de siècle* (Cambridge, MA: Harvard University Press, 1997)

'Thoughts on Coherence, Social Values and National Tradition in Private Law', in M. Hesselink (ed.), *The Politics of a European Civil Code* (Amsterdam: Kluwer Law International, 2006), 9

H. S. Maine, *Ancient Law: Its Connection with the Early History of Society, and Its Relation to Modern Ideas* (London: John Murray, 1861)

K. Mannheim, *Ideology and Utopia: An Introduction to the Sociology of Knowledge*, trans. L. Wirth and E. Shils (New York: Harcourt, Brace and World, 1936)

K. Marx, 'Essay on the Jewish Question', in Marx, *Writings of the Young Marx on Philosophy and Society*, ed. and trans. L. Easton and K. Guddat (Garden City, NY: Anchor, 1967)

U. Mattei, 'A Theory of Imperial Law: A Study on U.S. Hegemony and the Latin Resistance', (2003) 10 *Indiana Journal of Global Legal Studies* 383

E. Pashukanis, *Law and Marxism: A General Theory*, trans. B. Einhorn (London: Pluto, 1989)

M. Roe, 'Legal Origins, Politics and Modern Stock Markets', (2006) 120 *Harvard Law Review* 460

'Political Preconditions to Separating Ownership from Corporate Control', (2000) 53 *Stanford Law Review* 539

A. Santos, 'Labor Flexibility, Legal Reform and Economic Development', (2009) 50 *Virginia Journal of International Law* 1

A. Stone Sweet and J. Mathews, 'Proportionality, Balancing and Global Constitutionalism', (2008) 47 *Columbia Journal of Transnational Law* 73

G. Teubner, *Legal Irritants: Good Faith in British Law or How Unifying Law Ends Up in New Differences*, (1998) 61 *Modern Law Review* 11

M. Tushnet, 'Comparative Constitutional Law', in M. Reimann and R. Zimmermann (eds.), *The Oxford Handbook of Comparative Law* (Oxford University Press, 2006), 1225

M. Weber, *Max Weber on Law in Economy and Society*, ed. M. Rheinstein, trans. E. Shils (Cambridge, MA: Harvard University Press, 1954)

R. Zimmermann and S. Whittaker, *Good Faith in European Contract Law* (Cambridge University Press, 2000)

K. Zweigert and H. Kötz, *An Introduction to Comparative Law*, trans. T. Weir, 2nd rev. edn (Oxford: Clarendon, 1987)

Nuno Garoupa and Tom Ginsburg

3.1 Introduction: what is law and economics?

The economic analysis of law investigates the answer to two fundamental questions: (i) a positive question concerning the impact of laws and regulations on the behaviour of individuals, in terms of their decisions and the implications for social welfare; and (ii) a normative question concerning the relative advantages of laws in terms of efficiency and social welfare. To answer these two questions, law and economics applies the methodology of microeconomic analysis. Microeconomic analysis makes certain simplifying assumptions, namely that individuals respond to incentives and make their decisions in a rational way, comparing costs and benefits, given all the available information. More recent developments have relaxed the assumption of full rationality to adopt a more realistic limited rationality assumption in the context of the so-called behavioural law and economics. Another assumption is that the welfare of society is measured by aggregating the individual welfare of its members.[1]

Law and economics, or the economic analysis of law, is today one of the most influential scholarly methodologies in American legal thinking.[2] The origins of the field can be traced back to the eighteenth and nineteenth centuries, for example, with the writings of Bentham,[3] but economic analysis of law gained notoriety with the articles of Nobel laureates Ronald Coase[4] and

We are grateful to Gerrit de Geest and Francesco Parisi for comments. The usual disclaimers apply.

[1] S. Shavell, *Foundations of Economic Analysis of Law* (Cambridge, MA: Harvard University Press, 2004).

[2] N. Garoupa and T. S. Ulen, 'The Market for Legal Innovation: Law and Economics in Europe and the United States', (2008) 59 *Alabama Law Review* 1555.

[3] J. Bentham, *An Introduction to the Principles of Morals and Legislation* (London: Bensley, 1789).

[4] R. Coase, 'The Problem of Social Cost', (1960) 3 *Journal of Law and Economics* 1.

Gary Becker,[5] and the books of Guido Calabresi[6] and Richard Posner.[7] In the last forty years, law and economics has expanded to all areas of the law, starting with those with more obvious economic significance (antitrust and regulation, tax, corporate governance, bankruptcy, employment) to the hard core of legal studies (contracts, tort, property, crime, and civil and criminal procedure) and new areas of the law (such as family law, environmental law, or constitutional structure). Comparative law is no exception.[8] In fact, the extension of recent applications of economic methodology to comparative law has raised the question of the extent to which economic analysis of comparative law is by now a new, independent discipline.[9]

In this chapter we review the main literature in comparative law and economics. We start by looking at the micro level, where contributions have been made to different areas of the law. We then look at the macro level, where economics has addressed legal families and jurisdictional legal differences.

3.2 Economic analysis and comparative law at micro level: rules

3.2.1 Contracts

Law and economics develops the perspective that contractual parties engage in mutually beneficial exchanges that are efficient in nature. Contracts are stipulated to enhance the occurrence of such transfers. However, since they take place in the context of imperfect or asymmetric information, it is possible that at some point the social benefits do not justify the social costs of performance, raising the possibility of optimal breach. Law and economics investigates the extent to which remedies for non-performance induce optimal breach, in particular specific performance

[5] G. Becker, 'Crime and Punishment: An Economic Approach', (1968) 76 *Journal of Political Economy* 169.

[6] G. Calabresi, *The Costs of Accidents* (New Haven: Yale University Press, 1970).

[7] R. Posner, *Economic Analysis of Law*, 7th edn (London: Little Brown, 2007).

[8] U. Mattei, *Comparative Law and Economics* (Ann Arbor: University of Michigan Press, 1996).

[9] F. Faust, 'Comparative Law and Economic Analysis of Law', in M. Reimann and R. Zimmermann (eds.), *The Oxford Handbook of Comparative Law* (Oxford University Press, 2006), 837; G. De Geest (ed.), *The Economics of Comparative Law* (Cheltenham: Edward Elgar, 2009).

and damages.[10] This question has deserved attention from a comparative perspective, given the general sense that Anglo-American legal systems tend to prefer monetary damages, whereas civil law jurisdictions seem to favour specific performance even under conditions that make it unlikely to be efficient. Other important issues in contract law that have deserved attention from legal economists, taking into account that there are significant differences across jurisdictions, include pre-contractual liability in the context of the efficient breach theory, disclosure of information prior to contract formation, and regulation of cooling-off periods. Another significant difference across legal families concerns the use of consideration in contract formation and penalty clauses.[11]

3.2.2 Torts

The economic perspective on torts looks at the most efficient way of deterring accidents. Remedies and liability rules are assessed from the perspective of the benefit in avoiding accidents or tort wrongdoings (hence, deterring their occurrence) and the cost of prevention. Compensation of victims is discussed from the perspective of internalizing accident costs and providing the adequate incentives to potential tortfeasors.[12] Anglo-American tort doctrines have been compared to the civil law of obligations, and the way in which incentives are shaped in that context has been debated. Among the relevant topics addressed in the literature we can find a variety of tort law,[13] product liability, the different approach to strict liability and negligence rules across jurisdictions, quasi-contracts and *gestion d'affaires*, the principle of *non-cumul* in contractual and tort liability,[14] pure economic losses,[15] and the relationship between tort law as a deterrent mechanism and the legal system.[16]

---

[10] S. Shavell, *Foundations of Economic Analysis of Law* (Cambridge, MA: Harvard University Press, 2004).

[11] Mattei, *Comparative Law and Economics*.

[12] Shavell, *Foundations of Economic Analysis of Law*.

[13] Mattei, *Comparative Law and Economics*.

[14] A. Ogus, *Costs and Cautionary Tales: Economic Insights for the Law* (Oxford and Portland: Hart Publishing, 2006).

[15] M. Bussani, V. V. Palmer, and F. Parisi, 'Liability for Pure Financial Loss in Europe: An Economic Restatement', (2003) 51 *American Journal of Comparative Law* 113; F. Parisi, M. Bussani, and V. V. Palmer, 'The Comparative Law and Economics of Economic Pure Loss', (2007) 27 *International Review of Law and Economics* 29.

[16] M. L. Smith, 'Deterrence and Origin of Legal System: Evidence from 1950–1999', (2005) 7 *American Law and Economics Review* 350.

3.2.3 Property

From the viewpoint of law and economics, property law should be designed to assure maximization of property value, both in terms of transactions and use as collateral for development of capital markets. Moreover, following the basic insight of Coase,[17] the establishment of adequate entitlements and the adoption of legal rules that reduce transaction costs will help the necessary bargaining to internalize externalities. The fact that property law varies across jurisdiction has attracted the attention of legal economists to assess the extent to which certain aspects of property law are more or less efficient. A fundamental issue is of course titling of property.[18] Nevertheless, other significant topics include the different treatment of a bona fide purchaser,[19] the rise of anti-commons and its consequences for the property market and investment,[20] remedies in property law, codification in property law,[21] and the development of water law.

3.2.4 Litigation and civil procedure

There is a serious divergence between the private and the social motivation to litigate. Each party cares about the estimated benefit from litigation and the respective private costs. Society cares about the extent to which litigation incentivizes compliance with the law and helps the development of the legal system through articulating efficient rules. From this perspective, the rules of civil procedure and the institutional framework where litigation takes place should reduce transaction costs (thus favouring cheaper out-of-court settlements) and align the private interests of the litigants with the social-welfare-maximizing goals. Legal economists have used this perspective to access the design of civil procedure, settlement rates and litigation in

---

[17] Coase, 'Problem of Social Cost', p. 1.

[18] H. De Soto, *The Mystery of Capital: Why Capitalism Triumphs in the West and Fails Everywhere Else* (New York: Basic Books, 2000); B. Arruñada, 'Property Enforcement as Organized Consent', (2003) 19 *Journal of Law, Economics and Organization* 401; B. Arruñada and N. Garoupa, 'The Choice of Titling System in Land', (2005) 48 *Journal of Law and Economics* 709.

[19] Ogus, *Costs and Cautionary Tales*.

[20] M. Heller, 'The Tragedy of the Anticommons: Property in the Transition from Marx to Markets', (1998) 111 *Harvard Law Review* 621.

[21] Mattei, *Comparative Law and Economics*.

different jurisdictions,[22] pre-trial discovery and rules of evidence, litigation financing, in particular the American versus the English rule concerning whether the winner or loser pays lawyers' costs, the regulation of class actions, and the court system more generally.[23]

3.2.5 Criminal procedure

Criminal procedure establishes the rules under which criminal law is litigated. From the viewpoint of the economic theory of optimal law enforcement, criminal procedure should be designed to achieve efficient deterrence at minimal cost.[24] From a comparative perspective, the main differences that have attracted attention from legal economists are inquisitorial versus adversarial criminal procedure, the introduction of plea-bargaining,[25] the role of prosecutors,[26] and the principle of double jeopardy.[27]

3.2.6 Corporate law and governance

Corporate law and economics has probably attracted most attention from legal economists. There is a vast literature on the economic reasoning and consequences of the different legal frameworks under which companies are formed, investors operate, and managers make decisions. The way in which legal systems have tackled the separation of control and ownership has been at the heart of the debate, in particular the advantages and disadvantages of

---

[22] M. Ramseyer and M. Nakazato, 'The Rational Litigant: Settlement Amounts and Verdict Rates in Japan', (1989) 18 *Journal of Legal Studies* 263; T. Ginsburg and G. Hoetker, 'The Unreluctant Litigant? An Empirical Analysis of Japan's Turn to Litigation', (2006) 35 *Journal of Legal Studies* 31.

[23] S. Djankov, R. La Porta, F. Lopez-de-Silanes, and A. Shleifer, 'Courts', (2003) 118 *Quarterly Journal of Economics* 453; F. Cabrillo and S. Fitzpatrick, *The Economics of Courts and Litigation* (Cheltenham: Edward Elgar, 2008); A. Balas, R. La Porta, F. Lopez de Silanes, and A. Shleifer, 'The Divergence of Legal Procedures', (2009) 1 *American Economic Journal: Economic Policy* 138.

[24] Shavell, *Foundations of Economic Analysis of Law*.

[25] N. Garoupa and F. Stephen, 'Why Plea-Bargaining Fails to Achieve Results in So Many Criminal Justice Systems: A New Framework for Assessment', (2008) 15 *Maastricht Journal of European and Comparative Law* 319.

[26] N. Garoupa, 'Some Reflections on the Economics of Prosecutors: Mandatory v. Selective Prosecution', (2009) 29 *International Review of Law and Economics* 25.

[27] N. Garoupa and F. Gomez Pomar, 'Punish Once or Punish Twice: A Theory of the Use of Criminal Sanctions in Addition to Regulatory Penalties', (2004) 6 *American Law and Economics Review* 410.

the Anglo-American market-based system versus the long-term large-investor model of Germany.[28] Recent literature has developed a new field, law and finance, that investigates the extent to which corporate performance, ownership, and organization is influenced by potential legal determinants[29] or what particular forms of law enforcement provide a more successful regulation of the market for securities.[30] Another area that has been addressed is the significant differences in the legal treatment of trusts.[31]

3.2.7 Bankruptcy law

The sharp contrast between corporate and personal bankruptcy law in the United States and in Europe has raised questions concerning the economic adequacy of each model. Corporate reorganization, liquidation, fresh start in the US tradition and the extent to which employment goals should prevail in bankruptcy in the French tradition have been analysed by legal economists.[32] At the same time, how the differential use of bankruptcy law affects credit markets, contractual performance, and the business environment has deserved attention.[33] Finally, the identification of successful procedural and substantive rules of bankruptcy has been related to the broader issue of legal origin.[34]

---

[28] M. J. Roe, M. Ramseyer, and R. Romano, 'Some Differences in Corporate Structure in Germany, Japan, and the United States', (1993) 102 *Yale Law Journal* 1927; H. Hansmann, G. Hertig, K. J. Hopt, H. Kanda, E. B. Rock, R. Kraakman, and P. Davis, *The Anatomy of Corporate Law: A Comparative and Functional Approach* (Oxford University Press, 2004).

[29] R. La Porta, F. Lopez de Silanes, A. Shleifer, and R. W. Vishny, 'Law and Finance', (1998) 106 *Journal of Political Economy* 1113; R. La Porta, F. Lopez de Silanes, A. Shleifer, and R. W. Vishny, 'Agency Problems and Dividend Policies around the World', (2000) 55 *Journal of Finance* 1; R. La Porta, F. Lopez de Silanes, and A. Shleifer, 'Corporate Ownership around the World', (1999) 54 *Journal of Finance* 471.

[30] R. La Porta, F. Lopez de Silanes, and A. Shleifer, 'What Works in Securities Laws?', (2006) 61 *Journal of Finance* 1.

[31] Mattei, *Comparative Law and Economics*; H. Hansmann and U. Mattei, 'The Functions of Trust Law: A Comparative Legal and Economic Analysis', (1998) 73 *New York University Law Review* 434.

[32] M. White, 'The Costs of Corporate Bankruptcy: A U.S.–European Comparison', in J. Bhandari and L. Weiss (eds.), *Corporate Bankruptcy: Economic and Legal Perspectives* (Cambridge University Press, 1996), 467.

[33] K. Ayotte and H. Yun, 'Matching Bankruptcy Laws to Legal Environments', (2009) 25 *Journal of Law, Economics and Organization* 2.

[34] S. Djankov, O. Hart, C. McLiesh, and A. Shleifer, 'Debt around the World', (2008) 116 *Journal of Political Economy* 1105.

3.2.8 Antitrust and intellectual property law

Alongside corporate and bankruptcy, antitrust and intellectual property law form the fields that have come more rapidly under the scrutiny of law and economics. The convergence between US antitrust law and European competition law, the development of competition law in Asia and in Latin America, specific substantive differences (concerning cartel behaviour, unilateral conduct, and mergers and acquisitions) and procedural approaches (judicial versus administrative enforcement of competition law), or the treatment of intellectual property have generated an extensive economic literature.[35] For example, with respect to intellectual property, the different treatment of authors' and artists' rights across jurisdictions has been assessed in terms of incentives.[36]

3.2.9 Employment law

The disparity between the labour-market-oriented approach in Anglo-American law and the more heavily regulated approach in civil law countries to employment contracts has raised an important debate in terms of economic implications.[37] The extent to which ease of hiring and firing (and other characteristics of labour law) affects economic performance or influences corporate governance have raised controversy in the literature.[38]

3.2.10 Family law

The issue in family law most debated in the United States by legal economists has been the extent to which the introduction of no-fault divorce has changed marriage and divorce. Inevitably the controversy has been carried out to a comparative perspective.[39]

---

[35] E. Elhauge and D. Geradin, *Global Antitrust Law and Economics* (New York: Foundation, 2007).

[36] H. Hansmann and M. Santilli, 'Authors' and Artists' Moral Rights: A Comparative Legal and Economic Analysis', (1997) 26 *Journal of Legal Studies* 95.

[37] J. Botero, S. Djankov, R. La Porta, F. Lopez de Silanes, and A. Shleifer, 'The Regulation of Labor', (2004) 119 *Quarterly Journal of Economics* 1339.

[38] B. Ahlering and S. Deakin, 'Labor Regulation, Corporate Governance and Legal Origin: A Case of Institutional Complementarity?', (2007) 41 *Law and Society Review* 865.

[39] C. Coelho and N. Garoupa, 'Do Divorce Law Reforms Matter for Divorce Rates? Evidence from Portugal', (2006) 3 *Journal of Empirical Legal Studies* 525; L. Gonzalez and T. Viitanen, 'The Effect of Divorce Laws on Divorce Rates in Europe', (2009) 53 *European Economic Review* 127.

3.3 Economic analysis and comparative law at the macro level: structure

Economic analysis has also been utilized to understand issues related to the structure of legal systems and the incentives of legal actors who work within the system.

3.3.1 Judges and prosecutors

As central actors in any legal system, judges are an understandable focus of comparative analysis. Judicial independence has been the focus of some important empirical work.[40] Georgakopolous[41] distinguishes 'career' judiciaries, in which judges serve in a bureaucratic hierarchy for an entire career, from 'recognition' judiciaries, in which judges are appointed to the bench relatively late in life. These systems can be distinguished as emphasizing different forms of monitoring agents: the career system emphasizes ex post controls on judicial decision-making, while the recognitions system involves ex ante screening of agents; distinguishing the systems in this way is an approach further expanded by Posner.[42]

Selection mechanisms are also the focus of some attention. Ginsburg and Garoupa[43] analyse the structure of judicial councils from the perspective of efficient design. The incentives provided by different institutional audiences and the way in which different legal systems tackled them have also been addressed.[44] Such work has given rise to the development of a more nuanced approach than relying on the traditional common law–civil law distinction,

---

[40] M. Ramseyer and E. Rasmusen, *Measuring Judicial Independence* (University of Chicago Press, 2006).

[41] N. Georgakopoulos, 'Discretion in the Career and Recognition Judiciary', (2000) 7 *University of Chicago Law School Roundtable* 205.

[42] R. Posner, 'Judicial Behavior and Performance: An Economic Approach', (2005) 32 *Florida State University Law Review* 1259.

[43] N. Garoupa and T. Ginsburg, 'The Comparative Law and Economics of Judicial Councils', (2009) 27 *Berkeley Journal of International Law* 52.

[44] G. Hadfield, 'The Levers of Legal Design: Institutional Determinants of the Quality of Law', (2008) 36 *Journal of Comparative Economics* 43; G. Hadfield, 'The Dynamic Quality of Law: The Role of Judicial Incentives and Legal Human Capital in the Adaptation of Law', (2011) 79 *Journal of Economic Behavior and Organization* 80; N. Garoupa and T. Ginsburg, 'Judicial Reputation and Audiences: Perspectives from Comparative Law', (2009) 47 *Columbia Journal of Transnational Law* 451.

examining micro-incentives and distinguishing judiciaries even within the same legal tradition. For example, Posner[45] argues that the UK judiciary is more like its continental counterparts than that of the United States.

There has to date been relatively little comparative work on prosecutors. In their analysis of Japanese conviction rates, Ramseyer and Rasmusen look at judicial incentives to help explain why judges are so conviction-prone, but also point out that prosecutorial incentives matter.[46] In an under-resourced environment we should expect that prosecutors will only bring cases they are likely to win. A high conviction rate thus may provide insight into prosecutor incentives as well as judicial propensities. Risk aversion and career goals also vary across legal systems.[47]

3.3.2 Constitutional law

Constitutional law and economics overlaps significantly with public choice theory.[48] The two fields share a focus on the role of rules in structuring and constraining decision-making, shifting the terrain from choice within rules to the choice of higher order 'constitutional' rules. Constitutions are generally viewed as devices to minimize agency costs. By establishing structures that prevent capture by certain interest groups, constitutions can ensure superior governance. Another tradition emphasizes the role of constitutions in constraining inter-temporal choice through pre-commitment.[49] According to this line of thought, constitutions function to take certain high-stakes issues off the table and to help ensure that winners do not overly dominate losers.

Although generally pursued through the development of abstract propositions, some analysts draw on real-world institutional designs to inform optimal choice.[50] Others draw on economic analysis to examine and evaluate real constitutions. For example, Brennan and Pardo[51] evaluate the

---

[45] R. Posner, *Law and Legal Theory in England and America* (Oxford University Press, 1996).

[46] M. Ramseyer and E. Rasmusen, 'Why is the Japanese Conviction Rate So High?' (2001) 30 *Journal of Legal Studies* 53.

[47] Garoupa, 'Some Reflections'.

[48] R. Cooter, *The Strategic Constitution* (Princeton University Press, 2000).

[49] C. Sunstein, *Designing Democracy: What Constitutions Do* (New York: Oxford University Press, 2000).

[50] Cooter, *Strategic Constitution*.

[51] G. Brennan and J. C. Pardo, 'A Reading of the Spanish Constitution (1978)', (1991) 2 *Constitutional Political Economy* 53.

Spanish Constitution of 1978 critically, normatively questioning the provision of economic and social rights in the document. A separate branch considers the impact of constitutions on such dependent variables as economic growth. Elkins, Ginsburg, and Melton[52] take up the question of what factors help constitutions to endure, drawing on a large new database that should facilitate much more empirical testing of hypotheses generated by law and economics. Clearly, there is room for much more work informed by law and economics on comparative constitutional law from both positive and normative perspectives.

3.3.3 Lawyers, legal education and legal scholarship

A comparative perspective on the legal profession and the structure of law firms has looked at entry regulation, legal fees (the existence of contingent and conditional fees, in particular), the organization of law firms, the regulation of publicity and information disclosure in legal services, and rules of conduct.[53] This vast literature provides important economic insights into the regulation of the market for legal services around the world.

Important differences in legal education and legal scholarship on both sides of the Atlantic have been the object of economic analysis. Rather than relying exclusively on cultural preferences and path dependence, legal economists use incentives and a market approach to understand why legal education and the production of innovations in legal analysis have been persistently different across the world. A particular topic of interest is the asymmetric influence of law and economics in legal thinking in different jurisdictions.[54] Generally speaking, it is safe to say that law and economics has been more influential in North America than in other regions of the world, and this fact itself is an interesting question for analysis.

---

[52] Z. Elkins, T. Ginsburg, and J. Melton, *The Endurance of National Constitutions* (New York: Cambridge University Press, 2009).

[53] N. Garoupa, 'Providing a Legal Framework for the Reform of the Legal Profession: Insights from the European Experience', (2008) 9 *European Business Organization Law Review* 463.

[54] N. Garoupa and T. S. Ulen, 'The Market for Legal Innovation: Law and Economics in Europe and the United States', (2008) 59 *Alabama Law Review* 1555; K. Grechenig and M. Gelter, 'The Transatlantic Divergence in Legal Thought: American Law and Economics vs. German Doctrinalism', (2008) 31 *Hastings International and Comparative Law Review* 295.

3.3.4 Legal families and economic growth

At the macro level the economic literature has investigated the hypothesis that the common law system is particularly conducive to economic growth as opposed to civil law, in particular French law. This is a vein of literature essentially empirical.[55] This new literature defends the notion that legal systems originated in the English common law have superior institutions for economic growth and development than those of French civil law. According to the proponents of this view, there are essentially two reasons for the links between the common law and economic growth. First, common law provides more adequate institutions for financial markets and business transactions generally, and that factor in turn fuels more economic growth.[56] These institutions might include more efficient substantive rules, as well as mechanisms by which the common law tends to develop such rules.[57] Second, civil law presupposes a greater role for state intervention that is detrimental to economic freedom and market efficiency.[58] The relationship between growth or economic performance and the legal system carries an implicit assumption: law and legal institutions matter for economic growth.[59] This has been a staple of institutional economics for decades,[60] but nevertheless remains debatable.[61]

The alleged pro-market bias of the common law (the idea of some Hayekian bottom-up efficiencies in the English legal system and top-down inefficiencies in the French legal system) might be an important argument, but the existence of some anti-market bias in French law is debatable.[62] Even the thesis that French law is less effective than the

---

[55] P. Mahoney, 'The Common Law and Economic Growth: Hayek Might be Right', (2001) 30 *Journal of Legal Studies* 503; R. La Porta, F. Lopez de Silanes, and A. Shleifer, 'The Economic Consequences of Legal Origins', (2008) 46 *Journal of Economic Literature* 285.

[56] La Porta, Lopez de Silanes, and Shleifer, 'Economic Consequences of Legal Origins'.

[57] G. Priest and B. Klein, 'The Selection of Disputes for Litigation', (1994) 13 *Journal of Legal Studies* 1.

[58] Mahoney, 'Common Law and Economic Growth', 503.

[59] F. B. Cross, 'Law and Economic Growth', (2002) 80 *Texas Law Review* 737.

[60] D. North, *Institutions, Institutional Change and Economic Performance* (Cambridge University Press, 1991).

[61] D. Acemoglu, S. Johnson, and J. A. Robinson, 'Colonial Origins of Comparative Development: An Empirical Investigation', (2001) 91 *American Economic Review* 1369; D. Acemoglu and S. Johnson, 'Unbundling Institutions', (2005) 113 *Journal of Political Economy* 949.

[62] B. Arruñada, 'Property Enforcement as Organized Consent', (2003) 19 *Journal of Law, Economics and Organization* 401.

common law in protecting property rights from state predation has been disputed.[63] In fact, the current models developed to explain these differences have been subject to serious criticism.[64] Stability of the law is another possible argument in favour of judge-made law with deference to precedent against systematic and chaotic legislative production. However, in this respect, empirically it is not clear that case law is more stable than legislation.[65] In addition, the argument that the common law is more stable undercuts other claims that the mechanism for its efficiency lies in the selection of disputes for litigation.[66]

Another possible channel by means of which the common law might support growth is the enhanced willingness in common law jurisdictions to allow choice of law.[67] But globalization of business transactions has exerted enormous pressure for change in civil law jurisdictions in this respect. Overall, it might well be that the common law is more efficient and positively correlated with economic growth, but the causation remains under-theorized to a larger extent.[68] The mechanism for the efficiency of the common law versus (French) civil law is intrinsically convoluted and debatable. Furthermore, the analysis is complicated by the fact that it is now largely the model for legal reform as embodied in the Doing Business project promoted by the World Bank. There are good reasons to be careful about the implications of the Doing Business reforms for the economy.[69]

---

[63] B. Arruñada and N. Garoupa, 'Choice of Titling System in Land'; B. Arruñada and V. Andonova, 'Judges' Cognition and Market Order', (2008) 4 *Review of Law and Economics* 665.

[64] E. L. Glaeser and A. Shleifer, 'The Rise of the Regulatory State', (2001) 41 *Journal of Economic Literature* 401; E. L. Glaeser and A. Shleifer, 'Legal Origins', (2002) 117 *Quarterly Journal of Economics* 1193; F. B. Cross, 'Identifying the Virtues of the Common Law', (2007) 15 *Supreme Court Economic Review* 21; D. Klerman and P. Mahoney, 'Legal Origin?', (2007) 35 *Journal of Comparative Economics* 278; M. J. Roe, 'Juries and the Political Economy of Legal Origin', (2007) 35 *Journal of Comparative Economics* 294; H. Rosenthal and E. Voeten, 'Measuring Legal Systems', (2007) 35 *Journal of Comparative Economics* 711; G. Hadfield, 'The Levers of Legal Design: Institutional Determinants of the Quality of Law', (2008) 36 *Journal of Comparative Economics* 43.

[65] Cross, 'Identifying the Virtues of the Common Law'.

[66] Priest and Klein, 'Selection of Disputes'.

[67] E. Carbonara and F. Parisi, 'Choice of Law and Legal Evolution: Rethinking the Market for Legal Rules', 139 *Public Choice* 461 (2009); E. O'Hara and L. Ribstein, *The Law Market* (Oxford University Press, 2009).

[68] Cross, 'Identifying the Virtues of the Common Law', 21.

[69] B. Arruñada, 'Pitfalls to Avoid when Measuring the Institutional Environment: Is "Doing Business" Damaging Business?', (2007) 35 *Journal of Comparative Economics* 729; K. E. Davis and M. Krause, 'Taking the Measure of Law: The Case of the Doing Business Project', (2007) 32 *Law and Social Inquiry* 1095.

3.3.5 Convergence of legal systems

Legal economists have entered on the debate about the convergence of legal systems and the role of harmonization. When there is freedom of choice as to the legal regime to be used, competition between legal systems will emerge. Consequently convergence is expected in facilitative areas of the law, whereas divergence due to different local preferences could be sustainable in interventionist areas of the law not subject to market pressure.[70] This would be true so long as jurisdictions are not constrained to adopt rules and have good information about the effects of alternative arrangements.

Divergences of legal systems are not necessarily a sign of inefficiency. There is no reason to think that there is only one single efficient rule for every legal problem.[71] Yet there are obstacles to convergence that result from local rent-seeking (essentially by the legal professions), legal culture, and other forms of transaction costs.[72]

In this context, harmonization that has so often been justified on economic grounds has encountered in legal economists a hostile audience.[73] The clear preference for interjurisdictional competition and choice of law as a form to promote the emergence of rules of law has found wide support in law and economics.[74] Hybrid legal systems can benefit from the competition of different legal arrangements within a single jurisdiction.[75]

---

[70] A. Ogus, 'Competition between National Legal Systems: A Contribution of Economic Analysis to Comparative Law', (1999) 48 *International and Comparative Law Quarterly* 405; A. Ogus, 'The Economic Approach: Competition between Legal Systems', in E. Örücü and D. Nelken (eds.), *Comparative Law: A Handbook* (Oxford and Portland: Hart Publishing, 2007), 155; N. Garoupa and A. Ogus, 'A Strategic Interpretation of Legal Transplants', 35 *Journal of Legal Studies* 339.

[71] Ogus, 'Competition between National Legal Systems', 405; Ogus, 'Economic Approach', 155.

[72] Ogus, 'Competition between National Legal Systems', 405; A. Ogus, 'The Economic Base of Legal Culture: Networks and Monopolization', (2002) 22 *Oxford Journal of Legal Studies* 419; Ogus, 'Economic Approach', 155; Garoupa and Ogus, 'Strategic Interpretation'.

[73] U. Mattei, 'Efficiency in Legal Transplants: An Essay in Comparative Law and Economics', (1994) 14 *International Review of Law and Economics* 3; Ogus, 'Competition between National Legal Systems', 405; Ogus, 'Economic Approach', 155; Garoupa and Ogus, 'Strategic Interpretation', 339; E. Carbonara and F. Parisi, 'The Paradox of Legal Harmonization', (2007) 132 *Public Choice* 367.

[74] Carbonara and Parisi, 'Choice of Law', 461; O'Hara and Ribstein, *Law Market*.

[75] Ogus, 'Economic Approach', 155.

3.3.6 Transplants

Legal transplants raise two significant economic questions. First, when will a given jurisdiction prefer merely to adopt a solution already available in a different jurisdiction rather than develop its own rule (incurring the possibility of rediscovering the wheel)? The development of internal rules or the adoption of transplants responds to a trade-off between benefits in terms of facilitating international interaction (economic or otherwise) and the internal costs of legal consistency and local preferences.[76] The existence of a strategic motivation that ignores externalities derived from the adoption of particular transplants might generate an inefficient level of transplant adoption.[77]

The second set of issues involves what legal systems or legal families are more prone to import or export legal rules successfully. It has been argued that the local conditions for transplanting and adopting a particular law are more important than the supply from a particular legal family. Predisposition and familiarity with the transplanted laws are more important than legal origin in assuring effective transplants.[78]

3.3.7 Conflicts of law

The economic approach to conflicts of law does not see them as a problem, but rather as an opportunity to benefit from international jurisdictional plurality and search for the appropriate legal rule across jurisdictions. The efficient solution to conflict of laws should internalize the externalities created by the interaction of individuals located in different jurisdictions. A strategy oriented to apply the legal rule of the jurisdiction where the harm has been produced is not always efficient, since there might be important detrimental incentives.[79]

3.3.8 Rule of law

Rule of law is supposed to be associated with legal certainty, an independent judiciary, and serious limits to both private and state expropriation.

---

[76] Garoupa and Ogus, 'Strategic Interpretation', 339.   [77] Ibid.

[78] D. Berkowitz, K. Pistor, and J.-F. Richard, 'Economic Development, Legality and the Transplant Effect', (2003) 47 *European Economic Review* 165.

[79] A. Sykes, 'International Law', in A. M. Polinsky and S. Shavell (eds.), *Handbook of Law and Economics* (Amsterdam: Elsevier, 2007), 757.

Immediately, a positive correlation is anticipated between a high adherence to rule of law, investment, and economic development. Although generally there is a strong relationship between the rule of law and economic development, the reasons are debatable once we recognize that the fastest growing economies do not have an effective court system. The interaction between the rule of law and economic development might be more complex than was initially anticipated; in particular the direction of causation is still unclear.[80] The extent to which there is a direct relationship between rule of law and legal origin has also been considered.[81]

3.3.9 Law-making

Law-making varies across legal families. This raises the question whether there is a particular mix of statute law or codification with judge-made law that is more efficient. In other words, it is debatable whether there is a 'one size fits all' efficient law-making arrangement.[82] Depending on preferences, the role of precedent, and the idiosyncrasies of a particular legal system, different mixes of case law and statute law can be efficient.[83]

3.4 Conclusion

Comparative law and economics has generated a vast literature in the last decade, in terms of both micro and macro analysis. However, as with economics itself in the mid-twentieth century, a microeconomic foundation of the macroeconomics of comparative law is still missing. The important

---

[80] E. L. Glaeser, R. La Porta, F. Lopez de Silanes, and A. Shleifer, 'Do Institutions Cause Growth?', (2004) 9 *Journal of Economic Growth* 271; D. Kaufmann, A. Kraay, and M. Mastruzzi, 'Governance Matters VII: Governance Indicators for 1996–2007', (2007) *World Bank Policy Research Working Paper* 4654.

[81] R. La Porta, F. Lopez de Silanes, C. Pop Eleches, and A. Shleifer, 'Judicial Checks and Balances', (2004) 112 *Journal of Political Economy* 445.

[82] B. Depoorter, V. Fon, and F. Parisi, 'Litigation, Judicial Path-Dependence, and Legal Change', (2005) 20 *European Journal of Law and Economics* 43; V. Fon and F. Parisi, 'Judicial Precedents in Civil Law Systems: A Dynamic Analysis', (2006) 26 *International Review of Law and Economics* 519; G. A. M. Ponzetto and P. A. Fernandez, 'Case Law versus Statute Law: An Evolutionary Comparison', (2008) 37 *Journal of Legal Studies* 379; F. Parisi and V. Fon, *Economics of Lawmaking* (Oxford University Press, 2009).

[83] Ponzetto and Fernandez, 'Case Law versus Statute Law', 379; Parisi and Fon, *Economics of Lawmaking*.

empirical literature that points out significant differences at the macro level between the Anglo-American legal family and the civilian families needs a sound micro-based theoretical foundation. On the other hand, the economic analysis of particular legal rules in many areas of the law has been developed to a large extent without recognizing the macro implications. Legal economists and comparatists are in an excellent position to mitigate this gap soon.

Further reading

G. De Geest (ed.), *The Economics of Comparative Law* (Cheltenham: Edward Elgar, 2009)

F. Faust, 'Comparative Law and Economic Analysis of Law', in M. Reimann and R. Zimmermann (eds.), *The Oxford Handbook of Comparative Law* (Oxford University Press, 2006), 837

U. Mattei, *Comparative Law and Economics* (Ann Arbor: University of Michigan Press, 1996)

Comparative law and anthropology 4

Lawrence Rosen

4.1 The encounter of anthropology and law

Anthropology is a schizophrenic discipline. Often riven by mutually excluding factions and orientations – sometimes embodied in rival sub-disciplines,
sometimes displayed over the course of a single individual's career – the main
fault line commonly separates claims of cultural uniqueness from claims to
the discovery of universal features of human social and conceptual life. To
some the question is not unlike that posed in philosophy and other disciplines:
are human communities so incommensurable as to frustrate any useful
generalizations, or may one overcome this seeming diversity by the discovery
of deeper structures and principles that demonstrate unity at the level from
which variation is itself generated? From the side of the particularists comes
the claim that such generalizations are either trivial or untrue; from the side of
the universalists comes a set of theories – functionalist, structuralist, evolutionary – each of which may claim total explanatory power. Whether the
particular domain for pursuing this debate lies in a sub-field of the economic,
the familial, the political, or the religious, the capacity of the ideas generated
in one domain to contribute to the broader issues raised in the discipline as a
whole are, notwithstanding the more exaggerated claims, often simultaneously significant and limited. Nowhere is this truer than in the contributions
of anthropology to the study of law.

In one sense, of course, law is a particularly appropriate domain in which to
sort out the arguments over uniqueness versus commonality. If there are
regularities to any society must they not be expressed in some features of
authorized enforceability, clearly articulated precepts, and acceptable modes
of coping with changed circumstances? If all humans comprise a single
species with the capacity to create the categories by which they attend to
reality, must they not also share in this propulsion towards the regularization
of relationships? Of course, the moment one sets up the issue in this fashion
the field of contention often turns into definitional debate – what, after all, is

'religion' if some imagine it as a set of abstract moral principles and others imagine their gods infesting inanimate objects? What is 'law' if some reduce precepts to rules and meaning to sanction while others seem to eschew all abstraction and standardized evaluation? Whether it was manifested in those early students of social organization, such as L. H. Morgan and Sir Henry Maine, whose knowledge of law in their own cultures led them to consider its forms in pre-modern and non-Western contexts, or in the next two generations of scholars – B. Malinowski, Max Gluckman, Paul Bohannon, E. A. Hoebel – who were equally ready to use law as a vehicle for assessing social structure more broadly, the attraction of law as a testing ground for the particular or the universal was irresistible. If, for example, one was to argue (as E. E. Evans-Pritchard did) that the Nuer had a religious system that was entitled to be called a 'theology', why should the Barotse not have a system of legal thought entitled to be called a 'jurisprudence'? From such starting points the studies of kinship, religion, and political systems had produced ideas of general anthropological import: why should the same not be true for studies that take as their point of departure the law? To understand the contribution of law-based studies to the discipline as a whole – and more particularly why that contribution has been far more limited than it would seem to have promised – one has to consider first some of the ways in which anthropologists have approached the question of comparison more generally.

Evolutionism was, of course, one of the earliest theories that embraced comparison and generalization. In Britain its Spencerian implications so poisoned anthropology, however, that to this day many remain fearful that evolutionism will return to threaten structure with inevitability. Even their flirtation with Lévi-Straussian structuralism in the 1960s only reinforced the British anthropologists' aversion to history, and it is only recently that they have regained enough confidence to be able to consider the past as part of a culture and not a temptation to reductionist causality. Moreover, anthropological studies of law shared two elements common to other British concerns: the desire to establish non-literate societies as having orderly legal systems, whether in contradiction to colonial policy or in its service, and the assumption that law was a relatively discrete domain that could benefit from the application of analytical categories developed by formal legal scholars.

In the United States, by comparison, under Boas's lash evolutionary approaches largely went into abeyance (except among the archaeologists) until their brief revival in the 1960s when Leslie White, Marshall Sahlins,

Elman Service, and others attempted to formulate typologies based not on ineluctable progression but on ever greater modes of capturing energy, developing adaptations, and producing complexity. Where the neo-evolutionary theories were constructed mainly from ethnographic studies of kinship, economics, ecology, and politics, other domains – particularly law – got shunted aside. While the reasons for this will be discussed later, the point to emphasize here is that at each step along the path of theoretical develop-ment – whether in the United States or the United Kingdom – the domain of law became less and less central to the formulation of grand theory.

On both sides of the Atlantic a second major theoretical orientation also dominated the twentieth century. Functionalism was a theory (or set of theories) that was deeply embedded in its time. For those who were intent on showing that all societies are orderly it stood as a counter to the political and racist claims that 'primitive' societies were not organized and hence were in need of oversight by Western cultures. To theoreticians, function-alism had the advantage of showing connections among seemingly dis-connected aspects of a social and cultural system and thus could account for the resonances across domains that knit a society together. But, as Judith N. Shklar points out in her discussion of legalism, functionalism 'tends to reduce differences in content by dwelling on similarity of forms', 'insensibly becomes purpose, and approved purpose at that', and in its utilization of examples of 'primitive law' inevitably 'seeks one world under law'.[1] If 'prefabricated laws' simply await discovery, even in 'simple' societies, then as legal systems grow more complex functionalism helps to establish a claim to some grander law that all world powers should support. In Britain, many legal ethnographies were so entangled with Colonial Office projects – including the ill-fated attempts at writing unified laws for such diverse regions as east Africa, a project that naively assumed that there was an inherent unity to the customs of a given region – that many scholars avoided the field for fear of being tarred by its involvements. For some time in the United States limited studies of law, particularly among Native Americans, continued, although not without similar implications of being in service to national policy. When, however, the United Nations Universal Declaration of Human Rights was denounced by the American Anthropological Association as an imposition of Western values, law, as a subject for anthropological inquiry, became increasingly marginalized for

---

[1] J. N. Shklar, *Legalism* (Cambridge, MA: Harvard University Press, 1964), 83.

having the appearance of colonial complicity and denial of the right to cultural diversity.

4.2 Grounds for comparison

Given these political and intellectual associations, the stage was set for comparison to retreat into particularistic ethnographies of law, a process that further isolated the field from the development of broader anthropological theory. In some respects the anthropologists of law thus replicated the orientations of their colleagues in other fields of inquiry. And like colleagues working in other areas of the discipline, those who came at society and culture through their legal systems tended to employ comparison in one of four ways.

There were, for example, those who regarded each legal system either as equal in jurisprudential quality to any other, or as a specific instance of the universal features found in all legal structures. Max Gluckman, for example, had described the Barotse in much the same evaluative (to say nothing of analytic) terms he would use to describe British law; others (like Sally Falk Moore and Leopold Pospisil) emphasized common problems faced by any legal system – whether it be the nature of obligations or the formulation of certainty in the face of the indeterminate. A second (often overlapping) approach to comparison measured any given system against the standard of some other, invariably Western, system of law. Sometimes this was very explicit, as in Pospisil's belief that Roman law is an altogether superior system from which we can best draw concepts to describe and assess all other legal systems. Some scholars did not appreciate the ethnocentrism of their own legal studies, as when they would apply continental dichotomies (e.g., custom v. law, case law v. statutory law) to foreign systems with little awareness that these categories are by no means those through which other systems draw their conceptual and organizational distinctions. So central did the question of applying universal versus culturally specific concepts become in the anthropology of law, as it was in the substantivist/formalist debate in economic anthropology, that Bohannon and Gluckman went at one another for years over the appropriateness of using the terms of one system to describe the workings of legal systems in Africa and elsewhere.

A third approach to comparison treated law as a unique realm, rather than as part of an integrated cultural array. Here, emphasis was given to the existence of legal specialists, concepts restricted to the legal domain, distinctly legal modes of appraising contending factual claims, and the law's special need to assert and enforce the kind of certainty not found in many other domains of social life. Here, too, the biases of the anthropologist's own culture may have played a role, as we shall see, inasmuch as the belief among many Westerners that law is indeed a separate and often suspect domain came to influence the treatment of law in the ethnographic context as well.

Finally, comparison often centred on the more exotic elements of the legal. Ordeals and oaths, witchcraft accusations and irrational modes of fact-finding became central, with less attention paid to methods of mediation, out-of-court settlement, the role of contentious situations as vehicles of alliance formation and solidarity, or law as an instrument for creating a sense of the cosmos. Phrases like 'alternative dispute resolution' seemed to promise practical benefits that could be gained from comparative studies, when in fact the emphasis on 'resolution' suggested unrealistic closure and ignored the possibility that law could be as much about asserting a view of the world as aimed at resolving arguments. Of course these were topics of interest to students of religion, politics, and economy and, just as anthropologists working from those domains made comparisons to the history of Western and non-Western institutions, so, too, the legal anthropologists made use of the exotic as much for effect as for grasping the distinctive. But there was also a tendency, not present for the other sub-fields, to keep legal anthropology strictly within the bounds of the so-called legal, rather than to explore the styles of thought, the modes of generating categories, or the structured implications that cross-cut numerous domains of social and cultural life – a style of anthropological explication that was far more characteristic of other sub-disciplines that were thus able to contribute more readily to broader anthropological theory. By always circling back to the 'legal' the anthropologists of law forsook the opportunity for greater impact within their discipline as a whole.

4.3 Difficulties and disappointments

Thus while it is imperative to acknowledge the contributions that anthropologists of law have made to comparative law and anthropological knowledge – as we shall do below – it is not unfair to begin with the difficulties and disappointments of the field. Why, to put the matter bluntly, can it be argued that anthropology of law studies have contributed less to general anthropological theory than such fields as kinship, religion, political anthropology, and gender studies? Several key reasons come immediately to mind. First, many anthropologists (like many others in the West) share a strong prejudice against law and lawyers in their own societies. Lawyers always rank low in terms of public admiration and law is commonly thought, even by the well-educated, to be an area of obscured knowledge, strange terminology, and greater concentration on exercising domination or scoring points than on revealing truth. This attitude carries over into academia in numerous ways. Any anthropologist who has gone to law school in the United States can attest to the tendency of many of their anthropological colleagues to make derogatory comments about how they have sold out or how they are now in a non-intellectual field of study. Jealousy over the salaries of law professors, personally unpleasant encounters with the legal establishment, and feelings of relative powerlessness pervade the remarks.

Moreover, there is an assumption that law is so specialized and arcane that one must have special training to deal with it. This is particularly odd since no claims are made for those who study religion that they should have advanced training in theology before being qualified to approach their subject, nor are those who study the marketplace expected to have training in economics, or those who study gender to be certified in biology. That specialized training should be necessary to study legal systems is usually just a further way of distancing law from mainstream anthropology, rather than a rational approach to an academic necessity. Similarly, access to legal materials, especially in the absence of training in the legally arcane, is thought to be relatively difficult: Where do I go to read a relevant legal case, and how will I understand what I am reading without professionalized training? Again, this question is never asked of kinship, politics, and so on, and since legal materials are among the most thoroughly organized and accessible of all data the short amount of time needed to learn how to use them is clearly more a matter of attitude than of legitimate academic concern. That legal material might be a rich source for all kinds of non-legal information is thus precluded by the associations made with law generally.

Nor can it be argued that a number of concepts developed by anthropologists of law were particularly powerful. Is it not rather obvious that there are various 'legal levels' and 'plural' systems that may operate simultaneously and from which disputants may be able to choose? Is it really more than a formalization of the obvious to draw a branching diagram of legal terms like those used by linguistic anthropologists but to ignore ambivalence, humour, and irony in the process? And what field of social life is not, in some sense, 'semi-autonomous'? It is precisely the fact that these approaches tend to limit themselves to the realm of the formally legal rather than to open up law as a part of culture that renders their claims so unproductive to the discipline as a whole. Surely even for those interested in legal pluralism the more interesting questions to ask would be about how choice, uncertainty, or differences in cultural viewpoint among men and women, powerful and powerless, are reinforced as they play out across numerous domains of a culture.

There is, of course, a sociology to any discipline, and the ways in which knowledge has been construed in the anthropology of law have deeply affected the choice of topics and orientations. Given the prejudice against law noted above there has always been some risk in the United States to being identified as a legal anthropologist. Tags stick and since few departments feel that they must hire such a specialist opportunities may become limited if one is identified too thoroughly with the field. It is, of course, true that attachment to various sub-disciplines – psychological anthropology perhaps key among them in the United States – can also limit opportunities, as fashion and bias play out over the discipline. And it is also true that when a field of study is very lightly populated the few important figures in it can have a disproportionate impact, whether positive or not. In the anthropology of law, too, it would be impossible to account for the view its practitioners conjure up in the minds of their colleagues without attending to the fashions and the personalities of the dominant figures training the next generation of students.

For example, in her appraisal of various sub-fields of anthropology, Jane Collier begins her analysis of anthropology and law by noting Laura Nader's 1965 statement that 'It must be confessed that the anthropological study of law has not to date affected, in any grand way at least, the theory and methodology of the anthropological discipline, in the way that studies of kinship and language have, for example.'[2] Although Collier refers to Nader's Berkeley Village Law Project of the 1960s, she does not, however, note how much Nader sought to exclude those who did not follow her lead from the

---

[2] L. Nader, *The Ethnography of Law* (Menasha: American Anthropological Association, 1965), 3.

field and how (like her famous brother Ralph) she actually did not believe in the efficacy of law for social change, thus reinforcing the very prejudice against law that undermined the attention that might have been given to her own students' contributions. Nader had also noted that at a meeting of legal anthropologists in the late 1960s many of the scholars present 'disagreed on both personal and intellectual levels', resulting in a 'turbulent' event (quoted in Collier[3]). Collier herself attributes the lack of legal anthropology's influence on anthropology at large to three factors: it mainly developed during the hiring crises of the 1970s, such that many legal anthropologists could not find academic jobs; legal anthropology was absorbed into broader issues of power and privilege, thus losing its distinctive domain; and organizations like the Law and Society Association were drawing anthropologists away from contacts within their own discipline.[4] Collier does not, however, note that a number of these young scholars went to law school after their anthropology training and left to practise or teach law, or that the turn towards gender and power, for example, should have placed anthropologists of law at the centre of matters had it not been for the broader prejudice against law. The 1970s was also a period in the United States when attention was turning away from such arid fields as ethnoscience and more towards the study of systems of symbols, an area in which, on both sides of the Atlantic, law was not seen as a particularly fruitful area of investigation, probably for many of the reasons relating to its seemingly enclosed nature.

Nor were the law schools a particularly congenial venue for the practice of anthropology of law, even for those few who settled there. Here, the forces that limited the impact of law in anthropology were paralleled by forces limiting the impact of anthropology in law. Most legal scholars tend to see Western law through rather ethnocentric, indeed exceptionalist, eyes; they rarely think that there is terribly much to learn from the legal systems of the societies anthropologists study. In addition, many comparatists remain focused on the kinds of nineteenth-century typologies that anthropology has abandoned, thus limiting the legal anthropologists' sense of community with these scholars.[5] Even when social scientists study Western

---

[3] J. F. Collier, 'The Waxing and Waning of "Subfields" in North American Sociocultural Anthropology', in A. Gupta and J. Ferguson (eds.), *Anthropological Locations* (Berkeley: University of California Press, 1997), 117, 121.

[4] Collier, 'Waxing and Waning', 122.

[5] L. Rosen, 'Beyond Compare', in P. Legrand and R. Munday (eds.), *Comparative Legal Studies: Traditions and Transitions* (Cambridge University Press, 2003), 493.

law the mainstream lawyers tend to marginalize them if they do not emphasize a practical, case-law, treatise-like, or legislative orientation to the subject. Projects like those on law in developing nations that flourished briefly at Yale Law School in the 1960s ended in the proponents not receiving tenure, while the critical legal studies movement was equally unproductive of theory and readily marginalized by law faculties. While taking a Ph.D. in economics became de rigueur for many and the forces of the marketplace propelled some with doctorates in history to take law degrees and law school professorships, to this day the few anthropologists serving full-time on American law faculties are there mainly for the other bread-and-butter courses they teach and suffer the intellectual limitation that, in order to succeed with their law faculty colleagues, they must constantly bring their scholarly work back to questions of the legal rather than follow issues into whatever domains may prove most efficacious. As a result, these anthropologists are largely replicating in the law school domain the limited contribution to anthropological theory that the anthropologists of law inflicted on themselves by commonly choosing topics that remained tightly within the field of the legal.

4.4 Notable contributions

This is not, however, to suggest either that anthropologists have failed to make real contributions when discussing law or that they have forsaken all opportunity to add to general theory in the future. Some of the contributions, although little known to most anthropologists, surely deserve mention. When, for example, lawyers in the United States refer to the provision of the Uniform Commercial Code that allows a judge to alter or dismiss a contractual provision because it is 'unconscionable', almost none of them knows that this concept was included in the Code by its main author Karl Llewellyn following his experience with anthropologist E. Adamson Hoebel studying the pre-contact Cheyenne system of law. Llewellyn saw in that system the use of concepts which, although they seemed vague, became filled with constantly adaptable meaning as cases developed, and he thought it would be equally true that the concept of the unconscionable provision would develop in similar ways in a code for the American business community. In another example, Margaret Mead, hardly one identified with legal anthropology, had argued that the incest taboo was based not on biology, psychology, or alliance theory, but carved out a zone of intimate household arrangements where, say, partial nudity or caressing should carry no sexual overtones, and her view was actually adopted by courts that had to rethink the meaning of incest as American family forms were changing. And almost no anthropologist seems to know that Thurgood Marshall (lead counsel in the desegregation cases and later a justice of the US Supreme Court) said of Robert Redfield – who few realize obtained a law degree before he became an anthropologist – that without his testimony the claims to scientific racism could not have been undercut, testimony that contributed markedly to the Supreme Court overturning its earlier ruling in favour of racial segregation. Far from viewing these as contributions to anthropological theory these 'practical' applications remain largely unknown within the profession and even then are not categorized as advancements coming from the anthropology of law.

If we look at the contributions of the sub-field proper, a rather significant list of accomplishments could also be noted. For example, by emphasizing the oral elements in the legal systems of literate cultures anthropologists have contributed to our understanding of the ways in which such orality remains crucial notwithstanding the seemingly dominant role of literacy. Thus studies by Conley and O'Barr have shown that the speech styles of relatively powerless persons may adversely affect their credibility as witnesses in a court of law. Others have shown that narrative styles lead jurors to build a story as a case proceeds and for the outcome of their deliberations to be influenced by the thrust of that story as much as through any neutral evaluations of the facts presented. Linguistic anthropologists working in the domain of law have further shown that the meaning of terms is deeply embedded in larger cultural contexts, such that the role of copyrighted terms or the comprehensibility of contractual clauses for members of a class action suit may be swayed by cultural associations as much as by the lexical definitions of the vocabulary employed. Other anthropologists have been deeply involved in the role of oral history, particularly in the legal claims of indigenous peoples, suggesting, among other things, that just as the oral transmission of a sacred text may be less distorted than frequent transcription, so too the place of the oral may inscribe information that is easily misunderstood by societies in which literacy is a valued aspect of social status. By emphasizing local meanings ethnographers of law also demonstrate that globalization may be an overdrawn concept, and that there is a countercurrent – visible in legal decision-making and dispute processes – to which anthropologists working in other domains would be wise to attend. And while typology formation has garnered less interest as grand theory itself has declined, the contributions of anthropologists to rethinking systems of law as systems of categorization rather than as steps on some evolutionary scale hold out the possibility of reconsidering why, for example, some cultural features move more easily across boundaries than others.

All of these contributions are, however, unlikely to be among those non-specialist anthropologists or comparatists would immediately note, mainly because they often do not read law-related works, assuming them to be too specialized or irrelevant to their own concerns. As we have seen, this is both for reasons of segregating law studies from general social studies and because of the tendency of many of the contributors themselves to posit their arguments mainly in terms of law rather than using the legal setting as one in a series of domains that would connect with the work of fellow scholars. A good example of this latter approach is the title essay in Clifford Geertz's *Local Knowledge*. Like Gluckman's *The Ideas in Barotse Jurisprudence*, it was initially delivered as the prestigious Storrs Lectures at Yale Law School. In that essay Geertz argues that the ways in which the legal systems of Indonesia and Morocco fashion facts and create categories of appraisal are part and parcel of the overall systems of category formation that characterize those societies. Law, while a discrete area, is thus anything but an isolated one: it configures in its own zone ideas and relationships that cross-cut the whole of any socio-cultural system. Yet if Geertz is one of the most influential and widely read anthropologists of the past generation, it is equally true that this essay is one of his least known and least cited. Many other fine studies – Fallers on the Busoga,[6] Schlegel on the Tiruray[7] – never appeared in paperback and, like other works in anthropology of law, rarely make it onto introductory course reading lists. Is it because of the focus on law that these excellent studies have received so little attention? Is it that the lawyers, too, rarely note work of this sort because it is too concerned with societies they feel incompetent to discuss or from which they feel they can borrow no useful practices? Whatever the reasons, the results are indicative of the forces that have made it difficult, even when the scholar is famous and not predominantly identified with the anthropology of law, for works of this sort to impact the discussion of anthropological theory.

[6] L. A. Fallers, *Law Without Precedent* (University of Chicago Press, 1969).
[7] S. A. Schlegel, *Tiruray Justice* (Berkeley: University of California Press, 1970).

4.5 Future orientations

The picture that emerges, then, is one in which the contribution of studies in the anthropology of law, notwithstanding some first-rate publications, has been of very limited import to comparative law generally and to anthropological theory in particular. But this need not have been the case – nor need it be so in the future. Consider, for example, some of the ways in which the existing literature could be used and some of the directions in which future research could be oriented. Law is an incredibly rich domain for studying cultural modes of perceiving others. Faced with contending parties or challenges to the clarity of a society's assumptions, law-like settings confront a people with having to articulate their deepest orientations. When, say, a witness appears in a legal setting intriguing questions arise: Through what conceptual apparatus is he or she perceived? How are character, believability, and truth assessed? What other cultural concepts do people bring to the process to help them sort through the repertoire of available cultural categories? And when existing categories are unable to cope with new social arrangements (same-sex marriage, artificial insemination, permissible sex when two people bring children from earlier marriages), how do the modes of appraisal reverberate through a wide range of cultural domains? Law is hardly the only place where facts must be created, where skeletalization of the plethora of alternatives must produce comprehensible categories – or where the dearth of certainty means that the available 'facts' must themselves be fleshed out. But if notions of common-sense probability or levels of acceptable uncertainty exist in the legal aspects of a culture they must certainly share features with their operation in religion, politics, and so on. Would the use of theories about fractal approximations, chaos theory, fuzzy logic, or indeterminacy aid in sorting out the style of dealing with the open-textured nature of concepts in an entire culture if the starting point for theorizing came from the realm of legal process? It can even be argued that people live most of their lives in a world of considerable ambivalence and ambiguity, but that at moments of great stress they resort to less flexible social and cultural norms ('because I am your mother, that's why!'), a process that law may regularize and even ritualize. Indeed, one of the dominant theories that anthropology contributed to the social sciences and humanities very broadly was the idea that cultures are primarily composed of systems of shared symbols through which people orient their actions towards one another and create a sense of the orderliness of the cosmos. But where the scholars of the 1960s–1980s focused on the 'symbols' portion of that equation, it was the 'shared' aspect that subsequently became more problematic. So much of the seminal work showing that women or the powerless may not share the same orientations as others in their society has, however, ignored the insights that might come from looking at these issues as they play out in legal domains. Law-related studies could also address broader theoretical questions: Is passing acquaintance sufficient to hold a society together? Can a society be organized around essentially contested or negotiable principles, as may be true in certain legal systems? And was Margaret Thatcher right when she said that there is no such thing as 'society', only contending individuals?

Additional possibilities abound. Elizabeth Colson once suggested that as people observe disputing they learn the bounds of the permissible. How those lessons relate to their explication in religious, familial, and other contexts would, once again, bring law studies into the fold of the social and not keep it as somehow separable. If the plethora of television shows about everyday court cases is any indication, law may have become for many Westerners, as tragedy and comedy were for the ancient Greeks or elaborate rituals for many Asians, a crucial way of telling themselves about themselves, and not just about peculiarly legal issues. One of the great powers of the legal setting is its use as a forum through which the terms of discussion are set. If (as in many Islamic countries) persons of greater social import are held to higher standards than others or if relations are cast more in terms of 'justice' than of 'rights', unpacking those concepts through a thicker study of the nested sets of symbols employed throughout the culture would contribute enormously to resultant social theories. Indeed, if (as Stuart Hampshire put it) justice is conflict – because viewpoints are explicated, interdependencies reinforced, and communal approaches at least momentarily worked out – then the construction of a moral order in and out of court can only be grasped by moving constantly across a culture's multiple domains. And what richer area than law exists for starting an analysis of ideas of intentionality or responsibility and then seeing how those concepts are repeated and varied in such a way as to seem to those who engage their lives in those terms to be both immanent and natural?

Comparison, then, is more than marking point-for-point associations. Nor must its only goal be the elucidation of universals. Indeed, the dichotomy of the particular and the universal is especially harmful to comparative studies, law included. In an insightful passage, Clifford Geertz once wrote, 'Santayana's famous dictum, that one compares only when one is unable to get at the heart of the matter is the precise reverse of the truth; it is through comparison, and of incomparables, that whatever heart we can actually get to is to be reached.'[8] Among the better aims, therefore, may be the sort formulated by Geoffrey Samuel, when he says, 'What comparative law should have as its primary object are the models which can be used for constructing facts ... Comparative law, in other words, can go far in testing each system's construction of its perceived social reality.'[9] Albert Camus, however, may have been even closer to the mark when he said, 'Indeed it is not so much identical conclusions that prove minds to be related as the contradictions that are common to them.'[10] In the study of other societies' forms of law – however narrowly defined, however widely conceptualized – the opportunity continues to enter the broader world of social and cultural life and to see, in contexts where people must act on their deepest concerns, the ways in which they organize their relationships to one another and to the world they seek to comprehend.

Further reading

'Anthropology and Indian Claims Litigation', (1955) 2 *Ethnohistory* 287

P. Bohannon, *Justice and Judgment among the Tiv* (Oxford University Press, 1957)

J. F. Collier, 'The Waxing and Waning of "Subfields" in North American Sociocultural Anthropology', in A. Gupta and J. Ferguson (eds.), *Anthropological Locations* (Berkeley: University of California Press, 1997), 117

E. Colson, *Tradition and Contract: The Problem of Order* (Chicago: Aldine Publishing, 1974)

J. Comaroff and J. L. Comaroff (eds.), *Law and Disorder in the Postcolony* (University of Chicago Press, 2006)

J. L. Comaroff and S. Roberts, *Rules and Processes: The Cultural Logic of Dispute in an African Context* (University of Chicago Press, 1981)

J. M. Conley and W. M. O'Barr, *Rules versus Relationships: The Ethnography of Legal Discourse* (University of Chicago Press, 1990)

Just Words: Law, Language, and Power (University of Chicago Press, 1998)

---

[8] C. Geertz, *Local Knowledge: Further Essays in Interpretative Anthropology* (New York: Basic Books, 1983), 233.

[9] G. Samuel, 'Comparative Law and Jurisprudence', (1998) 47 *International and Comparative Law Quarterly* 817, 836.

[10] A. Camus, *The Myth of Sisyphus and Other Essays* (London: Vintage Books, 1983), 96.

L. A. Fallers, *Law without Precedent* (University of Chicago Press, 1969)

R. R. French, *The Golden Yoke: The Legal Cosmology of Buddhist Tibet* (Ithaca, NY: Cornell University Press, 1995)

C. Geertz, *Local Knowledge* (New York: Basic Books, 1983)

M. Gluckman, *The Judicial Process among the Barotse of Northern Rhodesia* (Manchester University Press, 1955)

  The Ideas in Barotse Jurisprudence (New Haven: Yale University Press, 1965)

S. Hampshire, *Justice is Conflict* (Princeton University Press, 2001)

P. Just, *Dou Donggo Justice: Conflict and Morality in an Indonesian Society* (Lanham, MD: Rowman & Littlefield, 2001)

K. N. Llewellyn and E. Adamson Hoebel, *The Cheyenne Way* (Norman: University of Oklahoma Press, 1941)

H. S. Maine, *Ancient Law* (London: John Murray, 1870)

B. Malinowski, *Crime and Custom in Savage Society* (New York: Harcourt, Brace, 1932)

B. M. Messick, *The Calligraphic State* (Berkeley: University of California Press, 1993)

S. F. Moore, *Law as Process: An Anthropological Approach* (London: Routledge & Kegan Paul, 1978)

L. H. Morgan, *Ancient Society* (New York: Henry Holt, 1877)

L. Nader and H. F. Todd, Jr (eds.), *The Disputing Process: Law in Ten Societies* (New York: Columbia University Press, 1978)

L. J. Pospisil, *Kapauku Papuans and their Law* (New Haven: Yale University Press, 1958)

  'Social Change and Primitive Law: Consequences of a Papuan Legal Case', (1958) 60 *American Anthropologist* 832

  The Ethnology of Law (Menlo Park: Cummings, 1978)

L. Rosen, *The Anthropology of Justice: Law as Culture in Islamic Society* (New York: Cambridge University Press, 1989)

  The Justice of Islam: Comparative Perspectives on Islamic Law and Society (Oxford University Press, 2000)

  'Beyond Compare', in P. Legrand and R. Munday (eds.), *Comparative Legal Studies: Traditions and Transitions* (Cambridge University Press, 2003), 493

  Law as Culture: An Invitation (Princeton University Press, 2006)

G. Samuel, 'Comparative Law and Jurisprudence', (1998) 47 *International and Comparative Law Quarterly* 817

S. A. Schlegel, *Tiruray Justice* (Berkeley: University of California Press, 1970)

J. N. Shklar, *Legalism* (Cambridge, MA: Harvard University Press, 1964)

5 Comparative law and language

Barbara Pozzo

5.1 Introduction

In the work of comparative lawyers, language is essential to the process of acquiring knowledge of foreign law.[1] Information on foreign law is in fact embedded in the language, which is expression of the culture, of the particular set of values, and – finally – of the mentality of lawyers, representing the legal system under analysis.[2] Law and language are cultural phenomena that must be studied taking into account time and context.[3]

That is why translation of legal information has always been considered one of the core questions of comparative law.[4] At the same time reflection on legal translation has offered comparative lawyers the occasion to learn more about the multiple relationships between law and language.[5]

On the one hand such reflection has developed a specific interest on the history and the development of legal languages,[6] while on the other hand it has focused on the technicalities and the specific problems of legal translation.[7]

More recently, comparative lawyers have focused their attention on more specific topics that highlight the various interconnections between law and language, like the policies of multilingualism in the European Union,

---

[1] K. Kredens and S. Gozdz-Roszkowski (eds.), *Language and the Law: International Outlooks* (Frankfurt am Main and New York: Peter Lang, Internationaler Verlag der Wissenschaften, 2007).

[2] D. J. Gerber, 'Authority Heuristics: Language and Trans-system knowledge', in B. Pozzo (ed.), *Ordinary Language and Legal Language* (Milan: Giuffrè, 2005), 41; I. Kitamura, 'Brèves réflexions sur la méthode de comparaison franco-japonaise', (1995) 47 *Revue internationale de droit comparé* 861, 862.

[3] About the changes in the meaning of language, compare J. Boyd White, *When Words Lose Their Meaning, Constitutions and Reconstitutions of Language, Character and Community* (University of Chicago Press, 1984).

[4] See 'Further reading'.

[5] R. Sacco, 'Language and Law', in B. Pozzo (ed.), *Ordinary Language and Legal Language* (Milan: Giuffrè, 2005), 1.

[6] J.-C. Gémar and N. Kasirer (eds.), *Jurilinguistique: entre langues et droits/ Jurilinguistics: Between Law and Language* (Montreal: Éditions Thémis, 2005).

[7] S. Šarčević, *New Approach to Legal Translation* (The Hague: Kluwer, 1997).

the use of English as a legal lingua franca, and the related problems of translation.

5.2 Ordinary language and legal language

The language of law has been analysed from various perspectives,[8] law being a kind of language on its own.[9]

From a broad and general perspective, it has been said that legal language is characterized by a number of specific features, being a language for a special purpose,[10] and one that must be distinguished from ordinary language.[11] Legal language is a technical language, in the sense that it is for experts only – that is, lawyers.[12] Moreover, it can acquire specific meanings, according to the particular field taken into consideration,[13] and it can employ metaphors or particular ways of saying that are typical of that particular context.[14]

For these reasons it has been underlined that legal language can be perceived as opaque by the layman,[15] often indicating the necessity for a plainer language in the field of law.[16]

From a historical perspective it has been emphasized that in the Western legal tradition[17] this particular language emerged when the Romans began

[8] G. Cornu, *Linguistique Juridique*, 2nd edn (Paris: Montchrestien, 2000), 11 ff.

[9] F. Oppenheim, 'Outline of Logical Analysis of Law', (1944) 11 *Philosophy of Science* 142.

[10] M. J. Morrison, 'Excursions into the Nature of Legal Language', (1989) 32 *Cleveland State Law Review* 271; H. Battifol, 'Observations sur la spécificité du language juridique', in *Mélanges Gabriel Marty* (Toulouse: Université des Sciences Sociales Editions, 1978), 35.

[11] A. Phillips, *Lawyers' Language: How and Why Legal Language Is Different* (London and New York: Routledge, 2003).

[12] C. Hutton, *Language, Meaning and the Law* (Edinburgh University Press, 2009).

[13] Cf. the essays in N. Molfessis (ed.), *Les mots de la loi* (Paris: Economica, 1999). For criminal law, cf. G. P. Fletcher, *The Grammar of Criminal Law: American, Comparative, and International* (Oxford and New York: Oxford University Press, 2007).

[14] D. Veronesi, *Wege, Gebäude, Kämpfe: Metaphern im deutschen und italienischen rechtswissenschaftlichen Diskurs* (Heidelberg: Synchron, 2011).

[15] A. Wagner and S. Cacciaguidi-Fahy (eds.), *Obscurity and Clarity in the Law: Prospects and Challenges* (Aldershot: Ashgate, 2008); S. Chatillon, 'Droit et Langue', (2002) 54 *Revue internationale de droit comparé* 687, 690.

[16] D. Mellinkoff, *The Language of the Law* (Boston: Little, Brown, 1963); J. Kimble, 'Plain English: A Charter for Clear Writing', (1992) 9 *Cooley Law Review* 1; R. C. Wydick, *Plain English for Lawyers*, 3rd edn (Durham, NC: Carolina Academic Press, 1994).

[17] In the sense used by H. J. Berman, *Law and Revolution, The Formation of the Western Legal Tradition* (Cambridge, MA: Harvard University Press, 1983).

to develop abstract terms and definitions, which acquired over the course of time meanings that were different from the everyday ones.[18]

Legal Latin has since then assumed an important role in determining the distinguishing features of a legal language, influencing the evolution also of other ancient languages, such as Greek, that needed a translation from Latin of the legal terminology invented by the Romans.[19]

Legal translations have always existed,[20] although, most likely, Latin is – in the Western legal tradition – the language for which the problem of legal translation has been posed in a systematic manner for the first time.

The importance of Latin as the prominent legal language may be analysed from different viewpoints, all of great interest for the current comparative law analysis.

On one hand, you might study the history of translations from the sources of law written in Latin as the history of the expansion of Roman law throughout the empire, acquiring knowledge of the profound and common roots that many legal systems share even today. This kind of approach might help us in shedding light on common backgrounds and in understanding the etymology of legal concepts.

From another viewpoint, it is interesting to study the history of legal Latin as it remained a lingua franca for centuries, until in medieval times it began to compete with modern national languages. This approach might again help us to understand the various synergies occurring between languages used at local level and a language applied at a higher level, used as a common tool in order to overcome differences between local languages.

5.3 The study of legal languages as a study of legal transplants

Legal languages, as well as legal systems,[21] are the result of a historical evolution which did not happen on its own, as if in a vacuum, but in constant

---

[18] F. Sini and R. Ortu (eds.), *Scientia iuris e linguaggio nel sistema giuridico romano* (Milan: Giuffrè, 2001).

[19] D. Magie, *De Romanorum iuris publici sacrique vocabulis sollemnibus in Graecum sermonem conversis* (Aalen: Scientia Verlag, 1973 [1905]).

[20] One of the first legal translations was that of the Treaty of Quadesh, between the pharaoh Ramses II and the Hittite king Muwatalli II, around 1274 BC.

[21] P. Letto-Vanamo, 'Legal Systems and Legal Languages', in H. E. S. Mattila (ed.), *The Development of Legal Language* (Helsinki: Kauppakaari, 2000), 21.

interchange with other legal languages and legal systems. Language, as well as law, is not a static, but a dynamic phenomenon.[22]

Legal languages are often the construct of translations of concepts, ideas, schemes of reasoning, institutions, which have taken place because of the prestige that a foreign legal model acquired during history. Studying the history of legal languages is like studying the evolution of legal systems.[23]

Understanding the origin of concepts in a given legal language implies unveiling the various influences of foreign legal patterns on the language under analysis, shedding light on the reasons why innovation has taken place. That is why the study of legal translations becomes a new way to tell the history of legal transplants.[24]

So it is perfectly clear that, in medieval times, all vernacular languages developing on the European continent began to translate legal terms from Latin, so that, for example, French,[25] Italian,[26] and German[27] are all tributary to the terminology invented by the Romans[28] and rediscovered by the School of Bologna.[29] In other words, national legal languages arise out of the translation of legal Latin,[30] more often from the daily work of practising lawyers, such as notaries.

It is useful to point out that in those times we were not facing translation from one legal language to another, as we understand legal translation

---

[22] R. Sacco, 'Legal Formants, A Dynamic Approach to Comparative Law II', (1991) 39 *American Journal of Comparative Law* 343.

[23] R. Arntz, 'The Roman Heritage in German Legal Language', in H. E. S. Mattila (ed.), *The Development of Legal Language* (Helsinki: Kauppakaari, 2000), 34.

[24] On the concept of legal transplants cf. M. Graziadei, 'Legal Transplants and the Frontiers of Legal Knowledge', (2009) 10 *Theoretical Inquiries in Law* 693.

[25] S. Lusignan, 'Le français et le latin aux XIIIe–XIVe siècles: pratique des langues et pensée linguistique', (1987) 42 *Annales, Économies, Sociétés, Civilisations* 955; A. Carpi, 'Il francese giuridico', in B. Pozzo and M. Timoteo (eds.), *Europa e linguaggi giuridici* (Milan: Giuffrè, 2008), 83; Mattila, *Comparative Legal Linguistics*, 187.

[26] R. Caterina and P. Rossi, 'L'Italiano giuridico', in B. Pozzo and M. Timoteo (eds.), *Europa e linguaggi giuridici* (Milan: Giuffrè, 2008), 184.

[27] H. Hattenhauer, *Zur Geschichte der deutschen Rechts-und Gesetzessprache* (Hamburg: Joachim Jungius-Gesellschaft für die Wissenschaften, 1987); V. Jacometti, 'Il linguaggio giuridico tedesco', in B. Pozzo and M. Timoteo (eds.), *Europa e linguaggi giuridici* (Milan: Giuffrè, 2008), 123.

[28] P. Lepore, 'Note minime su alcuni caratteri della lingua del diritto romano', in B. Pozzo and M. Timoteo (eds.), *Europa e linguaggi giuridici* (Milan: Giuffrè, 2008), 3.

[29] A. Monti, 'Tra latino e volgare: il linguaggio giuridico in età medievale e moderna', in B. Pozzo and M. Timoteo (eds.), *Europa e linguaggi giuridici* (Milan: Giuffrè, 2008), 31.

[30] P. Fiorelli, 'L'italiano giuridico dal latinismo al tecnicismo', in Fiorelli, *Intorno alle parole del diritto* (Milan: Giuffrè, 2008), 74–75.

today. On the contrary, the task of the notaries was to explain the technical and artificial language of the Latin sources in a more simple and plain language, so that all laymen could understand what was going on.[31] This process of translation from Latin to national vernacular languages that began in medieval times was further enhanced in the Renaissance by the building of nation states and the concern of local rulers to shape 'their' laws according to 'their' languages.[32]

The further evolution of legal languages is also able to reveal various legal transplants happening in Europe.

During the nineteenth century, for example, the Italian legal system was first influenced by the French model and then by the German one, and – especially – by the Pandect-science. More specifically, the French model and the German model were both received in Italy, albeit with different methods and for different motivations.

If the French model initially circulated under Napoleonic expansion in Italy as in other European countries,[33] it was later appreciated by virtue of the legal and institutional prestige which it had achieved. While the main channel for the transplanting of the French model was the translation of important pieces of legislation, such as the Code Napoléon,[34] the German model was introduced in Italy through the writings of legal scholars, which were read in the original German language but also translated.[35]

These changes in the reference model implied an innovation in the Italian legal language. Let us take the example of Italian contract law.

In the first Italian Civil Code of 1865, which was in great part the translation of the French Code Napoléon,[36] Article 1300 considers the category

---

[31] F. Bambi, 'Le ragioni della storia. Tra due bilinguismi', in B. Pozzo and F. Bambi (eds.), *L'italiano giuridico che cambia* (Florence: Accademia della Crusca, 2012), 15.

[32] In France, for example, since 1539 the Ordinance of Villers-Cotterets, still in force today, proclaims that French is the official language of the courts.

[33] O. Cachard, 'Translating the French Civil Code: Politics, Linguistics and Legislation', (2005–6) 21 *Connecticut Journal of International Law* 41.

[34] M. Grimaldi, 'L'exportation du Code civil', (2003) 107 *Pouvoirs, Revue française d'études constitutionnelles et politiques, Le Code civil* 80.

[35] Among the most important translations of German scholars we may refer to F. Carl von Savigny, *Sistema del diritto romano attuale*, 8 vols. (Turin: Unione Tipografico-Editrice, 1886–92); C. F. Gluck, *Commentario alle Pandette* (Milan: Vallardi, 1888–1909); A. Dernburg, *Pandette* (Turin: Fratelli Bocca, 1903–7); B. Windscheid, *Diritto delle Pandette*, 5 vols. (Turin: Unione Tipografico-Editrice, 1925–6).

[36] It is important to point out that the Code Napoléon was first translated in 1806. On this topic cf. P. Cappellini, 'Note Storiche introduttive', in G. Cian (ed.), *Codice di Napoleone il Grande*

of *nullity* (nullità), which was further differentiated into *relative nullity* and *absolute nullity*, as Article 1304 of the French archetype of 1804 was teaching.

After the reception of the German model at the end of the nineteenth century, the Italian legal vocabulary slowly changed, dropping the French terminology in favour of the concepts of nullity and avoidability (Nichtigkeit/Anfechtbarkeit, nullità/annullabilità) of German origin. That explains why nowadays it is easier to translate from German into Italian and vice versa, than from French to Italian and vice versa.[37]

The language of the common law has its own history and peculiarities, due to the peculiar origins of this legal system in medieval England; it took a path independent of the evolution of the *jus commune* on the Continent, although mutual influences and interference continued.[38]

In common law language we find many Latinisms, but these are the result of the work of ecclesiastics within the Curia Regis, who were using Latin because it was the language of learned people at that time, and not necessarily because it was the language of Roman legal sources.[39] For a long period the evolution of a common law language was also profoundly indebted to French law, so that historians are always very prompt in stressing the importance of law French in the development of current legal English.[40]

The difficulties in translation from English into all other European continental languages derive from the autonomous evolution of the common law system from the rest of Europe, that render some of its institutions unique to the common law context and its legal concepts, such as *trust*, untranslatable.

pel Regno d'Italia (Padua: Cedam, 1806; repr. 1989), XI–XVII; R. Ferrante, 'Traduzione del codice e tradizione scientifica: la cultura giuridica italiana davanti al Codice Napoleone', in E. Tavilla (ed.), *Giuseppe Luosi, giurista italiano ed europeo. Traduzioni, tradizioni e tradimenti della codificazione. A 200 anni dalla traduzione in italiano del Code Napoléon (1806–2006). Atti del Convegno Internazionale di Studi (Mirandola-Modena, 19–20 otto-bre 2006)* (Modena: Assessorato alla Cultura, 2009), 223.

[37] B. Pozzo, 'Harmonisation of European Contract Law and the Need of Creating a Common Terminology', (2003) 11 *European Review of Private Law* 754.

[38] R. van Caenegem, *The Birth of the English Common Law*, 2nd edn (Cambridge University Press, 1988), 96.

[39] Even if there were authors like Bracton who followed Roman sources, such as the Digest. S. Ferreri, 'Il linguaggio giuridico inglese', in B. Pozzo and M. Timoteo (eds.), *Europa e linguaggi giuridici* (Milan: Giuffrè, 2008), 259.

[40] J. H. Baker, 'The Three Languages of the Common Law', (1998) 43 *McGill Law Journal* 5; Baker, 'Le Brickbat que narrowly mist', (1984) 100 *Law Quarterly Review* 544.

As a result of Britain's past as the centre of an empire, the common law system and its legal language spread all around the world,[41] so that nowadays we face on the one hand the existence of various forms of 'world Englishes',[42] and on the other English is gaining the role of a lingua franca.[43]

5.4 The problems of legal translation

As already mentioned, legal translation must be considered a crucial issue in comparative law analysis.[44] Every operation of translation implies complex intellectual work that should aim at understanding the 'deep' meaning of what we want to translate, and at identifying a possible correspondence in the language into which we want to translate it.[45] That is why translating always implies an interpretation issue.[46] The mere juxtaposition of legal concepts in the different languages should be avoided, because it could have a very superficial result.[47]

Legal translation needs to steer between the opposite dangers of unfaithfulness to the culture from which we translate, and unintelligibility to the target audience. It is certain that something gets *lost*, but comparative lawyers may also *find* something in this translation process.[48]

In practice, the comparative lawyer faces three main problems in translating.

---

[41] Y. Lacoste, 'Pour une approche géopolitique de la diffusion de l'anglais', (2004) 115 *Hérodote* 5.

[42] R. M. Bhatt, 'World Englishes', (2001) 30 *Annual Review of Anthropology* 527.

[43] R. W. Bailey, *Images of English: A Cultural History of the Language* (Cambridge University Press, 1992).

[44] The importance of legal translation for the comparative law discourse has been emphasized by the fact that the International Academy of Comparative Law dedicated a session at two conferences to this issue. The first was the conference in Sydney in 1986, whose proceedings were published in (1987) 28 (4) *Cahiers de Droit*. The second was in Bristol in 1998, whose proceedings were published in E. Jayme (ed.), *Langue et droit* (Brussels: Bruylant, 1999).

[45] C. Durieux, 'La terminologie en traduction technique: apports et limites', (1992) 2 *Terminologie et Traduction* 95.

[46] E. Ioriatti Ferrari (ed.), *Interpretazione e traduzione del diritto, Atti del Convegno tenuto a Trento presso la Facoltà di Giurisprudenza il 30 novembre 2007* (Padua: Cedam, 2008).

[47] P. Legrand, 'How to Compare Now', (1996) 16 *Legal Studies* 232, esp. 234 f.

[48] B. Pozzo, 'Lost and Found in Translation', in R. Sacco (ed.), *Les frontières avancées du savoir du juriste/The Advanced Frontiers of Legal Science: L'anthropologie juridique et la traductologie juridique/Legal Anthropology and Translation Studies in Law*, Actes du Colloque ISAIDAT, Turin, 25–28 avril 2007 (Brussels: Bruylant, 2011), 149.

The first problem is that of translating legal concepts, that are deeply culturally bound. The second corresponds to the difficulty of rendering in another language a particular style, or genius of the language, that reflects a particular legal mentality. Finally, the third concerns the detection of values that are not expressed in writing but are immanent in a specific community and influence the interpretation of legal concepts, the filling of textual gaps, and – more generally – the resolving of language indeterminacy.

5.4.1 The translation of legal concepts

Comparative lawyers need to translate legal concepts that are characterized by two main features. On the one hand, they are technical, and, on the other hand, they are culturally bound,[49] so that it has been suggested that the teaching of a foreign legal terminology could be a way of teaching comparative law.[50]

In the process of translating, one concern is related to the identification of meanings which correspond to the same concept,[51] as, even within a single language, each word, phrase, or sentence does not have a unitary meaning.[52]

Legal concepts – within a particular legal system – are the result of the stratification of different meanings which have been developed over the course of time, and identifying these meanings is the condition precedent to any translating operation. An example might serve to illustrate the problem better than a wordy exposition:[53]

Can the word 'Eigentum' be translated by the words 'propriété', 'property' or 'proprietà'? For the layman they mean 'almost the same thing', as Umberto Eco would have it.[54] However, a jurist would first define the

[49] F. Terral, 'L'empreinte culturelle des termes juridiques', (2004) 49 *Meta* 876.
[50] B. Bergmans, 'L'enseignement d'une terminologie juridique étrangère comme mode d'approche du droit comparé: l'exemple de l'allemand', (1987) 39 *Revue internationale de droit comparé* 89.
[51] S. Gu, *The Boundaries of Meaning and the Formation of Law: Legal Concepts and Reasoning in the English, Arabic, and Chinese traditions* (Montreal: McGill-Queen's University Press, 2006).
[52] J. Boyd White, *Justice as Translation: An Essay in Cultural and Legal Criticism* (University of Chicago Press, 1990).
[53] We have drawn this example from A. Candian, A. Gambaro, and B. Pozzo, *Property-Propriété-Eigentum* (Padua: Cedam, 1992), 316 ff.
[54] U. Eco, *Dire quasi la stessa cosa - Esperienze di traduzione* (Milan: Bompiani, 2003).

ambit of the translation and indicate that 'Eigentum', in the context of the German Civil Code (Bürgerliches Gesetzbuch, BGB) and consequently in relations between private parties, means something other than its significance in a constitutional context, where the same concept can be found in Article 14 of the Grundgesetz (German constitution).

The definition of the ownership regime under §903 BGB is indeed subject to the limitations imposed by §90 BGB, which provides that 'Sache im Sinne des Gesetzes sind nur körperliche Dinge' ('Things in the eyes of the law are only corporeal things').

'Goods' in the legal sense, as far as the private law property regime is concerned, consist solely of corporeal things, therefore excluding, in this context, any reference to incorporeal property.

Therefore, in Germany, the property paradigm has never offered any scope for providing protection to products of the intellect, something which occurs in other national contexts, where the notion seems to be of broader application.

Shifting to the constitutional context, 'Eigentum' under Article 14 of the current German constitution[55] has always been interpreted by the courts as including patents and copyrights.

On the basis of the assumption of 'functional equivalence' between the law on property and other legal positions, the German Constitutional Court, the Bundesverfassungsgericht,[56] has further broadened the constitutional concept of ownership so as also to include *some* public rights ('subjektive öffentliche Rechte'), where these are of equivalent status to the position of owner.[57]

Therefore, even within the German legal system itself, 'Eigentum' is not always 'Eigentum', and translating it by using 'property', 'propriété' or 'proprietà' could have problematic aspects, depending on the relevant context and with the further warning that this divergence in meaning, when applied to both private law contexts and to constitutional ones, may either not exist at all, or may have a different dimension in Swiss or Austrian law, where the term 'Eigentum' is also used.

---

[55] Art. 14 of the German constitution (Grundgesetz) derives from Art. 153 of the Weimar constitution.

[56] The leading case is *BVerfGE* 4, 240, on which see H. Sendler, 'Die Konkretisierung einer modernen Eigentumsverfassung durch Richterspruch', (1971) *Die Öffentliche Verwaltung* 20.

[57] G. Nicolaysen, 'Eigentumsgarantie und vermögenswerte subjektive öffentliche Rechte', in H. P. Ipsen (ed.), *Hamburger Festschrift für Friedrich Schack* (Berlin: Metzner, 1966), 109.

Furthermore, when we have to translate legal concepts, we have to remember their demarcation function, which may vary according to the legal system being considered as the reference context.

Take, for instance, the notion of *contract*:[58] in regard to this, vast differences exist between the various European legal systems which cannot be explained merely on the basis of the common law/civil law antithesis.[59] Just to frame the issue, we should perhaps remind ourselves that marriage is a 'contrat'[60] for the French, while it is not one so far as the Germans are concerned, nor the Italians or the English.

Donation is contractual for Germans[61] and Italians,[62] but not for the English.

Trusts are instruments governed by the law of property, but to the extent to which any effects of this institution are required to be transposed into civil law jurisdictions, recourse must be had to mechanisms which are for all purposes part of the law of contracts.

Bearing all this in mind, can we translate 'contratto' as 'Vertrag', 'contract', or 'contrat'?

The demarcation function of the notion of contract varies according to each individual reference context, which raises the problem of informing the interlocutor of the risk run by adopting a literal translation which fails to emphasize the limitations and lines of demarcation of the concept being translated.

Finally, legal concepts are intimately connected with intellectual reasoning processes and cultural issues in a given context and therefore with the language in which these things are expressed.[63]

A legal scholar belonging to a particular country is reined in by his or her own legal language and objects to any innovation which comes along in the train of some line of thought or other.

---

[58] R. Sacco, 'Diversity and Uniformity in the Law', (2001) 49 *American Journal of Comparative Law* 171; Sacco, 'Il contratto nella prospettiva comparatistica', (2001) *Europa e Diritto Privato* 479.

[59] H. Kötz, *European Contract Law*, trans. T. Weir (Oxford: Clarendon, 1997); J. Gordley, *The Philosophical Origins of Modern Contract Doctrine* (Oxford: Clarendon, 1991).

[60] Code Napoléon, Arts. 1387 and ff.: 'Du contrat de mariage et des régimes matrimoniaux'.

[61] Bürgerliches Gesetzbuch, § 516: 'Eine Zuwendung, durch die jemand aus seinem Vermögen einen anderen bereichert, ist Schenkung, wenn beide Teile darüber einig sind, dass die Zuwendung unentgeltlich erfolgt.'

[62] Italian Civil Code, Art. 769: 'La donazione è il contratto col quale, per spirito di liberalità, una parte arricchisce l'altra, disponendo a favore di questa di un suo diritto o assumendo verso la stessa un'obbligazione.'

[63] Gerber, 'Authority Heuristics', 46 ff.

Some concrete examples will show the exact terms of the discussion.

What happens if an Italian lawyer wants to explain the difference existing between 'decadenza' and 'prescrizione', or 'interessi legittimi' and 'diritti soggettivi' to a foreign colleague? These are terms with which the Italian lawyer is accustomed to dealing, but the difficulty of explaining them without going into the whole historic and cultural background will soon become apparent – a background which has caused the distinctions to develop, and which is unknown in other European systems.

And thus a reminder[64] will be needed that, in order to understand the origin of the differentiation of 'decadenza' and 'prescrizione' in the Italian civil code, unknown to other systems, it is necessary to go back to the mid-nineteenth century and the studies which were being pursued on the legal effect of prescription periods and how time runs in legal terms. The subject was set in a single framework from the conceptual point of view and referred to one single legal regime – that of prescription.

This method of proceeding was accepted by both French and German academic commentators. The notion of prescription embraced several institutions which would be collocated today in a quite different way. Prescription included at one and the same time not only its extinguishing aspect, but also that of acquisition (*usucapione*). The 1865 Italian civil code reproduced this single archetype.[65]

However, after the 1865 civil code had been decreed, Italian academic lawyers came under the influence of their German counterparts, in particular the work of Grawein[66] and Weiss.[67]

German legal thought started to make a distinction between 'Präklusivfristen' and so-called 'Verjährungsfristen',[68] but in the German civil code (the BGB), which came into force on 1 January 1900, no specific provisions in the field of *decadenza* were included. However, the German

---

[64] We have taken this example from B. Pozzo, 'Constitutional Review of Disproportionately Different Periods of Limitation of Action (Prescription)', (1997) 5 *European Review of Private Law* 79, 92 ff., and esp. 98 n. 67.

[65] See Arts. 2105 ff. of the 1865 Italian Civil Code, 'Titolo XXVIII, Della prescrizione'.

[66] A. Grawein, *Verjährung und gesetzliche Befristung* (Leipzig: Duncker & Humblot, 1880).

[67] C. Weiss, *Verjährung und gesetzliche Befristung nach dem bürgerlichen Rechte des deutschen Reichs* (Munich: J. Schweitzer, 1905).

[68] In this connection see Andreas von Tuhr's classic treatment of this subject: A. von Tuhr, *Der Allgemeine Teil des Deutschen Bürgerlichen Rechts* (Leipzig: Duncker & Humblot, 1910), *Drittes Buch*, § 90, 500 ss.

code allowed that there were points which legal scholars may have wished to develop.[69]

In contrast to this, the Italian law-makers introduced a differentiation between *decadenza* and *prescrizione* in the 1942 civil code, a novelty with respect to the 1865 version, following the line of thought coming from German legal scholars which greatly influenced the debate in Italy in the early years of the century.[70]

The outcome of this is that the clear distinction between *decadenza* and *prescrizione*, which is a feature of the legal language of Italian jurists, is non-existent – as in the common law countries – or much more attenuated elsewhere, such as in France, where the expression 'délais prefix' is used by legal academics, but not in the code.[71]

In an analogous way, the origin of the differentiation between 'interesse legittimo' and 'diritto soggettivo' is directly related to the historic events which characterized the Italian system at the end of the nineteenth century,[72] following which a decision had to be reached, once Italy had been united, as to which model to follow regarding the organization of the administrative jurisdiction. Of the two models considered – the French model, with its system of administrative courts, and the Belgian one, with a single jurisdiction – the latter was preferred.

The consequence of this choice was that all disputes concerning *diritti soggettivi* to which the public administration was a party were heard by a *giudice ordinario*, that is to say a judge not presiding over specifically administrative courts.[73]

---

[69] In the 'Motive zu dem Entwurfe eines Bürgerlichen Gesetzbuches für das Deutsche Reich', Band I, Allgemeiner Theil, 374, there is the following statement on this point: 'Allgemeine Vorschriften über die im Entwurfe sich findenden zahlreichen Ausschlussfristen (Präklusivfristen) sind nicht aufgestellt. Der Begriff der Ausschlussfrist gibt, wie neuere Untersuchungen auf diesem Gebiete gezeigt haben, die maßgebenden Grundsätze ohne weiteres an die Hand.'

[70] See C. Fadda and P. Emilio Bensa, *Note a Windscheid, Diritto delle Pandette*, vol. IV (Turin: Utet, 1930), 586.

[71] As far as French academic commentary is concerned, see J. Carbonnier, *Droit civil, Introduction*, 20th edn (Paris: Presses Universitaires de France, 1991), 315.

[72] On this subject see B. Sordi, *Giustizia e amministrazione nell'Italia liberale. La formazione della nozione di interesse legittimo* (Milan: Giuffrè, 1985).

[73] Act no. 2248, annex E of 20 March 1865 abolished the ordinary courts under the administrative tribunal system (i tribunali ordinari del contenzioso amministrativo) and a new division of jurisdiction was created.

The *giudice ordinario*, however, did not hear claims on all those legal situations giving rise to actionable rights (*situazioni giuridiche soggettive*) outside the ambit of *diritti soggettivi*, namely those *interessi legittimi* (legitimate interests) which concerned an individual's assertion of the legitimate exercise of the administrative power. It was soon realized that citizens had thereby been deprived of all safeguards with regard to the normal actions of the public administration.

Subsequently, in 1889, a broader safeguard for citizens was achieved by instituting a Fourth Jurisdictional Section (IV Sezione giurisdizionale) in the Council of State, not yet having the status of judge, who was given general competence for judicial review of administrative action.[74] The establishment of this section was to mark the beginnings of *interessi legittimi*.[75]

It is therefore easy to appreciate that such a distinction does not exist, as far as other legal systems which opted for different institutional arrangements are concerned, while Italian jurists are accustomed to working with it.

5.4.2 About the translatability and the untranslatability of legal concepts

As we have seen, the legal language of a given system reverberates with specific taxonomies which have been developed over the course of years, decades, centuries, and millennia and which are an intrinsic part of the historical development of a given legal system.[76]

The result is often untranslatable so far as other legal realities are concerned.[77] How can we translate 'trust' in any other European continental language? How could we translate 'panchayat', the typical Indian institution, in any language which is not Hindi? How can we render the distinction existing in the Chinese system, between 'li' and 'fa', without using the very same words '*li*' and '*fa*'?

---

[74] Under Arts. 1447 ff. of the Italian civil code.   [75] By Act no. 5982 of 31 March 1889.

[76] U. Mattei, 'Three Patterns of Law: Taxonomy and Change in the World's Legal System', (1997) 45 *American Journal of Comparative Law* 5.

[77] Sofie M. F. Geeroms, 'Comparative Law and Legal Translation: Why the Terms Cassation, Revision and Appeal Should Not Be Translated', (2002) 50 *American Journal of Comparative Law* 201.

That is why Rodolfo Sacco, who has given much of his attention to translation problems, has pointed out that sometimes comparative lawyers must learn *not* to translate.[78]

The question of the untranslatability of legal concept anyway needs further attention. What is the significance of the apparent insusceptibility to translation? What meaning should be inferred from the inability to translate the Italian term 'rescissione' into German legal language?[79]

'Rescissione' is ruled by Articles 1447 ff. of the Italian civil code. In particular, Article 1447(1) provides that 'A contract by which one party assumes obligations under unfair conditions because of the necessity, known to the other party, of saving himself or others from a present danger of serious personal injury, can be rescinded on the demand of the party who assumes such obligations'; while Article 1448(1) provides that 'If there is a disproportion between the performance of one party and that of the other, and such disproportion was the result of a state of need of one party, of which the other has availed himself to his advantage, the injured party can demand rescission of the contract.' This ruling does not find a conceptual equivalent in German, but an analysis which merely indicates that the term 'rescissione' cannot be translated certainly seems to be unsatisfactory, unless it emphasizes that the lack of a German equivalent for the term does not necessarily imply that the legal system has not had to confront the issues which the Italian legal system deals with by the institution of *rescissione*. The practical effect of §138 BGB, which governs 'Rechtsgeschäft, das gegen die guten Sitten verstösst',[80] is that those legal circumstances which Italian law treats as coming under the rules governing *rescissione*, can be considered and resolved under this provision.

On the other hand we also have to highlight a different phenomenon, which appears to mirror that just set out – the sometimes straightforward possibility of translating a legal term literally into another language does not mean that the terms are effectively equivalent. To take once more the example

---

[78] R. Sacco, *Introduzione al diritto comparato*, 5th edn (Turin: Utet, 1992), 40 f.

[79] We have taken this example from Pozzo, 'Harmonisation of European Contract Law', 754.

[80] '§ 138. Legal transaction contrary to public morality, usury: (1) A legal transaction which is contrary to public morality is void. (2) In particular, a legal transaction is void by which a person, by exploiting the predicament, inexperience, lack of sound judgement or considerable weakness of will of another, causes himself or a third party, in exchange for an act of performance, to be promised or granted pecuniary advantages which are clearly disproportionate to the performance.'

of 'decadenza', already cited, it will be seen that, in France, a legal dictionary translates the Italian term 'decadenza' using the French word 'déchéance'.[81] However, when leafing through the French civil code it becomes clear that the term 'déchéance' only applies under particular circumstances, such as the case of an heir who has concealed assets which form part of the estate, and who is therefore barred from benefiting under the will.[82]

5.4.3 The genius of a language

In legal translation it is not only the particular meaning of legal concepts that have flourished in a specific legal and cultural humus that might be lost: it is the genius of the language itself that fades away.[83]

Legal discourse in every culture has its own structures and represents ways of reasoning: language shapes what the user knows. This knowledge-shaping (or cognitive) role is of fundamental importance, because it conditions all knowledge of foreign law.[84]

While translating the *Einführung in die Rechtsvergleichung auf dem Gebiete des Privatrechts* by Zweigert and Kötz into Italian, we became aware that the only translation possible was that envisaging it in short Italian sentences instead of the long German period with several commas and parenthetic clauses and finally the verb at the end. But we also knew that the style of the German sentence, especially that used in legal textbooks, would have got lost, and with it a mirror of the specific German legal mentality and legal culture.[85]

The problem of rendering in the translation the particular style, or genius, of the original language recalls the task of the translators of literary works; it is not specific to legal translation. Edith Grossman, the famous translator into English of the novels of Gabriel García Márquez, describes the huge

---

[81] G. Tortora, *Dizionario Giuridico Italiano–Francese, Francese–Italiano* (Milan: Giuffrè, 1991).

[82] This is the case envisaged by Art. 801 of the French Civil Code: 'L'héritier qui s'est rendu coupable de recélé, ou qui a omis, sciemment et de mauvais foi, de comprendre dans l'inventariee des effets de la succession, est déchu du bénéfice d'inventaire.'

[83] It was in particular the Historic School that maintained that law, like language, was part of the genius and culture of a people. On the particular genius of the French language cf. A. Dauzat, *Le génie de la langue française* (Paris: Payot, 1943).

[84] Gerber, 'Authority Heuristics', 41 ff.

[85] N. Kasirer (ed.), *Le droit civil, avant tout un style?* (Montreal: Centre de recherche en droit privé and comparé du Québec, 2003).

task of rendering in the translated language the flavour of the original language in the following words: 'In the process of translating, we endeavor to hear the first version of the work as profoundly and completely as possible, struggling to discover the linguistic charge, the structural rhythms, the subtle implications, the complexities of meaning and suggestion in vocabulary and phrasing, and the ambient, cultural inferences and conclusions these tonalities allow us to extrapolate.'[86]

It has been said that if one is translating a legal document all one need do is convey the meaning, but if one is translating literature one has to convey feeling as well as grammatical sense.[87]

I am in favour of the contrary opinion, that emphasizes in comparative law analysis the importance of a particular style in legal texts. This level of analysis could help comparative lawyers also to be more sensitive towards changes in the style due to the influence of other factors.

This approach has been taken in order to analyse, for example, the particular style of mixed jurisdictions, that – naturally – confront themselves with two or more particular styles, originating in different legal systems.

In the case of Israel, for example, it has been held that Hebrew is in general far less subtle than languages of European origin, that it discourages the expression of ambivalence, hesitation, nuance, doubt, and possibility, and encourages clear-cut statements and opinions. On the one hand, Hebrew should – for these reasons – be considered better suited to the kind of legal judicial writing that characterizes civilian systems.[88] On the other hand, it has been highlighted that English dominates in style: legal Hebrew is just expressed in local words, though not always in local syntax, so that ultimately modern legal Hebrew sounds like legal English expressed in Hebrew words.

5.4.4 Legal translation and the problem of immanent values

Our immediate perception of legal rules is that they seem inseparable from their written form. When speaking about legal languages and legal translation it is, however, important to remember that written language is only one of the possible forms of expression and manifestation of the law, and

---

[86] E. Grossman, *Why Translation Matters* (New Haven and London: Yale University Press, 2010), 9.

[87] A. Waley, 'Notes on Translation', (1958) *Atlantic Monthly* 107.

[88] C. Wasserstein Fassberg, 'Language and Style in a Mixed System', (2003) 78 *Tulane Law Review* 151, 158 ff.

that from a historical point of view, the law has not always and not in its entirety been laid down in written form.[89]

In the Western legal tradition we are accustomed to think of language in terms of writing, and we are trained to conceive law primarily in written terms. From this perspective only written law is considered authoritative.[90]

In other legal traditions, such as that of China[91] or those of Africa,[92] this perception might be different, as the unwritten character of customary rules could prevail in the law in action.

Furthermore, legal rules, whether oral or written, might be profoundly influenced by invisible patterns of ordering that need to be revealed before the rules are translated.[93]

We might say that the task of understanding the culture in which legal rules are rooted is a general one that every translation process implies, although in some particular cases this could be especially important.

In order to uncover the invisible patterns and ascertain the immanent values of a legal system, a comparative law analysis needs to understand the deep links between law and culture.[94]

Let us take few examples in order to render the problematic more clear: would it be possible to understand the concept of private property in China without keeping in mind the values of the socialist ideology in which this concept is embedded?[95] Or, would it be possible to understand the legislation on the remarriage of widows in India without knowing the values that Hindu traditional law attaches to the word 'widow' itself?[96]

---

[89] R. Sacco, 'Le droit muet', (1995) *Revue trimestrelle du droit civil* 783; Sacco, *Le fonti non scritte e l'interpretazione* (Turin: Utet, 1999).

[90] B. Grossfeld and E. J. Eberle, 'Patterns of Order in Comparative Law, Discovering and Decoding Invisible Powers', (2003) 38 *Texas International Law Journal* 291, 306.

[91] D. Cao, *Chinese Law: A Language Perspective* (Aldershot: Dartmouth, 2004), 161 ff.

[92] A. Allott, 'Law in the New Africa', (1967) 66 *African Affairs* 55, 63.

[93] Grossfeld and Eberle, 'Patterns of Order in Comparative Law', 297.

[94] On the interaction between law and culture cf. R. W. Gordon, 'Critical Legal Histories', (1984) 36 *Stanford Law Review* 57; M. Krygier, 'Law as Tradition', (1986) 5 *Law and Philosophy* 237; R. L. Abel, 'Comparative Law and Social Theory', (1978) 26 *American Journal of Comparative Law* 219.

[95] L. Chen, 'Private Property with Chinese Characteristics: A Critical Analysis of the Chinese Property Law of 2007', (2010) 18 *European Review of Private Law* 983.

[96] L. Carroll, 'Law, Custom and Statutory Social Reform: The Hindu Widow's Remarriage Act of 1856', in J. Krishnamurty (ed.), *Women in Colonial India: A Legal and Social Perspective* (Delhi: Oxford University Press, 1989).

5.4.5 The functions of legal translation

As we have seen, the difficulties that we can encounter in the process of translation may vary according to the inherent function of the text that needs to be translated. If the text has the purpose of creating rights or obligations – that is to say, if we are translating a normative text – we shall have to bear in mind that the precision of concepts will play a significant role, while if we are translating a purely informative text, such as that written by a scholar, the style or the genius of the language will play a major role.

More problems arise when the translation of a legal rule is aimed at harmonizing law in different legal systems, where different languages are spoken. The complexity of *legal* translation in a multilingual context has often been emphasized.[97] In Europe, for example, the task of harmonizing law has become in recent years the source of innumerable initiatives at EU level, where whatever rule, translated into twenty-three different languages, should achieve, once implemented in the twenty-seven national legal systems, the same result. This is a problem that we shall deal with in the next section.

5.5 Multilingualism in the European context

In recent years particular attention has been drawn to the specific aspects and problematics of multilingualism in the European context.[98]

European Community law has a multilingual character, which reflects the fact that the European Union is a multicultural and multilingual entity.[99]

Following the accession of ten new member states in May 2004 and then of Romania and Bulgaria in January 2007, there are now twenty-three official languages,[100] creating immense difficulties when translating from one language into the others.

---

[97] R. Sacco and L. Castellani (eds.), *Les multiples langues du droit européen uniforme* (Turin: L'Harmattan, 1999), 7 f.

[98] F. Müller and I. Burr (eds.), *Rechtssprache Europas: Reflexion der Praxis von Sprache und Mehrsprachigkeit im supranationalen Recht* (Berlin: Duncker & Humblot, 2004).

[99] See in this connection T. Judt and D. Lacorne (eds.), *Language, Nation, and State – Identity Politics in a Multilingual Age* (New York: Palgrave Macmillan, 2004), first published in French: *La politique de Babel: Du monolinguisme d'Etat au plurilinguisme des peuples* (Paris: Karthala, 2002).

[100] In 2004 the official languages were English, French, German, Danish, Dutch, Finnish, Greek, Italian, Portuguese, Spanish, and Swedish. On 1 May 2004 nine languages were added: Czech, Estonian, Hungarian, Latvian, Lithuanian, Polish, Slovakian, Slovene, and

Notwithstanding the many difficulties that working in a multilingual context implies, multilingualism is considered in some respects as undoubtedly being a treasure house of European culture. Respect for the diversity of its languages must be considered a founding principle of the European Union,[101] and this respect should not be limited to its official languages. On the contrary, national and regional authorities are encouraged to give special attention to measures, in line with the principles of the European Charter for Regional or Minority Languages, assisting those language communities where the number of native speakers is in decline from generation to generation.[102]

Multilingualism in Europe can create numerous challenges to the problem of translation.[103] One of the problems which needs highlighting arises from the *lack of definitions* for legal terms in directives, which then are given different meanings in the various national systems. Similar problems, relating to the difficulty in achieving a harmonized result, can be met in cases where the EU draftspersons opt for a deliberately *non-technical definition.*

An example can easily be supplied by the Directive of the European Parliament and Council issued on 21 April 2004 on environmental liability, with regard to the prevention and remedying of environmental damage.[104] There is a definition of damage in this directive which might perhaps seem technical, as far as scientists are concerned, but which, unfortunately, is not the case for lawyers. According to the definition under Article 2 of the directive itself, 'damage' means 'a measurable adverse change in a natural resource or measurable impairment of a natural resource service which may occur directly or indirectly'.

The definition employed, since it fails to supply the interpreter with unambiguous criteria, lends itself to being interpreted in quite different ways in the various national contexts, thereby undermining the very harmonization process which the directive was aiming to achieve.

Maltese; Irish was subsequently recognized as the twenty-first official language. In 2007 Bulgarian and Romanian became official languages.

[101] European Commission, *Action Plan 2004–2006*, Brussels, 24 July 2003, COM(2003) 449 final, 12.

[102] Council of Europe, European Charter for Regional or Minority Languages, Strasbourg, 5 November 1992.

[103] Cf. T. Salmi-Tolonen, 'Legal Linguistic Knowledge and Creating and Interpreting Law in a Multilingual Context', (2004) 29 *Brooklyn Journal of International Law* 1167.

[104] Directive 2004/35/CE of the European Parliament and of the Council of 21 April 2004 on environmental liability, with regard to the prevention and remedying of environmental damage, in OJ, 30 April 2004, L 143/56.

A further observation concerns the problem of lack of coherence in the application of terminology within the same language version, or when translated from one language to another.

Take, for instance, Council Directive 85/577 of 20 December 1985, on the protection of consumers in relation to contracts negotiated away from business premises. Article 4 of the directive, in the Italian-language version, governs the right of cancellation ('diritto di rescindere') of the contract by the consumer, not the right of withdrawal ('recesso').[105] The French version provides that the consumer has a 'right to resile from the effects of the contract' ('son droit de résilier le contrat'), using the terms 'résilier' and 'renoncer' as if they were equivalent, even though they are not; the former term, as we have seen, refers to the possibility of cancelling or withdrawing from a contract which is defective, while the latter concerns the possibility of renouncing an intention, as is the case when someone renounces or gives up a right to take legal action. The German version uses the term 'Widerruf', generally used in the BGB, at least before the 2002 reform of the law on obligations, to indicate the revocation of a unilateral act, for example an offer – certainly not a contract. However, in the German version of the directive itself, the term 'Rücktritt' is used, as if it were synonymous. The English version employs the following expressions without differentiation: 'to assess the obligations arising under the contract', 'right of cancellation', 'right to renounce the effects of his undertaking', 'right of renunciation'.

The complexity of the situation that characterizes drafting, translating and interpreting EU legal texts has led the European institutions to promote some efforts to rationalize the situation. Various initiatives have been taken, at different levels.

At an operative level it has often been said that translating into and from each official language is no longer a practical proposition, in that nowadays it is necessary to navigate among more than five hundred possible language combinations.

Some efforts have been made to cope with twenty-three official languages and the different needs and requirements of the European institutions. In the

---

[105] The common remedy of 'recesso' is laid down by Article 1373 of the Italian Civil Code, which provides that 'If one of the parties has been given the power to withdraw from the contract, such power can be exercised so long as there has been non commencement of performance. In contracts for continuous or periodic performance, such power can also be subsequently exercised, but the withdrawal has no effect as to performance already made or in the course of being made'.

daily business of the Commission, for example, the practice of using only three working languages appears to have been imposed, namely English, French and German; under this regime, drafts of policy documents and draft proposals for legislation are drawn up in one or two of these languages, and the texts are translated into the remaining official languages only in the final phases.

In this regard it is important to note that, while in the past, legislative drafts were often written in French, in recent years most of the European legislation is drafted in English. This must be considered to be a result of the fundamental will of facilitating communication. That is why the English used in these circumstances is a 'facilitated' English, which does not reflect the fundamental institutions, concepts, and categories of the common law.

The use of English with the purpose of facilitating communication must be put in the context of the various initiatives taken at EU level with a view to improving the drafting quality of EU legislation.

Since the 1992 European Council conference in Edinburgh, the need for better law-making through the use of clearer, simpler texts which respond better to the needs of good legislative practice has been recognized. Various provisions have been adopted to meet these requirements.

Among these are Declaration no. 39 on the quality of Community legislation,[106] in the final Act of the 1997 Amsterdam Treaty, and the interinstitutional Agreement of 22 December 1998[107] on common guidelines concerning the drafting quality of EU legislation, which emphasize that EU legislative acts should be drafted in a 'clear, simple and precise' way (first principle), and that 'concepts or terminology specific to any one national legal system are to be used with care'.

Finally there is the 'Joint Practical Guide of the European Parliament, the Council and the Commission, for Persons Involved in the Drafting of Legislation within the Community Institutions'.[108] In the 'General Principles' section of the Guide, the concept that the drafting of legislative acts must be clear, simple, and precise is reiterated (Principle 1.1), since the equality of citizens before the law requires that the law should be accessible and comprehensible for all (Principle 1.2).

---

[106] OJ C 340 of 10 November 1997.   [107] OJ C 73 of 17 March 1999.
[108] The Guide can be found at http://europa.eu.int/eur-lex/it/about/techleg/guide/index_it.htm#1.

The draftsman or author should attempt to reduce the legislative intention to simple terms, in order to be able to express it simply; as far as possible, everyday language should be used (Principle 1.4.1). The favoured solution therefore appears to be to opt for language which is as simple, common, and therefore non-technical, as possible. In Chapter 5 of the guide reference is made to the fact that throughout the process leading to its adoption, the draughtspersons should keep the multilingual nature of EU legislation in mind. Principle 5.2 requires that the original text must be particularly simple, and, as regards actual legal terminology, that terms which are too closely linked to national legal systems should be avoided (Principle 5.3.2). These guidelines will have a significant impact on the creation of a body of private European law, where the technical nature of legal language appears to conflict to some extent with the desired vagueness and non-technicality of the terms used. At the same time they let us understand why the English used at EU level must be considered a hybrid or neutral language.

5.6 English as a legal lingua franca

The English language necessarily brings with it the ideas of common law, but, in the EU context, further mediation is needed.

The first operation consists of understanding to what extent the English terms either correspond to their English meanings or allude to a non-autochthonous meaning.

The English as used in the EU is different from that of the common law: it is a new English. It is just one of twenty-three languages, and EU texts take their meaning from all language versions and are often drafted by non-native speakers, while they are negotiated and amended by all participants. Styles, concepts, and words are taken from other EU languages and adapted to English.

English becomes a 'neutral or descriptive language', which is associated with a classic civil law background. The language used in this context is, then, comprehensible in English, but not tied to technical concepts of English law.

English in this context has undergone an evolution. In order to translate civil law concepts neologisms have been introduced, such as 'unilateral withdrawal' (to translate the German 'Rücktritt') and 'collaboration' (to translate the German 'Mittäter und Beteiligte').

As Simon Tanner points out,

> The result, clearly, is a variety of legal English which is both simplified, having been drafted according to principles of plain English, and cross-cultural. The source system is, as mentioned, civil law in nature. Texts written in this variety of English are in themselves bound to have great influence, and their suitability for transposition into domestic legislation is bound to further boost the process not only of legal, but also of legal linguistic change in the UK … I would argue that this privileged position of English, and the fact that it is being used prevalently by non-native speakers, inevitably leads to simplification and the abandonment of excessive jargon.[109]

The problem of translating English as a lingua franca into the other official languages will be a new problem to face in the near future.[110] The work of legal translation will change. The problems will be different.

First, we shall not face the problem of transferring a legal concept from a legal language, which reflects the values, the mentality, and the architecture of a given legal culture, into another. We shall have to face a new problem: we shall have to translate from a hybrid language, which is not connected with a given system of values, into all other languages.

Second, we shall have to bear in mind that we are looking for correspondence not between two languages, but among twenty-three different languages. If we forget that, we shall be defeated by our challenge from the very beginning.

Third, in order to create correspondence among all languages, we can imagine using neologisms in the several official languages, but this will need to be under constant monitoring to maintain correspondence. That is neither absurd, nor impossible; a similar approach has been taken in francophone parts of Canada, where legal terminology has been standardized in more than one language.

The question remains: is English suitable for the task of standardizing a common legal terminology for Europe?

English is a forced choice, and we should not forget the contradiction behind it: English is at the same time the most widely spoken language and the least suitable for translating concepts of civil law.

---

[109] S. Tanner, 'The Past, Present and Future of Legal English in the UK and Abroad', in *Atti dell'Accademia Peloritana dei Pericolanti, Classe di Lettere e Filosofia e Belle Arti*, vol. 58 (Naples: Edizioni Scientifiche Italiane, 2006), 201–7.

[110] S. Traviano, *Translating English as a Lingua Franca* (Milan: Mondadori, 2010).

We often hear that English threatens other languages, but English as well is under threat. The cost of becoming a lingua franca will be to create a continental legal English which differs greatly from British legal English. We already speak in the English version of directives of 'unilateral withdrawal' in order to translate the German 'Rücktritt', of the 'right to renounce the effects of his undertaking' in order to translate 'le droit de résilier le contrat', of 'dissolving the contract' in order to translate 'den Vertrag zu kündigen'. It is no wonder that in this situation Continental English or Bruxelles English will develop its own path, its own terminology, independently from what the law lords in London think. It will become a new English dialect, one of many that we find around the world.

So it might be that in the near future we shall have to face a new task: to translate from EU English to British English, for the well-being of our translators.

Further reading

M. I. Ahmad, 'Interpreting Communities: Lawyering across Language Difference', (2006–2007) 54 *University of California Los Angeles Law Review* 999, in particular 1031

B. Bix, *Law, Language, and Legal Determinacy* (Oxford: Clarendon, 1993)

N. Bobbio, 'Scienza del diritto e analisi del linguaggio', in U. Scarpelli (ed.), *Diritto e analisi del linguaggio* (Milan: Edizioni di Comunità, 1976), 287

C. Boquet, *Pour une methode de la traduction juridique* (Vaud: Prilly, 1994)

D. Cao, *Translating Law* (Buffalo: Multilingual Matters, 2007)

E. Didier, *Langues et langages du droit: étude comparative des modes d'expression de la common law et du droit civil, en français et en anglais* (Montreal: Wilson & Lafleur, 1990)

J.-C. Gémar (ed.), *Langage du droit et traduction: essais de jurilinguistique/The language of the Law and Translation: Essays on Jurilinguistics* (Montreal: Linguatech, 1982)

Traduire ou l'art d'interpréter: langue, droit et société: élement de jurilinguistique (Sainte-Foy: Presses de l'Université du Québec, 1995)

J. Gibbons (ed.), *Language and the Law* (London and New York: Longman, 1994)

M. Goré, 'La traduction, instrument de droit comparé', in Marie Cornu and Michel Moreau (eds.), *Traduction du droit et droit de la traduction* (Paris: Dalloz, 2011), 109

G.-R. de Groot, 'Legal Translation', in J. Smits (ed.), *Elgar Encyclopedia of Comparative Law* (Cheltenham: Edward Elgar, 2006), 423

'La Traduction Juridique', (1987) 28 *Les Cahiers de Droit* 735

B. Grossfeld, 'Sprache und Recht', (1984) *Juristenzeitung* 1

B. Grossfeld and E. J. Eberle, 'Patterns of Order in Comparative Law, Discovering and Decoding Invisible Powers', (2003) 38 *Texas International Law Journal* 291

R. Guastini, *Il diritto come linguaggio: lezioni* (Turin: Giappichelli, 2006)

H. Guillorel and G. Koubi (eds.), *Langues et droits: Langues du droit, droit des langues* (Brussels: Bruylant, 1999)

J. E. Jacob, 'Language Policy and Political Development in France', in B. Weinstein (ed.), *Language Policy and Political Development* (Norwood: Ablex, 1990), 43

B. Kielar, *Language of the Law in the Aspect of Translation* (Warsaw: Wydawnictwa Uniwersytetu Warszawskiegi, 1997)

I. Kitamura, 'Problems of the Translation of Law in Japan', (1993) 23 *Victoria University of Wellington Law Review* 1

H. E. S. Mattila, *Comparative Legal Linguistics*, trans. C. Goddard (Aldershot: Ashgate, 2006)

D. Mellinkoff, *The Language of the Law* (Boston, MA: Little, Brown, 1963)

T. Morawetz (ed.), *Law and Language* (Aldershot: Ashgate, 2000)

M. Morris (ed.), *Translation and the Law* (Amsterdam and Philadelphia: John Benjamins, 1995)

B. Pozzo (ed.), *Ordinary Language and Legal Language* (Milan: Giuffrè, 2005)

B. Pozzo and V. Jacometti (eds.), *Multilingualism and the Harmonisation of European Law* (Alphen aan den Rijn: Kluwer, 2006)

B. Pozzo and M. Timoteo (eds.), *Europa e linguaggi giuridici* (Milan: Giuffrè, 2008)

M.-C. Prémont, *Tropismes du droit: logique métaphorique et logique métonymique du langage juridique* (Montreal: Liber, 2003)

M. Rathert, *Sprache und Recht* (Heidelberg: Universitätsverlag Winter, 2006)

E. Rotman, 'The Inherent Problems of Legal Translation', (1995) *Indiana International and Comparative Law Review* 187

R. Sacco, 'Language and Law', in B. Pozzo (ed.), *Ordinary Language and Legal Language* (Milan: Giuffrè, 2005), 1

'Langue et Droit', in E. Jayme (ed.), *Langue et Droit* (Brussels: Bruylant, 2000), 223

'La traduzione giuridica', in U. Scarpelli and P. di Lucia (eds.), *Il linguaggio del diritto* (Milan: Giuffrè, 1994), 475

'Traduzione giuridica', in *Digesto civ.*, Agg. (Turin: Utet, 2000), 722

R. Sacco (ed.), *Les frontières avancées du savoir du juriste/The Advanced Frontiers of Legal Science: L'anthropologie juridique et la traductologie juridique/Legal Anthropology and Translation Studies in Law, Actes du Colloque ISAIDAT, Turin, 25–28 avril 2007* (Brussels: Bruylant, 2011)

R. Sacco and L. Castellani, *Les multiples langues du droit européen uniforme* (Turin: L'Harmattan, 1999)

L. Sadat Wexler, 'Official English, Nationalism and Linguistic Terror: A French Lesson', (1996) 71 *Washington Law Review* 285

S. Šarčević, *New Approach to Legal Translation* (The Hague: Kluwer, 1997)

S. Schane, *Language and the Law* (London and New York: Continuum, 2006)

F. Schauer (ed.), *Law and Language* (New York: New York University Press, 1993)

P. Schroth, 'Legal Translation', (1986) 34 *American Journal of Comparative Law* 47

P. M. Tiersma, *Legal Language* (University of Chicago Press, 1999)

N. Urban, 'One Legal Language and the Maintenance of Cultural and Linguistic Diversity?', (2000) 8 *European Review of Private Law* 51

A. Wagner, *La langue de la common law* (Paris: L'Harmattan, 2002)

M. Weston, 'Problems and Principles of Legal Translation', (1983) 22 *Incorporated Linguist* 207

Part II

Comparative law fields

Comparative studies in private law 6
A European point of view
Franz Werro

Until recently, comparative legal studies were devoted essentially to private law. While this European-born, nineteenth-century focus survived emigration, it often caused legal comparison to stay at the periphery of legitimate scholarship, particularly in the post-war twentieth-century United States. An opening outside traditional private law studies has now presented itself, and comparative law research with broader concerns has increasingly appeared and gained proper recognition. However, because of its displacement from centre stage, comparative private law as it was usually understood in academia is today in a state of crisis and in search of a new profile. Even in practice, the proper content and role of comparative private law have faced new challenges. In the light of these changes, a specific chapter on comparative private law in a book dealing with legal comparison appears to be quite justified.

Indeed, while economic globalization and neoliberal ideology have given private ordering unprecedented importance, there is at the same time a growing sense that private law cannot be meaningfully separated from its operational context. Comparatists increasingly agree that an inquiry within confines of 'technical' private law betrays a laissez-faire bias and ignores the social and public dimension of the questions addressed. Further, a growing number of scholars claim that comparative research must derive from an interdisciplinary and theoretical approach, and no longer consist only of describing and comparing the static and mechanical content of positive foreign rules and precedents. In this approach, comparison in private law tries to give meaning to the functioning of law in its given social context. With this more comprehensive and less doctrinal understanding, private law

I wish to thank Daphne Lyman, Georgetown University Law Center JD 2010, for help in the editing of this chapter. I wish also to thank generous friends and colleagues who read an earlier version of this manuscript or with whom I simply had conversations about it. My gratitude goes in particular to Mauro Bussani, Christiana Fountoulakis, Pierre Legrand, Joseph Page, Geoffrey Samuel and Teemu Ruskola. Their comments were very helpful.

loses its mythical neutrality and reveals instead its cultural, economic, and political nature.

This evolution in comparative studies parallels the trends in the contemporary study of private law. It also echoes a critique against recent developments in practice, such as the current fashion of globalization. Giant private cross-border operators assume the prerogative of law-making, away from state interference and often from public scrutiny. In this self-regulated world, the law of private ordering has little visibility, except for broad transnational soft law principles, such as those of UNIDROIT (International Institute for the Unification of Private Law), designed to help private arbitrators solve disputes, again, though, away from public scrutiny. With the growing success of these principles and the decline in the importance of state boundaries, hard law appears more in disfavour than ever. The drafting of European principles appears also to be part of this evolution, when one considers the private nature of these non-binding principles and their focus on the functioning of the market. However, this development does not remain unchallenged, and part of the debates in comparative private law, which we shall echo in the present text, reflects the criticisms that have come along with the current evolution.

Yet in addition to this global and regional transnationalization of the law, on the European landscape there is also a growth of EU harmonizing legislation, which imposes new rules and principles in key sectors of private law and changes both the geographical and the conceptual boundaries of that law. Where law used to find its expression in national civil codes only, it is now often determined by European directives. This important phenomenon of legal denationalization puts into question the traditional divide between private and public law, as well as that between civil law and common law. Indeed, modern EU legislation tends to define consumers' and merchants' interests in a way that ignores or even contradicts national and systemic assumptions. Not surprisingly, it is against this somewhat confusing background that some have come up with the idea of a European Civil Code, with the hope that such a code would fix the disorderly situation in which private law finds itself, just as the codes of the nineteenth century did with respect to the laws of the various European nations. Not surprisingly, this idea has now given rise to a vigorous debate between those attached to law as the product of a local culture and those who think that private law should be a tool for increased efficiency.

Another way in which the boundaries of private law have changed, somewhat in contradiction to the transnationalization and Europeanization of the law just described, comes from the contemporary relevance of constitutional law in the definition of private entitlements. At the European level, this phenomenon stems from jurisprudence of the European Court of Human Rights: fundamental human rights tend to be used to put limits on the sanctity of contract and private autonomy in general. This is referred to as the 'constitutionalization of private law'.

Clearly, these European changes have an impact on the ways in which one can think of the role and the function of comparative legal studies devoted to private law in Europe. They pose fundamental and epistemological questions about law in general and private law in particular, and justify the more theoretical approach to comparison referred to before. Thus it is with these changes in mind that I have chosen to define the gist of the present contribution; because of the chosen focus, I shall mainly concentrate on the situation in Europe, but I shall do it, as much as possible, in the light of a more general and abstract concern. I shall give an overview of the constitutionalization of private law (section 6.1), and of its denationalization as influenced by consumer protection legislation and the drafting of common private law principles in Europe (section 6.2). Against this background, but with the ambition of transcending its geographical boundaries, I shall then try to discuss some implications for the use of comparison in academic private law studies as well as its method (section 6.3).

6.1 Some aspects of the constitutionalization of private law and the role of the European Court of Human Rights

As traditionally captured by the national civil codes in Europe, private law supposedly provided the sources of mores, the palladium of private property, and the guarantee of public and private peace.[1] Just as these codes were the fortresses designed to protect and define private autonomy, constitutions were made to guarantee and protect the fundamental rights of citizens against the state. Because state action was limited in the nineteenth century, private ordering had a central and essential place in the law.[2]

---

[1] J. E. M. Portalis, *Motifs et discours prononcés lors de la publication du Code civil* (Bordeaux: éd. Confluences, 2004), 15.

[2] See Duncan Kennedy, 'Three Globalizations of Law and Legal Thought: 1850–2000', in D. Trubek and A. Santos (eds.), *The New Law and Economic Development: A Critical Appraisal* (Cambridge University Press, 2006), 19 ff., 25 ff.; B. Schwartz, 'The Code and

Today, the picture has changed. According to the European Court of Human Rights (ECtHR), constitutional entitlements are not only understood negatively to protect citizens against the state, but also positively, to oblige the state to protect citizens against one another. As a consequence, courts must now engage in the balancing of conflicting human rights between individuals, with ultimate authority resting in the ECtHR, which can hold the state liable for making the wrong choice.[3]

The contemporary approach represents an important but controversial step because it places private autonomy on an equal and potentially competitive footing with other fundamental entitlements and questions the traditional dichotomy between private and public law. Instead of analysing this evolution in general terms, I shall narrow my inquiry to the law of privacy (subsection 6.1.1), although not without assessing some of the broader implications linked to the notion of positive obligations (6.1.2).

6.1.1 A short account of the constitutionalization of privacy in Europe

In Europe, privacy entitlements have for a long time been granted, both against other individuals and against the state. Courts defined the boundaries of private entitlements on the basis of national statutory provisions or general principles. For example, as of 1907, the Swiss Civil Code expressly recognized, next to the right to private property, a fundamental general entitlement to enjoy rights deriving from the very fact of being a person, the so called 'personality rights' (Art. 28 of the Swiss Civil Code). The German Code contained no such provision, but courts gradually also came to recognize a right to the protection of personality on the basis of general and deeply rooted principles, particularly after the Second World War.[4]

Public Law', in B. Schwartz (ed.), *French Administrative Law and the Common-Law World* (New York University Press, 1954), 247 ff.; see also S. Besson, 'Fundamental Rights and European Private Law', in M. Bussani and F. Werro (eds.), *European Private Law: A Handbook* (Berne: Staempfli: 2009), 7 ff.

[3] For a ban on a game considered to be against human dignity, see *Omega Spielhallen und Automataufstellung-GbmH* v. *Oberbürgermeisterin der Bundesstadt Bonn*, Case C-36/02, [2004] ECR I-0960; for an interesting comment see E. M. Belser, 'Grundrechte, Grundfreiheiten und Verträge – Wie sich die EMRK und der Binnenmarkt auf das Vertragsrecht auswirken?', in F. Werro (ed.), *Droit civil et Convention européenne des droits de l'homme* (Zurich, Basel, and Geneva: Schulthess, 2006), 133 ff.

[4] G. Brüggemeier and A. Colombi Ciacchi, 'Introduction', in G. Brüggemeier, A. Colombi Ciacchi, and G. Commandé (eds.), *Fundamental Rights and Private Law in the*

Courts tailored the limits of entitlements against the state on the basis of the national constitutions. Like many others, Swiss constitutional law delineated a right to private life and dignity. The Basic Law of Germany embraced the tradition of 'personality' protection in its Article 2.[5]

In disputes between private parties, civil courts defined the limits of private rights traditionally without making explicit reference to the constitution and the fundamental values it proclaimed. However, the overlapping values between private and public entitlements did exist, and judges ultimately engaged in the interpretation of open and undetermined private entitlements by taking into account constitutional imperatives; thus, for example, courts used the constitutional protection of privacy to specify the content of private free speech and, conversely, they used the constitutional protection of free speech or free information to construe the limits of the private right to privacy.

With time, the fading line between public and private law grew even more indistinct, particularly under the auspices of the ECtHR. The case law of this European court came gradually to recognize that the protection of fundamental rights was granted not only against the state, but, as mentioned above, also against private individuals and corporations. With the recognition of this horizontal effect of constitutional rights and the birth of the so-called 'positive obligation', it became the duty of courts and other state agents to ensure that constitutional rights traditionally limiting only state action would also be enforced against private actors.[6]

As a consequence, it is now largely recognized that defining the scope of personality rights in Europe is no longer a question of private national law only; it is also, and perhaps above all, a matter of European constitutional law.[7] National courts in Europe now resolve disputes between the press and private individuals, with the possibility of an appeal to the ECtHR, which

European Union (Cambridge University Press, 2010), vol. II, 4 ff., with further references; also J. Krzeminska-Vamvaka and P. O'Callaghan, 'Mapping out a Right to Privacy in Tort Law', in G. Brüggemeier, A. Colombi Ciacchi, and G. Commandé (eds.), *Fundamental Rights and Private Law in the European Union* (Cambridge University Press, 2010), vol. II, 111 ff.

[5] Art. 2 of the Grundgesetz guarantees that 'Every person has the right to free development of his personality, insofar as he does not injure the rights of others'. For an interesting comparative analysis see J. Whitman, 'The Two Western Cultures of Privacy: Dignity versus Liberty', (2004) 113 *Yale Law Journal* 1151.

[6] S. Besson, 'Comment humaniser le droit privé sans commodifier les droits de l'homme', in F. Werro (ed.), *Droit civil et Convention européenne des droits de l'homme* (Zurich, Basel, and Geneva: Schulthess, 2006), 1 ff., 12 ff.

[7] Besson, 'Comment humaniser', 42 ff.

might hold the defendant state liable for failing to furnish a private individual with adequate protection against the media. *Caroline von Hannover*[8] reflects this evolution. Caroline von Hannover had lost a claim in German courts for invasion of privacy against a magazine that had published pictures of her private life. Considering that the pictures were not newsworthy and that the plaintiff was not a politician or a public figure of comparable notoriety, the Strasbourg court held that Germany had violated a positive obligation under Article 8 of the European Convention on Human Rights (ECHR) to protect an individual's right to a private life.[9]

6.1.2 An assessment

Obviously, the exact definition and boundaries of entitlements result from a balancing process between two competing rights, the content of which depends on the particular circumstances of the case. However, the principle is clear: private autonomy must yield to other fundamental constitutional entitlements, and states have a duty to ensure that the proper balance is struck.

While the ECtHR openly recognizes that a general theory of positive obligations is still missing,[10] it has imposed such obligations not just in the law of privacy, as we saw, but also in other fields of law. For example, the Strasbourg court held in *Vgt Verein gegen Tierfabriken* v. *Switzerland* that the right of a monopolistic advertising company to refuse clients could come into conflict with their freedom of speech. The court took the same approach in *Pla and Puncernau* v. *Andorra*,[11] where it decided that a private contract could trigger state liability if it violated a constitutional right of one of the parties. In this case, Andorra was held responsible for allowing a private will to exclude non-biological heirs from the estate of their parents, in violation of a fundamental constitutional right to be treated equally.[12]

This constitutionalization of private law in Europe is unique, and certainly finds no similar counterpart in the United States. At the same time, it does not remain unchallenged in Europe, as some perceive it as a threat against private autonomy and the growth of commerce. While there is no

---

[8] *C. von Hannover* v. *Germany*, ECHR, 26 April 2004, Rec. 2004-VI 40 EHRR 1.

[9] Ibid., paras. 76 ff.

[10] F. Werro, 'La protection de la personnalité, les médias et la Cour européenne des droits de l'Homme: Une illustration de la constitutionnalisation et de l'européanisation du droit civil', in *Le centenaire du Code civil suisse* (Paris: LGDJ, 2008), 51 ff. n. 48.

[11] *Pla and Puncernau* v. *Andorra*, ECtHR, 13 July 2004, 42 EHRR 522.   [12] Ibid.

point in trying to convince anyone that the fear is unfounded, it may still be worthwhile to persuade some that the intrusion of human rights into private dealings does not really menace the existence of private autonomy. Rather than threatening individual freedom, the balancing of other fundamental rights against freedom of contract should actually favour an increased respect for the autonomy and the dignity of the individual by helping to protect the weak against the powerful.[13] This is not about submitting private law to a dogmatic old-fashioned public law, but about recognizing the functional differences between private and public law as well as the fundamental complementarity of the two.[14]

6.2 The denationalization of private law and the growing importance of EU law

Under the various treaties of the European Union, private law remains in principle in the sovereign hands of the member states. With the arguable exception of Article 114 of the Treaty on the Functioning of the European Union (TFEU) (ex-Art. 95 of the Treaty establishing the European Community (TEC)),[15] no provision gives the EU general authority to legislate in matters of private law. Treaty provisions do, however, empower the EU to make law promoting equal protection of consumers and imposing measures of harmonization in the field of commercial law. Those measures find a justification in the idea that legal divergences between the member states could expose enterprises to unequal conditions and create distortions in the functioning of free competition. Thus the EU has adopted a number of directives designed to harmonize the laws of the member states. This harmonization has to some extent taken place successfully. It has, however, also disrupted the functioning of national law and led to fundamental questions about its legitimacy. After

---

[13] For a critique of the human-rights tradition, accused of not taking human individuals seriously and of not being able to address human rights violations perpetrated by private actors, particularly in transnational settings, see G. Teubner, 'The Anonymous Matrix: Human Rights Violations by "Private" Transnational Actors', (2006) 69 *Modern Law Review* 327, 330.

[14] On this, see M. Schefer, 'Der zähe Überlebenwille einer überholten Dichotomie', in F. Werro (ed.), *Droit civil et Convention européenne des droits de l'homme* (Zurich, Basel, and Geneva: Schulthess, 2006), 223 ff., 244 ff.

[15] For such an argument see J. Basedow, 'A Common Law of Contract for a Common Market', (1996) 33 *Common Market Law Review* 1169 ff.

sketching this phenomenon and giving some illustrations (subsection 6.2.1), I shall proceed with a brief introduction to the debate surrounding the possible adoption of a European civil code or some more narrowly defined legislation, possibly limited to contract law (6.2.2).

6.2.1 The rise of consumer law protection and the disruption of national law

For a number of years the EU has adopted directives in traditional fields of private and commercial law with the double goal of protecting consumers in a uniform fashion and putting competing enterprises on an equal footing throughout the single market. The different directives have undoubtedly improved the level of consumer protection traditionally granted, at least in some member states. At the same time, the directives have also eliminated some legal divergences that had the potential of creating distortions in the functioning of free competition.[16]

That effort at harmonization has evolved over time. At first, the legislator chose to intervene very selectively in certain sectors of private law. Outside the field of corporate law, the directives in such specific areas as packaged travel arrangements, distance contracts, contracts concluded away from business premises, or products liability, reveal the piecemeal approach taken by the EU, which intervened only in those areas where special needs for protection were felt.[17] However limited, the approach taken was often quite detailed, and thus had significant impact. For example, the directive on products liability, while leaving certain areas to the wisdom of the member states, governs most essential aspects of this liability with a high level of precision, making the directives in many ways resemble an actual EU regulation.[18]

Over time, the European lawmaker has adopted more comprehensive schemes, including, for example, a directive on guarantees in sales.[19]

---

[16] For a general presentation see T. Wilhelmsson, G. Howells, and H.-W. Micklitz, 'European Consumer Law', in M. Bussani and F. Werro (eds.), *European Private Law: A Handbook* (Berne: Staempfli, 2009), 245 ff.

[17] This point has been made many times. See, e.g., F. Werro, 'Unification of Private Law in Europe: A Question of Cultural Legitimacy', in A. Furrer (ed.), *Europäisches Privatrecht im wissenschaftlichen Diskurs* (Berne: Staempfli, 2006), 109; but see already H. Kötz, 'Rechtsvereinheitlichung – Nutzen, Kosten, Methoden, Ziele', (1986) 50 *RabelsZ* 1.

[18] For a detailed analysis see J. Haas, *La responsabilité de l'entreprise en Europe: Un droit unique pour un marché unique?* (Berne: Staempfli, 2004), 163.

[19] Council Directive 1999/44 EEC of 25 May 1999.

Also, and for the sake of eliminating the risk of distortions in the functioning of competition, the directives have gradually imposed a maximal level of harmonization and disallowed the member states from extending the protection granted by the European legislation. Furthermore, the work done by the Acquis Group then demonstrated that the EU should move from a limited and scattered intervention in the private law of the member states to a broader scheme of legislation.[20] After various projects, the Council of the European Union adopted a new directive on consumer rights amending certain directives and repealing some others.[21]

This initiative is certainly a valid attempt to do away with the piecemeal and random nature of a legislative intervention that regulates certain questions but leaves out others, and thereby creates a complicated mixture of national and European rules.[22] Some of the rules adopted in certain directives have also been criticized for being intrusive and in contradiction to national conceptual frameworks.[23] That, for instance, is the case with the

---

[20] The Acquis Group was founded in 2002. It currently consists of more than forty scholars from nearly all EU member states. The group is directed by Professor Gianmaria Ajani and Professor Hans Schulte-Nölke. As a reaction to activities of EU institutions in the field of European contract law, the Acquis Group is working towards a systematic arrangement of Community law with the goal of elucidating the common structures of the emerging Community private law. For this purpose, the Acquis Group primarily concentrates on the existing EC private law within the *acquis communautaire*. See *Principles of the Existing EC Contract Law. Contract I. Pre-Contractual Obligations, Conclusion of Contract, Unfair Terms* (Munich: Sellier, 2007); *Contract II. General Provisions, Delivery of Goods, Package Travel and Payment Services* (Munich: Sellier, 2009).

[21] The Council of the EU decided on 10 October 2011; the text of the new directive is available at http://register.consilium.europa.eu/pdf/en/11/pe00/pe00026.en11.pdf; the idea was to merge some directives into a single instrument regulating the common aspects in a systematic fashion, simplifying and updating existing rules, removing inconsistencies, and closing gaps; for a previous (more ambitious) text, see the previous version at http://ec.europa.eu/consumers/rights/docs/Directive_final_EN.pdf.

[22] P.-C. Müller-Graff, 'EC Directives as a Means of Private Law Unification', in A. Hartkamp et al. (eds.), *Towards a European Civil Code*, 4th edn (Alphen aan den Rijn: Kluwer Law International, 2011), 149 ff.

[23] For a detailed analysis of the problem raised in the United Kingdom by the implementation of the directive of unfair terms, see H. Beale, 'Legislative control of Fairness: The Directive on Unfair Terms in Consumer Contracts', in J. Beatson and D. Friedmann (eds.), *Good Faith and Fault in Contract Law* (Oxford University Press, 1995), 231; on the question of the implementation of the directive on liability for defective products in France, see G. Viney, 'La marge de liberté laissée aux autorités nationales pour aménager la responsabilité du fait des produits défectueux dans les situations qui échappent au domaine d'application de la directive n. 85/374/CEE', (2009) *Revue des contrats* IV 1381 ff.; see also G. Viney, 'L'interprétation par la CJCE de la directive du 25 juillet 1985 sur la responsabilité du fait des produits', (2002) *Juris Classeur Périodique* 1945, 1947.

directive on products liability,[24] imposing a system of *cumul* that remains at odds with the French system of 'non-cumul'.[25] On a broader level, some also argue that while the directives may have given remedies to consumers, they have done so to distract them from raising deeper concerns about social justice and thus reinforce the predominance of the free market principle.[26]

Be that as it may, this European law has in effect transformed and modernized, but also destabilized, the law of the member states well beyond the scope of the directives. It has also jeopardized the legislative autonomy of the national lawmakers. Beyond the sometimes 'irritating' impact[27] of this arguably illegitimate intrusion, the national legislator is left alone when it comes to integrating these 'corps étrangers' into his own law, and one can relate to the point made by some defenders of the European civil code idea that more coherence would be welcome.

The *Leitner* case is a good illustration of the phenomenon just described.[28] In this case, the European Court of Justice (ECJ) decided to award financial compensation for the moral harm suffered by a tourist as a consequence of her ruined vacation.[29] It was a brave step to read this from the directive regulating the sale of package holidays and yet no doubt a correct one. Though, what is remarkable, and outside the scope of anyone's predictions, is the impact that this decision will have on the notion of compensable loss in general. The Advocate General was able to convince the ECJ to decide that a tourist who suffers the loss of enjoyment of her vacation as a result of the seller's breach of contract suffers a moral harm.[30] The member states are now left alone to determine what general implications this decision should have on losses suffered in cases involving other contractual or even non-contractual liability. Clearly, the decision has the potential to open up the traditionally narrowly defined 'tort moral', and to provide ammunition for an expansion of compensation in instances similar

---

[24] Council Directive 85/374/EEC of 25 July 1985, OJ L 210 of 7 August 1985, 29 ff.

[25] For a critical assessment early on, see J. Ghestin, 'L'influence des directives communautaires sur le droit français de la responsabilité', in B. Pfister and M. R. Will (eds.), *Festschrift für Werner Lorenz* (Tübingen: Mohr Siebeck, 1991), 631.

[26] U. Mattei and F. Nicola, 'A "Social Dimension" in European Private Law? The Call for Setting a Progressive Agenda', (2006) 41 *New England Law Review* 1.

[27] G. Teubner, 'Legal Irritants: Good Faith in British Law or How Unifying Law Ends Up in New Divergences', (1998) 61 *Modern Law Review* 11.

[28] *Simone Leitner v. TUI Deutschland GmbH and Co KG*, Case C-168/00, [2002] ECR I-2631.

[29] Ibid., pt. 24.

[30] See *Simone Leitner v. TUI Deutschland GmbH & Co. KG.*, case 168/00, ECR I-02631, pt. 30, Opinion of General Advocate Tizzano of 20 September 2001.

enough to that of the ruined vacation. Indeed, one fails to see why the victim of a tort jeopardizing the enjoyment of a vacation should not be entitled to the same protection as the package-deal tourist whose contractual partner breached his duties of care. However, the risk of legal divergences remains large and the effect of harmonization limited.

While the foregoing case triggers only an invitation to revisit the general notion of compensable loss beyond the scope of the directive, the 2002 ECJ cases on product liability are even more intrusive. In these cases, the ECJ held that the directive of 1985 deprives the member states of the power to give remedies extending the limits set forth by the directive when based on the defectiveness of the product alone.[31] As a consequence, the directive imposes the limits of no-fault liability and forbids the national lawmaker from granting additional protection to the victims of defective products. In defence of this business-friendly decision, commentators insisted that this was the price to pay for harmonization.[32] Opposing this attack on the protection of consumers, others immediately proposed tools to circumvent the limits of this decision, namely by introducing liability based on an irrebuttable presumption of fault.[33] Regardless of which point of view one adopts, it is clear that the ECJ took an intrusive step, potentially disruptive of an individual member state's consumer protection policy. The decision is all the more criticizable because it actually fails to harmonize the law as it pretends to do. Indeed, allowing national civil liability systems to remain in place on grounds other than defectiveness, such as fault or breach of warranty, does not take away the possibility of legal divergences between the member states and thus does not protect European business against distortion of competition.

6.2.2 The question of a European civil code and of the Common Frame of Reference

The shortcomings of the directives have triggered some anti-EU feelings, but have also given birth to the idea of alternative EU legislative tools,

---

[31] *Commission* v. *France*, Case C-52/00, [2002] ECR I-03969.

[32] C. Larroumet, 'Note sur les arrêts français et espagnol du 25 avril 2002', (2002) *Dalloz* 2462 ff.

[33] Viney, 'L'interprétation par la CJCE', 1945 ff.; also J. Calais-Auloy, 'Menace européenne sur la jurisprudence française concernant l'obligation de sécurité du vendeur professionnel (CJCE, 25 avril 2002)', (2002) *Dalloz* 2458 ff.

including that of a European civil code, deemed capable of promoting some degree of coherence and systemic integrity.

The argument was easy to coin: once a given market integrates, with the removal of trade barriers and customs tariffs as well as the introduction of a single currency, the need for unification of private law seems to impose itself. Nineteenth-century Switzerland and Germany offer examples of that kind of economic and legal integration. Despite the much more complex, multicultural, and plurilinguistic nature of the European enterprise, a number of political actors, including the European Parliament and – to some extent – the EU Commission, as well as small business and consumer advocates, have expressed their inclination towards the idea of comprehensive unified legislation in the field of private law, and have even proposed the adoption of common rules, mainly in contract law, but also in tort and even in property law; in 2002, the European Parliament adopted a resolution proposing the adoption of a European civil code by 2010.[34]

While highly controversial, the idea of a European civil code has generated the most interesting debate on the essence and function of private law since the French Revolution and the rise of the nation state in the nineteenth century. For the first time since 1804, the existence or the exclusivity of national civil codes has come under some threat. With this menace, all sorts of fundamental questions about private law and its relation to the nation and a given culture have arisen.[35]

Interestingly, the debate over European private law integration is not conducted cleanly along political lines. Big business and holders of vested interests, such as national bar associations, have rejected the idea. Some Euro-sceptic conservatives who embrace a defence of national law based on a somewhat chauvinistic pride have also voiced their disapproval. At the same time, the left has also expressed worries that the EU Commission

---

[34] See Resolution of the European Parliament on the approximation of the civil and commercial law of the Member States, [2002] OJ C140E/538.

[35] Study Group on Social Justice in European Private Law, 'Social Justice in European Contract Law: A Manifesto', (2004) 10 *European Law Journal* 653. See also P. Legrand, 'Antivonbar', (2006) 1 *Journal of Comparative Law* 13; Legrand, 'Sens et non sens d'un Code civil européen', (1996) 48 *Revue internationale de droit comparé* 779, 798, 802; for an interesting evaluation of Pierre Legrand's contribution to this debate, see R. Cotterrell, 'Is It So Bad To Be Different? Comparative Law and the Appreciation of Diversity', in E. Örücü and D. Nelken (eds.), *Comparative Law: A Handbook* (Oxford and Portland: Hart, 2007), 133 ff., 138 ff.

would be focusing on the functioning of the market only, while neglecting the social dimension of private law, and, as a result, promoting what is referred to as the 'anti-law movement'.[36] Further, the attacks against the civil law system launched by World Bank reports[37] have widened the circle of opponents to a European code. Recently, and perhaps also as a result of this, the point has been made that any attempt to codify should perhaps remain strictly civilian and thus continental only.[38]

The lack of simple alliances shows that prudence is thus necessary. It appears also more than ever that private law cannot meaningfully be seen as separated from a given culture and perhaps even from a given language.[39] Yet, at the same time, it seems equally true that culture is not static and that the boundaries of civil society evolve over time. Member states have stretched these societal boundaries as they have integrated into the European Union, and it seems quite reasonable to accept the fact that private law would lose a certain connection to national borders. It should thus not come as a surprise that national codes might have to cede some of their *raison d'être* to new European legislative instruments.[40]

As it is, the political nature of the enterprise and the controversies surrounding the proposed integration of private law have led to the re-dimensioning of the project. Instead of accepting the idea of a European civil code, as proposed by the European Parliament, the EU Commission rejected it as soon as 2004 and launched the possible adoption of a 'Common Frame of Reference' whose rules and principles – to be endorsed by the European legislators – would merely help the adaptation of national private

---

[36] Mattei and Nicola, 'A "Social Dimension" in European Private Law?', 29.

[37] See www.doingbusiness.org/Documents/DB2004-full-report.pdf.

[38] M. Bussani, 'Faut-il se passer du common law (européen)? Réflexions sur un Code civil continental dans le droit mondialisé', (2010) 62 *Revue internationale de droit comparé* 7 ff.

[39] S. Glanert, 'Speaking Language to Law: The Case of Europe', (2008) 28 *Legal Studies* 161; on the decline of a language as a loss, see D. Réaume, 'Official Languages Rights: Intrinsic Value and the Protection of Difference', in W. Kymlicka (ed.), *Citizenship in Diverse Societies: Theory and Practice* (New York: Oxford University Press, 2000). On the relation between law and language, in general, see R. Sacco, 'Langue et droit', in L. Castellani (ed.), *Les multiples langues du droit européen uniforme* (Turin: L'Harmattan, 1999), 163 ff.

[40] The same is true with respect to international commerce. The argument must even be made that the adoption of unified law is a means of providing a 'neutral' platform for parties who may not always trust the law of the other; for a detailed and convincing analysis, see C. Fountoulakis, 'The Parties' Choice of "Neutral Law" in International Sales Contracts', (2005) 7 *European Journal of Law Reform* 303 ff.

law to the requirements of the European market.[41] With that 'toolbox', whose vague definition evolved over time, the very notion of a European civil code gradually gave place to a more flexible and restricted project in the field of contract law that was not supposed to suppress the plurality of the legal systems and the sovereign autonomy of the member states' legislation.[42] In parallel, academics became involved and received substantial EU resources to put together a 'Draft Common Frame of Reference' (DCFR).[43]

After a relatively short period of nevertheless intensive work, the DCFR appeared in its full edition of over 6,000 pages at the end of 2009. Instead of focusing on business or contract law only, the DCFR offered a comprehensive set of definitions, principles, and model rules for European private law in general.[44] To that extent, this academic proposal went beyond the scope that the Commission had ultimately in mind, and it triggered various political and academic resistance and criticism.[45] Whatever the reasons, the Commission decided in spring 2010 to limit its efforts of unification specifically to contract law. In its decision of 26 April of that year, the Commission appointed a group of experts to help elaborate a proposal of a Common Frame of Reference in the field of European contract law, including consumer as well as business transactions.[46]

How the political condemnation of the overly comprehensive DCFR will affect the propositions that it contains remains to be seen, and we do not

---

[41] European Commission, COM(2004) 651 final (11 October 2004). In parallel, an empirical study commissioned by Clifford Chance revealed an interest on the part of the commercial practitioners in the adoption of some unified private law, mainly in the field of contract law; see S. Vogenauer and S. Weatherill (eds.), *Harmonisation of European Contract Law* (Oxford and Portland: Hart, 2006).

[42] On the open-endedness of the political project see N. Jansen, 'The Authority of an "Academic Draft of Reference"', in H. Micklitz and F. Cafaggi (eds.), *European Private Law after the Common Frame of Reference* (Cheltenham: Edward Elgar, 2010), 147 ff. See H. Beale, 'The Nature and Purpose of the Common Frame of Reference', (2008) *Juridica* 10 ff.; see also B. Fauvarque-Cosson, 'Droit européen et international des contrats: L'apport des codifications doctrinales', (2007) *Dalloz chronique* 96 ff.

[43] C. von Bar, 'A Common Frame of Reference for European Private Law – Academic Efforts and Political Realities', (2008) 12 *Electronic Journal of Comparative Law* 1 ff., available at www.ejcl.org/121/art121-27.pdf.

[44] C. von Bar et al. (eds.), *Principles, Definitions and Model Rules of European Private Law* (Munich: Sellier, 2009).

[45] See, e.g., on the law of tort, G. Brüggemeier, 'Non-contractual Liability Arising out of Damage Caused to Another: The Making of a Hybrid', in A. Somma (ed.), *The Politics of the Draft Common Frame of Reference* (The Hague: Kluwer, 2009), 179 ff.

[46] See http://ec.europa.eu/justice/policies/consumer/policies_consumer_intro:en.htm.

wish to enter here into a discussion of the merits and weaknesses of this instrument or of its possible substitutes.[47] Recently, the European Commission further limited the objective of a regulatory scheme and proposed the adoption of a regulation on an optional Common European Sales Law only.[48] Regardless of the merits of this text, it appears to be doubtful, and perhaps even conceptually impossible, that efforts of unification of private law be limited to the law of sales or even to the law of contract only; to that extent, the DCFR had it right, even if its authors went beyond the call of duty.[49] However, this does not take away the fact that some of the methodological and substantive choices made by the authors of the DCFR and of the new proposal will have to be questioned, examined, and discussed. On the one hand, before proceeding with legislating, one may want to find out more about how national courts actually decide concrete cases before coming to conclusions as to how they should be decided.[50] On the other hand, one will have to have a political debate on the legitimacy of many of the substantive solutions proposed. The choice of one solution deemed 'better' or 'more efficient' should not necessarily be the proposed solution, contrary to what the DCFR and other model laws sometimes suggest.[51] Even the very idea of a statutory scheme and of its functions should be examined more fundamentally. Contract law, no less than the rest of private law or law in general, rests on political choices and

---

[47] For some of the criticisms addressed to the DCFR that may have influenced the decision of the Commission, see B. Fauvarque-Cosson, 'Droit européen des contrats: bilan et perspectives pour la prochaine décennie', (2010) *Revue des contrats* 316 ff.; R. Zimmermann, 'The Present State of European Private Law', (2009) 57 *American Journal of Comparative Law* 479.

[48] European Commission, COM(2011) 635 final, Brussels 11 October 2011; the text of the proposal is available at http://ec.europa.eu/justice/contract/files/common_sales_law/regulation_sales_law_en.pdf.

[49] In our view, 'contract law', which is not a category recognized as such in the codes of the civil law system, cannot meaningfully be separated from the law of obligations, or from property law, or other areas of private law. Swiss codification shows that once the law of obligations and the law dealing with civil capacity were unified in the late nineteenth century, the idea of a Swiss civil code in its entirety imposed itself very soon after.

[50] See L. Antoniolli, F. Fiorentini, and J. Gordley, 'A Case-Based Assessment of the Draft Common Frame of Reference', (2010) 58 *American Journal of Comparative Law* 343, analysing the results of L. Antoniolli and F. Fiorentini (eds.), *A Factual Assessment of the Draft Common Frame of Reference* (Munich: Sellier, 2010).

[51] See F. Werro, 'What Is To Be Gained from Comparative Research and Teaching? Thoughts for an Ideal Agenda', in C. Godt (ed.), *Hanse Law School in Perspective – Legal Teaching and Cross Border Research under Lisbon* (forthcoming).

cultural preferences. It cannot meaningfully be detached from its social, linguistic, and cultural context. One does not adopt legal rules or principles in the name of so-called rationality, efficiency, or quality without debating concrete political implications.

In any event, and whatever role some type of European legislation might play in the future profile of private law in Europe, it seems to be crucial to keep in mind the active role of courts. If we assume for a moment that a single text regulating private law – whatever its scope – could be meaningfully adopted in the European Union, there still would be the problem of the interpretation of such a text. It is likely that local judges would read this law through their own national lenses. In the absence of a new European court system, resting on a common European legal education, the adoption of a single text regardless of its precision would still trigger different outcomes, determined in their variety by different linguistic and cultural assumptions.[52] The cultural or societal clashes that divide judges within the same country, easily demonstrated by the varying opinions of judges at different levels of appeal of the same case,[53] will no doubt be harsher across borders.

However, the purpose of this chapter, again, is not to analyse the pros and cons of a European regulation of private law or even to analyse its feasibility, but more to shed light on the possible role and function of comparative law in that context, and hopefully also beyond. Indeed, the questions that the constitutionalization or denationalization of private law trigger in

---

[52] Despite its crucial role, the ECJ cannot possibly bring the kind of unity that is required. On the fundamental role of the ECJ so far, see W. van Gerven, 'Bridging the Unbridgeable: Community Law and National Tort Laws after *Francovich* and *Brasserie*', (1996) 45 *International and Comparative Law Quarterly* 517 ff.; van Gerven, 'The ECJ Case Law as a Means of Unification of Private Law?', in A. Hartkamp et al. (eds.), *Towards a European Civil Code*, 3rd edn (Nijmegen: Kluwer, 2004), 101 ff. On the necessity of a new European court system in the case of unification of private law, see M. Bussani, 'European Tort Law – A Way Forward?', in M. Bussani (ed.), *European Tort Law: Eastern and Western Perspectives* (Berne: Staempfli, 2007), 365, 373–7.

[53] As illustrated by the swimming-pool cases in England and France; *Ruxley Electronics and Constructions v. Forsyth*, [1995] 3 WLR 118, [1996] AC 344; and Cass. Civ., 17 November 1984, reported in H. Beale, A. Hartkamp, H. Kötz, and D. Tallon, *Cases, Materials and Text on Contract Law* (Oxford and Portland: Hart, 2002), 689–90. On the comparative analysis of the French and English swimming-pool cases, see R. Sefton-Green, 'The European Union, Law and Society: Making the Socio-Cultural Difference', in T. Wilhelmsson, E. Paunio, and A. Pohjolainen (eds.), *Private Law and the Many Cultures of Europe* (The Hague: Kluwer, 2007), 37 ff.

Europe have general implications on legal comparison and its methodology beyond geographical boundaries.

6.3 Implications for comparative legal studies and its method

If legal integration and the functioning of markets require removal of legal divergences, as claimed by the proponents of a unified private law in Europe or even worldwide, one may well ask what will happen to comparative legal studies in that field once a unified law has been adopted. The 'founders' of comparative law as a discipline in 1900 are celebrated for having used their skills to erase legal differences and to promote the unification of law, but it is arguably because they have succeeded only very partially with a small number of international conventions that comparative studies still exist as they do.[54]

Instead, in part as a result of the contemporary unification efforts perceived to menace cultural diversity, a number of comparatists argue today that comparison should not encourage the finding of the same, but rather help recognize and discuss difference.[55] This new approach may not serve the immediate and concrete needs of the legal practitioner who seeks inspiration from foreign law. As an academic or political enterprise,[56] however, comparison should find a just cause in the possible exploration and understanding of that difference (subsection 6.3.1). Naturally, this raises questions of method and the selection of tools that help to give meaning to that difference (6.3.2).

---

[54] On this question see S. van Erp, 'Comparative Private Law in Practice: The Process of Law Reform', in E. Örücü and D. Nelken (eds.), *Comparative Law: A Handbook* (Oxford and Portland: Hart, 2007), 399 ff., who claims that unification projects regardless of their success do not actually threaten the need for comparative law.

[55] Pierre Legrand in this respect appears foundational. Among many other texts of his, see P. Legrand, 'Comparative Legal Studies and the Matter of Authenticity', (2009) 4 *Journal of Comparative Law* 366, who at the outset of his piece uses a nice quotation from Larkin: 'Insisting so on difference, made me welcome:/ Once that was recognized, we were in touch.'

[56] Again, that enterprise may at times be distinguished from the practical endeavour of someone in search of a foreign solution or of a form of reasoning helping towards the resolution of a particular case, either driven by clients' interests or a search for judicial inspiration. Also, on the need to keep in mind the purpose of the inquiry when embarking on a comparative study, see G. Dannemann, 'Comparative Law: Study of Similarity or Differences?', in M. Reimann and R. Zimmermann (eds.), *The Oxford Handbook of Comparative Law* (Oxford University Press, 2006), 383 ff.

6.3.1 Convergence versus divergence and the question of the functional equivalent

Mainstream comparative literature remains in general attached to the notion that divergences in legal rules are often variations on common principles. Fundamentally, law would be one; local specificities would only be superficial and incidental manifestations of the same truth. In effect, legal comparison is often presented as a way of using foreign law to understand what unites the different legal systems. It is understood as a scientific enterprise that looks at law rationally and without ideological prejudices. Beyond identifying and analysing some differences, the result of the inquiry is, more fundamentally, supposed to help identify and understand the underlying principles that give a coherent meaning to decisions and rules that otherwise do not reveal those principles.[57] Along with the faith in the truth of those principles often comes the proclaimed cardinal *praesumptio similitudinis*.[58] In this approach, a local rule is nothing but the more or less adequate expression of the particular function that the law is trying to serve. The search must lead to identifying the foreign rule or institution that constitutes a functional equivalent of the rule identified in the place where the inquiry starts.

This assumption certainly has its appeal and its justification. It rests in part on the belief that, where the mere recording of the surface would only reveal dividing difference, sophisticated reading and understanding reveal commonality and togetherness. One can relate to the idea that for comparatists, at times, and perhaps especially after the Second World War, this approach has borne the hope of peace and the possibility of overcoming destructive rivalries and differences between the cultures of different nationalities. Yet, at the same time, sameness, at least if proclaimed as a general principle of investigation, bears the risk of doing violence to some interesting and important differences.[59] It also celebrates one solution as

---

[57] James Gordley, 'Is Comparative Law a Distinct Discipline?', (1998) 46 *American Journal of Comparative Law* 607.

[58] K. Zweigert and H. Kötz, *Einführung in die Rechtsvergleichung*, 3rd edn (Tübingen: Mohr Siebeck, 1996), 2. For a critical discussion of this approach, see for instance Ralf Michaels, 'The Functional Method of Comparative Law', in M. Reimann and R. Zimmermann (eds.), *The Oxford Handbook of Comparative Law* (Oxford University Press, 2006), 369 ff.

[59] The term is often used by Legrand, and convincingly so: see for instance P. Legrand, 'Paradoxically, Derrida: For a Comparative Legal Studies', (2005) 27 *Cardozo Law Review* 631, 706 f.; the fact that this would reveal an 'emotional investment', as pointed out by Cotterrell, 'Is It So Bad', 138, does not undermine the legitimacy of Legrand's claim and choice of words.

superior to others. It assumes that the comparatist should find the same in the other, regardless of that other, and reject it in case it is different. As one can see, the risk of imperialism and hegemonic views is lurking, together with a threat to the right to be different.[60] The principle of sameness that ignores some notions celebrated in certain parts of the world may not find an equivalent elsewhere. This is, for example, the case with the very notion of 'private law' that may be problematic or irrelevant in certain contexts outside Europe.

In any event, if one is interested in respecting cultural identity and is thus tempted to investigate difference rather than operating by reference to the principle of convergence, one has to address the question of how to proceed. While the answer to this question does not impose one given method only, deciding in favour of the exploration of difference has methodological implications. Sacrosanct functionalism must surely leave room for other methods of investigation.

6.3.2 Investigating difference, rejecting positivism, and the question of interdisciplinarity

In addition to maintaining the assumption of convergence, traditional or orthodox legal comparison often assumes that foreign law has a firm given content that can be found in the legal sources in the country under scrutiny. Along with harbouring this positivistic and static assumption, legal comparison often consists only of describing legal outcomes and rules in a reportorial and, ultimately, not very informative way. By focusing on what is stated to be the law in official legal documents, the work often resembles that of presenting skeletons.[61] The tensions, controversies, debates, and

---

[60] We shall leave out here consideration of the ethical and political need also to recognize similarity. Indeed, there is a long orientalist tradition of 'recognizing' the non-West's difference (historic claims that China has had no tradition of civil and private law, but only penal law and despotic public law). Obviously it can be important to be able to see that what looks different can be reinterpreted as not so different from the European or Western standard. On this question see T. Ruskola, 'Legal Orientalism', (2002) 101 *Michigan Law Review* 179; also from a more general point of view, on the questionability of the representation of China as fundamentally different, see J.-F. Billeter, *Contre François Jullien* (Paris: Allia, 2006).

[61] G. P. Fletcher, 'Comparative Law as a Subversive Discipline', (1998) 46 *American Journal of Comparative Law* 683. For a similar point see H. P. Glenn, 'Com-paring', in E. Örücü and D. Nelken (eds.), *Comparative Law: A Handbook* (Oxford and Portland: Hart, 2007), 91,

lack of certitude that surround a given decisional process are to a large extent ignored.

As he tends to take things too literally, the orthodox comparatist fails to relate to the way in which culture permeates the foreign legal institution or rule, and he does not account for the uncertain reasoning process out of which a given rule has emerged. In so doing, he fosters conclusions that will most likely be incomplete and, certainly from the point of view of the indigenous lawyer, unacceptable in their simplicity. Again, to the extent that the search for convergence drives traditional comparison, the comparatist will often praise or blame a given foreign solution, depending on how well this solution matches his home rule or institution, and on how it appears to serve the home-defined function assigned to the matter under scrutiny. For example, the traditional comparatist may, as many civilians have done, look at common law 'consideration' in the formation of contracts and declare that it is a superfluous institution. In addition to being superficial and probably useless, this comparison leads to ignoring what decisive forces have led a given system to adopt this rule and to assuming the superiority of the rule with which one is familiar.

If it is accepted that difference and cultural diversity are assets rather than impediments to social and commercial exchanges, this certainly implies a different attitude and method for the comparatist from those just described. Rather than merely making the descriptive and formal inventory of foreign law and judging its value in the light of his own, the comparatist should engage in recognizing and respecting the foreign and the other as such. To study, recognize, and respect the foreign becomes a complex and unlimited exploration, in which the comparatist must 'avoid positioning himself as that by reference to which the other ought to be assessed'.[62]

One way of avoiding that self-centrism is to engage in a collective enterprise, where knowledge of foreign law is brought by different *rapporteurs* in order to discuss and analyse the information together. This is the method that has often been adopted in comparative settings. It was refined in the Common Core of European Private Law project, where the

where he makes the point that the way in which foreign law is often taught consists of bringing an understanding of 'what the foreign law somehow *is*, with very little or no place for discussion of why it might be the way it appears to be, and what consequences that might have for the law we have already learned in other courses'.

[62] P. Legrand, 'The Verge of Foreign Law – with Derrida', (2010) *Romanian Journal of Comparative Law* 73 ff., 78.

comparison made by the editor of a given volume dealing with a given subject is done on the basis of factual hypotheticals. These are prepared on the basis of information supplied by national *rapporteurs*, who display a cosmopolitan and open-minded attitude.[63] Accordingly, the result of the comparative analysis is not based just on law-in-the-books, but on some empirical and cultural investigation.

Regardless of whether work is done in a team or by one person alone, legal comparison should become an inquiry. Understanding the law of the other should be an investigation into the forces that justify its existence from within.[64] By definition, this appears to call for interdisciplinarity, as history, politics, literature, economics, and other forces determine what Legrand, using Derrida, calls the 'spectral' dimension of legal texts.[65] These disciplines thus become some of the indispensable tools for coming closer to give meaning to legal texts.[66] Along those lines, it is clearly not sufficient to assume that the same common Roman law representations have haunted private law texts for more than two thousand years. Within Europe, different cultures and languages, not to mention different forms of capitalism and respect for the state have shaped the law and the relation of individuals to it in ways that partially blur and erase the past Roman law heritage. Thus comparative studies will benefit from some form of law-and-ism, just as any serious academic legal research would if it pretends to do something other than mere doctrinal analysis.

Some object to this approach by stating that lawyers are not equipped to deal with interdisciplinarity.[67] It is certainly true that the practitioner rarely engages in an inter- or multidisciplinary investigation for the sake of

[63] M. Bussani and U. Mattei, 'Le fonds commun du droit privé européen', (2000) *Revue internationale de droit comparé*, 2000, 29 ff., 44.

[64] Legrand, 'Verge of Foreign Law', 85 ff.; in a similar way, one should try to investigate the psychology and the thinking of the lawyers of the foreign legal system when engaging in legal comparison; on this inquiry, see W. Ewald, 'What Was It Like To Try a Rat?', (1995) 143 *Pennsylvannia Law Review* 1889.

[65] Legrand, 'Verge of Foreign Law', 85 f.

[66] G. Samuel, 'Taking Methods Seriously (Part Two)', (2007) 2 *Journal of Comparative Law* 210, 229.

[67] On this objection, see B. Fauvarque-Cosson, 'Development of Comparative Law in France', in M. Reimann and R. Zimmermann (eds.), *The Oxford Handbook of Comparative Law* (Oxford University Press, 2006), 61, who argues that 'when Legrand advocates complex cultural and interdisciplinary comparison, his approach renders the discipline so complicated that it may well discourage and deter scholars from becoming involved in the first place'.

solving her clients' problems and, if she needs it, she will hire the required experts. Even academic jurists armed with the time and motivation to engage in such an inquiry may find the research impossible due to lack of expertise or the volume of material. In other words, interdisciplinary research may appear quite difficult, at least when done alone. However, this should not mean that one must give up on that challenge, at least if one claims to engage in useful and responsible studies. In effect, lawyers might want to revisit their simplistic and reductionist understanding of the world and consider working in teams with colleagues from other disciplines. But this question shows that not only competence, but also courage and independence are at stake. Indeed, it may be hard for scholars to find themselves without the reassuring support they enjoy from the world of practice. In that respect it is interesting to compare European professors with their US counterparts: whereas the former are making sure that courts refer to their work, and often engage in consulting, the latter are much more often exclusively involved in the pursuit of free theoretical reflections. These theory-minded professors are obviously not cited in court decisions and forgo additional revenues, but they can launch important debates and generate influential schools of thought.

Be that as it may, one manageable interdisciplinary method may be that which Lasser, borrowing from literary criticism, calls 'close reading'.[68] Specifically, Lasser suggests that the comparatist must do her research in a foreign legal system on the basis of a rigorous literary analysis of the discourses employed in and by the jurists within that system. However, this 'close reading' should not be practised only on the official and public output generated by formal state agencies, but also on the many other discourses that are produced in and around the legal system being studied.[69]

In whatever form, some interdisciplinary approach seems quite vital in academic comparative studies.[70] Alternatively, or as another form of

---

[68] M. Lasser, 'The Question of Understanding', in P. Legrand and R. Munday (eds.), *Comparative Legal Studies: Traditions and Transitions* (Cambridge University Press, 2003), 203.

[69] Lasser, 'Question of Understanding', 207–12; for a similar point see G. Samuel, 'Form, Structure and Content in Comparative Law: Assessing the Links', in E. Cashin Ritaine (ed.), *Legal Engineering and Comparative Law* (Zurich: Schulthess, 2009), 27 ff., 46.

[70] The question of the use of comparative law in practice remains in part a different question, mainly because the comparison will often be driven by the needs of the client. This need-based comparison will reduce the space made to the question of understanding required in academia.

interdisciplinary method, a repeated physical and emotional immersion in the country of the law being looked at may also help to achieve meaningful comparison. This immersion will yield contextual information that will guide the comparatist and reveal perspectives on the foreign law investigated. Indeed, the observation made by a knowledgeable lawyer immersed in the foreign culture may not only help the comparatist gain new insights into his own law, but add valuable information relevant for the local lawyer, whose perception is often limited by a lack of external feedback.[71]

Among other things, it is precisely this form of interdisciplinary or immersive method that seems to be lacking at times in the contemporary efforts of European private law-making. Perhaps work based on some deeper analysis would reveal that a common code makes no sense; on the contrary, however, it could perhaps show that the specificities of once sharply divided cultures have now evolved and that a common law is possible or, on the contrary, quite superfluous. The fact that cultures in general, as well as legal cultures, evolve must not be neglected. In any event, without comparative work willing to consider the law of the other seriously and to take into account its cultural dimension, a common private law codification, such as the one undertaken so far at the European level, may prove to be nothing more than a fallacy.

6.4 Conclusion

Private law used to monopolize comparative legal studies. Along with this hegemony, comparative private law often cultivated a positivistic view of the law, perhaps especially with respect to foreign law. Mainstream comparatists still appear to hold to this view. While this approach may be useful in practice, it is unsatisfying from a theoretical point of view. This positivistic conception leads to a comparison that is largely mechanical and quite superficial. Indeed, it often consists of presenting and analysing rules and precedents as they appear to the foreign eye, without taking into account what it takes to understand them from within. In effect, foreign

---

[71] R. Sacco, *La comparaison juridique au service de la connaissance du droit* (Paris: Economica, 1991), 115 ff.

law is thus defined as the law of the other, but without any insight into what drives that law to be different from the comparatist's own law. Instead, difference is perceived as an incident that can be either copied or corrected, but not as a richness that should be analysed and preserved. This way of comparing seeks to provide an insight into the good norm and help eliminate the bad one. This is what has given birth to unification projects, yielding some international conventions throughout the twentieth century. Despite the limited success that this conception has had, this is what feeds the current idea that local civil codes can be replaced by some form of European one.

However, the integrational changes that menace diversity in the private laws of Europe have put into question the mainstream approach to comparative private law. As the present chapter has tried to demonstrate, a critical, cultural, and anti-positivistic conception of what academic comparative legal studies should involve has emerged. The new conception grounded on an interdisciplinary methodology derives from the belief that foreign law can only be observed properly if it is respected and recognized as different. In order to give meaning to that difference, the new comparatists advocate the use of literature, linguistics, history, and politics, among other disciplines, to apprehend foreign law in a given context. While ambitious and not necessarily easy to adopt, even in academia, that approach seems to rest on the realization that without the use of these tools, the texts of law will not be given any truly relevant meaning.

In a time of transformation and legal integration of private laws in Europe such as those described in this chapter, it appears that this alternative – non-positivistic – way of engaging in the study of foreign law could be very useful, perhaps vital. Instead of ignoring differences in the name of efficiency, the proponents of this formidable enterprise of a European civil code would well be inspired to engage in an exercise of understanding difference. It could turn out that legal systems and cultures are converging, and one can only hope that Europeans will get a better sense of what unites them. Regardless of how cultures converge, this process must be one of dialogue and exchange, with a solid understanding of the political nature of the enterprise. If not, legal integration will appear to be an act of violence, and it will ultimately lead to a pitiful and hurtful failure. In an age of so-called globalization, *la pensée unique* appears more than ever to be a menace to, and not a tool for, peace.

Further reading

M. Bussani, 'The Contract Law Codification Process in Europe: Policies, Targets and Time Dimensions', in S. Grundmann and J. Stuyck (eds.), *An Academic Green Paper on European Contract Law* (The Hague: Kluwer, 2002), 159

    Il diritto dell'Occidente. Geopolitica delle regole globali (Turin: Utet, 2010)

M. Bussani and F. Werro (eds.), *European Private Law: A Handbook* (Berne: Staempfli, 2009), vol. 1

H. Collins, *The European Civil Code: The Way Forward* (Cambridge University Press, 2008)

V. Constantinesco, 'La "codification" communautaire du droit privé à l'épreuve du titre de competence de l'Union européenne', (2008) *Revue trimestrielle de droit européen* 711

R. Cotterrell, 'Comparative Law and Legal Culture', in M. Reimann and R. Zimmermann (eds.), *The Oxford Handbook of Comparative Law* (Oxford University Press, 2006), 709

B. Fauvarque-Cosson and A.-J. Kerhuel, 'Is Law an Economic Contest? French Reactions to the *Doing Business* World Bank Reports and Economic Analysis of the Law', (2009) 57 *American Journal of Comparative Law* 811

S. Glanert, 'L'européanisation des droits au risque de la littérature-monde', (2010) 65 *Revue interdisciplinaire d'études juridiques* 1

H. P. Glenn, *Legal Traditions of the World – Sustainable Diversity in Law*, 2nd edn (New York: Oxford University Press, 2004)

J. Gordley, 'Comparative Law and Legal History', in M. Reimann and R. Zimmermann (eds.), *The Oxford Handbook of Comparative Law* (Oxford University Press, 2006), 753

    'The Universalist Heritage', in P. Legrand and R. Munday (eds.), *Comparative Legal Studies: Traditions and Transitions* (Cambridge University Press, 2003), 31

J. Gordley and A. T. Von Mehren, *An Introduction to the Comparative Study of Private Law* (Cambridge University Press, 2006)

M. Graziadei, 'Comparative Law as a Study of Transplants and Receptions', in M. Reimann and R. Zimmermann (eds.), *The Oxford Handbook of Comparative Law* (Oxford University Press, 2006), 441

    'The Functionalist Heritage', in P. Legrand and R. Munday (eds.), *Comparative Legal Studies: Traditions and Transitions* (Cambridge University Press, 2003), 100

    'Legal Transplants and the Frontiers of Legal Knowledge', (2009) 10 *Theoretical Inquiries in Law* 693

B. Grossfeld, 'Comparatist and Languages', in P. Legrand and R. Munday (eds.), *Comparative Legal Studies: Traditions and Transitions* (Cambridge University Press, 2003), 154

V. Grosswald Curran, 'Comparative Law and Language', in M. Reimann and R. Zimmermann (eds.), *The Oxford Handbook of Comparative Law* (Oxford University Press, 2006), 675

'Cultural Immersion, Difference and Categories in US Comparative Law', (1998) 46 *American Journal of Comparative Law* 43

V. Grosswald Curran and B. Grossfeld, *Core Questions of Comparative Law* (Durham, NC: Carolina Academic Press, 2004)

S. Grundmann and J. Stuyck (eds.), *An Academic Green Paper on European Contract Law* (The Hague: Kluwer, 2002)

M. W. Hesselink, 'The Common Frame of Reference as a Source of European Private Law', (2009) 83 *Tulane Law Review* 919

N. Jansen, 'Comparative Law and Comparative Knowledge', in M. Reimann and R. Zimmermann (eds.), *The Oxford Handbook of Comparative Law* (Oxford University Press, 2006), 305

N. Jansen and R. Zimmermann, 'Restating the Acquis Communautaire? A Critical Examination of the "Principles of the Existing EC Contract Law"', (2008) 71 *Modern Law Review* 505

P. Jung and C. Baldus (ed.), *Differenzierte Integration im Gemeinschaftsprivatrecht* (Munich: Sellier, 2007)

N. Kasirer, 'English Private Law, Outside-In', (2003) 3 *Oxford University Commonwealth Law Journal* 249

D. Kennedy, 'The Methods and Politics of Comparative Law', in M. Bussani and U. Mattei (eds.), *The Common Core of European Private Law* (The Hague: Kluwer, 2002, repr. 2003), 131

P. Legrand (ed.), *Comparer les droits, résolument* (Paris: Presses Universitaires de France, 2009)

Le droit comparé, 3rd edn (Paris: Presses Universitaires de France, 2009)

'Econocentrism, Focus: Economics and Comparative Law', (2009) 59 *University of Toronto Law Journal* 215

P. Legrand and R. Munday (eds.), *Comparative Legal Studies: Traditions and Transitions* (Cambridge University Press, 2003)

P. Legrand and G. Samuel, *Introduction au common law* (Paris: La découverte, 2008)

U. Mattei, 'Comparative Law and Critical Legal Studies', in M. Reimann and R. Zimmermann (eds.), *The Oxford Handbook of Comparative Law* (Oxford University Press, 2006), 815

'A Theory of Imperial Law: A Study on U.S. Hegemony and the Latin Resistance', (2003) 3(2) *Global Jurist*

U. Mattei, T. Ruskola, and A. Gidi (eds.), *Schlesinger's Comparative Law*, 7th edn (New York: Foundation Press, 2009)

J. H. Merryman, D. S. Clark, and J. O. Haley (eds.), *Comparative Law, Historical Development of the Civil Law Tradition in Europe, Latin America, and East Asia* (New Providence: Lexisnexis, 2010)

R. Michaels, 'American Law (United States)', in J. M. Smits (ed.), *Elgar Encyclopedia of Comparative Law* (Cheltenham: Edward Elgar, 2006), 66

'Global Legal Pluralism', (2009) *Duke Public Law and Legal Theory*, Research Paper Series No. 259

R. Michaels and N. Jansen, 'Private Law and the State: Comparative Perceptions and Historical Observations', (2007) *Duke Law School Faculty Scholarship Series*, http://lsr.nellco.org/duke_fs/77

H. Micklitz and F. Cafaggi (eds.), *European Private Law after the Common Frame of Reference* (Cheltenham: Edward Elgar, 2010)

H. Muir Watt, 'Globalization and Comparative Law', in M. Reimann and R. Zimmermann (ed.), *The Oxford Handbook of Comparative Law* (New York: Oxford University Press, 2006), 579

H. Muir Watt and R. Sefton-Green, 'Fitting the Frame: An Optional Instrument, Party Choice and Mandatory/Default Rules', in H. Micklitz and F. Cafaggi (eds.), *European Private Law after the Common Frame of Reference* (Cheltenham: Edward Elgar, 2010), 201

E. Örücü, 'Comparatists and Extraordinary Places', in P. Legrand and R. Munday (eds.), *Comparative Legal Studies: Traditions and Transitions* (Cambridge University Press, 2003), 467

V. V. Palmer, 'Mixed Jurisdictions', in J. M. Smits (ed.), *Elgar Encyclopedia of Comparative Law* (Cheltenham: Edward Elgar, 2006), 467

Mixed Jurisdictions Worldwide: The Third Legal Family (Cambridge University Press, 2001)

P. Ranieri, *Europäisches Obligationenrecht. Ein Handbuch mit Texten und Materialien*, 3rd edn (Vienna/New York: Springer, 2009)

M. Reimann, 'Towards a European Civil Code: Why Continental Jurists Should Consult Their Transatlantic Colleagues', (1999) 73 *Tulane Law Review* 1337

M. Reimann and R. Zimmermann (eds.), *The Oxford Handbook of Comparative Law* (Oxford University Press, 2006)

G. Samuel, 'Comparative Law and the Courts', in G. Canivet, M. Andenas, and D. Fairgrieve (eds.), *Comparative Law before the Courts* (London: BIICL, 2004), 253

'Droit comparé et théorie du droit', (2006) 61 *Revue interdisciplinaire d'études juridiques* 1

'Interdisciplinarity and the Authority Paradigm: Should Law Be Taken Seriously by Scientists and Social Scientists?', (2009) 36 *Journal of Law and Society* 431

H. Schulte-Nolke, 'EC Law and the Formation of Contract – from the Common Frame of Reference to the "Blue Button"', (2007) 3 *European Review of Contract Law* 332

R. Schulze, *Common Principles of European Private Law: Studies of a Research Network* (Baden-Baden: Nomos, 2003)

I. Schwenzer, 'Development of Comparative Law in Germany, Switzerland and Austria', in M. Reimann and R. Zimmermann (eds.), *The Oxford Handbook of Comparative Law* (Oxford University Press, 2006), 69

J. M. Smits, 'Comparative Law and its Influence on National Legal Systems', in M. Reimann and R. Zimmermann (eds.), *The Oxford Handbook of Comparative Law* (Oxford University Press, 2006), 513

S. Vogenauer, 'Sources of Law and Legal Method in Comparative Law', in M. Reimann and R. Zimmermann (eds.), *The Oxford Handbook of Comparative Law* (Oxford University Press, 2006), 869

A. Watson, *Comparative Law: Law, Reality and Society* (Lake Mary: Vandeplas Publishing, 2008)

'Legal Transplants and European Private Law', (2000) 2 *Ius Commune Lectures on European Private Law* 1

S. Weatherill, 'Why Object to the Harmonisation of Private Law by the EC?', (2004) 12 *European Review of Private Law* 633

F. Werro, 'Liability for Harm Caused by Things', in A. Hartkamp et al. (eds.), *Towards a European Civil Code*, 4th rev. edn (Alphen aan den Rijn: Kluwer Law International, 2011), 921

J. Whitman, 'The Neo-Romantic Turn', in P. Legrand and R. Munday (eds.), *Comparative Legal Studies: Traditions and Transitions* (Cambridge University Press, 2003), 312

F. Wieacker, 'Foundations of European Legal Culture', (1990) 38 *American Journal of Comparative Law* 1 (1990)

W. Wiegand, 'The Reception of American Law in Europe', (1991) 39 *American Journal of Comparative Law* 229

T. Wilhelmsson, 'The Legal, the Cultural and the Political – Conclusions from Different Perspectives on Harmonisation of European Contract Law', (2002) *European Business Law Review* 541

T. Wilhelmsson, E. Paunio, and A. Pohjolainen (eds.), *Private Law and the Many Cultures of Europe* (The Hague: Kluwer, 2007)

R. Zimmermann, 'Comparative Law and the Europeanization of Private Law', in M. Reimann and R. Zimmermann (eds.), *The Oxford Handbook of Comparative Law* (Oxford University Press, 2006), 539

'The Present State of European Private Law', (2009) 57 *American Journal of Comparative Law* 479

Comparative administrative law 7

Francesca Bignami

7.1 Overview

The field of administrative law is inextricably bound to two phenomena that trace their origins to the nineteenth century: the rise of large state bureaucracies designed to fulfil a complex array of societal needs and the development of liberal democratic norms of social organization and public authority. Much of administrative law can be understood as an attempt to work out the tension inherent in these two phenomena: the recognition that the attainment of public purposes is contingent on a cadre of full-time employees, paid by the public purse and loyal to the state, and, at the same time, the belief that public authority is legitimate only if embedded in democratic politics and liberal societies. To put it more succinctly, these are the objectives, on the one hand, of neutrality and expertise, and, on the other hand, of democracy and liberal rights.

The common aspiration of making public administration both capable and accountable serves as the springboard for the comparative analysis in this chapter. I begin with a discussion of what, in the law, is taken to be the hallmark of modern bureaucracy – the legal guarantees of civil service employment – together with national variations in the professionalization of administration and contemporary efforts to cut back on civil service guarantees. I then turn to three important types of accountability: the contestation of administrative action before the courts, the involvement of organized interests in administrative policymaking, and informal accountability to the general public through parliamentary ombudsmen and transparency guarantees. These categories serve as a framework for exploring the similarities and differences that shape contemporary administrative law systems. The chapter concludes with the increasingly important phenomenon of the globalization of administrative law and the rapid migration of administrative principles across legal systems throughout the world, both national and international. In line with the intellectual purpose of this volume, I have omitted topics that have traditionally been considered peripheral to the field or that fall at the intersection with other disciplines, for instance the constitutional powers of the executive branch over public administration and the empowerment of private groups through self-regulation, and refer the reader to the bibliography at the end of the chapter for guidance.

7.2 Public administration

One of the defining elements of bureaucracy is civil service employment: the selection and promotion of public officials based on merit and insulated from political influence through tenured employment.[1] The legal guarantees of civil service employment emerged to serve multiple ends: autocratic rulers seeking to consolidate their authority (Prussia), political elites adapting the instruments of government to the demands of industrialization and urbanization (Britain), and government reformers intent on shielding administration from the instability and incompetence of party-patronage appointments (France and the United States). In Europe, Japan, and North America, civil service safeguards were introduced over the course of the nineteenth century, beginning in the 1840s in France, 1870 in Britain, 1873 in Prussia, 1882 in Canada, 1887 in Japan, and 1883 in the United States.

Modern civil service laws are designed to render public employees independent of partisan politics and competent to perform the business of the nation. Some legal systems go so far as to constitutionalize this ambition, including the Italian Constitution (Arts. 97 and 98) and the German Basic Law (Art. 33). The core features of civil service employment are: (1) life tenure absent grave misconduct; (2) merit-based recruitment; (3) promotion based on a mixture of seniority and merit (often accompanied by independent civil service commissions); (4) pay scales and benefits that are more standardized than in private enterprise; and (5) restrictions on political activity, speech, and union activities, although these are far less common now than in the past.

---

[1] S. Skowronek, *Building a New American State: The Expansion of Administrative Capacities, 1877–1920* (Cambridge University Press, 1982); J. Ziller, *Administrations comparées: Les systèmes politico-administratifs de l'Europe des Douze* (Paris: Montchrestien, 1993).

Notwithstanding the common impulse to develop a professionalized public administration, there remain significant differences in the degree to which recruitment is professional or political. At the top echelons of the bureaucracy, political appointments are more extensive in the United States than in other countries, based on the theory that electoral winners should have an opportunity to impose a new set of priorities on government administration through the selection of high-level personnel.[2] There are also significant differences in the extent of patronage appointments at the lower levels of the bureaucracy. Some countries appear to be particularly vulnerable to party-based infiltration of the public administration, notwithstanding a legal commitment to an independent, professionally competent civil service. Italy represents but one example of this phenomenon.[3] A number of mechanisms, related to the historically weak nature of party competition, have enabled political parties and party-affiliated trade unions to circumvent the civil service system and carve out the public administration among themselves. These mechanisms include the unofficial assignment of government sectors to certain political parties – for instance, in the past, the Ministry of Agriculture to the Christian Democrats – and the recruitment of personnel through temporary contracts, which are then converted into permanent employment by law or government decree.

The past twenty years or so have witnessed a number of challenges to the traditional model of civil service employment.[4] The most important is the wave of new public management reforms that hit most democracies in the 1980s. Reformers in this school have sought to render the public sector more efficient by making the terms of public-sector employment – pay, benefits, and promotion – more flexible and by tying them more closely to performance indicators. Even more radically, various service delivery functions have been taken away from government administration and are now handled by firms operating in the private sector. The scope of these reforms, however, varies dramatically. Privatization, for instance, is far less pervasive in Europe than in the United States, where core state

---

[2] R. Rose, 'Giving Direction to Government in Comparative Perspective', in J. D. Aberbach and M. A. Peterson (eds.), *The Executive Branch* (New York: Oxford University Press, 2005), 72.

[3] S. Battini, 'Il Personale', in L. Torchia (ed.), *Il Sistema Amministrativo Italiano* (Bologna: Mulino, 2009), 279; S. Cassese, 'Hypotheses on the Italian Administrative System', (1993) 16 *West European Politics* 325.

[4] E. Suleiman, *Dismantling Democratic States* (Princeton University Press, 2003).

functions such as running prisons and conducting military operations have been out-sourced to private contractors.[5]

7.3 Administration and the courts

7.3.1 Systems of judicial review

With the emergence of bureaucratic power in the nineteenth and early twentieth centuries came the question of justice. What was to be the relationship between the old mode of exercising public authority, through trials and courts, and this new form of state power, designed to expeditiously raise taxes, undertake public works, protect public health, and more? The right to contest administrative decisions in a trial-like proceeding before a state official removed from the original determination emerged in both civil law and common law systems as critical to the legitimacy of administrative authority. At the same time, what is generally understood to be the major difference between administrative law systems also took shape: jurisdiction vested in the ordinary courts in England versus litigation before specialized state officials connected to the executive branch in France.

The origins of the common law–*droit administratif* divide are extremely complex and have been the object of numerous distinguished studies.[6] For our purposes, it is enough to recall the very different historical circumstances surrounding the rise of bureaucracy and administrative law in France and England. In France, the drive to consolidate absolute authority in the seventeenth and eighteenth centuries was marked by intense conflicts between the royal officers responsible for administering the provinces (*intendants*) and the powerful regional courts in the hands of local elites (*parlements*). In an attempt to insulate the decisions of the *intendants* from interference by the *parlements*, legal oversight was entrusted to a special body directly controlled

---

[5] M. Minow, 'Outsourcing Power', in J. Freeman and M. Minow (eds.), *Government by Contract: Outsourcing and American Democracy* (Cambridge, MA: Harvard University Press, 2009), 110; S. Dolovich, 'State Punishment and Private Prisons', (2005) 55 *Duke Law Journal* 441.

[6] See, e.g., S. Cassese, 'La costruzione del diritto amministrativo: Francia e Regno Unito', in S. Cassese (ed.), *Trattato di diritto amministrativo*, 2nd edn, vol. I (Milan: Giuffrè, 2003), 1–93; M. D'Alberti, *Diritto amministrativo comparato* (Bologna: Mulino, 1992); J. D. B. Mitchell, 'The Causes and Effects of the Absence of a System of Public Law in England', (1965) *Public Law* 95, 96–101.

by the monarchy (*Conseil du Roi*). This system of a specialized review body was borrowed during the French Revolution, albeit motivated by a very different republican theory aimed at destroying the special privileges and vested interests of the *parlements* of the Ancien Régime and ensuring that government officials would not encounter resistance from the old elites in carrying out the will of the people. Napoleon, in turn, embraced this system with the founding of the Council of State (*Conseil d'État*). It was at this time that the distinctive French separation of powers doctrine was born, according to which 'to judge the administration is still to administer' (*juger l'administration c'est encore administrer*): judicial review by the ordinary courts represented an encroachment on the executive power and therefore oversight had to be entrusted to a specialized body connected with the executive branch.

By contrast, in England, the business of government was handled by local elites with relatively little central involvement until well into the nineteenth century, and appeals against government officers were heard by courts of general jurisdiction based on the same system of common law writs devised for private disputes. Although the Stuarts made a bid to improve royal control by creating a separate set of prerogative courts with jurisdiction over complaints against government officers, the attempt came to end with the victory of Parliament and the common law bar in the Revolutionary Settlement of 1688. At that time, the hated prerogative courts were abolished and the powers and independence of common law judges were formally established by Act of Parliament. Later, when a substantial, centralized bureaucracy emerged, largely in response to nineteenth-century industrialization, the stature of the common law was such that there could be no question of ousting the courts and transferring administrative disputes to a separate body.

Let us explore the common law–*droit administratif* difference in more detail. In 1885 the English scholar Albert Venn Dicey famously proclaimed that in England, unlike France, there was no such thing known as 'administrative law'.[7] Government officers could be held to account for their actions, like private individuals, before the ordinary courts of law. The same judges, applying the same rules and affording the same rights and remedies, had the power to decide both suits against the government and purely private

---

[7] A. V. Dicey, *Introduction to the Study of the Law of the Constitution* (London: Macmillan, 1885).

disputes. Dicey argued that by treating public administration and private individuals on the same footing, the English system did a better job of safeguarding basic liberties and therefore was superior to the French one.

This characterization of the English system of legal redress has rightly been debunked as inaccurate, not only from the perspective of the law as it has evolved today, but also at the time it was pronounced. For instance, the statute of limitations for tort actions against public officials was six months, compared with the six years for similar actions between private parties, and was only extended by the Law Reform (Limitation of Actions, etc.) Act of 1954. It is true, however, that the practice of common law adjudication did produce a marked tendency to deny any categorical difference between public and private law and led to a natural overlapping of legal concepts, writs, and forms of redress between cases brought against private parties and against the government.[8] Today, with the elaboration of numerous legal doctrines specific to administration, the creation of a specific procedure for judicial review, the widespread resort to administrative tribunals (explained below), and the establishment of a special section of the ordinary courts devoted to administrative law, it is evident that, even in England, administrative law is a field apart from private law. The main vestiges of the original model that have survived are to be found in the area of government torts and public contracts, which are considered part of the general law of torts and contracts, and in the continuing power of common law courts to hear, in the last resort, cases brought against the government.

In France, the Council of State was originally established by Napoleon.[9] Then, as now, it had the dual function of drafting government laws and rules and hearing cases against government administration. Originally, the Council of State's dispute-resolution function was subject to extensive limitations, but by the time of the Third Republic most had been abolished and the Council of State had become a powerful and respected arbiter of complaints against the government.

Institutionally, the critical difference between the Council of State and the judicial branch is the system of recruitment and management of personnel,

---

[8] M. Taggart, 'The Peculiarities of the English: Resisting the Public/Private Law Distinction', in P. Craig and R. Rawlings (eds.), *Law and Administration in Europe: Essays in Honour of Carol Harlow* (Oxford University Press, 2003), 107.

[9] This discussion of the Council of State is drawn largely from M. Fromont, *Droit administratif des États européens* (Paris: Thémis, 2006).

which gives rise to pronounced cultural and sociological affinities between the Council of State and public administration. Members of the Council of State are selected from graduates of the École Nationale d'Administration, the elite, state-run school designed to train the uppermost echelons of the civil service (about two-thirds), and from the ranks of experienced individuals already serving in the administration, either in the lower administrative courts or in the upper ranks of the civil service (about one-third). This stands in contrast to the judiciary, which is populated with law school graduates who receive professional training at the state-sponsored school for the judiciary. Moreover, at any given point in time, about one-third of the members of the Council of State are serving elsewhere in the public administration, in ministerial cabinets, public enterprises, and other government offices. The last distinguishing feature of the Council of State is the mix of functions performed by its members. There are five administrative sections, responsible for giving technical advice on legislation and regulation, and one adjudicatory section, which hears administrative law cases, and members are commonly assigned to both an administrative section and the adjudicatory section. It is also important to underscore what does not separate the Council of State from the judicial branch – independence. True, members of the Council of State, unlike the judiciary, are not formally guaranteed permanence in office (*inamovibilité*), which means that in theory they can be transferred from one post to another for any reason. In practice, however, this never occurs, and it is universally acknowledged that the Council of State enjoys the same independence from executive-branch meddling as do the courts.

Litigation in the Council of State is conceived in markedly different terms from litigation in the ordinary courts. Traditionally, administrative litigation was understood primarily as designed to guarantee the legality and propriety of government action in a republican system faithful to the rule of law. In other words, administrative litigation was perceived as serving 'objective' purposes, linked to the correct working of the bureaucracy within the overall system of government. Until recently, the 'subjective' purposes of promoting justice and safeguarding individual rights were believed to be secondary. This has had numerous consequences for the system of administrative law adjudication. The fact that an administrative decision takes the form of a generally applicable regulation, affecting broad classes of individuals based on general characteristics, is not a barrier to getting into court (i.e. standing) as in other countries, such as Germany, England, and, in the past, the United States. Because of the focus on the objective lawfulness of rules, any individual affected by a rule can come forward to contest its correctness. Another consequence of the French stylization of administrative adjudication was, until recently, a fairly tame system of judicial remedies. Before 1980, the Council of State could annul offending administrative acts but did not have the procedural tools necessary to force administration to come into compliance and to guarantee that victorious litigants would obtain relief from wrongful government action. Since the 1980s, however, the Council of State has gradually acquired a better remedial toolkit, first with the power to fine a non-compliant administration (*astreinte*), then with the power to issue injunctions (*injonction*), and finally with the power to grant temporary injunctions (*référé*).

Mirroring the institutional separation between the judiciary and the Council of State, the study and doctrinal elaboration of administrative law in France is marked by a self-conscious divide between public and private law. In public law thinking, state administration is granted extraordinary privileges (the prerogatives of the *puissance publique*) but is also subject to extensive duties designed to safeguard the rights and interests of citizens. One clear example of this is the important concept of 'public service'.[10] The notion of public service was invented to cover any state activity performed in the general interest, not simply the core functions of policing and defence. Once a government activity is classified as a 'public service', the state is empowered to take whatever measures are necessary to ensure the continuity of that service and adaptation to changing circumstances, but it is also under a duty to treat the citizen-users of the public service equally and neutrally. To ensure continuity and adaptability, the administration is permitted unilaterally to modify government contracts with private providers, but it is also required to compensate the provider for any loss suffered as a consequence.

Linked to this understanding of the special concerns of public law is the sweeping scope of the field. In contrast with common law systems like that of the United States, where public contracts and government liability are taught as specialty subjects and are omitted from most administrative law textbooks, in the French tradition, state liability and government contracts are integral to the discipline. The theoretical apparatus of government privileges and duties at the core of administrative law extends to all forms

---

[10] J. S. Bell, 'Comparative Administrative Law', in M. Reimann and R. Zimmermann (eds.), *The Oxford Handbook of Comparative Law* (Oxford University Press, 2006), 1261, 1274.

of administrative action and all attempts to obtain individual redress from government wrongs. As many have observed, however, public law is coming to borrow more and more from private law, and therefore, even in France, public contracts and governmental liability are losing some of their distinctiveness.[11]

An alternative to the English and French models of judicial review that has emerged is that of a specialized branch of the judiciary dedicated to hearing administrative law cases.[12] The first example is generally taken to be Germany. There the judicial branch is composed of the Federal Constitutional Court and five discrete judicial hierarchies, one for civil and criminal law, one for labour disputes, one for tax disputes, one for social security disputes, and one for administrative law disputes. The last three all handle variants of what would be called administrative law cases in other countries. The judges who serve in the tax, social security, and administrative law courts are recruited on the basis of the same system of university study, exams, and traineeships as their counterparts on other courts and share the same guarantee of independence. The only difference is the degree of specialization and familiarity with administrative disputes that the members of these three branches acquire.

The systems in this third category operate closer to the common law model than the French one. In Germany as well as other countries that have chosen to adopt a specialized judiciary, government contract and tort disputes are heard by the civil courts, not by the administrative courts, and the doctrine tracks the private law of contract and tort. Moreover, administrative litigation is designed to protect individual rights and interests, much as private law litigation, and therefore the conditions under which standing is granted are more limited than in French law while, at the same time, the remedial powers of courts are broader.

Most legal systems have adopted one of these three institutional models. Histories of colonial rule can go some way in explaining the patterns that we see today. The territories that were at some time ruled by the British and that adopted the common law have entrusted generalist courts with hearing disputes between individuals and public administration. These include Australia, India, Ireland, New Zealand, and the United States. Due

---

[11] See, e.g., E. Picard, 'The Public–Private Divide in French Law through the History and Destiny of French Administrative Law', in M. Ruffert (ed.), *The Public–Private Law Divide: Potential for Transformation?* (London: BIICL, 2009), 17.

[12] Fromont, *Droit administratif des États européens*, p. 128.

to the influence of US law after the Second World War, a number of other countries have adopted the generalist court model, including Japan and South Korea. Countries influenced by France in the 1800s and the first half of the 1900s today have Councils of State that operate separate from the judiciary. These include Belgium, Greece, Italy, Luxembourg, the Netherlands, Turkey, Algeria, Egypt, Lebanon, Morocco, Senegal, and Colombia.[13] However, the label can be deceptive, since some of these Councils of State only have policymaking powers (e.g. Luxembourg) and some only have powers of adjudication and are housed within the generalist court of last resort for civil and criminal disputes (e.g. Algeria, Morocco, Senegal). Moreover, unlike the French model, jurisdiction over government liability cases in Belgium, Italy, and the Netherlands is vested in the courts, not the Council of State, on the liberal theory that the ordinary courts are better placed to protect property and other rights against oppressive state action. It appears that the system of a specialized, administrative law branch of the judiciary, illustrated above with the German case, is even more widespread than the other two models: it has been adopted in Austria, the Czech Republic, Estonia, Finland, Hungary, Poland, Portugal, Romania, Slovenia, Spain, Sweden, Switzerland, and most of Latin America.

7.3.2 Principles of administrative action

7.3.2.1 Procedural principles

Traditionally, one of the differences that separated the common law from continental legal systems was its reliance on procedural principles of fair play in judging the correctness of administrative action.[14] The common law tended to equate important categories of administrative action with the adjudication of courts and to require analogous procedural safeguards. By contrast, the administrative law of continental Europe was more focused on the substantive correctness of administrative decisions in deciding

---

[13] Y. Gaudemet, 'L'exportation du droit administratif français: Breves remarques en forme de paradoxe', in Michel Borgetto (ed.), *Mélanges Philippe Ardant: Droit et politique a la croisée des cultures* (Paris: LGDJ, 1999), 431.

[14] This discussion only covers procedural rights in individualized administrative determinations, since they originated historically with courts and judicial standards of fair administrative action. For the comparative procedure of administrative rule-making, where the initiative has rested largely with legislatures, see the next section.

whether to let them stand.[15] In English law, this procedural emphasis was encapsulated by the principle of natural justice, which included the right to be heard and the right to an impartial adjudicator, also known as the rule against bias. In US law, these same guarantees have been developed in the constitutional case law on procedural due process. Although the French Council of State began fashioning procedural requirements for government administration as far back as 1944, with a line of cases on the 'rights of the defence' (*droits de la défense*), these rights were more limited than their common law counterparts: they generally excluded rights to an oral hearing and the disclosure of documents and they only applied to those administrative decisions that were cast as imposing sanctions.

Since the 1970s, however, this common law–continental law difference has faded. A number of national laws guarantee individuals, in the context of an individualized administrative determination, the right to receive notice of the proposed decision, to examine the supporting documents, to respond in writing, and to receive a statement of reasons with the final decision. These include French laws of 11 July 1979 and 12 April 2000, the Italian law of 7 August 1990, the Swedish Administrative Procedure Act of 1986, and the Danish Public Administration Act of 1985. The German case is somewhat exceptional, in that the proceduralization of individual decision-making began immediately in the post-war period, under the heavy influence of constitutional law, and was eventually codified with the Federal Administrative Procedure Act of 1977. Spain is another interesting case. Already in 1889, notice and hearing procedures for licensing, procurement, and other types of individualized decisions were set down in the Spanish Administrative Procedure Act. A number of countries in Latin America and east Asia have also adopted administrative procedure laws: Peru in 1972, Argentina in 1973, Costa Rica in 1978, Colombia in 1984, Japan in 1993, and South Korea in 1995.[16]

Notwithstanding this common trend, at least one important difference remains. Common law countries have institutionalized the judicial model within the administrative process to a greater extent than other legal systems. In Britain and Australia this takes the shape of administrative tribunals, while

[15] D. Custos, 'Droits administratifs: américain et français: sources et procédure', (2007) *Revue internationale de droit comparé* 285, 295–6.

[16] A. R. Brewer-Carias, *Etudes de droit public comparé* (Paris: LGDJ, 2001); T. Ginsburg, 'Dismantling the "Developmental State"? Administrative Procedure Reform in Japan and Korea', (2001) 48 *American Journal of Comparative Law* 585.

in the United States it comes under the heading of 'formal adjudication', governed by the Administrative Procedure Act and handled by administrative law judges.[17] Administrative tribunals and administrative law judges are responsible for hearing appeals from social security determinations, immigration decisions, and other high-volume regulatory areas, and their decisions are subject to judicial review on points of law before the ordinary courts. They are formally part of government administration even though they enjoy significant statutory guarantees of independence and their decision-making procedure is modelled after the courtroom. This institutionalization of dispute resolution stands in contrast to continental bureaucracies, where there is generally a right of appeal up the chain of command to administrative superiors, but where the main opportunity for an independent hearing is in judicial review before a fully fledged court.

7.3.2.2 Substantive principles

In reviewing the substance of an administrative decision to ban a product on safety grounds, to deny a building permit for a supermarket, or to accomplish one of the thousands of other purposes of bureaucracy, what criteria do courts use?[18] A multitude of doctrinal headings are used by courts to examine the substance of administrative decisions and decide whether or not to let them stand. Nevertheless, the intervention of courts in the activity of bureaucracy can be seen to fall under three distinct headings: rule of law, individual rights, and policy rationality. In the section below, I explore the local expressions of these judicial review practices and discuss the important variations in how and the extent to which these powers are exercised.

Much judicial review is geared towards furthering the rule of law, understood as the principle of a government of laws and not of men.[19] Public administration must respect the purposes and limits set down in laws – generally passed by parliaments, but also, in some places executive

---

[17] Peter Cane, 'Judicial Review in the Age of Tribunals', (2009) *Public Law* 479.

[18] Due to space constraints, the principles of government torts and public contracts are omitted from this discussion.

[19] I take this as the lowest-common-denominator definition of rule of law. It is also important to note, however, that the definition varies considerably from one legal system to the next. Among the most comprehensive conceptions is probably the German one, which includes substantive principles of fundamental rights and social justice as part of the definition of 'law' and which does not recognize inherent executive powers, but, rather, requires that all administrative action be authorized by parliamentary law. Bell, 'Comparative Administrative Law', 1272.

decrees – or turn into the arbitrary action of tyrannical despots. The task of courts is to enforce those limits. To understand the pervasiveness of this understanding of the relationship between courts and the bureaucracy, it suffices to peruse the main types of challenges contemplated in the administrative law of France, the United States, and England. Administrative acts can be overturned in France in the case of 'incompetence' or a 'violation of the law',[20] in the United States, if they are 'in excess of statutory jurisdiction, authority, or limitations, or short of statutory right',[21] and in England if the court finds an 'error of law'[22] or 'illegality'.[23] Thus, to take an example from US administrative law, in 2000 the Supreme Court struck a regulation of the Food and Drug Administration severely restricting the sale and advertising of tobacco products on the grounds that the statute under which the government was acting could only be interpreted to give it authority over medical drugs, not tobacco.[24] The same challenge would be styled as incompetence or a violation of law in France and an error of law or illegality in England.

A second type of substantive review of administrative action is the protection of basic liberties against government action. This was true even in the absence of a written bill of rights enforceable by the courts, as was the case in most countries until the 1950s, given the importance of property rights in both the common law and civil law codes. With the spread of written constitutions in the twentieth century, as well as international human rights instruments, in particular the European Convention on Human Rights, the catalogue of rights that courts are expected to defend against administrative action has expanded: freedom of expression and association, the right to privacy and human dignity, personal liberty, the right to engage in trades, and much more. All of these rights can be readily breached by the decisions of immigration authorities, social security agencies, licensing boards, and other government bodies, and they are commonly invoked before the courts.

On this aspect of judicial review, let us dwell on Germany for a moment, where fundamental rights guarantees are particularly pervasive and

---

[20] Fromont, *Droit administratif des États européens*, 167.

[21] Administrative Procedure Act §706(2)(B).

[22] P. Craig, *Administrative Law*, 6th edn (London: Sweet & Maxwell, 2008), 437.

[23] Ibid., 5–18, 531–49.

[24] *Food and Drug Administration* v. *Brown and Williamson Tobacco Corp.*, 120 S.Ct. 1291 (2000). Here, as in most statutory interpretation cases, the Supreme Court did not specify which of the judicial review provisions of the Administrative Procedure Act were being applied, but, rather, relied on its precedent.

administrative law has been thoroughly constitutionalized, more so than in other European systems and the United States. The most conspicuous sign of this is probably the declaration, made in 1959 by the president of the Federal Administrative Court, that administrative law is 'concretized constitutional law' (*konkretisiertes Verfassungsrecht*).[25] The German courts have developed a number of cross-cutting principles that are designed to limit administrative action to the benefit of individual liberties. Three in particular bear mention: proportionality, equality, and legitimate expectations.

Any measure that interferes with a right must satisfy a proportionality test. In this sequential inquiry, the government must demonstrate that the measure is capable of achieving the declared public ends; that it is necessary to achieve those ends and that no other, equally effective and less rights-restrictive, measures are available for accomplishing the same purposes; and that the public benefit from the measure outweighs the burden to the individual right. Thus, for instance, in the domain of administrative sanctions, the Federal Constitutional Court has held that the forfeiture of unemployment benefits for two weeks, in response to the recipient's failure to notify the public employment office regularly of his employment status, was disproportionate. To take another example, in 1958 the Constitutional Court declared a restriction on the number of pharmacies to be a disproportionate interference with the right freely to choose one's profession. The German courts engage in a similar inquiry when administrative programmes are challenged due to alleged discrimination based on economic or other characteristics: under the equality principle '[d]ifferences must be of such a kind and weight so as to justify a differentiation'.[26] And the principle of legitimate expectations, the rough equivalent of the duty of non-retroactivity and the protection of reliance interests in the United States, and derived in Germany from the rule of law and the right to freedom of action, significantly limits the ability of public administration to reverse benefit-conferring determinations. As a result of this legal doctrine, beneficiaries of public programmes involving agricultural subsidies, housing benefits, and other types of entitlement have a right to significant notice

[25] For this and the rest of the discussion of German law, see G. Nolte, 'General Principles of German and European Administrative Law – A Comparison in Historical Perspective', (1994) 57 *Modern Law Review* 191, 201.
[26] 85 BVerfGE 191, 210 (1992).

(generally one year) or compensation before the government may alter the terms of the programme or withdraw a benefit improperly granted.[27]

These rights, albeit with numerous modifications and with significant differences in judicial practice, have gone on to influence the case law of the European Court of Justice (ECJ) and other European legal systems.[28] The constitutionalization of European administrative law stands in marked contrast to the United States, where the Supreme Court is highly deferential to government action that burdens the economic rights protected under the Fourteenth Amendment of the Constitution.[29] These are the very rights that are most commonly implicated by administrative determinations, yet so-called 'rational basis' review under the Fourteenth Amendment is a tremendously lenient standard when compared with the principles of proportionality and equality in German law.

The last form of judicial review of administrative action is review for policy rationality. Doctrinally, rationality review picks up where legality review leaves off: when controlling legislation does not contain standards to guide administrative action and thus effectively leaves decision-making to bureaucratic discretion, the courts nonetheless can evaluate administrative action based on criteria related to sound policymaking. Doctrinal expressions of this form of review give the impression that only acts of confirmed insanity will be struck by the courts: review for 'arbitrary and capricious' decision-making in the United States[30] and review for 'manifest error of assessment' (*erreur manifeste d'appréciation*) in France.[31] Even better is the English articulation of the principle:

By 'irrationality' I mean what can now be succinctly referred to as 'Wednesbury unreasonableness' ... It applies to a decision which is so outrageous in its defiance of logic or accepted moral standards that no sensible person who had applied his mind to the question to be decided could have arrived at it.[32]

---

[27] E. J. Eberle, 'The West German Administrative Procedure Act: A Study in Administrative Decision Making', (1984) 3 *Dickinson Journal of International Law* 67.

[28] A. Sandulli, *La proporzionalità dell'azione amministrativa* (Padua: Cedam, 1998); J. Schwarze, *European Administrative Law* (London: Sweet & Maxwell, 1992).

[29] B. Ackerman, *We the People: Transformations* (Cambridge, MA: Harvard University Press, 1998).

[30] Administrative Procedure Act §706(A)(2). It should be noted that, doctrinally speaking, arbitrary and capricious review is required under the Administrative Procedure Act and is unrelated to weak rational-basis review under the Constitution.

[31] Ziller, *Administrations comparées*, 296.

[32] *Council of Civil Service Unions* v. *Minister for the Civil Service*, [1985] AC 374, Lord Diplock.

In the United States, however, arbitrary and capricious review has become a demanding test, and, indeed, it has come to represent a distinctive feature of the US administrative law system. It became common judicial practice in the late 1960s and the 1970s and was associated with the fall of the post-war consensus on economic growth, growing distrust in technologies and government, new social movements such as the environment and civil rights, and the spread of public interest lawyering. The Supreme Court's statement in *State Farm* remains the emblematic articulation of arbitrary and capricious review of administrative policymaking in US law:

> the agency must examine the relevant data and articulate a satisfactory explanation for its action including a 'rational connection between the facts found and the choice made' ... Normally, an agency rule would be arbitrary and capricious if the agency has relied on factors which Congress has not intended it to consider, entirely failed to consider an important aspect of the problem, offered an explanation for its decision that runs counter to the evidence before the agency or is so implausible that it could not be ascribed to a difference in view or the product of agency expertise.[33]

In *State Farm*, the Supreme Court struck an administrative decision revoking a passenger-safety rule requiring automobiles to be fitted with automatic seatbelts or airbags. It found that the tests and studies in the agency's record did not support a determination that the rule would fail to produce safety benefits and it faulted the agency for failing to consider other policy options for ensuring passenger safety, namely an airbag-only rule.

Although European rights-based proportionality review and American arbitrary and capricious review overlap in some respects, their essence is fundamentally different. In the former, the focus is on the individual right, and the decision to overturn the administrative act rests on an assessment of the importance of the right as compared to the public purpose as well as the ability of the administration to articulate a close connection between the government measure and the public purpose. In the latter, the focus is on the quality of the science and policymaking assessments behind the administrative decision and the ability of the government to justify its chosen course of action in the face of alternative scientific evidence and the policy options put forward by its opponents.

---

[33] *Motor Vehicle Manufacturers Ass'n* v. *State Farm*, 463 US 29, 42 (1983).

7.4 Administration and organized interests

In the conventional image of public administration, bureaucrats and courts
are the main protagonists. State officials deploy their considerable expertise
and technical prowess to accomplish public purposes, and courts watch over
them to ensure that they stay within the four corners of the law. The role
of social and economic groups in administrative governance has generally
been ignored in legal scholarship, largely a reflection of the normative
theories used to legitimate administration according to which elections,
representative assemblies, and independent courts operate as the primary
agents of democracy and are to be regarded with suspicion.

A growing literature, however, now recognizes that many elements of
administrative law are designed to enable social and economic actors to
inform and participate in administrative governance, and that the legitimacy
of administration rests as much on accountability to civil society as it does on
judicial review and legislative oversight.[34] Industry associations, trade unions,
professional associations, environmental and consumer groups, and various
other actors are routinely called on to advise on government rule-making,
manage public programmes, and engage directly in standard-setting and
rule enforcement through powers of self-regulation. Due to space constraints,
this section will address only one of these forms of administrative law: the
procedures that empower social and economic groups to participate in government rule-making.

A distinctive feature of US administrative law is what is known as notice-
and-comment rule-making. Before administrative agencies decide on the new
policies contained in government rules – for instance, worker-safety standards for coal mines, maximum chemical concentrations for drinking water,
and consumer protection rules for the banking industry – they must first give
notice of the proposed rule, allow the public an opportunity to comment on
the rule, and respond to any objections in a 'concise general statement'
explaining the rationale for the rule.[35] If commentators are disappointed
with the final result, they may go to court. Besides reviewing the rule on the
substantive grounds discussed in the previous section, the court will also
decide whether the agency adequately responded to the public comments or,

---

[34] See, e.g., J. Freeman, 'Collaborative Governance in the Administrative State', (1997) 45
   University of California Los Angeles Law Review 1.
[35] Administrative Procedure Act §553.

if no such procedure was held, whether the administration was correct in deciding that one of the exceptions to the requirement of notice-and-comment rule-making applied. Thus notice-and-comment rule-making significantly limits administrative discretion, both on when and whom to consult and on what weight, if any, to give to objections from the regulated community. Although notice-and-comment rule-making is formally open to anyone, a number of studies have found that, in practice, organized interests and market actors are the main participants, both because of the resources necessary to respond convincingly to administrative proposals and, in the event of defeat, to call the administration to task before the courts, and because of the broad-reaching and abstract nature of the policies being decided, which rarely prompts action from individual citizens.[36]

Notice-and-comment rule-making was first introduced in 1946, with the adoption of the Administrative Procedure Act. It was then amplified in the 1960s and 1970s by a series of court decisions that required administration to alert the public to all aspects of a proposed rule and to give careful consideration to public comments in the administrative statement supporting the final rule.[37] This judicial turn was driven by the sense that administration had been 'captured' by industry actors and that public interest groups, which were rapidly proliferating at the time, should be guaranteed an equally prominent role in the policymaking process.[38] The original creation and subsequent development of notice-and-comment rule-making reflects what, in the political science literature, is known as the American system of pluralist interest representation.[39] In the theoretical stylization of pluralism, multiple organizations, representing a variety of different interests, compete to influence government decisions in what, formally speaking, is a policymaking process open to all, and government officials seek to mediate neutrally among these diverse interests. Pluralist thinkers like Arthur Bentley, David Truman, and Robert Dahl saw immense democratic promise in this system of interest-group competition, because they believed that government decisions would reflect the entire range of interests at play in the nation rather than cater

[36] J. Webb Yackee and S. Webb Yackee, 'A Bias Towards Business? Assessing Interest Group Influence on the U.S. Bureaucracy', (2006) 68 *Journal of Politics* 128; M.-F. Cuellar, 'Rethinking Regulatory Democracy', (2005) 57 *Administrative Law Review* 411.

[37] See, e.g., *US* v. *Nova Scotia Food Products*, 568 F.2d 240 (2d Cir. 1977).

[38] R. B. Stewart, 'The Reformation of American Administrative Law', (1975) 88 *Harvard Law Review* 1669.

[39] Ibid., 1669.

to any one group or set of groups. Of course, as many have observed, this positive assessment rests on a number of often questionable assumptions – that all groups are equally capable of mobilizing, that all organizations have the resources necessary to participate in the political process, and that government officials mechanically responding to self-regarding interests, even a wide variety of pluralist interests, is a process capable of generating morally worthy government policies.[40] Nevertheless, the theory of pluralism is extremely powerful in American politics and legal procedures such as notice-and-comment rule-making reflect and perpetuated it.

By contrast, in Europe, the favourite device for obtaining outside advice on government rules is the civil society committee. Established by law, these committees are composed of representatives of the major organizations active in the policy area and are generally chaired by a government bureaucrat. Their consultation can be either mandatory or optional, depending on the policy area and the type of government proposal, and they often also exercise powers of proposal. In France, Italy, the European Union, and other legal systems, there are hundreds of these committees in areas as diverse as welfare and industrial policy, consumer policy, environmental policy, and equal protection. To give but one example, in France, the High Council on Professional Equality between Men and Women gives advice on new equal protection initiatives, and is composed of nine members of the administration, nine members selected by the five major national trade unions, nine members chosen by a variety of employer organizations, and nine policy experts and representatives of women's rights organizations selected by the responsible government ministry. In committees such as the French High Council, the organizations entitled to comment on government policies are the handful mentioned in the enabling legislation or tapped by the administration to sit on the committee, and therefore influence over policymaking is more restricted than in notice-and-comment rule-making, as it is limited to those groups that have established themselves as reputable and powerful members of the regulatory community. Moreover, unlike notice-and-comment rule-making, which is mandatory for most forms of administrative rule-making, consultation of civil society committees is often entirely within the discretion of public administration. And, finally, while American

---

[40] See, e.g., R. B. Stewart, 'Madison's Nightmare', (1990) 57 *University of Chicago Law Review* 335.

officials must reply meticulously to comments or risk being sued, their European counterparts are not legally required to respond in any particular fashion to the comments and proposals authored by such committees.

It is certainly true that, today, European regulators also stage broad-based consultations, using the possibilities afforded by the Internet to make their policy proposals widely known and to solicit the reactions of all those organizations that care to comment.[41] Therefore the privileged access in the past through the committee system has been attenuated somewhat through the use of new technologies. However, in contrast with US notice-and-comment rule-making, these consultations are permeated by administrative discretion, both in the decision to call them in the first place and subsequently in the decision on what kind of response, if any, to give to public opposition. Regulators, therefore, are still in a strong position to control access to the policymaking process.

The institution of the civil society committee is rooted in the theory and politics of what, in the political science literature, is known as neo-corporatism.[42] In many European countries, producer groups are represented by a few, all-encompassing and broadly representative labour unions, employer associations, farmer groups, and professional associations, and these organizations are given an essential role in the policymaking process. As politics have changed and non-material interests have become more prominent, this model of all-encompassing organizations and privileged access has been extended to environmental and consumer protection groups, human rights organizations, and other types of associations. Neo-corporatist theory portrays the state and society as intertwined: public administration nurtures the many producer organizations on which social cohesion and economic prosperity depended and, in turn, those producer groups are entitled to influence the policies of the state. These ideas were developed in the law by thinkers such as Harold Laski in England, Otto von Gierke in Germany, Léon Duguit and Maurice Hauriou in France, and Santi Romano in Italy, and

---

[41] See, e.g., D. Rubinstein Reiss, 'Participation in Governance from a Comparative Perspective: Citizen Involvement in Telecommunications and Electricity in the United Kingdom, France and Sweden', (2009) *Journal of Dispute Resolution* 381.

[42] P. C. Schmitter, 'Still the Century of Corporatism?', in P. C. Schmitter and G. Lehmbruch (eds.), *Trends Toward Corporatist Intermediation* (London: Sage, 1979), 13; W. Streeck, 'The study of organized interests: before "The Century" and after', in C. Crouch and W. Streeck (eds.), *The Diversity of Democracy* (Cheltenham: Edward Elgar, 2006) 3, 17–18, 29–30.

stand in marked contrast to the depiction of interest group politics as conflictual and government actors as passive arbiters in pluralist theories of democracy.

7.5 Administration and the public

In a number of administrative law systems, informal, wide-ranging public oversight has become critical to the legitimacy of bureaucracy. Although this form of diffuse accountability is achieved through a wide range of legal tools and institutional arrangements, two are particularly prominent: ombudsmen appointed by parliaments with oversight and complaint-resolution functions and laws guaranteeing all citizens a right of access to government documents. Sweden is generally believed to be the first Western legal system to have established an ombudsman and freedom of information. There the expansion of parliamentary power and the establishment of a constitutional monarchy was accompanied by the passage of the Law on Liberty of the Press (1766, re-enacted in 1809), abolishing censorship and giving a right of public access to government documents, and the creation of a parliamentary ombudsman (1809). For a long time, Sweden stood out as an anomaly, but, beginning in the 1970s, momentum got under way in a number of countries for broader public accountability in government administration, and today a vast array of legal systems have freedom-of-information laws and ombudsmen.

Ombudsmen share a number of characteristics.[43] They are institutionally linked to parliaments, not the executive branch, by virtue of the fact that they are appointed by parliament, generally for a fixed term, and are legally obligated to report periodically to parliament on their activities. The principal function of ombudsmen is to settle complaints filed by members of the public against the bureaucracy. The process is informal, in that a simple letter or online complaint form is sufficient to trigger an investigation and the grounds for complaining are extremely broad – anything linked to maladministration – and do not need to be styled as one of the grounds

---

[43] Early accounts include W. Gellhorn, *Ombudsmen and Others: Citizens' Protectors in Nine Countries* (Cambridge, MA: Harvard University Press, 1966), and D. Rowat, *The Ombudsman: Citizen's Defender* (London: George Allen & Unwin, 1968). A good example of the more recent literature is K. Heede, *European Ombudsman: Redress and Control at the Union Level* (The Hague: Kluwer, 2000).

for obtaining legal redress in the courts. 'The public officer was extremely rude' or 'I never received an answer to the query that I filed with the tax office' is enough to warrant a response from the ombudsman.[44] The ombudsman system, therefore, offers the promise of redress to individuals without the resources to go to court and in circumstances that fail to meet the stringent legal criteria that have been developed by courts to make a successful claim against the administration.

Once the ombudsman comes to a decision on a complaint, the powers of the office are limited compared to courts. The ombudsman cannot order civil servants to comply with his or her decision but rather must rely on bureaucratic goodwill and the threat of bad press and public embarrassment to induce compliance.[45] The triangular relationship between the ombudsman, the press, and parliament is critical to ensuring the effectiveness of the institution. The threat of public censure and hostile parliamentary questions is the main tool in the ombudsman's arsenal and underscores the diffuse public accountability inherent in this area of administrative law. Ombudsmen in Sweden, France, Denmark, and many other countries are also involved in policymaking and regularly recommend changes to administrative law and practice to bring administration into line with rule of law ideals and fundamental rights guarantees.

Laws on the right of access to public documents also broaden public oversight of administration.[46] The right to government documents expands public scrutiny by giving individuals a right to examine the decisions of government even absent a claim of having been wronged or having a particular interest in the matter. Simply by virtue of being a citizen, individuals are assumed to have a stake in the correct workings of their government and are entitled to request government documents without having to put forward a justification for their request. Freedom-of-information laws, however, also restrict the types of documents that are accessible. For instance, documents filed with government by industry and containing commercial secrets and documents related to national security are either excluded from

[44] See, e.g., European Ombudsman, *The European Code of Good Administrative Behaviour* (Luxembourg: OPOCE, 2005), Art. 12.

[45] On the enforcement dimension, the powers of the office of the Swedish ombudsman are exceptional because it can initiate disciplinary proceedings or bring criminal prosecutions against individual civil servants.

[46] J. M. Ackerman and I. E. Sandoval-Ballesteros, 'The Global Explosion of Freedom of Information Laws', (2006) 58 *Administrative Law Review* 85.

the right of access or subject to extensive redaction before they may be released to the public. Preliminary drafts, notes, and memoranda are entirely exempted from disclosure in Sweden and Denmark if they are not circulated outside the responsible government agency and are exempted until the relevant government decision becomes final in Finland and the United States. These laws also differ in how they organize access to documents: an official register of government documents, open to public consultation, exists in Sweden, Finland, and the European Union, but not in Denmark, the Netherlands, and the United States, where petitioners must designate the issue of interest and trust the responding agency to locate the relevant documents.

Both ombudsmen and freedom-of-information laws have been popular over the past decades. In Europe, Finland (1919), Denmark (1954), the United Kingdom (1967), France (1973), Spain (1981), the Netherlands (1984), Ireland (1984), Portugal (1991), and Romania (1991) have established ombudsmen at the national level, and other countries, such as Germany and Italy, have established them at the regional level. New Zealand (1962), Hong Kong (1989), and South Korea (1994) are examples of other jurisdictions with parliamentary ombudsmen. As for freedom of information, according to one study, almost seventy countries throughout the world have at the time of writing adopted the necessary legislation.[47]

These overviews give an idea not only of the extent of diffuse public accountability as a feature of administrative law, but also of the remaining variations. Legal systems still differ in the degree to which individuals seek formal recognition of their grievances through the courts or rely mostly on informal avenues of redress through ombudsmen. In some countries, parliamentary ombudsmen are absent, as in the United States and Germany (at the federal level), and in others the ombudsman system is considered ineffective. By contrast, in countries like Sweden and Denmark, the informal administrative justice offered by ombudsmen is immensely popular and tends to function as a substitute for courts. Freedom-of-information laws also have not taken root everywhere. In Europe alone, Italy and Greece are notable exceptions to the trend.

---

[47] Privacy International (David Banisar), *Freedom of Information Around the World 2006: A Global Survey of Access to Government Information Laws*, available at www.freedominfo.org/documents/global_survey2006.pdf.

7.6 The globalization of administrative law

This discussion would be incomplete without mention of the accelerating diffusion of administrative principles among legal systems, spurred by the forces of globalization. Traditionally, one of the reasons that public law was said to be the poor cousin of private law in comparative studies was that public law was too idiosyncratic and contingent on domestic politics and national history for comparison to yield any fruitful insights. There is no doubt that administrative law is profoundly shaped by distinct national experiences with state formation. Today, however, the rise of a liberal consensus and the growing power of international organizations have prompted political actors in a variety of jurisdictions to adopt a common set of good governance reforms involving administrative procedures and principles of judicial review. Therefore, at least on the books, administrative law appears to be converging.

Transparency, where the last section ended, is a good example of the globalization phenomenon. As explained earlier, legislation on the right of access to government documents was first adopted in Sweden in 1766 and it was immediately copied in Finland, which at the time was a Swedish colony. Two hundred years later, it still was limited to those two countries. Then, in the 1970s and 1980s, the United States and a handful of other European countries adopted freedom-of-information legislation. In 1993 the European Union followed suit, obliging not only its own institutions to hand over documents to the public, but also putting heavy pressure on all of its member countries to do the same. Since then, the United Nations, the Organization of American States, and a number of other international organizations have urged their member countries to adopt freedom-of-information laws. By 2006, one survey found that nearly seventy countries had such laws and an additional fifty countries were in the process of drafting them.[48] And, according to a recent analysis, the many transnational and international regulatory authorities that have sprung up over the past decades also have made commitments to transparency.[49] In sum, since the 1990s the right of access to government documents has become a commonplace of public life, and this is due in no small measure to the growing influence of international bodies in world politics.

---

[48] Privacy International, *Freedom of Information*.

[49] B. Kingsbury, 'The Concept of "Law" in Global Administrative Law', (2009) 20 *European Journal of International Law* 23.

One of the main challenges facing comparative law scholars today is to understand the operation, utility, and, ultimately, desirability of these common procedures and principles in the multiple legal settings in which they now exist. To do so, it is necessary for comparative scholarship to move beyond the traditional national focus and to recognize the growing importance of international legal systems as objects of study in their own right and as catalysts for change at the domestic level. At bottom, however, comparative law is well equipped to handle this new task. It requires a deep appreciation of the historical diversity of national legal traditions and a familiarity with the many ways in which legal transplants can be transformed in the process of migration from one place to another. These are concerns that have traditionally been at the heart of comparative law scholarship and that offer an essential platform for coming to grips with globalization.

Further reading

J. S. Bell, 'Comparative Administrative Law', in M. Reimann and R. Zimmermann (eds.), *The Oxford Handbook of Comparative Law* (Oxford University Press, 2006), 1259

F. Bignami, 'From Expert Administration to Accountability Network: A New Paradigm for Comparative Administrative Law', (2011) 59 *American Journal of Comparative Law* 859

S. Cassese, 'La costruzione del diritto amministrativo: Francia e Regno Unito', in S. Cassese (ed.), *Trattato di diritto amministrativo*, 2nd edn, vol. 1 (Milan: Giuffrè, 2003), 1

P. P. Craig and A. Tomkins, *The Executive and Public Law: Power and Accountability in Comparative Perspective* (Oxford University Press, 2006)

M. D'Alberti, *Diritto amministrativo comparato. Trasformazioni dei sistemi amministrativi in Francia, Gran Bretagna, Stati Uniti, Italia* (Bologna: Mulino, 1995)

D. Fairgrieve, M. Andenas, and J. Bell, *Tort Liability of Public Authorities in Comparative Perspective* (London: BIICL, 2002)

M. Fromont, *Droit administratif des États européens* (Paris: Thémis, 2006)

P. L. Lindseth, '"Always Embedded" Administration? The Historical Evolution of Administrative Justice as an Aspect of Modern Governance', in C. Joerges, B. Stråth, and P. Wagner (eds.), *The Economy as a Polity: The Political Constitution of Contemporary Capitalism* (London: UCL Press, 2005), 117

G. Napolitano (ed.), *Diritto Amministrativo Comparato* (Milan: Giuffrè, 2007)

S. Rose-Ackerman, *Controlling Environmental Policy: The Limits of Public Law in Germany and the United States* (New Haven: Yale University Press, 1995)

From Elections to Democracy: Building Accountable Government in Hungary and Poland (Cambridge University Press, 2005)

S. Rose-Ackerman and P. L. Lindseth (eds.), *Comparative Administrative Law* (Cheltenham: Edward Elgar, 2010)

H. Schepel and J. Falke, *Legal Aspects of Standardisation in the Member States of the EC and EFTA: Comparative Report* (Luxembourg: OPOCE, 2000)

K. Strøm, W. C. Müller, and T. Bergman (eds.), *Delegation and Accountability in Parliamentary Democracies* (Oxford University Press, 2003)

L. Verhey and T. Zwart (eds.), *Agencies in European and Comparative Perspective* (The Hague: Kluwer, 2003)

Comparative constitutional law 8

Günter Frankenberg

8.1 Constitution as law, instrument, and culture

'Constitution' – like 'nation', 'state', 'democracy', and 'sovereignty' – appears as one of the central icons and also one of the most ambiguous ideological structures in the pool of cultural representations of modernity. Constitutions react to the individual and societal need for orientation by offering a language of rights and values and to the requirement of authoritative decisions by allocating and balancing power within an institutional arrangement. Hence constitutions are not cages of norms, but texts situated in contested fields of ideas and interests and run through by competing interpretations.

In general, comparative constitutional scholarship, rather than expressly addressing the question 'what is a constitution?', pragmatically settles on a couple of meanings – or less. Dominant is the notion of the constitution as a higher or supreme law. Superiority is ascertained, technically, by the systematic ranking of constitutional norms at the top of the legal hierarchy, above the ordinary laws, and by the methodological rule that laws have to be interpreted in conformity with the constitution. Genetically, a constitution qualifies as law when it is produced by a law-making body, such as a constitutional assembly or convention, and then is adopted according to legally prescribed procedures (referendum or qualified parliamentary decision). What looks like a routine under the rule of law implies a paradoxical *creatio ex nihilo*: a people constitutes itself in performing the act of adopting a constitution and has always already been presupposed as empowered to sign the said constitution.[1] This self-empowerment of 'we the people', or 'we the nation', belies the mystical basis of constitutional authority.[2]

---

[1] M. Loughlin and N. Walker (eds.), *The Paradox of Constitutionalism, Constituent Power and Constitutional Form* (Oxford University Press, 2007).

[2] J. Derrida, 'Force of Law: The "Mystical Foundation of Authority"', (1990) 11 *Cardozo Law Review* 919.

Framers of constitutions try to solve or, rather, cover up the paradox with recourse to a specific constitutional style that seeks to remove constitutions from the world of normal law-making. Unlike ordinary laws, constitutions are not just passed but are 'solemnly declared', 'proclaimed', or even 'ordained' – a semantic usage bestowing on them the aura of quasi-sacred documents. Some constitution-makers elevate the document's making and their legitimacy by invoking the presence of a transcendent authority – God, a sacred religion or church, the crown, the Holy Trinity or Divine Providence. Similarly, the makers of socialist constitutions appeal to the authority of history, science, the Party, or, with the charm of vagueness, to 'the requirements of the new situation and tasks' (Vietnam 1992).

Superiority is also underscored by the language of the document which distinguishes its substantive content as consisting of inalienable, sacred, and natural rights or 'humble obligations' (Ireland) and 'lofty duties' (China), or as sanctioning outright constitutional support for religion (the Catholic Apostolate in Argentina 1853; Islam in Afghanistan). At times even the constitutional design reveals the framers' romance with a 'higher', preferably religious, authority. If not purposely intended, it seems like a more than happy coincidence that the original amendments to the United States Bill of Rights correspond to the biblical Ten Commandments.

Proceeding from the concept of higher law, comparison has to deal with the related prescriptive aspects of constitutions as an instrument of *governance* and *government* allocating, balancing, and controlling political power, as well as a *charter* laying down the ground rules for social conflicts. From this triad – higher law, governmental organization, and ground rules – one may infer the visions of order imposed by elites or desired by the constitutions' addressees. Most commonly, constitutions present variations on the theme of self-government and fantasies of a kind of domination where the subjective factor is magically neutralized – within a 'government of laws and not of men'. Comparative constitutional law can tell fascinating stories about how the self is first elevated as popular sovereign and then reduced and fragmented within schemes of representation, delegation, and the transfer of power away from the collective self consenting to being governed by secular (or religious) authorities. Comparison similarly informs about how conflicts between citizens and their governors and among citizens themselves are removed from where they arise – the workplace, the family, gender relations, civil society, and so on – then shifted to public arenas and transformed into controversies under constitutional law to be settled by constitutional or supreme courts.

Once comparatists consider constitutions as phenomena of *culture*,[3] they transgress the borders of a formalist or instrumental understanding and address the symbolic dimension, thus leaving the world of legal positivism (rules and principles, cases and legal methods) behind and entering a terrain which stakes out 'the collective ensemble of artifacts, practices, and spaces enmeshed in the production and dissemination of *meanings* and *knowledges*'.[4] In the cultural terrain 'the real' is imagined, reconstructed, and made sense of within a constitutional framework. Consequently, the quasi-sacred texts are decanonized and placed in the context of the everyday, once comparison focuses also on the ideas and practices of ordinary people, on the programmatic visions of social movements, or group or elite interests, and so forth. Informed by a *constitutive theory*, comparatists regard constitutions as reflecting and shaping the practices and even literary translations of the everyday[5] and, in particular, the imagination of political unity and collective identity – such as the notion of 'human rights as the foundation of every human community' (German Basic Law, Art. 1), a state based on 'the coexistence with minorities' (Albania 1998) or a 'State of the people, by the people, and for the people' (Vietnam 1992, Art. 2), as well as offering a framework for ideology. Within this perspective constitutions are regarded as not passively reflecting culture, but actively intervening and, under certain circumstances, transforming culture. Hence comparison operates with a reflexive relationship between culture and constitution.

Whether and to what extent constitutions are integrated in the symbolic everyday depends on their popular appeal, readability, and age. Whether or not they capture the people's utopian fancy and the popular desire for authoritative higher-law settlement, unification, and orientation remain open questions. Liberal constitutions (United States, France, Germany, or

---

[3] Concerning the concept of culture see R. Williams, *Keywords: A Vocabulary of Culture and Society* (Oxford University Press, 1976), 76–82; E. W. Said, *Culture and Imperialism* (New York: Alfred A. Knopf, 1994).

[4] J. D. Leonard, 'Introduction', in J. D. Leonard (ed.), *Legal Studies as Cultural Studies – A Reader in (Post)Modern Critical Theory* (Albany: State University of New York Press, 1995), 3 (emphasis in original).

[5] Concerning the influence of a constitution on culture see M. Meltzer, *Secular Revelations: The US Constitution and Classical American Literature* (Cambridge, MA: Harvard University Press, 2005).

India) usually keep aloof from notions of community and solidarity and make do, in passing, with a generalized 'People' or the abstract 'Nation', 'Union' or 'State'. By way of contrast, socialist constitutions recast the atomized society of individuals or groups as the 'people of all nationalities' or 'the alliance of workers and peasants' (China, Vietnam) or 'working people' (North Korea). Constitutions of recently united countries tend to imagine the end of ethnic diversity (Weimar Constitution 1919) and a unity above the fractured society of groups or regions as a 'democratic society' (Angola 1992, Namibia 1990), or 'civil society' (Afghanistan 2004).

8.2 Comparing constitutions as an academic discipline

As a matter of tradition or established routine, the order of knowledge requires scientific studies to be carried out in the sense and according to the rules of a 'discipline'. Academic disciplines are generally distinguished by (a) a discrete subject matter, such as law, philosophy, or, more narrowly, civil law, (b) a corresponding set of theories, such as positivism or legal realism, (c) methods ascertaining its scientific analysis, and usually (d) a curriculum organizing the education and the reproduction of knowledge within a given discipline. Both the external perception and the internal understanding of research and studies as being governed by the theoretical and methodological rules of a specific discipline qualify a discipline as 'normal science' (Thomas Kuhn) and distinguish it from other fields of investigation and teaching. Over time such rules, borders, and perceptions establish a disciplinary identity and project that may serve as a point of departure for 'interdisciplinary' enterprises.

While comparative law qualifies as an academic discipline, the (re)production and ordering of comparative constitutional knowledge has not yet been elevated to the level of a discrete science. The constitutional comparatist still appears to be an 'intellectual nomad'[6] bereft of a genuine, demarcated field of research. This may be due to the porous boundaries limiting the subject matter, to methodological problems, and to the still marginal status of comparative constitutional studies within legal education. Many scholars agonize

---

[6] V. Grosswald Curran, 'Cultural Immersion, Difference and Categories in U.S. Comparative Law', (1998) 46 *American Journal of Comparative Law* 657.

over the accurate label for their work, some favouring 'comparative constitutional law', others preferring 'comparative constitutional studies'.[7] Not everyone associates different comparative projects with this semantic distinction. In general, the 'law faction' tends to follow the formalist and positivist path to constitutional law as higher law and instrument of government: rules and principles, constitutional adjudication and institutions, whereas constitutional realists analyse constitutions in their historical, political, and social contexts. By way of contrast, the 'studies faction' prefers to look beyond constitutional provisions, cases, and institutions so as to grasp them as artifacts of culture, thus looking for the context *in* constitutional law. Even if taken as designations of different comparative projects, these labels do not argue against a discipline, though, but only for a contested internal division over theory and method common to other disciplines.

A more serious threat to the disciplinary identity is raised by scholars advocating a 'societal constitutionalism' that dismisses the traditional world of constitutions.[8] Under the theoretical umbrella of legal pluralism these approaches, transgressing the field of written or unwritten constitutions, depart from legal formalism and positivism, and question both the traditional canon of comparative constitutional law and the framework of the nation state for constitutions, thus turning comparative studies into an interdisciplinary venture.

The tradition of comparative constitutional studies arguably dates as far back as Aristotle's abstract comparison of different forms of state and types of constitution in his search for the perfect constitution as defined by their stability, usefulness, and justice.[9] Aristotle may be invoked as having inspired three strands of more or less comparative studies: first, philosophical constructions of an ideal constitution for a polis or republic (from Locke and Rousseau to Rawls); second, sociological analyses of constitutions (including non-legal factors as context); and, third, constitutional engineering focusing on the best fit of constitutions in a given historical national or supranational environment. Aristotle's sporadic references to contextual aspects, such as the geography of Crete, were more systematically and sociologically elaborated by Montesquieu in his *De l'esprit des lois* (The spirit of laws) (1748),

---

[7] D. Nelken, 'Comparative Law and Comparative Legal Studies', in E. Örücü and D. Nelken (eds.), *Comparative Law: A Handbook* (Oxford and Portland: Hart, 2007), 3.

[8] D. Sciulli, *Theory of Societal Constitutionalism* (Cambridge University Press, 1992).

[9] Aristotle's typology in *Politics* is presumed to be based on a (missing) survey of 158 city states.

where he related the laws of a country to climate, mentality, religion, customs, and other extra-legal aspects. In his 'Constitutional Project for Corsica' (1765) and his 'Considerations on the Government of Poland' (1772) Rousseau adopted the role of constitutional consultant and developed a constitutional plan that would be adequate for the people and the government. In pursuit of his aim to 'move the hearts of men' he argued for the crucial importance of education to 'give souls a national formation'.

In the following centuries comparative constitutional studies, rather than consciously establishing themselves as a discipline, oscillated between and borrowed from political science, philosophy, and comparative law. They more or less followed the cycles of constitution-making and were energized by revolutions and counter-revolutions (at the end of the eighteenth/beginning of the nineteenth century and in the middle of the nineteenth century), the hegemonic redesigning of dependent countries according to spheres of colonial interests (post-First World War), the decolonization and liberation movements (post-Second World War), and finally the breakdown of socialism and restructuring of post-socialist countries (after 1989).

Nevertheless, comparative constitutional law has remained a department of comparative law rather than an autonomous discipline. This may change, however, as recent publications, notably handbooks,[10] and journals specializing in constitutional comparison (*I•CON*) as well as projects of constitutional engineering[11] testify to a developing disciplinary identity and energy. More importantly, some constitutional courts have begun to give up the 'four walls' doctrine[12] and to enter into transnational dialogues with other courts, thus moving towards a practice of comparative constitutional interpretation and the still tentative recognition of a transnational body of

---

[10] M. Troper (ed.), *Traité International de Droit Constitutionnel* (Paris: Dalloz, 2011); A. von Bogdandy, P. Cruz Villalón, and P. M. Huber (eds.), *Handbuch Ius Publicum Europaeum*, Vol. I *Grundlagen und Grundzüge staatlichen Verfassungsrechts*, Vol. II *Offene Staatlichkeit – Wissenschaft vom Verfassungsrecht* (Heidelberg: C. F. Müller, 2007 and 2008); N. Dorsen et al., *Comparative Constitutionalism: Cases and Materials* (Eagan: West, 2003); V. C. Jackson and M. V. Tushnet, *Comparative Constitutional Law*, 2nd edn (New York: Foundation Press, 2006).

[11] G. Sartori, *Comparative Constitutional Engineering: An Inquiry into Structures, Incentives and Outcomes*, 2nd edn (New York: New York University Press, 1996).

[12] Meaning that a constitution is 'primarily to be interpreted within its four walls and not in the light of the analogies drawn from other countries' (*Gov. of Kelantan* v. *Gov. of Malaysia*, [1963] MLJ 355/358 (Malaysia)).

constitutional law.[13] These dialogues incidentally shift scholarly attention away from the traditional preoccupation with the legitimacy of constitutional review[14] to the actual practices of constitutional adjudication.

8.3 Comparison as a critical practice: methodological problems

According to Abbé Sieyès, Napoleon, and, arguably, some of the American founding fathers, constitutions are required to be 'short and dark'. They bear a close relationship to politics and ethics – closer than most other laws. Therefore they are permeated by ideas, ideals, and ideology, which account for their strangeness and, by the same token, imply a great deal of constructive work and cause problems of understanding. The constructive work begins with the reading of texts written by constitutional elites, consultants, courts, and commentators. Next, the comparatist writes about the fruits of her readings and 'navigate[s] past the wrecks of a dozen sunken philosophies'[15] of comparative studies. Her writing is both selective and constructive as it deals with the selection, arrangement, and interpretation of information.[16]

Comparatists reconstruct a variety of texts that are shot through with vague and obscure passages, with contradictions and internal tensions, empty spaces and redundancies, with tendentious commentaries, misleading dichotomies, and dangerous supplements. Therefore they introduce a variety of methods which are meant to discipline the 'explosion of fact' and the textual and contextual richness. However much one may compare, in the end one still has to settle for incomplete knowledge and less than total cognitive control. To grasp as much as is possible of the picture, a combination of approaches may help: a reconstruction of constitutional history, a careful tracing of the anatomy of constitutions, and an analysis of how constitutional institutions, provisions, doctrines, and arguments are transferred from one context to another.

---

[13] J. Waldron, 'Foreign Law and the Modern *Ius Gentium*', (2005) 119 *Harvard Law Review* 129; S. Choudry (ed.), *The Migration of Constitutional Ideas* (Cambridge University Press, 2006).

[14] Jackson and Tushnet, *Comparative Constitutional Law.*

[15] C. Geertz, 'Thick Description: Toward an Interpretive Theory of Cultures', in Geertz, *The Interpretation of Cultures*, 2nd edn (New York: Basic Books, 2000), 14.

[16] G. Frankenberg, 'Comparing Constitutions: Ideas, Ideals and Ideology – Toward a Layered Narrative', (2006) 4 *International Journal of Constitutional Law* 439.

Comparison as a critical practice requires operating within 'nets of meaning' and 'webs of signification'.[17] And once the comparatist begins to look at constitutional law not just as a body of norms but as 'a view of the way things are', as imaginations of reality – like science or religion, ideology or art – as well as an ensemble of 'practical attitudes toward the management of controversy', she has to cope with translations of constitutions 'between a language of imagination and one of decision'.[18] Guided by a constitutive theory of law, she will discard the fact/law and law-in-the-books/law-in-action distinctions and deal, instead, with how she will present in her comparative studies the legal representations of local conflicts, contexts, and visions. Therefore a combination of methodological approaches appears to be more suited to cope with the problem of strangeness as well as the tension between the global and local aspects of constitutions.

8.4 Dimensions and projects of comparative constitutional studies

In the light of the complex work of constructing and reconstructing constitutions and of their strangeness, comparative constitutional studies call for a historical perspective and a variety of structuralist and non-structuralist analyses, some of which are briefly outlined below. Similarly, some authors advocate a 'multi-factor analysis'.[19]

8.4.1 Comparing constitutional archetypes

The higher-law concept implies that constitutions are law. From a historical perspective this implication turns out to be both too narrow and too broad. In tracing and mapping the development of modern constitutions, not counting hybrids, one may reconstruct four models as defined by distinct features and styles: constitution as (a) contract, (b) manifesto, (c) programme, and (d) law. These models qualify as Weberian ideal types or archetypes. Their gestalt is represented – not altogether unlike Jungian

---

[17]   C. Geertz, 'Local Knowledge: Fact and Law in Comparative Perspective', in Geertz, *Local Knowledge* (New York: Basic Books, 1983), 167; Geertz, 'Thick Description', 3.

[18]   Geertz, 'Local Knowledge', 174.

[19]   M. J. Horwitz, 'Constitutional Transplants', (2009) 10 *Theoretical Inquiries in Law* 535.

archetypes[20] – on the symbolic level by documents. Rather than elucidating a 'constitutional unconscious', however, they shape the flow of constitutional imagination and the practice it informs and therefore qualify as specimens for copies and variations.

(a) The constitutional *contract* dates as far back as Magna Carta, arguably one of the founding documents of modern constitutionalism. After receding to the realm of philosophy as social contract, the contractual archetype experienced a renaissance throughout the nineteenth century and very recently returned to the supranational level (Europe). While the early contracted constitutions established a relationship between the monarch and the barons, presupposing membership of the contracting parties of one of the feudal estates, later contracts since the nineteenth century either laid down a compromise among competitors claiming sovereignty (monarch/estates; monarch/people) and/or set up a relationship between independent territorial political units, mostly states, within a newly constituted federal or confederate system of government.

Typically, the contractual constituent power refers to an empirical, internally structured plurality: 'We the Undersigned'. Constitutional contracts tend to focus on the modalities of government. They limit the exercise of political power or sovereignty by placing an obligation on the central public authority (king, federal government) to respect the rights of individuals or members of an estate or the competences reserved to the contracting parties and states. As organizational contracts – such as the Articles of the Federation in 1781 or the Imperial German Constitution in 1871, where 'the five Majesties present ... contracted an eternal alliance', or the Treaty on European Union (1992) as amended by the contested Treaty of Lisbon (December 2009) – they address rather straightforwardly the problems of sovereignty and allocation of power within a multi-level system of government.

In contrast to 'real' organizational contracts, which span the whole conceptual grid from higher law to ideology, *social contracts* are neither prescriptive nor descriptive, but dwell in the realm of theory and philosophy as narratives of legitimation, where they serve as metaphors or hypothetical constructions for the transformation of a state of nature (anarchy) into a social state (order, society), or of a 'society of individuals' into an imaginary

---

[20] C. G. Jung, *The Archetypes and the Collective Unconscious*, 2nd edn (Princeton University Press, 1981).

'body politic' (civil society, *civitas*, or *État politique*) based on an infinite number of virtual, reciprocal agreements. Framers or commentators have borrowed the philosophical idea of a social contract to elevate a constitution above the horizon of partisan interests and thus to dignify its making and contents.

(b) The constitution as *political manifesto* or 'aspirational document'[21] is epitomized by the French Déclaration des Droits de l'Homme et du Citoyen (1789). This declaration and its predecessors, the English freedom proclamations of the seventeenth century and the Declaration of Independence (1776), as well as the later Universal Declaration of Human Rights (1948) and the Arab Charter on Human Rights (2004), arose from political struggles, revolutionary uprisings, liberation movements, and human catastrophes. As normative speech acts they turn the performative into a mere statement by claiming that they do not constitute, but only confirm or reaffirm what is already beyond dispute as common knowledge (the traditional rights of Englishmen; human rights) or self-evident truth – notably '[t]hat all men are created equal' or the supremacy of the Shari'a as the only 'true religion' – or what expresses a presumed political consensus – 'that these united [New England] colonies are, and of right ought to be, free and independent states'. The confessional message of manifestos lends itself to narratives regarding the ends of government (protecting rights) or the basis of a good society (fundamental rights and values).

As distinct from constitutional contracts, manifestos are unilateral proclamations of elected, delegated, or self-styled elites who claim to have a special foundational mission. They invariably document the result, closure, or summary of a political discourse. With the rise of the other constitutional archetypes the manifesto does not altogether disappear from the constitutional stage but is submitted to the discipline and routines of higher lawmaking. Manifesto elements are relegated to the preambles, where they may provoke doctrinal debates concerning their nature as binding norms, or to constitutional provisions, where they reappear under the guise of fundamental values, promotional goals, or constitutional mandates.

(c) 'Real-existing socialism' introduced the third archetype: the constitution as *programme* or plan of development that translates the 'laws of scientific socialism' and historical materialism into ideological blueprints

[21] Horwitz, 'Constitutional Transplants', 541, 543.

for socio-economic and political-cultural progress. From a Western higher-law viewpoint they are often dismissed as 'façade constitutions'. Such a biased perspective, exclusively informed by liberal constitutionalism, misses the interesting stories programme-constitutions can tell.[22] They are not meant to serve as regulatory law, instruments of government, or enforceable ground rules. For conflicts between citizens and the socialist 'powers that be' that would otherwise warrant civil rights, are inconceivable within authoritarian socialist regimes because it is always the people's state and party cadres that are acting. And on the way to that state, conflicts are not admissible as they would compromise the prerogative of the 'laws of socialism'.

Hence such constitutions imitate semantically the higher-law style of Western constitutionalism, while serving as positive ideology with a strictly symbolic purpose in the socialist context. They offer a frame of reference for political unity and collective identity, and they mirror and project stages of development, such as 'the primary stage of socialism' (China, Art. 6), along the guidelines provided by the theoretical authorities, primarily Marx/ Engels and Lenin. Consequently, programme constitutions become obsolete and need to undergo revision, once the ruling cadres decide, on the basis of their superior insight into the authoritative scriptures, that a certain developmental stage has been passed. Accordingly, the Soviet Union, 'constituted' in 1921–2, was reconstituted in 1936, the new Soviet Constitution proclaiming the 'victory of socialism', somewhat prematurely as it turned out. In 1978, the Soviet Union underwent yet another reconstituting. The German Democratic Republic (East Germany) and Vietnam followed a similar pattern and were constitutionally revamped several times in response to the new situation and developmental circumstances (Vietnam 1992), respectively 'in correspondence with the processes of historical development' (German Democratic Republic 1974).

The proclamatory style and unilateral declaration of programme constitutions by a self-established avant-garde bear a certain resemblance to the manifesto. Interestingly enough, even contracted or legislated constitutions have preserved programmatic elements, and authors rejecting the idea of a European constitution have unwillingly and ironically invoked the concept of

---

[22] M. Sidel, 'Analytical Models for Understanding Constitutions and Constitutional Dialogue in Socialist Transitional States: Reinterpreting Constitutional Dialogue in Vietnam', (2002) 6 *Singapore Journal of International and Comparative Law* 42.

a programme constitution when arguing that the union as a 'system in flux' contradicts the idea of one ultimate document with rigid legal constraints.

(d) Although constitutional history does not follow the path of evolution, one can discern a secular trend from manifesto and contract constitutions to the fourth archetype, the constitution as *statute*, which is to say, as a product of a qualified law-making process. This sequence was first illustrated by the incorporation of the French Déclaration into the Revolutionary Constitution of 1791, then by two Supreme Court decisions declaring the US Constitution as directly applicable law superior to all ordinary laws and as the basis of judicial review.[23] Subsequently, legislated constitutions and in their wake constitutional reviews of legislation have proliferated all over the world since the early nineteenth century.

In sharp contrast to the other archetypes, the constitutional elites invoke the absent people as an imaginary collective and constituent power. They claim popular sovereignty for and popular participation in constitution-making as the foundational and legitimatory source and lay the foundation stone for the impressive career of 'We the People' (US Constitution) which was copied and modified in many versions, such as 'We the Japanese people', 'In the name of God, the Merciful, the Compassionate, We the people of Afghanistan', 'We inscribe the following as the Constitution of the Kingdom of Cambodia', and so on.

The legislated or statutory constitution qualifies as the most flexible archetype – flexible enough to incorporate elements of the other archetypes. At times, it appears to imply a foundational social contract while, at others, it draws from the confessional style of manifestos and incorporates programmatic visions in the guise of goals of the state with constitutional mandates or promotional goals and principles addressed to the lawmaker, such as the promotion of women's rights (Bangladesh 1972, Art. 10; German Basic Law, Art. 3(2)), the establishment of a system guaranteeing social security (Albania 1998, Art. 59), or the renunciation of war (Japan 1947, Art. 9; German Basic Law, Art. 26). Some legislated constitutions even include contractual elements uniting ethnic groups (Afghanistan), nationalities (China), or communities and territories (Fiji Islands). Therefore the benefit of comparative studies may be to elucidate variations of the archetypical design and hybrids mixing different constitutional styles.

---

[23] *Marbury* v. *Madison*, 5 US 137 [1803], and *McCulloch* v. *Maryland*, 4 Wheat. 316 [1819].

8.4.2 Comparative analysis of constitutional architecture

The architecture and structural elements of constitutions deserve attention in comparative studies because the anatomy may reveal how fundamental questions of life in society are addressed: the distribution of justice, the definition of the common wealth, the allocation and control of power, and the amendment, interpretation, and protection of the constitution. Four building elements characterize the architecture or anatomy of modern constitutions all over the world.

(a) In the liberal tradition the most prominent element deals with questions of justice or agency, which constitutions invariably attribute to the individual members, groups, and parties of the sovereign body politic. They reveal an originally novel but today common and routinized political imagining of the subject as an active participant in social life and political decision-making who is expected to master her personal destiny and the problems arising from life in society and the polity. Nearly all modern constitutions translate this activist expectation into *rights* and *principles* that are meant to guarantee equal freedom within an overall political scheme of self-rule translated into a regime of law-rule. Some constitutions, not only socialist constitutions, deviate from the liberal lack of social ambition and complement the catalogue of civil and political rights with social rights (Japan, Vietnam, Angola). Most constitutions underscore their rights-catalogues with rule-of-law principles safeguarding the equal distribution of freedom (prohibition of discrimination, principle of proportionality, institutions for legal redress of grievances). Both rights and principles of justice have proven immune to the critiques of their indeterminate texture, ideological content, and possessive-individualist connotations.

(b) Constitutions address questions of the good life or public interest in terms of *values* derived from political or social ethics and *duties* considered essential for social coexistence. The duties contained in this building block are not correlatives of rights, but responsibilities, virtues, and rules of conduct. Prominent among constitutionally sanctioned shared values are social peace, human dignity, security, friendship among nations, protection of the natural environment, unity, and solidarity – the modern version of *fraternité*[24] (Angola 1992).

---

[24] E. Denninger, 'Solidarität als Verfassungsprinzip', (2009) 92 *Kritische Zeitschrift für Gesetzgebung und Rechtswissenschaft* 20.

Unlike the general and universal duty to respect the rights of others, value-oriented civic duties correspond asymmetrically to rights and have a tendency to come into conflict with them. The implementation of duties transgresses the horizontal relationship among citizens. Rather than empowering the citizenry, values and duties call for their top-down enforcement by public authorities.

(c) Compared with the glamour of rights and the popular, albeit vague, appeal of values, regulations concerning the *allocation* and *control of power* within an institutional framework seem to incite less interpretive enthusiasm and popular excitement. Such neglect comes as a surprise, since organizational regulations shape the very 'constitution of politics' and, hence, directly affect the exercise and viability of rights and rule-of-law guarantees.

The organizational building block involves practical questions of historical experience and political risk management, all of which is embodied in systems of horizontal and vertical balance of powers, election rules, the management of public debts, the imposition of duties and taxes, and so forth. In constitutional theory, organizational rules have often been played off against fundamental rights and vice versa. Quite prophetically, the authors of the French Déclaration anticipated the necessary coexistence of both rights and separation of powers (Art. 16).

(d) The fourth component of any modern constitution concerns questions of constitutional *validity*, *amendment*, and *protection*. Some of the relevant provisions – establishment of a constitutional court, judicial review, and amendment procedures – superficially resemble organizational regulations. However, they have to be distinguished as *meta-rules* or rules of *collision*. Meta-rules define the *pouvoir constituant* and lay down the conditions for the repeal, revision, and interpretation of a constitution, thus trying to strike a balance between the contradictory imperatives of stability and flexibility. Rules of collision determine in cases and controversies the legal hierarchy within a legal order. They also situate a constitution and a national legal regime with regard to supranational and international law.

Within and through meta-rules and collision rules constitutions talk about themselves and establish their reflexive and modern nature. By the same token, they are designed to defend a constitution's dignity as 'supreme law' vis-à-vis ordinary laws and their interpretation by adding 'interpretation in conformity with the constitution' to the canons of legal interpretation. Meta-rules operate as closure, with regard to the paradox of the constitutional moment, while keeping open the permanent discourse on legitimacy.

Comparative analysis reveals that constitutions almost everywhere share these structural properties. Such similarity on the surface, however, only characterizes the way polities dress for their appearance on the global theatre's stage as secular and rule-of-law-abiding regimes. Remarkable differences come into view if the architecture of constitutions is not read schematically as a result of globalization, but if one looks more closely at the peculiar national arrangements of the different building elements – how they are designed and internally related and interact in the constitutional everyday. Comparative studies may bring to the fore which of the conceptual varieties (higher law, instrument of government, cultural artifact) is accentuated by structure and how certain structural arrangements are privileged by certain archetypes. Furthermore, comparative studies may investigate whether the combination of an elaborate organizational scheme with a narrow rights basis points towards a preoccupation with and uneasiness about power on the part of the constitutional elites (US Constitution), or a conglomerate of values (Angola, Cameroon, Tanzania) and duties (Algeria, Azerbaijan) can be interpreted as reacting to problems of social integration, notably in decolonized societies.[25]

8.5 Comparative analysis of constitutional transfer

The Watson/Legrand controversy concerning the (im)possibility of legal transplants has triggered an ongoing scholarly debate also in comparative constitutional studies. From the numerous semantic offers – 'transplant', 'adaptation', 'borrowing', 'contamination', 'migration', 'translation', and so on – 'transfer' seems preferable as a general term which conveys both the change of context and its problematic nature.

8.5.1 The focus on the global: constitutional transfer

In comparing transfer processes one has to deal with two striking features. First, constitutions – across national boundaries, language barriers, epistemic communities, and diverse political-cultural contexts – appear to share a

---

[25] O. Akiba, *Constitutionalism and Society in Africa* (Farnham: Ashgate, 2004).

similar grammar and vocabulary, follow almost uniform patterns of structural design, and can be traced back to comparable institutional paths. Globalization, one is tempted to assume, has streamlined the ideas, practices, and results of the framing, amending, and – to a lesser degree – interpreting of constitutions.[26] Second, however, most constitutions contain items that have so far resisted globalization. The coexistence of global and local items call for a theory, informed by comparison, that gives analytical clues as to how constitutional transfer happens, why it is problematic or fails, and what kind of constitutional order it produces.

Such theoretical account[27] has to start at the point of origin, however questionable, where constitutional ideas, institutions, norms, and arguments are (or were) fabricated in a specific historical and cultural context. It is here, within a set of initial circumstances, where transfer and transformation may start. The second phase of transfer focuses on the process of de-contextualization: how the vocabulary, design, and institutional arrangements are taken out of their formative environment and 'shock-frozen'. In media reports, scholarly journals, and other publications they are reified and standardized as constitutional commodities, for example the 'We the People' formula; the Supreme Court model of judicial review; the Westminster type of parliament or the European Convention on Human Rights. At times, they are then idealized as constitutional universals. In their disassembled or de-contextualized state they are then transmitted – one might say that they migrate – to the global reservoir of constitutionalism, a collective memory which is constantly controlled, filled, and revised by the intersecting discourses on constitutional law and the practices of constitution-making. There they are available for constitutional architects, legal consultants, political elites, or civil society associations shopping for a better constitution, a constitutional court or other items, or intending to update a catalogue of rights or a set of values as happened in post-colonial and post-socialist countries.

During the third phase the prefabricated, purchased items are transferred to a host context where they have to be reassembled, fitted into a new constitutional scheme or tradition, and adapted to a different cultural

---

[26] W. Menski, *Comparative Law in a Global Context: The Legal Systems of Asia and Africa*, 2nd edn (Cambridge University Press, 2006).

[27] For a more elaborate account see G. Frankenberg, 'Constitutional Transfer – the IKEA-Theory Revisited', (2010) 8 *Journal of International Constitutional Law* 563.

environment. This process involves a great deal of translation, *bricolage*[28] or 'selective imitation'.[29] It implies considerable uncertainties and risks because the *bricoleurs* have to operate without knowing the original master plan of the purchased item and instead have to rely on the fairly general manual of (global) constitutionalism. During the process of assembly, adaptation, and *bricolage* they are confronted with the risk of bad fit as the transferred item may be rejected by the power elites or civil society, or may not be adaptable to the existing constitutional culture or institutional arrangement. Furthermore, the adaptation may involve a politically difficult and time-consuming readjustment or even replacement of constitutional items. In the end the result may not look like a copy of the original – such as the Hungarian Constitutional Court modelled after the German Constitutional Court – but a pastiche, a hybrid or ironic imitation: the deconstruction of the mythical *unum* by the concept of a plural 'We the multinational people of the Russian Federation', the submission of rights to 'the interests of the State, of society, and of the collective' (China, Art. 51) or the detailed and lengthy Swiss Constitution of 1874 that is said to have been modelled after or at least inspired by the US Constitution. Any 'original meaning', if at all distinguishable, one may conclude, gets lost or deconstructed and reshaped in the complex processes of de- and re-contextualization.

8.5.2   The focus on difference: transfer-resistant aspects

Comparative study uncovers an impressive richness of constitutional items that have resisted transfer because they are obviously bound to the local context. While the methodological problem that consists in identifying them may be solved by comparison, a theoretical explanation of why these items are non-marketable seems to be quite elusive. In order to identify examples of transfer-resistance comparatists have to give up the global perspective of convergence and be open to surprising, unusual provisions that may strike them as odd. By focusing on markers of difference they will then recognize the peculiar configuration of traditional, socialist, and capitalist values

---

[28] C. Lévi-Strauss, *The Savage Mind* (University of Chicago Press, 1966); J. Derrida, 'Structure: Sign and Play in the Discourse of the Human Sciences', in J. Derrida, *Writing and Difference*, trans. A. Bass (University of Chicago Press, 1966), 278.

[29] M. Graziadei, 'Legal Transplants and the Frontiers of Legal Knowledge', (2009) 10 *Theoretical Inquiries in Law* 723, 732.

shaping the style and content of the Constitution of Vietnam; or the uncommon combination of pre-constitutional with constituted institutions (the emperor in Japan, Arts. 1–7; the traditional Loya Jirga in Afghanistan; or the comparable, if less powerful, Great Council of Chiefs in the Fiji Islands). Other transfer-resistant items are, for instance, the renunciation of war (Japan, Art. 9); the constitutional duty to display the portrait of the president in governmental offices and embassies (Bangladesh, Art. 4); the provision that 'the prisons of the nation shall be healthy and clean' (Argentina, S. 18); and the unusually elaborate scheme of social rights of urban and rural workers, including the provision that they be entitled to 'paid weekly leave, preferably on Sundays' (Brazil, Art. 7(XV)).

In pursuing the search for difference comparatists may also identify a group of less parochial constitutional items that point towards a regionally limited transfer or societies sharing a cultural or religious tradition or political experience, such as the right to a marriage based on consent (Albania; Azerbaijan, Art. 34; Japan, Art. 24); the personal character of criminal punishment (Afghanistan, Burkina Faso); the duty of children who are of age to care for their parents (Azerbaijan, Art. 34; Uzbekistan, Art. 66); or the abolition of untouchability (India).[30] This group of constitutional commodities indicates that resistance to transfer may yield over time and that originally context-bound provisions may later be included in the global reservoir, notably clauses 'entrenching' parts of a constitution (Azerbaijan, Arts. 155, 158; German Basic Law, Art. 79; Morocco, Art. 106; Namibia, Art. 131; Iran, Art. 177), or proliferate regionally.

It would be misleading to treat the context-bound aspects of constitutions as marginal or irrelevant because they do not follow the widely presumed trend towards constitutional internationalization. Surprising and unusual items deserve special attention and methodological care as they may give away crucial information about local struggles and experiences, about popular or elitist visions of the good life in society and an 'imagined future',[31] once the comparatist not only places them in their historical, political, and social contexts but, more importantly, looks for the context they contain.

---

[30] Translated into clauses prohibiting discrimination on the grounds of caste in the constitutions of Bangladesh, Pakistan, and Sri Lanka.
[31] Graziadei, 'Legal Transplants', 727.

Further reading

O. Akiba, *Constitutionalism and Society in Africa* (Farnham: Ashgate, 2004)

L. W. Beer, *Constitutional Systems in Late Twentieth Century Asia* (Seattle: University of Washington Press, 1992)

A. von Bogdandy, P. Cruz Villalón, and P. M. Huber (eds.), *Handbuch Ius Publicum Europaeum, Vol. I Grundlagen und Grundzüge staatlichen Verfassungsrechts, Vol. II Offene Staatlichkeit – Wissenschaft vom Verfassungsrecht* (Heidelberg: C. F. Müller, 2007 and 2008)

N. J. Brown, *Constitutions in a Non-constitutional World: Arab Basic Laws and the Prospects for Accountable Government* (Albany: State University of New York Press, 2002)

S. Choudry (ed.), *The Migration of Constitutional Ideas* (Cambridge University Press, 2006)

N. Dorsen et al., *Comparative Constitutionalism: Cases and Materials* (Eagan, MN: West, 2003)

G. Frankenberg, 'Critical Comparisons: Rethinking Comparative Law', (1985) 26 *Harvard International Law Journal* 411

R. Gargarella, *The Legal Foundations of Inequality: Constitutionalism in the Americas, 1776–1860* (Cambridge University Press, 2010)

C. Geertz, 'Local Knowledge: Fact and Law in Comparative Perspective', in C. Geertz, *Local Knowledge* (New York: Basic Books, 1983), 167

'Thick Description: Toward an Interpretive Theory of Cultures', in C. Geertz, *The Interpretation of Cultures*, 2nd edn (New York: Basic Books, 2000), 3

M. Graziadei, 'Legal Transplants and the Frontiers of Legal Knowledge', (2009) 10 *Theoretical Inquiries in Law* 723

V. Grosswald Curran, 'Cultural Immersion, Difference and Categories in U.S. Comparative Law', (1998) 46 *American Journal of Comparative Law* 657

G. Hassall and C. Saunders, *Asia-Pacific Constitutional Systems* (Cambridge University Press, 2002)

M. J. Horwitz, 'Constitutional Transplants', (2009) 10 *Theoretical Inquiries in Law* 565

V. C. Jackson and M. V. Tushnet, *Comparative Constitutional Law*, 2nd edn (New York: Foundation Press, 2006)

J. D. Leonard, 'Introduction', in J. D. Leonard (ed.), *Legal Studies as Cultural Studies – A Reader in (Post)Modern Critical Theory* (Albany: State University of New York Press, 1995)

M. Loughlin and N. Walker (eds.), *The Paradox of Constitutionalism, Constituent Power and Constitutional Form* (Oxford University Press, 2007)

W. Menski, *Comparative Law in a Global Context: The Legal Systems of Asia and Africa*, 2nd edn (Cambridge University Press, 2006)

D. Nelken, 'Comparative Law and Comparative Legal Studies', in E. Örücü and D. Nelken (eds.), *Comparative Law: A Handbook* (Oxford and Portland: Hart, 2007), 3

J. Oloka-Onyango, *Constitutionalism in Africa: Creating Opportunities, Facing Challenges* (Kampala: Fountain Press, 2001)

G. Sartori, *Comparative Constitutional Engineering: An Inquiry into Structures, Incentives and Outcomes*, 2nd edn (New York University Press, 1996)

D. Sciulli, *Theory of Societal Constitutionalism* (Cambridge University Press, 1992)

M. Sidel, 'Analytical Models for Understanding Constitutions and Constitutional Dialogue in Socialist Transitional States: Re-interpreting Constitutional Dialogue in Vietnam', (2002) 6 *Singapore Journal of International and Comparative Law* 42

M. Troper (ed.), *Traité International de Droit Constitutionnel* (Paris: Dalloz, 2011)

M. Tushnet, 'The Possibilities of Comparative Constitutional Law', (1999) 108 *Yale Law Journal* 1225

W. Van Caenegem, *A Historical Introduction to Western Constitutional Law* (Cambridge University Press, 1995)

J. Waldron, 'Foreign Law and the Modern *Ius Gentium*', (2005) 119 *Harvard Law Review* 129

Comparative criminal justice 9

Elisabetta Grande

9.1 Comparative criminal justice: a long neglected discipline on the rise

9.1.1 A past of oblivion

Traditionally, legal comparison has been mostly associated with private law. One of its masters, Gino Gorla, pointed out that '[comparative law] methodology has been conceived essentially, if not exclusively, in connection with civil law'.[1] Born and developed within the private law arena therefore, comparative law in its modern foundation has for years paid almost no attention to criminal justice. Things today are rapidly changing, however. New international dynamics ask for a deep understanding of the similarities between criminal legal systems rather than of their differences, pushing criminal justice into the realm of a modern comparative law methodology, one that takes an integrative approach instead of a contrastive one.[2]

The search for a common grammar among legal systems has been typical, indeed, of the private law domain since the second half of the twentieth century, when the need for legal uniformity stemmed from galloping globalization. Under the impact of a dramatic worldwide intensification of the transnational exchange and movements of persons, goods, and capital, private comparative law scholars began to search for a common core of legal systems. Since the Cornell seminars, they have incrementally succeeded in refining a methodology that looks beyond the narratives and discourses to grasp the deep similarities between legal systems.[3] Closely associated with the

---

[1] G. Gorla, 'Diritto Comparato', in *Enciclopedia del Diritto*, vol. XII (Milan: Giuffrè, 1964), 940 (author's translation).

[2] R. Schlesinger, 'Past and Future of Comparative Law', (1995) 43 *American Journal of Comparative Law* 477.

[3] See, for an application and a development of the 'Cornell' methodology, the Common Core of European Private Law project, conducted by Ugo Mattei and Mauro Bussani at www.commoncore.org.

principle of state sovereignty, however, criminal law and criminal procedure instead remained consigned within the boundaries of a contrastive comparison, one that limits itself to the analysis of the differences between legal systems (rather than searching for similarities) and that consequently is less interested in challenging the representation that each system gives of itself.

Because of its search for a common core of rules, comparison in private law meant a deep look into legal systems, producing a critical understanding of each other through 'cross-participation', or 'cultural immersion'.[4] To the contrary, comparison in criminal law and procedure for a long time simply meant to learn from a distance a good or bad example of a foreign law, if not passively to accept the cultural hegemony of a foreign legal system. And where the bases for criminal jurisdiction other than territoriality were recognized, the task of the comparative criminal lawyers became to ascertain the applicable foreign law in order to comply with the well-recognized rule that an offender acting outside the jurisdiction of the forum state will be punished only if the act is criminal both in the forum state and in the state where the act was committed.

This is why still, today, as has been pointed out, 'textbooks on comparative law feel no need to address, or even acknowledge the existence of, comparative studies in criminal law' and 'the massive *International Encyclopedia of Comparative Law* does not cover criminal law, devoting itself instead to virtually every aspect and variety of "civil, commercial and economic law"'.[5]

9.1.2 A shining future?

And yet, in the very recent past, comparison in criminal matters has received a strong boost towards an integrative approach by the advent of a supranational criminal justice system, both at the international level and at that of the European Union. While marking a new attitude by national jurisdictions to the existence of a supranational criminal authority, which was strongly resisted in the past in the name of the principle of state sovereignty, the internationalization and the 'harmonization' of criminal law and procedure led in fact for the first time towards the search for common ground among different criminal legal traditions.

---

[4] V. Curran, 'Cultural Immersion, Difference and Categories in U.S. Comparative Law', (1998) 46 *American Journal of Comparative Law* 43.

[5] M. D. Dubber, 'Comparative Criminal Law', in M. Reimann and R. Zimmermann (eds.), *The Oxford Handbook of Comparative Law* (Oxford University Press, 2006), 1287, 1288.

At the international level, the formation of temporary international tribunals (each designed to deal respectively with crimes committed in the former Yugoslavia, Rwanda, Sierra Leone, and Lebanon) and the implementation in 2002 of the permanent International Criminal Court (ICC, intended to deal with genocide, crimes against humanity, and war crimes) involved the creation of a supranational substantive and procedural criminal law. This required a careful look at the norms and legal traditions of *all* the members of the international community. A comparison between different legal systems searching for similarities and not only for differences became thus essential from the perspective of shaping the rules for the new international institutions. Therefore comparative criminal justice finally entered into the realm of an integrative approach. With the advent of the international criminal tribunals, comparative criminal justice moreover abandoned the appearance of a purely theoretical discipline to cross the threshold of a practical one, and this is particularly true when considering that the ICC applies not only 'the Statute, Elements of Crimes and its Rules of Procedure and Evidence' or, in second place, 'applicable treaties and the principles and rules of international law', but also, 'failing that, general principles of law derived by the Court from national laws of legal systems of the world' (Art. 21 ICC Statute). Hence, in deciding a case the ICC itself has to engage in an integrative comparative search in order to find out the applicable law.

At the European level, criminal justice has for a long time been excluded from the province of Community law. With the conclusion of the Treaty of Maastricht in 1992, criminal law and procedure were finally brought into the arena of EU law, but criminal matters were confined to the sphere of the 'third pillar' (related to co-operation in the areas of freedom, security, and justice), preserving consequently an international character. It is only very recently, in 2005, that through its decisions the European Court of Justice (ECJ) anticipated the convergence of the 'pillars'.[6] It also acknowledged in advance the full mandate to make criminal laws that in 2010 the Treaty of Lisbon gave to the European Parliament and the European Council. In fact the Treaty in its Articles 82 and 83 today provides for Union competence in establishing minimal standards for criminal procedural rules and criminal provisions in specific, although not exhaustive, areas of crime having a cross-border dimension.

---

[6] *Criminal proceedings against Maria Pupino*, 16 June 2005, Case C-105/03, [2005] ECR I-5285; *Commission* v. *Council*, 13 September 2005, Case C-176/03, [2005] ECR I-7879; *Commission* v. *Council*, 23 October 2007, Case C-440/05, [2007] I-9097.

A true process of the Europeanization of national criminal law has therefore only just started. Yet it is since 2000 that the EU, by means of various framework decisions, has abandoned a restriction of focus on the area of co-operation in criminal matters to tackle the sphere of substantive criminal law and, to a lesser extent, of criminal procedure. Since the turn of the millennium, indeed, in their 'third pillar' capacity, the organs of the European Union have legislated in areas such as drug trafficking, terrorism, corruption, counterfeiting, and organized crime, stimulating in so doing a growing body of literature on 'European criminal law'. In 2000, a multi-state comparative scholarly effort towards harmonization of national criminal laws even resulted in a legislative draft named 'Corpus Juris – Penal Provisions for the Protection of European Finances', addressing both substantive and procedural rules in the area of violations of financial interests of the European Union.[7]

In spite of the so-called 'democracy deficit problem', which in criminal matters puts the legality principle in serious jeopardy even when directives – as is the case – are mandatorily prescribed as legislative instruments, the star of the Europeanization of national criminal law and procedure seems on the rise. Its expansion is going to be accompanied by the creation of new European criminal justice authorities such as the European prosecutor, who in the near future is envisaged as being assigned the role of appearing before the criminal courts of any member state to prosecute cases involving the interests of the EU. After the Lisbon Treaty and in the wake of the above-mentioned 'Corpus Juris', the endeavour towards the making of a European substantive and procedural criminal 'code' dealing with common minimal rules will therefore certainly continue, and this will definitively transform comparative criminal justice from an abstract and marginal discipline into a practical as well as a crucial one.

9.2 Methodological problems

9.2.1 Comparative criminal law

9.2.1.1 Studying foreign law

There is a long-standing tradition of comparative criminal law in the very limited sense of studying foreign criminal laws. Foreign criminal laws have

---

[7] M. Delmas-Marty and J. A. E. Vervaele (eds.), *The Implementation of the Corpus Juris in the Member States* (Antwerp: Intersentia, 2000).

sometimes been studied for reform purposes, leading occasionally to more or less successful legal transplants. At other times they have been studied in order to become acquainted with concepts and categories typical of a different and prestigious legal culture, such as the German one, for the purpose of their use in the domestic setting, regardless, however, of any real need. Occasionally they have been studied to display erudition in enriching the footnotes of criminal law textbooks with the criminal code provisions of other countries.

Comparative criminal law as the study of foreign laws can be traced back to Paul Johan Anselm von Feuerbach (1775–1833), the acknowledged founding father of the discipline, and to his interest in Islamic, European, east Asian, south Asian, Middle Eastern and US criminal law, for the very ambitious purpose of deriving a universal legal science. The later editions of his *Textbook of the Common Criminal Law in Force in Germany* were heavily interlarded by Karl Joseph Mittermaier (1787–1867) with detailed descriptions of foreign solutions to individual questions, thus transforming Feuerbach's textbook into a little encyclopaedia of foreign criminal law. An even more ambitious project in the same direction was undertaken some years later by a group of German law professors, who between 1905 and 1909 published a sixteen-volume work entitled *Vergleich des deutchen und des ausländischen Strafrechts* (A comparative account of German and foreign criminal law), in connection with proposals for reform of the German criminal code. In the same period Franz von Liszt, the Austrian pioneer of comparative criminal law, under the auspices of the Union internationale de droit pénal edited the first volume of an impressive series of essays on the criminal law of the states of Europe (*Le droit criminel des Etats Européens*, 1894), with the aim of expounding in a subsequent, but never published, volume the common core of the criminal laws of Europe. Since then, similar accounts and studies of foreign criminal laws have proliferated, often adding an exotic flavour to domestic Italian, German or French criminal law textbooks. None of these can be considered, however, to be a veritable work of comparative law. They are mere juxtaposition of different foreign criminal laws, most of the time depicted with no consciousness of the often distortional perspective of the foreign observer not immersed in the observed legal system, and usually only portrayed by means of their formal and abstract legal provisions.

9.2.1.2 Getting the other right

Comparison in the legal field – as much as in non-legal ones – instead means first of all 'getting the other right'. To do that one must become totally acquainted with the other system and abandon the cultural lenses worn at home. Different systems draw on different sources of criminal law; or give a different importance to the same sources; or apply different methods of interpreting the law; or make use of different conceptual categories for framing the same issue; or employ the same conceptual category to mean different things. Judge-made law, statutory law, academic literature, or customary law can play a role in making the 'legal rule' in the foreign legal system which is different from that at home. 'Negligence', as a mental element of the crime, can mean at home something other than in the foreign system; 'recklessness' may not even exist as a conceptual category in the foreign system, and its equation with foreign categories describing a similar actor's state of mind can be misleading. Even the basic patterns of structuring the offence – that is, the analytical conceptual framework through which the crime is constructed – can be radically different in different legal traditions (as is the case for the common law notion of the offence as opposed to that of the many criminal systems influenced by the German theory of crime).[8] In order to get the foreign criminal law right, therefore, the observer needs to free herself not only from all kinds of positional superiority that may affect her observation of the 'other' in order to humbly adopt the insider perspective of the foreign legal system, but she also needs to liberate herself as much as possible from any domestic cultural constraint that would inevitably distort her perspective.

'Getting the other right' also means looking beyond the formal and abstract foreign legal rules, putting them into a broader context and checking them against the operative level. In so doing one could discover for instance that criminal strict liability in England, even if acknowledged in theory, has been in practice routinely avoided by means of prosecutorial discretion or of a mere nominal punishment (so called 'absolute discharge').[9] Or, conversely, that a 'necessity' defence may not be acknowledged as a general ground for exclusion of criminal liability, but nonetheless by the same means is given practical application.[10] Analogously, 'mistake of law' or the 'entrapment defence' doctrines may not formally exclude criminal liability, but a

---

[8] A. Eser and G. P. Fletcher (eds.), *Justification and Excuses: Comparative Perspectives* (Huntington, NY: Juris Publishing, 1987).

[9] M. Wasik, 'The Grant of Absolute Discharge', (1985) 5 *Oxford Journal of Legal Studies* 211, 221.

[10] D. Ormerod, *Smith and Hogan's Criminal Law*, 13th edn (Oxford University Press, 2011), 371, 373.

closer look at the sentencing praxis of the system can reveal their strong operative relevance.[11] The dynamics at play among different sources of law in the observed foreign system can be very different from what it at first glance appears, so that, in contrast to the continental narrative, German criminal law is much more the product of the scholarly literature and of its influence on the courts than of the legislator and the code.[12] By the same token, even if only recently explicitly abjured, the long and firmly asserted judicial power in the making of the criminal law in England has in fact been substantially over for a couple of centuries.[13]

This is why, in order to get the foreign law right, it is essential for the researcher to question her first impressions, to make connections among different levels of normative and practical rules, to address the system as a whole, to take into consideration the structural institutions as well as the foreign mentality and to avoid limiting herself to the study in isolation of the formal provisions of the law.

9.2.1.3 Through the others' mirror

Challenging her own as well as others' legal narratives is even more typically the job of the comparatist, the very one that engages in the search for differences and similarities among different systems, particularly if she is seeking a common core of rules. For the sake of a harmonization of laws, the researcher cannot be satisfied without a serious integrative comparison, one that from the beginning makes the researcher mirror herself and her own legal world and perspective in those of others, by a regard that goes beyond mere appearances and formal assertions. By means of a subversive attitude,[14] the comparatist in search of common ground among different criminal law systems needs to question the apparent diversity or similarity of the rules in the observed legal systems, looking not only

---

[11] Wasik, 'Grant', 225 f.

[12] Dubber, 'Comparative Criminal Law', 1318. As clear evidence of the crucial creative role of the German professors in creating the criminal law, among many other examples, it is sufficient to draw attention to the origins of para. 17 Strafgesetzbuch (StGB), dealing with unavoidable mistake of law, or para. 35 StGB, dealing with excusing necessity, both the product of the academic genius, afterwards internalized and applied by the courts and finally adopted in the criminal code.

[13] G. Williams, *Criminal Law: The General Part*, 2nd edn (London: Sweet & Maxwell, 1961), 594.

[14] G. P. Fletcher, 'Comparative Law as a Subversive Discipline', (1988) 46 *American Journal of Comparative Law* 689; H. Muir-Watt, 'La fonction subversive du droit comparé', (2000) 52 *Revue internationale de droit comparé* 503.

to what legislative provisions, scholars, or judges say, but also to what in practice happens in the life of the law. The third eye that this kind of comparison offers to the observed as well as to the observer makes possible a critical understanding of the attitudes, beliefs, and practices of each one, unveiling surprising divergences or convergences among legal traditions.

Checked against the operative level, the Anglo-American subjective approach to the inchoate crime of attempt – that is, an approach that aims to punish the *actor*'s dangerousness – can thus turn into an objective one – that is, an approach that focuses on the punishment of the *act*'s dangerousness – and, conversely, the Italian objective approach can give way to a subjective one; the crime of conspiracy, apparently unique to the common law tradition, could reveal some unsuspected similarities of function with the parties to crime doctrine of the continental tradition;[15] and protection against a retroactive criminal punishment can in practice turn out to be better assured (by means of such devices as 'mistake of law' doctrine – in the United States – or 'absolute discharge' and concurrent sentencing practices – in England) in a common law criminal system that acknowledges the law-making power inherent in the judicial interpretation of a statute than in a civil law one, dominated by the principle of strict legality, therefore psychologically and practically not equipped to defend its citizens against a judicial overruling of a favourable interpretation of the law.[16]

With no pressure to use the 'other' as a mirror, the criminal law scholar traditionally did not look at her own legal system through foreign eyes and did not bring her own perspective to the foreign criminal system. Nevertheless, she is nowadays required to engage in such a new comparative

---

[15] Details for both statements in E. Grande, *Accordo criminoso e conspiracy. Tipicità e stretta legalità nell'analisi comparata* (Padua: Cedam, 1993), reviewed by G. P. Fletcher, 'Is Conspiracy Unique to the Common Law?', (1995) 43 *American Journal of Comparative Law* 171 ff.

[16] E. Grande, 'Principio di legalità e diritto giurisprudenziale: un'antinomia?', (1996) 27 *Politica del diritto* 469. For the US system see Model Penal Code §2.04(3)(b); W. R. LaFave, *Criminal Law*, 4th edn (Eagan: Thomson & West, 2003), 101 and 295; S. Pomorski, *American Common Law and the Principle Nullum Crimen sine Lege* (Berlin: Mouton, 1975), especially 181 ff. For the English system see Williams, *Criminal Law*, 303, and the many cases where, although the law was extended by 'judicial legislation', the accused was also convicted on a well-established ground, and the two sentences were ordered to run concurrently, making the 'judicial legislation' in reality a pronouncement for the future (e.g. *R* v. *Caldwell*, [1982] AC 341, [1981] 1 All ER 961; *Button* v. *DPP*, (1965) 66 Cr. App. R. 36, 44; *R* v. *Howe and others*, (1987) 85 Cr. App. R. 32). For a different technique, also giving future effect to a decision that broadens the criminal law, see the decision of the ECtHR, *S. W.* v. *United Kingdom*, judgment of 22 November 1995.

endeavour by the mentioned internalization and harmonization of the criminal law. And yet an integrative and subversive comparison can be of particular difficulty for the criminal lawyer, especially if she is trained in the continental tradition. The submission to the principle of strict legality, with its underlying idea that a democratic system can accept one and only one source of the criminal law – legislation through parliament – makes it especially difficult to acknowledge the complexity of the legal rule, the existence of an operative level possibly working in a different way from the declamatory one, and the adequacy of a search for the criminal rule beyond its formal provision. Moreover, the special need for certainty felt when dealing with criminal law asks for a special caution in subverting dogmas and firm beliefs in this area of the law, and this, too, may contribute to explaining the long delay accumulated by comparative criminal law as a field of study as compared to other comparative disciplines. A delay, it is worth pointing out, that has built up notwithstanding the fact that in 1971 Marc Ancel was already teaching comparative criminal lawyers that 'comparative law allows the researcher a better knowledge and a better understanding of her own law, the peculiar characters of which are better revealed by means of comparison with the foreign system'.[17]

9.2.2 Comparative criminal procedure

9.2.2.1 Moving beyond stereotypes

Marc Ancel's lesson was unquestionably learned in the field of criminal procedure. Starting from the 1970s, comparative scholarship in criminal procedure developed a methodology that carefully questioned previous stereotypes and rhetoric, thoroughly checked discourses against practices, and conscientiously tried to make use of the study of the foreign law for the sake of a better understanding of the domestic one and vice versa (thus gaining a critical perspective on both legal experiences), arriving therefore at the appointment with the internationalization and harmonization of the end of the century better equipped than criminal law scholarship.

Around the 1970s, two different taxonomies were devised as fresh analytical tools for understanding the complexity of the criminal process. They both maintained an enormous influence on comparative scholarship. The

---

[17] M. Ancel, *Utilité et méthodes du droit comparé* (Neuchâtel: Editions Ides et Calendes, 1971), 10 (author's translation).

first one – stemming from the genius of Herbert Packer – did not expressly address the comparatist audience but, as a classification against which any criminal procedure system could be checked, it represented a first step towards a comprehension of *all* criminal process practices in the world, outside any stereotypical intellectual constraint. According to Packer's theory, two criminal-procedure value systems can be imagined at work in a criminal process, the 'crime control' model and the 'due process' model; the first one resembling an 'assembly line' or a 'conveyor belt', aiming at a speedy repression of criminal conduct, the second one looking instead like an 'obstacle course', pointing at the control of the quality of the result. These models, short of being labelled by the author as good or bad, proved to be very useful for perceiving, in Packer's words, 'the normative antinomy that runs deep in the life of the criminal law', in the common law as much as in the civil law tradition.[18]

The second seminal taxonomy, this time especially devoted to comparative criminal procedure, came from the intellect of an academic belonging to two legal worlds: Mirjan Damaška. In 1973 Damaška, a scholar educated in the civil law/socialist tradition but exposed to the common law one, freed the comparatist from the previous dominating sterile and ideological dichotomy in comparative criminal procedure, the very one that, in a purely normative stance, related the continental procedure to an *inquisitorial* model and the common law procedure to an *accusatorial* one.[19] As normative categories, 'accusatorial' and 'inquisitorial' were used to refer to two normative ideals of procedure, the first being associated with full respect for the rights of the defendant, the second with authoritarian and bloodthirsty practices.[20] Using the expressions '*adversary* system' and '*non-adversary* system' as heuristic categories for grasping the essence of the two procedural styles, Damaška organized the two rival procedural models outside stereotypical contrapositions and rhetorical claims to superiority, turning his attention instead to their different structural arrangements. His observation of the systems in

---

[18] H. Packer, *The Limits of the Criminal Sanction* (Palo Alto: Stanford University Press, 1969), expanding H. Packer, 'Two Models of the Criminal Process', (1964) 113 *University of Pennsylvania Law Review* 1, 5.

[19] M. Damaška, 'Evidentiary Barriers to Conviction and Two Models of Criminal Procedure: A Comparative Study', (1973) 121 *University of Pennsylvania Law Review* 506.

[20] For the unfortunate resistance of such a view maintaining the Continental-inquisitorial/ common law-accusatorial dichotomy in the American legal culture, which still makes use of the 'inquisitorial system' as 'a kind of negative polestar for American criminal procedure', see D. A. Sklansky, 'Anti-inquisitorialism', (2009) 122 *Harvard Law Review* 1634, 1638.

action thus made him articulate the core contrast between contemporary common law and continental criminal procedure as one involving alternative patterns of distributing procedural control. The essence of the common law style – that is, of the 'adversary model' or 'contest model' – was located in the allocation of control over the proceeding to the conflicting parties, in sharp contrast to the fundamental matrix of the continental style – that is, of the 'non-adversary model' or 'inquest model' – where that same control is allocated to non-partisan officials. In the contest model, the prosecution and the defence, in a position of theoretical equality, are responsible for presenting the evidence proving their conflicting positions in front of a passive adjudicator whose function is to ensure – whenever asked to do so – that parties play by the rules. In the inquest model, court officials are in charge of a thorough inquiry and have the responsibility for gathering and evaluating the evidence, the role of the prosecution and the defence in the proof process being marginal and subordinate to the court's function of searching for the truth. Along the spectrum of these two extreme ideal types, any particular system can find a place outside any ideological stance. This new dividing line between criminal procedural traditions, together with a later devised dichotomy based on 'hierarchical' as opposed to 'co-ordinated' organizational structures,[21] helped comparatists to move beyond old intellectual constraints in explaining the internal logic of criminal procedures, and opened up a fruitful dialogue among legal cultures.

9.2.2.2 Reaching maturity

In the wake of Damaška's intuitions, during the decade of the 1970s, comparative research on criminal procedure abandoned the stage of its infancy and – not for the sake of the harmonization of the law, but in a reform-oriented spirit – scholars started to engage in deep comparisons, challenging foreign as well as domestic self-images. The debate that went on in 1977–8 in the pages of the *Yale Law Journal* about comparative prosecutorial discretion – opposing Abraham Goldstein and Martin Marcus on one side and John Langbein and Lloyd Weinreb on the other – gives an early account of the fact that scholars were not willing to accept foreign descriptions of foreign laws without checking them against the operative level. They wanted to go beyond pure narratives and searched for 'dissonances between legal norms and legal

---

[21] M. Damaška, 'Structures of Authority and Comparative Criminal Procedure', (1975) 84 *Yale Law Journal* 480.

operations',[22] without forgetting, however, to put the foreign system in its own institutional and cultural setting, different from the one at home.[23]

Since then the application of such a methodology has underlain the vast majority of the comparative projects, allowing a better understanding of each other's organizing features and the internal logic of the process, opening the way to critical approaches to one's own system[24] and to empirical studies,[25] unveiling unsuspected practices and ideologies,[26] and shedding new light on foreign as well as domestic law, in the awareness that 'each system acts as something of a foil against which to understand the other'.[27]

Over time, comparative criminal procedure scholarship moved beyond a simple reform-oriented approach. It looked for a deeper cross-cultural comprehension of fundamental questions such as the pursuit of the truth in criminal processes;[28] it provided the basis for a shared framework of reference to give practical solutions to problems of transnational co-operation in the investigation of criminal matters;[29] it granted a better understanding of the cultural dynamics at play in international criminal courts, where the

---

[22] A. S. Goldstein and M. Marcus, 'The Myth of Judicial Supervision in Three "Inquisitorial" Systems: France, Italy, and Germany', (1977) 87 *Yale Law Journal* 240, 245.

[23] J. H. Langbein and L. L. Weinreb, 'Continental Criminal Procedure: "Myth" and Reality', (1978) 87 *Yale Law Journal* 1549.

[24] E.g., W. T. Pizzi, *Trials without Truth: Why Our System of Criminal Trials Has Become an Expensive Failure and What We Need to Do to Rebuild It* (New York University Press, 1999); J. H. Langbein, 'Mixed Court and Jury Court: Could the Continental Alternative Fill the American Need?', (1981) *American Bar Foundation Research Journal* 195; Langbein, 'Money Talks, Clients Walk', *Newsweek* (17 April 1995), 32; A. W. Alschuler, 'Implementing the Criminal Defendant's Right to Trial: Alternatives to the Plea Bargaining System', (1983) *University of Chicago Law Review* 931.

[25] E.g., J. Hodgson, *French Criminal Justice: A Comparative Account of the Investigation and Prosecution of Crime in France* (Oxford and Portland: Hart, 2005).

[26] E.g., A. Goldstein, 'Reflections on Two Models: Inquisitorial Themes in American Criminal Procedure', (1974) 26 *Stanford Law Review* 1009; M. D. Dubber, 'American Plea Bargains, German Lay Judges, and the Crisis of Criminal Procedure', (1997) 49 *Stanford Law Review* 547; W. T. Pizzi, 'The American "Adversary System"', (1998) 100 *University of West Virginia Law Review* 847; Pizzi, 'Sentencing in the US: An Inquisitorial Soul in an Adversarial Body?', in J. Jackson, M. Langer, and P. Tillers (eds.), *Crime Procedure and Evidence in a Comparative and International Context* (Oxford and Portland: Hart, 2008), 65; J. Ross, 'Do Rules of Evidence Apply (Only) in the Courtroom? Deceptive Interrogation in the United States and Germany', (2008) 28 *Oxford Journal of Legal Studies* 443.

[27] Hodgson, *French Criminal Justice*, 1.

[28] Already and extensively Damaška, 'Evidentiary Barriers', 578 ff.; Damaška, 'Truth in Adjudication', (1998) 49 *Hastings Law Journal* 289; T. Weigend, 'Is the Criminal Process about Truth?: A German Perspective', (2003) 26 *Harvard Journal of Law and Public Policy* 157.

[29] J. Ross, 'Undercover Policing and the Shifting Terms of Scholarly Debate: The United States and Europe in Counterpoint', (2008) 4 *Annual Review of Law and Social Science* 239.

actors act, react, and understand procedural issues in different ways according to their own different legal tradition.[30]

Scholarly efforts in comparative criminal procedure supplied, therefore, the essential material on which in the last twenty years the European Court of Human Rights (ECtHR) has built a basic common core of criminal procedure rules for European countries. The realignment of European criminal procedures along the lines indicated by the ECtHR, giving rise – according to some scholars – to a unique European 'participatory model' transcending the contest/inquest divide and rooted in a philosophical and political tradition common to both sides of the English Channel,[31] could not have been realized but for the understanding of the different or similar internal logic of the criminal process in different countries provided by comparative scholarship. The recent emerging vast literature on not only European criminal procedure but also worldwide, confirms the growth of the discipline and the increasing need for it.

9.3 Criminal justice and legal transplants

9.3.1 Cases . . .

Since the seminal work of Alan Watson in 1974,[32] legal transplants – that is, the borrowing by a legal system of rules, concepts, and categories from another legal system – have always captured comparatists' attention. Comparative criminal justice represents no exception, and the interest in grasping the dynamics at play in the game of the lending and the borrowing of legal ideas is strongly retained in criminal matters.[33] The criminal justice landscape can be

---

[30] M. Langer, 'The Rise of Managerial Judging in International Criminal Law', (2005) 53 *American Journal of Comparative Law* 837, 864 ff.

[31] J. D. Jackson, 'The Effect of Human Rights on Criminal Evidentiary Processes: Towards Convergence, Divergence or Realignment?', (2005) 68 *Modern Law Review* 737; S. J. Summers, *Fair Trials: The European Criminal Procedural Tradition and the European Court of Human Rights* (Oxford and Portland: Hart, 2007); D. M. Amann, 'Harmonic Convergence? Constitutional Criminal Procedure in an International Context', (2000) 75 *Indiana Law Journal* 809, 818–20, 870; M. Delmas-Marty, 'Towards a European Model of the Criminal Trial', in M. Delmas-Marty (ed.), *The Criminal Process and Human Rights: Towards a European Consciousness* (Vienna and New York: Springer, 1995), 191.

[32] A. Watson, *Legal Transplants* (Edinburgh: Scottish Academic Press, 1974).

[33] E.g., M. Damaška, 'The Uncertain Fate of Evidentiary Transplants: Anglo-American and Continental Experiments', (1997) 45 *American Journal of Comparative Law* 839; M. Langer,

particularly useful in understanding the most basic question related to legal transplants, namely what motivates a legal system to look to a foreign one for adoption of the latter's rules and categories. Differently stated, criminal justice terrain can be very helpful to the intellectual endeavour of explaining why some legal systems export their own ideas and features, being perceived as fascinating and prestigious by others.

Legal hegemony does not appear to be a simple reflection of the military and economic power of a country. On the contrary, it seems to maintain – at least in part – its own autonomous explanation. A rapid glance at legal 'fluxes' in the criminal justice field shows, for example, that the US system (admittedly still the most powerful one, militarily and economically), while being the major exporter of categories and concepts in substantive civil law, does not perform the same role in substantive criminal law. US substantive criminal law culture looks indeed to be more on the importing side, borrowing – since the publication of the Model Penal Code – the building blocks of criminal liability from the (worldwide) hegemonic German criminal law tradition. American scholars' interest in the German theory of crime is obvious in the many criminal law scholarly works that – somehow surprisingly for an otherwise self-centred culture – look at the German experience and engage in a close dialogue with their German counterparts.[34] The American borrowing attitude is especially clear in the works of those prominent and influent American scholars who, subverting the traditional 'holistic'/'one-storey bungalow' common law notion of the criminal offence – 'which treats "actus reus" and "mens rea" as well as any defences to one of those as elements of the same order' – construct instead the crime concept in a German perspective as a 'structured'/'multi-storey house' 'in which one must, in order to reach full punishability, ascend floor by floor to reach the highest level', each floor representing a different grade of criminal involvement.[35] Henceforth, for the sake of accommodating the need to look

'From Legal Transplants to Legal Translations: The Globalization of Plea Bargaining and the Americanization Thesis in Criminal Procedure', (2004) 45 *Harvard International Law Journal* 1; E. Grande, 'Italian Criminal Justice: Borrowing and Resistance', (2000) 48 *American Journal of Comparative Law* 227.

[34] E.g., G. P. Fletcher, *Rethinking Criminal Law* (New York: Oxford University Press, 1978); P. H. Robinson, *Fundamentals of Criminal Law* (New York: Little, Brown, 1988); M. D. Dubber and M. G. Kelman, *American Criminal Law: Cases, Statutes, and Comments* (New York: Foundation Press, 2005).

[35] A. Eser, 'Justification and Excuse: A Key Issue in the Concept of Crime', in A. Eser and G. P. Fletcher (eds.), *Justification and Excuses: Comparative Perspectives* (Huntington, NY: Juris Publishing, 1987), 22, 23.

at the offence in the United States by way of the analytical conceptual framework created in Germany since the beginning of the twentieth century, Paul Robinson – by approaching the crime construction from the back instead of the front[36] – transformed the common law procedural notion of (affirmative) defence into a civilian substantive one;[37] while Markus Dubber rearranged the paragraphs and stretched the words of the Model Penal Code beyond their ordinary sense.[38]

In the area of criminal procedure, however, the US system is a great exporter of legal product, spreading, as it does, its procedural features, such as plea bargaining, jury trials, witnesses' cross-examination, illegally obtained evidence, or hearsay exclusionary rules, and sometimes even the 'fruits of the poisonous tree' doctrine, to western continental Europe, Japan, eastern Europe, the Middle East, and even Africa.[39]

The law of sentencing provides an inverse legal flux different again from the one noticed above on the criminal theory terrain, since the 'three strikes'/'tough on crime' US policy is vigorously travelling and rapidly reaching Europe.[40]

9.3.2 . . . and reasons

While proving that legal transplants can not be credited to the mere economic or military strength of the exporting country, since even the

---

[36] In line with a path also indicated by A. Eser: 'Justification and Excuse: A Key Issue in the Concept of Crime', 24.

[37] P. H. Robinson, 'Criminal Law Defenses: A Systematic Analysis', (1982) 82 *Columbia Law Review* 199; Robinson, *Criminal Law Defenses*, 2 vols. (St. Paul: West, 1984).

[38] M. D. Dubber, *Criminal Law: Model Penal Code* (New York: Foundation Press, 2002); Dubber and Kelman, *American Criminal Law*, 182 ff.

[39] E.g., S. C. Thaman, 'Europe's New Jury Systems: The Cases of Spain and Russia', (1999) 62 *Law and Contemporary Problems* 233; M. Langer, 'Revolution in Latin American Criminal Procedure: Diffusion of Legal Ideas from the Periphery', (2007) 55 *American Journal of Comparative Law* 617; R. Vogler, 'Spain, Criminal Procedure: A Worldwide Study', in C. M. Bradley, *Criminal Procedure: A Worldwide Study* (Durham, NC: Carolina Academic Press, 1999), 361; R. Vogler, *A World View of Criminal Justice* (Aldershot: Ashgate, 2005); M. M. Feeley and S. Miyazawa (eds.), *The Japanese Adversary System in Context. Controversies and Comparisons* (London: Palgrave Macmillan, 2002); U. Mattei, 'The New Ethiopian Constitution: First Thoughts on Ethnical Federalism and the Reception of Western Institutions', in E. Grande (ed.), *Transplants Innovations and Legal Tradition in the Horn of Africa/Modelli autoctoni e modelli di importazione nei sistemi giuridici del Corno d'Africa* (Turin: L'Harmattan, 1995), 111.

[40] M. Cavadino and J. Dignan, *Penal Systems: A Comparative Approach* (New York: Sage, 2006), 11; E. Grande, *Il terzo strike. La prigione in America* (Palermo: Sellerio, 2007); French Loi n. 2007-1198 du 10 août 2007.

most powerful state – namely the United States – is sometimes importing from less powerful ones, this rapid glance at legal fluxes in the criminal justice field asks for a better understanding of the reasons underlying them.

It is the claim of the scientific superiority of a legal scholarship, which is simultaneously metapositivistic in its methodological approach and perceived by foreign scholars as leading within its own borders, that may explain both the spreading since the 1930s of American general legal ideas in substantive civil law matters and the worldwide dissemination over the past century of German criminal law doctrine and theory.[41] Yet it is by invoking a political/philosophical superiority, referring to a still resistant image of the common law adversary model as one of limited state power – therefore better equipped than any other to protect the individual against state abuse – that US government and organizations representatives (such as USAID or CEELI) are nowadays able to promote US criminal procedure in the entire world.[42] Rather than the product of a scholarly endeavour – as in the first case – this second kind of flux seems to be the result of a political and ideological venture, and more than with the diffusion of legal categories or concepts – as in the first kind of flux – it seems to have to do with the circulation of the image and the ideal of a morally superior legal arrangement. Checked against the reality, such an image can nevertheless crumble before the discovery of an actual (and to some extent inevitable) disparity of power between the parties to which procedural control is handed over, so that the US adversary system ideal of a maximum freedom from state interference may easily turn into the reality of a lack of state protection of the weaker party – that is, the defendant – against the mighty one – that is, the prosecutor. Therefore the US adversary model has usually not been taken by other countries in its entirety, and especially not its party-controlled internal logic (i.e. the logic of a trial contest between partisan parties refereed by a passive judge); rather, only some of its features have been exported. This allows receiving states to gain the rhetorical licence of 'morally advanced

---

[41] U. Mattei, 'Why the Wind Changed: Intellectual Leadership in Western Law', (1994) 42 *American Journal of Comparative Law* 195; E. Grande, *Imitazione e diritto. Ipotesi sulla circolazione dei modelli* (Turin: Giappichelli, 2000).

[42] For the vigorous pushing forward of the US criminal procedure model by US governmental agencies in Latin America and East Europe, see Langer, 'Revolution in Latin American Criminal Procedure', 647 ff., and Vogler, *World View*, 172 ff., 177ff.

procedural systems' for which they were looking when importing the foreign model, but at the same time selective acceptance gave them the opportunity to continue to rely on their own mechanism of protection of the individual against state and non-state abuses. In this sense the spirit of a communal search for the truth (the 'rumba' as opposed to the 'tango' model of procedure[43]) typical of the European participatory model mentioned above, keeps alive a different way of protecting defendant's rights, despite acoustic reception of the adversary model in European countries.[44]

Looking back at the past, this same kind of 'symbolic' circulation can also be detected in the inverse circulation of the nineteenth-century French codes from Europe to the United States, which, more than the diffusion of their rules, proved to be the diffusion of the protection of the individual-rights ideal that they represented. By the same token, however, the flux ended up in a mere restyling of the US criminal law system[45] – which had its own, different, way of protecting individuals against judicial legislation – making it, however, able to claim to itself as much as before the entire world the status of a 'morally advanced criminal law system'.[46]

The third kind of legal flux, the one that related to the law of punishment execution and sentences, can finally be associated with the globalization of economic power, rather than with the economic power of one single state. As the vast bulk of studies of the so-called 'prison industrial complex' acknowledge, it is in fact prison corporatization that seems to explain, more than anything else, the spreading of the 'toughness on crime movement' to Europe and elsewhere.

---

[43] E. Grande, 'Dances of Criminal Justice: Thoughts on Systemic Differences and the Search for Truth', in J. Jackson, M. Langer, and P. Tillers (eds.), *Crime Procedure and Evidence in a Comparative and International Context* (Oxford and Portland: Hart, 2008), 145.

[44] For a detailed description of the European participatory model which enhances the defence rights and her participation in the criminal proceeding, while requiring a protective stance towards defendants on the part of those acting on behalf of public authority, see Jackson, 'Effect of Human Rights', p. 759.

[45] 'In the Field Code, the codification spirit had not simply matured, it had died. Having begun with Bentham as, in Sir Arthur Maine's phrase, "the clearing of the brain," it became at the end a rearranging of the attic', notes S. H. Kadish, 'Codifiers of the Criminal Law: Wechsler's Predecessors', (1978) 78 *Columbia Law Review* 1098, 1137.

[46] For further details see Grande, *Imitazione e diritto*, 113 ff, especially 130 ff.

Further reading

C. M. Bradley, *Criminal Procedure: A Worldwide Study*, 2nd edn (Durham, NC: Carolina Academic Press, 2007)

E. Cape et al. (eds.) *Suspects in Europe: Procedural Rights at the Investigative Stage of the Criminal Process in the European Union* (Antwerp: Intersentia, 2007)

G. Corstens and J. Pradel, *European Criminal Law* (The Hague: Kluwer, 2002)

M. R. Damaška, *Evidence Law Adrift* (New Haven: Yale University Press, 1997)

H. R. Dammer and E. Fairchild, *Comparative Criminal Justice Systems*, 3rd edn (Belmont: Thompson-Wadsworth, 2006)

M. Delmas-Marty and J. R. Spencer (eds.), *European Criminal Procedures* (Cambridge University Press, 2002)

M. D. Dubber, 'Comparative Criminal Law', in M. Reimann and R. Zimmermann (eds.), *The Oxford Handbook of Comparative Law* (Oxford University Press, 2006), 1287

P. Fennell, C. Harding, N. Jörg, and B. Swart, *Criminal Justice in Europe: A Comparative Study* (Oxford: Clarendon, 1995)

G. P. Fletcher, *Basic Concepts of Criminal Law* (New York: Oxford University Press, 1998)

G. Fornasari and A. Menghini, *Percorsi europei di diritto penale* (Padua: Cedam, 2008)

E. Grande, *Imitazione e diritto: Ipotesi sulla circolazione dei modelli* (Turin: Giappichelli, 2000), also available in Portuguese, trans. F. Sgarbossa, *Imitação e direito. Hipóteses sobre a circulação dos modelos* (Porto Alegre: Sergio Antonio Fabris, 2009)

J. Hatchard, B. Huber, and R. Vogler (eds.), *Comparative Criminal Procedure* (London: BIICL, 1996)

K. J. Heller and M. D. Dubber (eds.), *The Handbook of Comparative Criminal Law* (Stanford: Stanford Law Books, 2011)

J. Jackson, M. Langer, and P. Tillers (eds.), *Crime, Procedure and Evidence in a Comparative and International Context* (Oxford and Portland: Hart, 2008)

A. Klip, *European Criminal Law: An Integrative Approach* (Antwerp: Intersentia, 2009)

F. Pakes, *Comparative Criminal Justice* (Cullompton: Willan Publishing, 2004)

F. Palazzo and M. Papa, *Lezioni di diritto penale comparato* (Turin: Giappichelli, 2000)

J. Pradel, *Droit Pénal Comparé* (Paris: Dalloz, 1995)

P. L. Reichel, *Comparative Criminal Justice Systems: A Topical Approach* (Upper Saddle River: Pearson Prentice Hall, 2008)

C. Sotis, *Il diritto senza codice. Uno studio sul sistema penale europeo vigente* (Milan: Giuffrè, 2007)

R. J. Terrill, *World Criminal Justice Systems*, 6th edn (Cincinnati: Anderson Publishing, 2009)

S. C. Thaman, *Comparative Criminal Procedure: A Casebook Approach*, 2nd edn (Durham, NC: Carolina Academic Press, 2008)

S. Trechsel, *Human Rights in Criminal Proceedings* (Oxford and New York: Oxford University Press, 2005)

R. Vogler, *A World View of Criminal Justice* (Aldershot: Ashgate, 2005)

R. Vogler and B. Huber (eds.), *Criminal Procedure in Europe* (Berlin: Strafrechtliche Forschungsberichte, 2008)

T. Weigend, 'Criminal Procedure: Comparative Aspects', in J. Dressler (ed.), *Encyclopedia of Crime and Justice*, 2nd edn (New York: Macmillan, 2002), 444

'Criminal Law and Criminal Procedure', in J. Smits (ed.), *Elgar Encyclopedia of Comparative Law* (Cheltenham: Edward Elgar, 2006), 214

C. Van Den Wyngaert (ed.), *Criminal Procedure Systems in the European Community* (London: Butterworths, 1994)

10 Comparative civil justice

Oscar G. Chase and Vincenzo Varano

10.1 Introduction

The civil justice system of every modern state presents a tapestry of intertwined threads. The resulting image reflects the laws providing for redress
of selected grievances, the remedies available to the aggrieved parties, the
institutions available for resolving disputes, and the processes followed by
those institutions. All of these are informed by the fundamental elements of
the society – its political system, its economic arrangements, and its culture.
In this chapter we are concerned primarily with dispute-processing institutions. All modern states have established judicial systems designed to
accomplish the basic tasks of finding the relevant law and applying it in
an efficient and fair manner to the actual facts underlying the dispute. The
differences among them are about how to achieve these goals. We shall
describe significant features of modern systems, discuss the difficulties of
categorizing them, and try to account for the differences among them by
looking at broader issues of politics, culture, and history. We close with
some observations about the future of procedure in an ever-globalizing
world and of the challenges for procedural comparatists.

Before we parse the varieties of disputing in the modern world, we alert
the reader to the tunnel-vision dangers of assuming that 'official' dispute
institutions tell the whole story. Even in the most 'officialized' countries,
informal systems, usually grouped under the catch-all heading of alternative dispute resolution or 'ADR', supplement the formal, court-based processes. Still more is this the case in those societies that have yet to succumb
completely to modernity. As Werner Menski powerfully reminds us, large
groups of people are still at least partially, or even predominantly, oriented

Oscar G. Chase thanks Sarah Brodie, NYU School of Law Class of 2011, for her excellent
research assistance and gratefully acknowledges the financial support of the Filomen
D'Agostino and Max E. Greenberg Research Fund.

towards traditional ways of thought and living.[1] Taking a different path, H. Patrick Glenn argues that the informal law of the less developed world (what he calls 'chthonic' law) is but one of several – perhaps many – legal traditions, including the Talmudic, Islamic, Hindu, civil law, and common law.[2] The dispute processes, or 'civil justice' (as we might call it) of each of these traditions largely mirror the world views of those who are steeped in them.[3]

As we explore the similarities and differences among the dispute process-ing systems of modern legal traditions we are struck by the simultaneous resilience and mutability seen everywhere. Glenn rightly emphasizes the capacity of legal traditions to maintain an essential integrity while absorb-ing the learning of others. 'The interdependence of complex traditions is evident both from the difficulty in defining the starting points of major legal traditions . . . and by the ongoing, major forms of communication and debate between complex traditions.'[4] This suggests the difficulties of plac-ing particular countries in one or another tradition or, as René David and John E. C. Brierley prefer to call them, 'legal families'.[5] One of the most interesting tasks facing the contemporary procedural comparatists is that of at once respecting and challenging the traditional taxonomies. What are these taxonomies and what are their distinguishing features?

The world's modern legal systems are for convenience usually divided into two major groupings, the 'common law' and the 'civil law' countries. The common law family includes England (whence it arose), Australia, Canada, India, the United States, and other countries with historic ties to England. Most other countries share the civil law tradition, which traces its earliest origins to the Roman Empire but then spread throughout continen-tal Europe by virtue of the influence of the great European universities, beginning with the university of Bologna in the eleventh century, and the Catholic Church and its ecclesiastical processes. The adoption of a proce-dural system based on civil law concepts may be the result of prior colo-nialism (as with Latin America) or conscious adaptation from foreign

[1] W. Menski, *Comparative Law in a Global Context*, 2nd edn (Cambridge University Press, 2006).

[2] H. P. Glenn, *Legal Traditions of the World*, 3rd edn (Oxford University Press, 2007).

[3] O. G. Chase, *Law, Culture and Ritual: Disputing Systems in Cross-Cultural Context* (New York University Press, 2005).

[4] Glenn, *Legal Traditions of the World*, 356.

[5] R. David and J. E. C. Brierley, *Major Legal Systems in the World Today*, 3rd edn (London: Stevens & Sons, 1985), 20–31.

systems (as with China, Japan, South Korea, and Russia). Although there are significant differences in the historical development and styles of legal reasoning between the common and civil law systems, most important for this chapter are the differences in the rules that govern disputes in court.

Differences in the rules historically typifying the two systems led to the controversial and misleading labels of 'adversarial' and 'inquisitorial'.[6] Some commentators had come to refer to procedure under common law as 'adversarial' because this system vested a good deal of control over the proceedings in the parties and their attorneys, allowing for a sharper clash of forensic skills in the courtroom. Under the civil law system, on the other hand, process tended to reserve more authority over the lawsuit to the presiding judge, even including responsibility for questioning witnesses; this prompted the 'inquisitorial' label. More contemporary literature, however, sharply criticizes this terminology, in part because the categories are imperfect at best – differences between countries within a category can be considerable. Moreover, the words 'adversarial' and 'inquisitorial' are mischievous in this context, in that the term 'inquisitorial' has an unavoidably pejorative connotation. Modern scholars reject any implication that civil law processes are similar to the infamous Inquisition of the medieval Church, noting that '[t]o Anglo-Americans, ... the two concepts are suffused with value judgments: the adversary system provides tropes of rhetoric extolling the virtues of liberal administration of justice in contrast to an antipodal authoritarian process'.[7] And it is certainly the case that the dispute resolution procedures of all modern states share such fundamental principles as the right to be heard and to present evidence, the right to representation by counsel, and the right to an impartial adjudicator.

Still, from a historical perspective one can identify certain key differences between the common law and the civil law systems. As is well known, the use of a lay jury to decide the facts in civil cases was at the heart of the common law process and explains the main features of that procedure. The concentration, orality, and immediacy of procedure, especially at the proof-taking stage, are certainly related to the presence of the jury. On the civil law side, no significant lay participation similar to the jury has ever been an important aspect of procedure. The fact-finding process has always

---

[6] U. Mattei, T. Ruskola, and A. Gidi (eds.), *Schlesinger's Comparative Law*, 7th edn (New York: Foundation Press, 2009), 786–90.

[7] M. Damaška, *The Faces of Justice and Authority* (New Haven: Yale University Press, 1986), 4.

been entrusted to a professional judge endowed with initiative powers, and the proceedings have been characterized by a piecemeal unfolding, and by the predominance of writing, with a resulting lack of immediacy – that is, the decision was made by an official who had not directly heard the witnesses. Some aspects of these differences remain salient in the contemporary world, although we should bear in mind that uniformity within systems is a thing of the past – if it ever existed. There are as many differences among civil law countries as there are between the English and the US model of procedure (which diverged especially after the virtual abolition of the jury in England, and still further after the sweeping reform of the Civil Procedure Rules of 1998).[8]

Subject to the foregoing reservations, one can identify some 'typical' features of the civil law process that distinguishes it from the common law model: (i) the use of a professional 'career' judiciary, as opposed to the typical common law practice of a judicial appointment after an extensive career at the bar; (ii) the division of the judiciary into discrete subject-matter courts, including not only trial but also appellate stages; (iii) a first-instance process marked by a series of discrete appearances before the judge rather than a concentrated single hearing; (iv) the lack of all but rudimentary forms of the pre-trial discovery so prominent in the United States particularly; (v) the predominance of judicial questioning of witnesses and the concomitant absence of cross-examination by counsel; (vi) judicial selection of expert witnesses; and (vii) 'Supreme Courts' with mandatory jurisdiction.

10.2 Courts

The main components of the machinery for the administration of civil justice are the courts, which are set up to solve disputes and to sentence crimes and misdemeanours according to predetermined procedures. Although the basic scheme of many systems of the administration of justice provides for a set of courts of first instance of general jurisdiction, and often for courts of first instance of limited jurisdiction, one or more intermediate courts of appeal, and one supreme court, there are some variations, even crucial ones, which deserve to be mentioned.

---

[8] On the significance and impact of the English reform, see A. Zuckerman, *Civil Procedure* (London: LexisNexis UK, 2003), ch. 1.

The first variation is presented by those legal systems, typically in the orbit of the civil law tradition, which provide for several separate hierarchies of courts. The basic hierarchy deals with civil and criminal cases. Invariably, due to a more rigid adherence to the principle of separation of powers, there is a separate set of administrative courts which have jurisdiction, generally speaking, over public law disputes – although the criteria for the division of labour between the two sets of courts may vary considerably – and there are legal systems such as that of Germany which, for the sake of specialization, add separate fiscal, labour, and social jurisdictions. In this respect, as in many others, Japan followed the civil law tradition model, but the administrative jurisdiction was abolished by the new Constitution of 1946, which brought about a considerable Americanization of the Japanese legal system.[9] China, in turn, seems to have courts which have various separate divisions. Most of them have the criminal, civil, and administrative divisions, but some courts of general jurisdiction also have other divisions such as the economic, the intellectual property, and the bankruptcy division. There are also over one hundred specialized courts, including railway, forestry, maritime, and military courts.[10]

The second important variation to the scheme concerns the structure and role of supreme courts. While the common law supreme courts, and those of the legal systems which are at least in part in their orbit, such as Japan's, are characterized by a compact, manageable, unitary structure which tends to strengthen their authority and the precedential effect of their decisions, the supreme courts of the civil law tradition are generally composed of several dozen judges (roughly two hundred in France, and four hundred in Italy, for instance), divided into several civil and criminal panels, with the possibility of deciding more important issues or resolving divergences of interpretation in plenary sessions. We return to this structural difference in section 10.7, when we treat appeals.

A third crucial variation is that courts in many legal systems lack the power of judicial review vested in the US courts. Certainly, the American influence was felt in such countries as Japan, where constitutional adjudication is vested in the ordinary Supreme Court, and some Latin American

---

[9] O. G. Chase and H. Hershkoff (eds.), *Civil Litigation in Comparative Context* (St. Paul, MN: Thomson West, 2007, ch. 3, and, with special reference to Japan, esp. 124.

[10] S. B. Lubman, *Bird in a Cage: Legal Reform in China after Mao* (Palo Alto: Stanford University Press, 1999), 251.

countries.[11] However, the dominant model of constitutional adjudication which found its way into post-Second World War constitutions, as well as the constitutions which followed the collapse of dictatorships in Spain and in Portugal, and in the countries of eastern and central Europe formerly in the Soviet orbit, provides for the institution of special constitutional courts. Judges of constitutional courts are generally appointed politically, for a predetermined and usually non-renewable term, and are not necessarily career judges. Access to constitutional courts is by way of judicial referral – that is, referral by a court where a proceeding is pending and the doubt arises as to the constitutionality of a provision to be applied in the case at hand, by way of political initiative – that is, direct actions brought by certain government officials, or by individual recourse for the protection of fundamental rights of the applicant as it happens in Germany with the *Verfassungsbeschwerde*, and in Spain and many Latin American countries (*recurso de amparo*). A solitary position has been occupied for a long time by France, where the Constitution of 1958, as amended, provided for a truly political body, the Constitutional Council, before whom the constitutionality of a statute could be attacked only before its promulgation and only by certain political officials, and, following a 1973 amendment, by a parliamentary minority. A very recent and important evolution is represented by a constitutional amendment of 21 July 2008,[12] according to which access to the Council may also take place by way of referral from the highest courts of the country – that is, the Cour de Cassation and the Conseil d'État – and the legislative provision which will be declared unconstitutional following the referral shall be repealed.

A final variation concerns the selection of judges. As described in more detail in the following section on the legal profession, in most civil law countries the judiciary is staffed by career judges, while in common law regimes judges are chosen from the ranks of experienced attorneys.

This quick comparative introduction to courts cannot be concluded without a reference to a couple of supranational courts, which have a regional, but not for this reason a less important, jurisdiction. One of these courts is the Court of Justice of the European Union. Under the treaty, this court, which sits in Luxembourg and now consists of twenty-seven judges, one

---

[11]   J. H. Merryman, D. S. Clark, and J. O. Haley, *The Civil Law Tradition: Europe, Latin America, and East Asia* (Charlottesville, VA: Michie, 1994), 819.

[12]   Available at www.assemblee-nationale.fr/english/8ab.asp.

from each member state, has a wide jurisdiction such as that on the legality of Community acts, and on violations of Community rules by the member states. By Art. 267 (formerly 234) of the Consolidated version of the TFEU, as modified by the Lisbon Treaty, in force since 1 December 2009, the Court can be asked by national courts, in the course of a proceeding, to give a preliminary ruling on the interpretation of the treaties or the validity and interpretation of acts of the institutions of the Union. A decision of the European Court of Justice (ECJ) binds the court which has referred the question but also other national courts within the EU where the same problem is raised.

The European Court of Human Rights sits in Strasbourg, and is the 'judicial arm' of the European Convention for the Protection of Human Rights and Fundamental Freedoms (the European Convention on Human Rights, ECHR), signed in Rome in 1950 and effective as of 1953. The ECHR has now been ratified by forty-seven states, including Russia and Turkey, and, as a consequence, forty-seven judges presently sit on the court. Any individual who feels that her rights under the Convention have been violated by a state can take a case to the Court, after having exhausted all available domestic remedies. The Court cannot force the states to change their law so as to make it compatible with the European Convention, but it has a high persuasive authority and the power to award damages to the party whose rights have been violated. There is no other international human rights covenant which provides for such a high degree of individual judicial protection.

10.3 The legal professions

The legal profession is essential to the proper functioning of the administration of justice, but it is very difficult, if not impossible, to give in a short space an account of the many significant differences which concern its structure in the various legal systems. First of all, we should perhaps mention the fact that legal education may be graduate and very much professionally oriented, as in the United States and, because of recent reforms, in Japan,[13] or undergraduate, as in the rest of the world. Admission to the practice of law generally requires the passing of a bar examination, and, in many legal systems, a

---

[13] Chase and Hershkoff, *Civil Litigation in Comparative Context*, 93.

period of training and apprenticeship. This is true in civil law legal systems including China (Lawyer Law of the People's Republic of China of 1996, as amended in 2001[14]), Japan,[15] and Russia (according to the new Law on Advocacy of 1 July 2002), but also in those common law systems more strictly connected with England.

The second important observation which we must make is that while the Americans think of the legal profession as a single entity with a considerable amount of lateral mobility,[16] most other legal systems provide for a variety of legal professions, which are quite separate from each other, open only to law graduates, who have to pass a difficult examination and whose initial choice tends to be final. The professions we refer to are that of attorney, notary, and judge.

To begin our description with the judiciary, we must underline that a career judiciary and a bureaucratic selection of judges prevails in the civil law tradition, and in such countries as China (Art. 9 of the Judges Law of the People's Republic of China of 1995 as amended in 2001[17]), whereas in common law countries, and also such countries as Russia (Constitution of Russia, Arts. 119, 128) and Japan,[18] judges are appointed – usually by the executive – from among more experienced lawyers. In the United States the popular election of judges is required in many states, a practice virtually unknown elsewhere.[19] The judges of the US federal courts are appointed by the president, subject to Senate confirmation. Although the independence of judges is a value proclaimed by most, if not all, contemporary legal systems, the reality of a number of them, including China[20] and Russia,

---

[14] D. C. K. Chow, *The Legal System of the People's Republic of China in a Nutshell* (St. Paul, MN: West, 2003), 225–54.

[15] Chase and Hershkoff, *Civil Litigation in Comparative Context*, 89, 93.

[16] J. H. Merryman and R. Peréz-Perdomo, *The Civil Law Tradition: An Introduction to the Legal Systems of Europe and Latin America*, 3rd edn (Palo Alto: Stanford University Press, 2007), 102.

[17] Chow, *Legal System of the People's Republic of China*, 203; J. A. Cohen, 'Reforming China's Civil Procedure: Judging the Courts', (1997) 45 *American Journal of Comparative Law* 793, 795.

[18] Chase and Hershkoff, *Civil Litigation in Comparative Context*, 87–94.

[19] Judicial elections can become problematic because large donations are sometimes made to candidates for judicial office, even by lawyers or persons whose cases may come before the judge elected. Addressing this problem, the Supreme Court has held that under certain circumstances a judge who has received substantial contributions from a litigant must recuse himself from taking part in the case, *Caperton* v. *A. T. Massey Coal Co.*, (2009) 129 S. Ct. 2252.

[20] Cohen, 'Reforming China's Civil Procedure', *passim.*

shows a different picture of a diffuse lack of independence and of corruption of judges.[21]

Throughout the civil law world the notary has for centuries been a very important legal professional, whose similarity to the common law notary public is limited only to the name. The civil law notary must pass a highly competitive exam to enter a profession which enjoys many privileges, including that the number of notarial offices is generally limited. Notaries draft, authenticate, preserve in their office, and release certified copies of many important documents from wills to corporate charters to contracts for the transfer of land. Acts drafted by a notary are called 'public acts' and have a strong evidentiary value, which can be upset only by means of a special proceeding with criminal connotations.[22] As a consequence, notaries are holders of a public office (in China the Public Notary Office is a subordinate agency of the Ministry of Justice[23]), but at the same time they are often private professionals of considerable affluence and high standing in the community.

A typical feature of the profession of attorney in many legal systems, both of common and civil law, has been its division into at least two categories, the parties' agent and representative (the solicitor in England, or the *avoué* in France), and the advocate or barrister pleading in court. However, the present trend is that of unifying the various branches of the legal profession. This has taken place in England, where the two branches have not been fused, but, following the Courts and Legal Services Act 1990, and the Access to Justice Act 1999, barristers no longer have the monopoly on the right of audience before the superior courts, and consequently the monopoly on judicial appointments. Solicitors, in turn, have lost after centuries their monopoly on conveyancing.[24] France, which had traditionally a highly fragmented legal profession, has drastically reduced the categories of professionals: after the enactment of the Law no. 2011–94 of 25 January 2011 – according to which *avoués près la cour d'appel* automatically became *avocats* on 1 January 2012 – the French legal profession will remain with a unified profession of *avocat*, just like most other

---

[21] R. Peerenboom, *China's Long March toward Rule of Law* (Cambridge University Press, 2002), 367–9; X. He, 'Enforcing Commercial Judgments in the Pearl River Delta of China', (2009) 57 *American Journal of Comparative Law* 419, 430.

[22] Chase and Hershkoff, *Civil Litigation in Comparative Context*, 81, 85–6.

[23] http://legalinfo.gov.cn/english/Legal-Service/node_7635.htm.

[24] Chase and Hershkoff, *Civil Litigation in Comparative Context*, 94.

legal systems in the world, and a small group of *avocats* admitted to practise before the highest courts.

Almost everywhere, the legal profession has been rigidly regulated as far as rules of ethics are concerned, as is the salary of lawyers. Some of these rules are now being relaxed, if not abolished, in order to allow for more competition in the delivery of legal services. This phenomenon is particularly interesting in the European Union. On the one hand, the freedom of circulation of persons provided for by the European treaties – freedom of establishment (Art. 49 TFEU), freedom to provide services (Art. 56 TFEU) – has been gradually extended to attorneys as well as to any other private professional. On the other hand, several traditional restrictions on the exercise of the legal profession, such as the prohibition of contingency fee agreements, the prohibition of advertising, and the prohibition or limitation of partnerships, are attenuated if not eliminated. Changes in the attitude towards contingency fee agreements are particularly meaningful. In Italy, for instance, the Law of 4 August 2006, no. 248, has eliminated from Article 2233 of the Civil Code the prohibition of contingency fee agreements. In Germany the Constitutional Court has held unconstitutional the absolute prohibition of contingency fee agreements, and required the German parliament to modify the relevant statute.[25] The reform law was enacted on 12 June 2008.[26] Some commentators report that contingency fees are increasingly used in central European states, and rightly suggest that this general change of attitude towards contingency fee agreements is due to the fact that '[T]he provision of significant government expenditure on legal aid is no longer consistent with the prevailing economic policy.'[27] Contingency fee agreements (i.e. agreements that the lawyer will receive a fee only if the client recovers a judgment) have also been introduced in Russia,[28] while England and France have opted for the conditional fee agreement, under which the client agrees to an increased fee if a judgment is recovered, but which does not make the fee entirely dependent on a favourable judgment, and the 'honoraire complémentaire' respectively, going, at least in part, in

---

[25] BVG, 1BvR2576/04 vom 12.12.2006, www.bverfg.e/entscheidungen/rs/20061212.

[26] BGBl I, 1000.

[27] C. Hodges, 'Europeanisation of Civil Justice: Trends and Issues', (2007) 26 *Civil Justice Quarterly* 96, 107.

[28] S. Budylin, F. E. Gill, and O. Kibenko, 'International Legal Developments', (2008) 42 *International Lawyer* 1083.

that direction, even though the rule prohibiting fees based only on the result to be obtained has been maintained.[29]

10.4 Proceedings of first instance

An important difference in terminology between the common law and civil law systems is the label given to the procedure leading to the decision of the court of original jurisdiction: It is the 'trial' in the common law and the 'first instance proceeding' in the civil. In this chapter we use the latter term to include the former. However one labels them, the proceeding of first instance lies at the heart of any system of civil justice. In principle, it is there that the facts are, or should be, conclusively determined and ascertained, while the higher courts should perform a more limited role of review of first instance judgments.

Historically, as we have already mentioned in the introduction, there are several crucial differences between the common law and the civil law models. The former was certainly shaped since the very beginning by the presence of the jury as adjudicator of the facts. This led, first of all, to a sharp distinction between a pre-trial stage aimed at identifying through a variety of techniques (foremost among them the discovery process) the issues of fact that were in genuine dispute and had to be referred to the jury, as well as at disposing of the controversy prior to trial if possible. The jury's role also mandated a concentrated trial at which the evidence had to be taken and the case decided without indulging in adjournments that would have conflicted with the need of the jurors to go back to their everyday life. The second consequence was the preponderance of oral testimony over written evidence, and the array of exclusionary rules which were meant to protect the jurors from unreliable evidence. The third quite natural feature was that of immediacy – that is, the need for an immediate contact between the jury and the facts and their proofs, without possibility of delegating the taking of evidence to other persons. Last but not least, the judge presiding over the trial had to be passive, so as not to appear to the jury to lean in favour of one of the parties. Nothing like the common law jury has ever characterized the civil law model of procedure. The adjudicator has always been a

---

[29] For England, see §58 of the Courts and Legal Services Act 1990, as amended by §27 of the Access to Justice Act 1999. For France, see Art. 10 of the L.71-1130, as amended.

professional judge, usually entrusted with active initiative powers; the proceeding unfolded in a piecemeal, diluted fashion rather than in concentrated fashion; written evidence prevailed over oral evidence; the decision of the judge was frequently based on evidence taken by other officials, which also served to protect weak judges from intimidation by powerful parties and witnesses. Both systems, on the other hand, have always relied on special proceedings, such as summary proceedings and provisional remedies, often used as short cuts when the outcome was already clear and further proceedings unnecessary.

Against this historical background of profound differences, a quick look at proceedings of first instance in the contemporary world shows what can be considered to be the most important development of civil procedure in recent decades – that is, a clear trend towards approximation or convergence. This phenomenon is even more striking if one considers that, traditionally, the administration of justice, jurisdiction, and rules of procedure have always had strong local connections, and have been identified with the state, its authority, and its physical and political borders. The approximation movement is very clear in the sweeping reform movement which has recently affected many civil justice systems, from England to France, from Germany to Spain, from Japan to Australia, from Russia to Austria, from Switzerland – where a new federal code of civil procedure has been enacted to replace the old cantonal codes effective 2011 – to Norway, and even including the United States. One of the motivations for approximation emerges, for example, in the words of the report accompanying the reform proposal of the Norwegian Code, in force since 1 January 2008: 'It is important that procedure be in principle familiar and understandable also for parties coming from abroad. Courts deal more and more frequently with cases originating in transnational activities which involve non Norwegian parties.'[30]

Even the contrast between an allegedly 'adversarial' common law model, and an allegedly 'inquisitorial' civil law model has lost much of its appeal, as we have previously noted. Both procedural models, beyond the differences which distinguished them historically (foremost among them the jury), share the same fundamental principles (independence and impartiality of the adjudicator; right to be heard, as enshrined among others by Art. 6

[30] NOU 2001, 32, Rett pŒ sak; I. B. Backer, 'The Norwegian Reform of Civil Procedure', (2007) 51 *Scandinavian Studies in Law* 41.

of the European Convention on Human Rights), and attribute the same purposes to civil procedure – the efficient and just dispatch of private disputes. As Professor Jolowicz realistically put it in an article he published in 2003, 'a pure adversarial procedure is no more capable of existing in the real world than a purely inquisitorial one ... the most that can be said is that some systems are more adversarial – or more inquisitorial – than others'.[31]

But let us now turn to some of the trends which show the movement towards the approximation of procedural systems. The first trend shows that the judge is being vested increasingly with an active power of case management, which means the power to handle individual cases in the most appropriate and efficient way. The shift from the parties to the judge of the power to conduct litigation is the essence of the English revolution brought about by the new Procedural Code of 1998,[32] but characterizes procedural reform in other legal systems as well. Case management has become an important aspect of procedural reform practically everywhere in the world, including the United States[33] and Australia;[34] Germany, Austria, and China,[35] which have always been characterized by an active judge;[36] France,[37] Spain,[38] and Russia,[39] whose recent reforms strengthened the

[31] J. A. Jolowicz, 'Adversarial and Inquisitorial Models of Civil Procedure', (2003) 52 *International and Comparative Law Quarterly* 281.

[32] N. Andrews, *The Modern Civil Process* (Tübingen: Mohr Siebeck, 2008), 24–5, 48–53; A. Zuckerman, *Zuckerman on Civil Procedure, Principles of Practice*, 2nd edn (London: Thomson/Sweet & Maxwell, 2006), 32–49, and, in greater depth, ch. 10.

[33] Chase and Hershkoff, *Civil Litigation in Comparative Context*, 28–30.

[34] J. A. Epstein, 'The Quiet Revolution in Australia – The Changing Role of the Judge in Civil Proceedings', in N. Trocker and V. Varano (eds.), *Civil Procedure Reform in Comparative Perspective* (Turin: Giappichelli, 2005), 185, 192–200.

[35] Chase and Hershkoff, *Civil Litigation in Comparative Context*, 49; Cohen, 'Reforming China's Civil Procedure', 794.

[36] In China, however, 'the responsibility for preparing the case, presenting arguments, and examining witnesses has now been transferred primarily to lawyers'. Peerenboom, *China's Long March*, 286.

[37] F. Ferrand, 'The Respective Role of the Judge and the Parties in the Preparation of the Case in France', in N. Trocker and V. Varano (eds.), *Civil Procedure Reform in Comparative Perspective* (Turin: Giappichelli, 2005), 117, 7–32.

[38] I. Díez-Picazo Giménez, 'The Principal Innovations of Spain's Recent Civil Procedure Reform', in N. Trocker and V. Varano (eds.), *Civil Procedure Reform in Comparative Perspective* (Turin: Giappichelli, 2005), 33.

[39] D. Maleshin, 'The Russian Style of Civil Procedure', (2007) 21 *Emory International Law Review* 543.

judge; while countries like Japan have maintained an active role for the judge, although somewhat mitigated by American influence.[40]

The second reform trend is connected to the idea of flexibility. If the goal of civil justice is to guarantee effectively the protection of rights in a reasonable time at a reasonable cost, this goal cannot be achieved through the same model of procedure rigidly conceived as applicable in every case or through special proceedings for particular types of controversy (labour, discrimination, corporate, etc., as is the case in Italy, for instance). It needs, rather, flexibility, it needs different models of procedure to be adopted depending on the peculiar features of each individual case. This is another significant aspect of the English reform, which provides for three different 'tracks' – the small-claims track, the fast track, and the multi-track. The choice between them depends on the amount at stake and the complexity of the case. In order to avoid, then, the choice being made in the abstract, the rules require that the judge, in the exercise of her case management powers, and the parties select the most appropriate track at the initial stage of the proceeding.[41] A similar solution has been adopted also by the French Nouveau code de procédure civile (NCPC), providing for three tracks (*circuits*) – the short, the middle, and the long track. The choice between them depends again on the complexity of the case. The idea of a flexible procedural model has been pursued by a number of other countries in recent reforms, including Germany,[42] Austria,[43] Japan,[44] and Norway.[45]

The need for adequate preparation of the case in view of a concentrated dispositive hearing and to obtain a rapid, rational, and orderly disposition is quite familiar to the common lawyers, but much less so to the civilian lawyers. Civil law countries, in fact, have traditionally dealt with cases in a very protracted way through a series of hearings without any 'precise

---

[40] Chase and Hershkoff, *Civil Litigation in Comparative Context*, 35–45.

[41] Andrews, *Modern Civil Process*, 50–2.

[42] G. Walter, 'The German Civil Procedure Reform Act 2002: Much Ado About Nothing?', in N. Trocker and V. Varano (eds.), *Civil Procedure Reform in Comparative Perspective* (Turin: Giappichelli, 2005), 67–89; P. L. Murray and R. Stürner, *German Civil Justice* (Durham, NC: Carolina Academic Press, 2004), 209–13.

[43] E.-M. Bajons, 'Civil Procedure for Austria Revisited: An Outline of Recent Austrian Civil Procedure Reforms', in N. Trocker and V. Varano (eds.), *Civil Procedure Reform in Comparative Perspective* (Turin: Giappichelli, 2005), 115, 118–21.

[44] Chase and Hershkoff, *Civil Litigation in Comparative Context*, 44.

[45] F. Valguarnera, 'Le riforme del processo civile in Norvegia: qualche riflessione comparativa', (2008) 42 *Rivista trimestrale di diritto e procedura civile* 885, 894–6.

boundaries between preliminary, evidentiary and plenary proceedings'.[46] In
order to reduce delay and achieve the rationalization of the litigation
process, a number of procedural systems are following a third reform
trend and adopting a bifurcated model of procedure (France and Spain,
for instance, or one might also cite Japan or Russia), or consolidating the
multiple stages with the goal of a concentrated final hearing (e.g. Germany
and Austria). The first stage of the proceeding is directed at the preparation
(if not the anticipated solution) of the case, while the second stage, the main
hearing, is dedicated to proof taking and reaching a decision. In order for
the preparatory stage to be effective, strong powers have on the whole been
granted to the judge, whose function is that of clarifying in a timely fashion
the matters in genuine dispute. Some German[47] and Spanish[48] scholars
argue that their respective systems have become very similar to the Anglo-
American systems, with the activities of the main hearing concentrated in a
single event in order to assure immediacy to the proof-taking stage, and
increase the use of orality.[49] Meanwhile, the 'trial' supposedly at the heart of
the common law has been shown actually to be used with less and less
frequency in the United States.[50] While this has many causes, we cannot
neglect the growing emphasis by the US Supreme Court on procedural short
cuts such as dismissals based on inadequate pleadings[51] or insufficient
proof to justify a trial.[52] These developments manifest a move away from
the traditional orality of the US civil trial.

Last but not least, the approach to discovery is changing in the civil law
world – once dominated by the principle that no party has to help her
opponent in her investigation of the facts, and therefore by the lack of
effective instruments capable of eliciting information relevant for the
decision of the case. So, for instance, Article 10 of the French Civil Code,
as amended in 1972, introduces a general duty of procedural disclosure, by
providing that 'each party must bring her contribution to the administration
of justice in view of the ascertainment of the truth', and that the party who

[46] Murray and Stürner, *German Civil Justice*, 14.
[47] Walter, 'German Civil Procedure Reform Act 2002', 71–80.
[48] Díez-Picazo Giménez, 'Principal Innovations of Spain's Recent Civil Procedure Reform', 42–4.
[49] Chase and Hershkoff, *Civil Litigation in Comparative Context*, 8; as to Russia, see Maleshin, 'Russian Style of Civil Procedure', 546.
[50] M. Galanter, 'The Vanishing Trial: An Examination of Trials and Related Matters in Federal and State Courts', (2004) 1 *Journal of Empirical Legal Studies* 459.
[51] *Bell Atlantic Corp.* v. *Twombly*, 550 US 544 (2007).   [52] *Scott* v. *Harris*, 550 US 372 (2007).

defaults without justification can be forced to fulfil her duty through the imposition of an *astreinte*. In turn, Article 11 of the *dispositions liminaires* of the NCPC reaffirms the duty of the parties to contribute to the proof-taking, and specifies that their non-compliance will again be sanctioned with the imposition of an *astreinte*.[53] Even more interestingly, French courts have interpreted Article 145 of the NCPC so as to facilitate the securing of documents from the opponent or a third party before, and independently of, litigation, even beyond the need to conserve or establish facts on which a solution of the dispute may depend.[54] If we turn to Germany, the 2001 amendments of §§142 and 144 have granted the courts the power to order parties or third parties to disclose documents in their possession on the simple basis that they may be relevant to the issues raised for the decision – a nearly revolutionary reform with regard to the German tradition of procedural law.[55] Similar devices have been introduced in the Netherlands and Spain, not to mention Japan,[56] and China, where 'if a party seeks evidence that may be in the custody of the opposing party the party would need to make a request to the court to direct the opposing party to turn over any relevant materials to ensure cooperation'.[57]

Obviously, there remain quite a few differences between the various models of procedure: limiting ourselves to the law of evidence, mention could be made of the preponderance of written over oral evidence in the civil law (but recall the US cases *supra*, moving away from orality). We should mention also the civil law adherence to the principle of free evaluation of evidence (which does not leave too much room for the exclusionary rules of the common law) and its distrust of the parties as witnesses, and, of course, the interrogation of witnesses by the judge rather than through cross-examination. Also, there continue to be differences between procedural systems within the same legal tradition: suffice it here to refer to the differences between the English system, where the jury has practically disappeared from civil cases, and a new revolutionary code has been enacted, and the US system. Nonetheless, legislators throughout the world seem to pursue convincingly objectives of approximation, as we have seen; and there are other forces at work whose goal is to promote the

---

[53] N. Trocker and V. Varano, 'Concluding Remarks', in Trocker and Varano (eds.), *Civil Procedure Reform in Comparative Perspective* (Turin: Giappichelli, 2005), 243, 255.
[54] Ibid., 256–7.   [55] Walter, 'German Civil Procedure Reform Act 2002', 75–7.
[56] Trocker and Varano, 'Concluding Remarks', 255–7.
[57] Chow, *Legal System of the People's Republic of China*, 283.

harmonization of procedural systems. The 'Principles of Transnational Civil Procedure', approved in 2004 by the American Law Institute (ALI) and the Institut International pour l'Unification du Droit Privé/International Institute for the Unification of Private Law (UNIDROIT), are an example of soft law. Their main goal is to provide a uniform process for the solution of transnational controversies, but they pursue an even more ambitious goal, that of offering to legislators worldwide a model for national reform projects, so that the differences between the various procedural systems may be further attenuated. On a regional level, it is undeniable that the harmonization process is taking place also at the level of the European Union. As a consequence, a number of regulations and directives have been issued with effects on the law of procedure of the member states. Among the most important is Regulation 44/2001, which, based on the experience of the 1968 Brussels Convention and the 1988 Lugano Convention, affects one of the aspects of possible greater friction among the various national systems, and pursues the freedom of circulation of civil and commercial judgments by prescribing the rules concerning jurisdiction, recognition, and enforcement of judgments.[58] It is also clear that certain goals of community policy, such as that of enhancing access to justice, are having a remarkable impact on the member states. The change of attitude towards contingency fee agreements, and their spreading throughout the community, is a clear answer to the European demand for more access and the crisis of state-funded legal aid systems; the same is true with regard to ADR or the mechanisms for bringing multiple actions.[59] Last but not least, a pivotal role in the process of harmonization has been played by the remarkable jurisprudence of the ECJ, which has repeatedly stressed the importance of the right to effective judicial protection – a right recognized by the common constitutional traditions of the member states and by Articles 6 and 13 of the ECHR.

10.5 The preclusive effect of judgments

All modern systems have means of insuring finality to valid judgments through rules often referred to as rules of preclusion or *res judicata*. All such doctrines serve some basic goals: avoiding duplicative or inconsistent

---

[58] [2001] OJ L12/1.   [59] Hodges, 'Europeanisation of Civil Justice', *passim*.

judgments, preserving public and private resources, and putting an end to disputes. Nonetheless, there are important variations, and, as we shall see, the differences tend to reflect other features of the procedural system in which they are found and to split along common law/civil law lines.

Any system that allows some prior determinations to affect later cases must include a rule for deciding *which* determinations get preclusive effect. There is wide agreement that parties should not be given a second opportunity to litigate claims that have already been decided,[60] but that generality begs the question of how much similarity there must be before 'claims' are held to be the same. In France and some other civil law countries, claim preclusion is rather narrow, requiring three identities: identity of the object of the suit (roughly the relief sought), identity of the cause (the facts and legal principle that entitles relief), and identity of parties.[61] Germany's relatively restrictive system grants preclusive effect only to the specific claims actually brought and decided. A different view of claim preclusion is taken in Japan, where claims are viewed in terms of the substantive rights that they represent. A plaintiff who has lost an action for tort damages can bring a subsequent suit for unjust enrichment based on the same set of facts, since the two rights represented are distinct. However, a plaintiff who has lost a claim of ownership based on a theory of purchase is barred from asserting ownership based on inheritance, since the underlying right, ownership, is the same.[62]

The most expansive approach to claim preclusion is found in the United States, where a plaintiff is precluded from bringing not only any claims which were in fact adjudicated in a prior action but also those that could have been brought in that action and which arose out of the same transaction, occurrence, or series of transactions or occurrences.[63] The transactional analysis is a pragmatic one which focuses on the connections in time and space between the events in question, as well as the expectations of the parties.[64] This approach encourages claimants to consolidate in one lawsuit all legal claims plausibly arising from a transaction, or related series of

---

[60] Chase and Hershkoff, *Civil Litigation in Comparative Context*, 436–8.
[61] R. H. Field, B. Kaplan, and K. M. Clermont, 'Supplement to Materials for a Basic Course in Civil Procedure', as repr. in O. G. Chase and H. Hershkoff (eds.), *Civil Litigation in Comparative Context* (St. Paul, MN: Thomson West, 2007), 456.
[62] Y. Taniguchi, P. C. Reich, and H. Miyake (eds.), *Civil Procedure in Japan*, 2nd rev. edn (Huntington, NY: Juris Publishing, 2008), §7.09[8][b], [d].
[63] Restatement (Second) of Judgments, §26.   [64] Ibid.

transactions, into one suit. The US approach serves the causes of judicial economy and finality at the expense of the litigant's power to choose how and when to pursue legal claims. Interestingly, Spain, which has recently adopted an entirely new code of civil procedure, has adopted by statute a rule very similar to that in the United States. It gives preclusive effect to all claims that could have been brought in a prior action.[65]

In addition to preventing double litigation of *claims*, most common law countries, including England and the United States, grant preclusive force to some *issues* that are decided in the course of resolving entire claims.[66] This is called issue preclusion, issue estoppel, or collateral estoppel. When applicable, the doctrine prevents parties from relitigating particular issues that have been decided against them in a previous action, even if the previous 'claim' was different from that at issue in the later action. Issue preclusion applies only to issues that were essential to the determination of the first claim, presumably because these are the issues on which the court and parties focused. England's formal doctrine of preclusion is narrower than that of the United States, but the related power to prevent abuse of process gives the English courts discretion to prevent repetitious litigation of both claims and issues, even when preclusion doctrines would not, strictly speaking, be applicable. Civil law countries generally reject any use of issue preclusion.[67] As has been said, Spain, a new and notable exception to this rule, has adopted by statute a system of issue preclusion similar to, but narrower than, that in the United States.

Once we know what kinds of determinations are granted preclusive effect in a particular legal system, a further question arises: what parties are bound? Traditionally, non-parties could neither benefit from nor be harmed by the preclusive effects of prior determinations. This rule is still very much in force in most of the world,[68] with the United States the most notable exception.

In the United States, and to a lesser extent in other jurisdictions, non-parties can benefit from determinations made in prior litigation.[69] This

---

[65] R. C. Casad, 'Issue Preclusion and Foreign Country Judgments: Whose Law?', (1994) 70 *Iowa Law Review* 53, 63.

[66] Zuckerman, *Civil Procedure*, 812.

[67] Murray and Stürner, *German Civil Justice*, 359 (discussing the German rejection of issue preclusion).

[68] Ibid.; Casad, 'Issue Preclusion and Foreign Country Judgments', 63.

[69] Zuckerman, *Civil Procedure*, 805.

practice, known as non-mutual issue preclusion, can be used in two ways. It can be used defensively, for example when a defendant prevents a plaintiff from asserting a claim by using a prior determination obtained by another party against that plaintiff in a different action. An example would be when a defendant in a patent infringement suit invokes a prior suit (to which it was not a party) that found the plaintiff's patent invalid.[70] Non-mutual issue preclusion can also be used offensively in the United States.[71] For example, in a products liability case a defendant manufacturer may be bound by a finding in a previous case that it had negligently designed the product at issue. Under US law an important limitation provides that a person can not be bound by a judgment in a prior case in which she was not a party, because each party is entitled to their own 'day in court'.[72]

A possible explanation for the divergence of views on claim preclusion is the difference in evidentiary rules in common law and civil law countries. Civil law countries allow prior judgments to be used as evidence, obviating the need for the strong formal system of preclusion.[73] Systems that have evolved in reliance on a jury show residual reluctance to treat prior decisions as evidence,[74] and the United States, which still relies heavily on juries, and where avoiding trial altogether is particularly appealing, has developed a particularly robust system of preclusion. Spain's adoption of a US-style preclusion doctrine does suggest that the efficiency-enhancing benefits of preclusion can extend beyond common law systems.

Other aspects of a country's civil practice and procedure necessarily influence its approach to finality. In common law countries, which traditionally used an adjudicative process that imposed time, energy, and monetary costs on the public (in the form of a jury), the parties, and the courts, preclusion is strong. These considerations help explain the particularly expansive scope of preclusion authorized in the United States because of the greater resources parties must expend not only at trial but also in conducting the pre-trial discovery that is such a prominent feature of procedure there. In civil law countries, where civil juries have never been

---

[70] *Blonder-Tongue Laboratories, Inc.* v. *University of Illinois Foundation*, 402 US 313 (1971).

[71] *Parklane Hosiery Co.* v. *Shore*, 439 US 322 (1979).

[72] *Taylor* v. *Sturgell*, 553 US 880 (2008).

[73] Field, Kaplan, and Clermont, 'Supplement to Materials', 12–13.

[74] However, for discussions of the limited use of prior judgments as evidence in the United States and England, see H. Motomura, 'Using Judgments as Evidence', (1986) 70 *Minnesota Law Review* 979, at 982, and Zuckerman, *Zuckerman on Civil Procedure*, 816.

used and large 'pre-trial' expenses are not an issue, rules preventing the re-litigation of some matters are less onerous.

To put the matter in broader context, the aggressive preclusion rules found in the United States seem to go against the grain of the often asserted American individualism and litigiousness. Perhaps the rules arose precisely as a reaction to those very American traits that inform so much of its legal system.[75]

10.6 Mass harms, aggregation of claims, and access to justice

Modern societies are characterized by the massive scale of legal and social relationships. Standardized contracts, the wide dissemination of information, and mass-produced products create the possibility that the rights of numerous individuals will be harmed in similar or identical ways.[76] The traditional modes for vindicating such claims are often impractical because of the expense of litigation, power imbalances between the perpetrator and the victim, or because the wronged party is unaware of the right.[77] Public solutions, too, are often ill suited to address such harms because the harms are too minor to capture the legislator's attention, or because of the forward-looking nature of legislation. Moreover, government actions can themselves be the cause of mass harms through discriminatory or other rights-impairing actions. In the absence of legal institutions suited to dealing with diffuse harms, perpetrators are effectively immunized from redress. The problem can be seen as but one aspect of the broader problem of financial barriers that limit access to justice (discussed below). For many of the same reasons supporting vindication of claims in general – deterrence, compensation, and basic justice – legal systems are finding ways to deal effectively with mass harms. But all such approaches must themselves be respectful of litigant autonomy and the individual's interest in controlling litigation affecting the rights at stake.

[75] O. G. Chase, 'American "Exceptionalism" and Comparative Procedure', (2002) 50 *American Journal of Comparative Law* 277.

[76] M. Cappelletti, 'Vindicating the Public Interest through the Courts: A Comparativist's Contribution', (1976) 25 *Buffalo Law Review* 643.

[77] Ibid., 647.

Societies can respond to mass harms by using legislative or administrative powers or by facilitating litigation by private parties, or as is often the case by some version of each. Mass harms can be addressed by legislation providing for compensation from public or private funds. Such was the legislative response in India to the Union Carbide disaster in Bhopal.[78] There, as in the Japanese response to mass toxic drug exposure torts involving thalidomide, legislation was enacted compensating victims of mass torts.[79] The advantages of governmental, rather than adversarial, resolution are many; legal expenses are reduced if not eliminated, courts are not directly burdened, and remedies can be tailored to achieve equity across the board.[80] These legislative schemes often include ex ante regulation to ensure that similar harms do not occur in the future.[81] The United States, however, has generally been resistant to legislative creation of compensation systems for victims of mass torts.

Another approach is to allow representative private parties to assert the claim in court on behalf of similarly situated victims. The most controversial type of group litigation is the US class action. In a class action, one or more people sue (or, less commonly, are sued) on behalf of a very large group of those similarly situated. The prerequisites for a class action are (1) the class members must be too numerous to make joinder practical, (2) there must be questions of law or fact common to all class members, (3) the claims or defences of the class representative must be typical of the class, and (4) the representatives must fairly and adequately protect the interests of the class.[82] Class actions can involve injunctive relief or monetary damages. Where damages are sought, the requirements for class certification are stricter and each member of the class is entitled to individual notice of the pendency of the action and may opt out of the action. A person who does opt out is not bound by the result and does not share in any eventual settlement or judgment, but those who do not opt out are bound by the judgment according to normal rules

---

[78] L. S. Mullenix, 'Lessons from Abroad: Complexity and Convergence', (2001) 46 *Villanova Law Review* 1, 27.

[79] Ibid.; A. Bernstein, 'Formed by Thalidomide: Mass Torts as a False Cure for Toxic Exposure', (1997) 97 *Columbia Law Review* 2153, 2158–61.

[80] K. R. Feinberg, 'Speech: Negotiating the September 11 Victim Compensation Fund of 2001: Mass Torts Resolution without Litigation', (2005) 19 *Washington University Journal of Law and Policy* 21, 23–6.

[81] Bernstein, 'Formed by Thalidomide', 2158–61.   [82] Fed. R. Civ. Pro. 23(a).

of preclusion.[83] To protect against unfairness to class members, courts are required to examine carefully the putative class before allowing the action to go forward, class certifications can be appealed immediately after they are made, and settlements are subject to judicial scrutiny.[84]

The possibility that the class members will be bound makes the class action extremely powerful, but also creates a potential for abuse. A serious problem is the conflict between the interests of the lawyers for the class and the class members they represent, especially when a defendant offers a settlement that provides generous fees for the plaintiff class's lawyers but only very modest benefits for the class. Conflicts of interest among the class members can also arise and may be so intractable that the court will not allow the action to go forward.[85] Despite these problems, the US class action allows the resolution of claims that would be practically impossible under any other system and is thought to serve as an effective deterrent against certain kinds of wrongdoing, such as securities fraud.

Other features of a country's civil procedure and legal culture will affect which mechanisms it selects to deal with mass claims. In the end, as seems to be the trend in modern systems, most societies will likely use a combination of strategies to deal with mass claims, and there is a contemporary interest in class action-like devices in many parts of the world.[86]

In Germany, a recent scandal involving alleged misleading capital markets information which prompted suits by 15,000 individual claimants led to the creation of a new procedure for dealing with group claims. The new law provides for a test case to be selected and for all the other claims to be stayed pending resolution of the lead case. The original court decides which questions are common, and submits those questions to a higher court. The findings of the higher court are then applied to all the pending cases.[87]

Another type of group litigation, the representative action, has been used in England for over two hundred years, yet it is not particularly common, owing to the restrictive rules governing damages, a general rule that the

---

[83] For an example of a system similar to that in the United States, but in which plaintiff class members are never bound by an adverse judgment, see A. Gidi, 'Class Actions in Brazil – A Model for Civil Law Countries', (2003) 51 *American Journal of Comparative Law* 311.

[84] Fed. R. Civ. Pro. 23.   [85] *Amchem Products, Inc.* v. *Windsor*, 521 US 591 (1997).

[86] Walter, 'German Civil Procedure Reform Act 2002', n. 4; Gidi, 'Class Actions in Brazil'.

[87] Hodges, 'Europeanisation of Civil Justice', 117–18; M. Stürner, 'Model Case Proceedings in the Capital Markets – Tentative Steps Towards Group Litigation in Germany', (2007) 26 *Civil Justice Quarterly* 250, 256–66.

loser pays all litigation costs, and the unavailability of contingent fees.[88] Recent changes to the English Civil Procedure Rules adopt group litigation orders, a judge-driven method of consolidating similar claims and issues. In group litigation orders, the group members must opt in, so that problems with inadequate representation are minimized.[89]

Japan has followed a trajectory similar to England, but has recently gone further, adopting a consumer organization suit[90] similar to those in the European Union.[91] In consumer organization suits, the plaintiff is not an individual acting as a representative, but an entity.[92] The entity can be either public, such as an administrative agency, or private, such as a consumer group. The organization must be authorized by the government to act in such suits,[93] and since individuals are not parties to the suit, they can never be bound by its outcome.

Limitations on collective or class actions raise the question of how ordinary citizens can obtain a hearing of their grievances – that is, of access to justice. Of course, that problem is much greater than when prosecuting relatively small claims. It is still more serious when even substantial claims of rights or damages cannot be pursued for lack of funds. One response is to allow lawyers to charge contingency or conditional fees so that the attorney is paid out of the recovery. Thus even impecunious persons with promising claims can secure an attorney (*supra*, sections 10.2, 10.4). Another, which is

---

[88] E. F. Sherman, 'Group Litigation under Foreign Legal Systems: Variations and Alternatives to American Class Actions', (2002) 52 *DePaul Law Review* 401, 422–4.

[89] Sherman, 'Group Litigation', 422–4; N. Andrews, *English Civil Procedure: Fundamentals of the New Civil Justice System* (Oxford University Press, 2003), 977.

[90] These suits are called consumer injunction suits, but they may seek damages as well as injunctive relief.

[91] Chase and Hershkoff, *Civil Litigation in Comparative Context*, 423.

[92] Sherman, 'Group Litigation', 418–19.

[93] R. H. Dreyfuss, 'Class Action Judgment Enforcement in Italy: Procedural "Due Process" Requirements', (2002) 10 *Tulane Journal of International and Comparative Law* 5, 10. A new damages class action reserved to consumers has been introduced in Italy by Art. 140-bis of the Consumer Code of 2005, as amended by Law No. 99 of 23 July 2009. Arts. 139 and 140 of the same code provided for an injunctive group action to be brought by selected consumers' associations. Art. 140-bis grants standing to sue to individual consumers adequately representing the class; other individuals who wish to avail themselves of the new class action must 'opt in', unless they prefer to bring their individual suits; the action can be brought only before certain courts of first instance of general jurisdiction (Art. 140-bis (4)); the class action will have to be 'certified' by the court in a preliminary hearing; the effects of the judgment do not extend beyond the members of the class. For a positive appraisal of the new provision see R. Caponi, 'Italian Civil Justice Reform 2009', (2009) 14 *Zeitschrift für Zivilprozess International* 143, 154–8.

now very common in Germany, is legal cost insurance that indemnifies litigants for the fee of their own lawyer and for any costs assessed against them for opposing counsel.[94] Some jurisdictions have attempted to reduce the financial barriers to access by making available ADR processes such as mediation and arbitration, and sometimes even mandating their use prior to litigation.[95] But while these 'alternatives' may make rough justice available and dispense with the need for lawyers for certain kinds of disputes, they do not afford equal justice to those who must resort to them because of lack of funds. The traditional safety net for persons needing access to court has, of course, been state-funded legal aid. With the possible exception of Germany,[96] while it remains available in many parts of the world, the sums allocated to funding legal aid are insufficient to meet the actual needs of the poor.[97] Despite aspirational statements by some governments there has been little progress and some retrogression due to political and economic challenges beginning in the 1990s.[98] We note that significant funding increases have been discussed in several major countries[99] and – we hope – may some day bear fruit.

10.7 Appeals

Although appeals serve the goals of error correction and uniformity of law in all systems, appellate procedures vary greatly, especially when one compares common and civil law countries. The variations are most stark in three areas: (1) the structure of appellate courts, (2) the right to appeal, and (3) the scope of review.

As we discussed in section 10.2, the structural contrast between common and civil law appellate courts is one of unity versus specialization. In common law systems, appellate courts have general subject matter jurisdiction. These courts can review all types of disputes, civil and criminal.[100]

---

[94] Murray and Stürner, *German Civil Justice*, 123–5.

[95] Chase, *Law, Culture and Ritual*, 94–102; U. Mattei, 'Access to Justice: A Renewed Global Issue?', in K. Boele-Woelki and S. van Erp (eds.), *General Reports to the XVIIth Congress of the International Academy of Comparative Law* (Brussels: Bruylant, 2007), 398–403.

[96] Murray and Stürner, *German Civil Justice*, 116–23.

[97] Hodges, 'Europeanisation of Civil Justice', 98–100; Mattei, 'Access to Justice', 403–6.

[98] Hodges, 'Europeanisation of Civil Justice', 98–100.

[99] Mattei, 'Access to Justice', 403–6.

[100] Chase and Hershkoff, *Civil Litigation in Comparative Context*, 1067.

Civil law systems often divide cases according to subject matter and funnel them into specialized courts, both of first instance and of appeal.

Although almost all jurisdictions allow one appeal from first instance as of right (England being a notable exception), appeal to the highest court is a matter of right only in civil law countries. It is contrariwise dependent on the grant of discretionary review in common law systems. Guaranteed access to the highest court of any jurisdiction predictably leads to an enormous caseload staffed by many judges who perforce sit on panels or 'senates' that constantly struggle against excessive backlogs. These problems have led to reforms in a few countries aimed at reducing the volume of cases at the highest level of appeal. Spain recently limited appeal by right to controversies over a certain value, where the appeal deals with fundamental rights, or where the decision below contrasts with the case law of the highest court. Germany, too, has tightened its appellate leave-granting, with the highest court now enjoying substantial discretion in deciding which cases to accept, and is now approaching the level of discretion that common law courts have always enjoyed.[101] In Italy, a statute of 2009 allows the court of cassation to dispose of cases peremptorily, when the challenged decision has decided the issues of law consistently with the jurisprudence of the court, and examination of the grounds of the appeal does not offer elements to confirm or amend the same opinion. Although it is still too early to tell how significant the change will be, it does not seem likely that the new law is going to solve the problem of the workload of the court.[102]

In the US federal system, appeals to the highest court are subject to the discretion of the Supreme Court, which is extremely selective, typically granting leave to appeal in fewer than 3 per cent of cases in which it is sought.[103] England, on the other hand, has no appeal by right. Even intermediate appellate courts generally grant leave to appeal only where the appeal has a real chance of success or there is another public interest in granting the appeal.[104]

---

[101] Trocker and Varano, 'Concluding Remarks', 265.

[102] Law No. 69 of 18 June 2009, in *Gazzetta Ufficiale*, n. 140 of 19 June 2009. See Caponi, 'Italian Civil Justice Reform 2009', 150. For a more optimistic view see M. De Cristofaro and N. Trocker (eds.), *Civil Justice in Italy*, Nagoya University Comparative Study of Civil Justice 8 (Tokyo: Jigakusha, 2010), 248–50.

[103] A. B. Morrison, 'Litigation', in A. B. Morrison (ed.), *Fundamentals of American Law* (New York: Oxford University Press, 1996), 61–82.

[104] Zuckerman, *Zuckerman on Civil Procedure*, §23.5.

The final area of variation in appellate procedure concerns the scope of review exercised. Common law countries, which evolved with the jury as fact finder, generally do not allow appellate courts to disturb findings of fact made by the trial court. Review is confined to the law, and is based entirely on the written record.[105] No new evidence or pleadings are permitted.[106] In most civil law systems, on the other hand, there is an intermediate court, which considers both fact and law, and a high court. Traditionally, the highest courts in civil law countries were courts of *cassation*. Courts of cassation typically consider only questions of law, and, instead of replacing the defective decision of the lower court with a decision of their own, they simply quash it.[107] There are also high courts of *revision*, which similarly consider only law, but which replace the defective decision below with a new decision. Recent reforms have blurred the distinction.[108]

Civil law courts vary with regard to the scope of appellate review permitted, with some countries allowing for what amounts to a re-hearing of the case, and others following a stricter approach and relying almost exclusively on the record (e.g. Portugal and Austria). New evidence is often admitted, with restrictions of varying degree.[109]

10.8 Conclusion

A leitmotif of this chapter and of contemporary comparative procedure law scholarship is the approximation (or 'harmonization') of procedural systems. In part this is an aspirational theme, exemplified by the ALI/ UNIDROIT Principles of Transnational Civil Procedure. It is also, however, descriptive. Distinguished scholars have observed a variety of points on which representatives of the common law and civil law traditions are converging. This has led some to question not only the well-undermined distinction between 'adversarial' and 'inquisitorial' systems but the continuing utility of the common law/civil law categories, at least where

---

[105] American Law Institute, *Principles of Transnational Civil Procedure* (Cambridge University Press, 2004), 47.

[106] Morrison, 'Litigation', 79.

[107] J. A. Jolowicz, 'Introduction: Recourse against Civil Judgments in the European Union: A Comparative Survey', in J. A. Jolowicz and C. H. van Rhee (eds.), *Recourse against Judgments in the European Union* (The Hague: Kluwer Law International, 1999), 2.

[108] Ibid., 4.   [109] Ibid., 9–10.

procedure is concerned.[110] In section 10.4, 'Proceedings of first instance', we observed an increasing role for the judge in the supposedly 'adversarial' systems, a trend towards concentrated hearings in the civil law world, and even, in the latter, tentative steps towards involuntary 'discovery' by the litigants. But it is not the case that every common law system has changed in exactly the same way or that every civil system (whether Romanist or Germanic in orientation) has adopted the same features of the traditional common law process. The outcome of some of the more radical reforms of civil justice systems could well be described as diversifying in some respects, even as approximation proceeds in other regards. The United States in particular has often gone its own way and in many respects remains an outlier. In any event, the two paradigms that have shaped comparative procedural thinking for centuries no longer have the descriptive or normative power that has in the past been both useful shorthand and an obscurant over-generalization. As some common law/civil law systems become more like each other, it is arguable that they at the same time become (ironically) less like their formerly fellow-category constituents. These developments raise important and as yet unresolved questions for scholars of procedure, including the basic question whether the categories remain descriptively valid and helpful or have become misleading barriers to understanding.

Further reading

American Law Institute, *Principles of Transnational Civil Procedure* (Cambridge University Press, 2004)

N. Andrews, *English Civil Procedure: Fundamentals of the New Civil Justice System* (Oxford University Press, 2003)

The Modern Civil Process (Tübingen: Mohr Siebeck, 2008)

I. B. Backer, 'The Norwegian Reform of Civil Procedure', (2007) 51 *Scandinavian Studies in Law* 41

E.-M. Bajons, 'Civil Procedure for Austria Revisited: An Outline of Recent Austrian Civil Procedure Reforms', in N. Trocker and V. Varano (eds.), *Civil Procedure Reform in Comparative Perspective* (Turin: Giappichelli, 2005), 115

[110] O. G. Chase and J. Walker, 'Common Law, Civil Law, and the Future of Categories: An Introduction', in J. Walker and O. G. Chase (eds.), *Common Law, Civil Law, and the Future of Categories* (Markham, Ontario: LexisNexis Canada, 2010), 1.

A. Bernstein, 'Formed by Thalidomide: Mass Torts as a False Cure for Toxic Exposure', (1997) 97 *Columbia Law Review* 2153

S. Budylin, F. E. Gill, and O. Kibenko, 'International Legal Developments', (2008) 42 *International Lawyer* 1083

W. Burnham and A. Trochev, 'Russia's War between the Courts: The Struggle over the Jurisdictional Boundary between the Constitutional Court and Regular Courts', (2007) 55 *American Journal of Comparative Law* 381

R. Caponi, 'Italian Civil Justice Reform 2009', (2009) 14 *Zeitschrift für Zivilprozess International* 143

M. Cappelletti, 'Vindicating the Public Interest through the Courts: A Comparativist's Contribution', (1976) 25 *Buffalo Law Review* 643

R. C. Casad, 'Issue Preclusion and Foreign Country Judgments: Whose Law?', (1994) 70 *Iowa Law Review* 53

'Issue Preclusion in the Law of Spain: Cosa Juzgada Positiva', in J. A. R. Nafziger and A. T. von Mehren (eds.), *Law and Justice in a Multistate World* (Ardsley, NY: Transnational, 2002), 595

O. G. Chase, 'American "Exceptionalism" and Comparative Procedure', (2002) 50 *American Journal of Comparative Law* 277

Law, Culture, and Ritual: Disputing Systems in Cross-Cultural Context (New York University Press, 2005)

O. G. Chase and H. Hershkoff (eds.), *Civil Litigation in Comparative Context* (St. Paul, MN: Thomson West, 2007)

O. G. Chase and J. Walker, 'Common Law, Civil Law, and the Future of Categories: An Introduction', in J. Walker, and O. G. Chase (eds.), *Common Law, Civil Law, and the Future of Categories* (Markham, Ontario: LexisNexis Canada, 2010)

D. C. K. Chow, *The Legal System of the People's Republic of China in a Nutshell* (St. Paul, MN: West, 2003)

J. A. Cohen, 'Reforming China's Civil Procedure: Judging the Courts', (1997) 45 *American Journal of Comparative Law* 793

R. David and J. E. C. Brierley, *Major Legal Systems in the World Today*, 3rd edn (London: Stevens & Sons, 1985)

M. Damaška, *The Faces of Justice and Authority* (New Haven: Yale University Press, 1986)

M. De Cristofaro and N. Trocker, *Civil Justice in Italy*, Nagoya University Comparative Study of Civil Justice 8 (Tokyo: Jigakusha, 2010)

I. Díez-Picazo Giménez, 'The Principal Innovations of Spain's Recent Civil Procedure Reform', in N. Trocker and V. Varano (eds.), *Civil Procedure Reform in Comparative Perspective* (Turin: Giappichelli, 2005), 33

R. H. Dreyfuss, 'Class Action Judgment Enforcement in Italy: Procedural "Due Process" Requirements', (2002) 10 *Tulane Journal of International and Comparative Law* 5

J. A. Epstein, 'The Quiet Revolution in Australia – The Changing Role of the Judge in Civil Proceedings', in N. Trocker and V. Varano (eds.), *Civil Procedure Reform in Comparative Perspective* (Turin: Giappichelli, 2005), 185

K. R. Feinberg, 'Speech: Negotiating the September 11 Victim Compensation Fund of 2001: Mass Torts Resolution without Litigation', (2005) 19 *Washington University Journal of Law and Policy* 21

J. E. Ferejohn, 'Constitutional Review in the Global Context', 6 *New York University Journal of Legislation and Public Policy* 49 (2003)

F. Ferrand, 'The Respective Role of the Judge and the Parties in the Preparation of the Case in France', in N. Trocker and V. Varano (eds.), *Civil Procedure Reform in Comparative Perspective* (Turin: Giappichelli, 2005), 117

R. H. Field, B. Kaplan, and K. M. Clermont, 'Supplement to Materials for a Basic Course in Civil Procedure', as repr. in O. G. Chase and H. Hershkoff (eds.), *Civil Litigation in Comparative Context* (St. Paul, MN: Thomson West, 2007)

M. Galanter, 'The Vanishing Trial: An Examination of Trials and Related Matters in Federal and State Courts', (2004) 1 *Journal of Empirical Legal Studies* 459

A. Gidi, 'Class Actions in Brazil – A Model for Civil Law Countries', (2003) 51 *American Journal of Comparative Law* 311

H. P. Glenn, *Legal Traditions of the World*, 3rd edn (Oxford University Press, 2007)

X. He, 'Enforcing Commercial Judgments in the Pearl River Delta of China', (2009) 57 *American Journal of Comparative Law* 419

C. Hodges, 'Europeanisation of Civil Justice: Trends and Issues', (2007) 26 *Civil Justice Quarterly* 96

J. A. Jolowicz, 'Adversarial and Inquisitorial Models of Civil Procedure', (2003) 52 *International and Comparative Law Quarterly* 281

'Introduction: Recourse against Civil Judgments in the European Union: A Comparative Survey', in J. A. Jolowicz and C. H. van Rhee (eds.), *Recourse against Judgments in the European Union* (The Hague: Kluwer Law International, 1999), 1

H. Kštz, 'Civil Justice Systems in Europe and the United States', (2003) 13 *Duke Journal of Comparative and International Law* 61

S. B. Lubman, *Bird in a Cage: Legal Reform in China after Mao* (Palo Alto: Stanford University Press, 1999)

D. Maleshin, 'The Russian Style of Civil Procedure', (2007) 21 *Emory International Law Review* 543

U. Mattei, 'Access to Justice. A Renewed Global Issue?', in K. Boele-Woelki and S. van Erp (eds.), *General Reports to the XVIIth Congress of the International Academy of Comparative Law* (Brussels: Bruylant, 2007), 398

U. Mattei, T. Ruskola, and A. Gidi (eds.), *Schlesinger's Comparative Law*, 7th edn (New York: Foundation, 2009)

W. Menski, *Comparative Law in a Global Context*, 2nd edn (Cambridge University Press, 2006)

J. H. Merryman and R. Pérez-Pérdomo, *The Civil Law Tradition: An Introduction to the Legal Systems of Europe and Latin America*, 3rd edn (Palo Alto: Stanford University Press, 2007)

J. H. Merryman, D. S. Clark, and J. O. Haley, *The Civil Law Tradition: Europe, Latin America, and East Asia* (Charlottesville, VA: Michie, 1994)

A. B. Morrison, 'Litigation', in A. B. Morrison (ed.), *Fundamentals of American Law* (New York: Oxford University Press, 1996)

H. Motomura, 'Using Judgments as Evidence', (1986) 70 *Minnesota Law Review* 979

L. S. Mullenix, 'Lessons from Abroad: Complexity and Convergence', (2001) 46 *Villanova Law Review* 1

P. L. Murray and R. Stürner, *German Civil Justice* (Durham, NC: Carolina Academic Press, 2004)

R. Peerenboom, *China's Long March toward Rule of Law* (Cambridge University Press, 2002)

M. Reimann and R. Zimmermann (eds.), *The Oxford Handbook of Comparative Law* (Oxford University Press, 2006)

E. F. Sherman, 'Group Litigation under Foreign Legal Systems: Variations and Alternatives to American Class Actions', (2002) 52 *DePaul Law Review* 401

M. Stürner, 'Model Case Proceedings in the Capital Markets – Tentative Steps towards Group Litigation in Germany', (2007) 26 *Civil Justice Quarterly* 250

Y. Taniguchi, 'Japan's Recent Civil Procedure Reform: Its Seeming Success and Left Problems', in N. Trocker and V. Varano (eds.), *Civil Procedure Reform in Comparative Perspective* (Turin: Giappichelli, 2005), 91

Y. Taniguchi, P. C. Reich, and H. Miyake (eds.), *Civil Procedure in Japan*, 2nd rev. edn (Huntington, NY: Juris, 2008)

N. Trocker and V. Varano, 'Concluding Remarks', in N. Trocker and V. Varano (eds.), *Civil Procedure Reform in Comparative Perspective* (Turin: Giappichelli, 2005), 243

N. Trocker and V. Varano (eds.), *Civil Procedure Reform in Comparative Perspective* (Turin: Giappichelli, 2005)

F. Valguarnera, 'Le riforme del processo civile in Norvegia: qualche riflessione comparativa', (2008) 42 *Rivista trimestrale di diritto e procedura civile* 885

G. Walter, 'The German Civil Procedure Reform Act 2002: Much Ado about Nothing?', in N. Trocker and V. Varano (eds.), *Civil Procedure Reform in Comparative Perspective* (Turin: Giappichelli, 2005), 67

A. Zuckerman, *Civil Procedure* (London: LexisNexis UK, 2003)

Zuckerman on Civil Procedure, Principles of Practice, 2nd edn (London: Thomson/Sweet & Maxwell, 2006)

K. Zweigert and H. Kötz, *Introduction to Comparative Law*, trans. T. Weir 3rd rev. edn (Oxford: Clarendon; New York: Oxford University Press, 1998)

Comparative law and international organizations

George A. Bermann

The term 'international organization' covers a wide field, from the International Red Cross to the Food and Agricultural Organization, the World Trade Organization and the European Union. The place of comparative law in the establishment and functioning of these institutions will thus vary greatly according to the organization. It is nevertheless possible to identify certain recurring aspects relating to the establishment, functioning, and control of international organizations in which comparative law has an actual or potential role to play. This is unsurprising because law itself is present in all these dimensions of international organization activity.

First, international organizations themselves represent the result of decisions of both a legal and a political character. Second, international organizations, once created, become legally anchored within one legal system or another, the characteristics of which must be understood by all who may come into contact with it. Third, international organizations commonly engage in prescriptive or normative activity by which secondary law (i.e. law generated by the organization as distinct from the law that created the organization itself) comes into being. Fourth, some of the most important international organizations from a legal point of view have as a mission the developing of draft treaties that are intended to be signed and ratified by a sufficient number of states to come into force or the production of model legislation that national legislatures may enact into law. Fifth, whether an international organization generates legal norms or engages in a quite different set of activities, it is more likely than not operating according to a more or less formal set of procedures that may either have been prescribed for the organization on its founding or established by the organization itself as and when it began conducting its activities. In either case, for the organization itself, those procedures very much constitute law. Sixth, more and more international organizations perform adjudicatory functions, which require that they both apply legal norms and observe legal procedures. Seventh, and finally, international organizations may be subject to external legal norms that further constrain their freedom of action.

To the extent that law figures in these and other ways in the landscape in which international organizations operate, comparative law also stands to come into play. By definition, an international organization draws members from a multiplicity of legal systems, and if it produces effects of any kind, those effects will likewise be felt within a multiplicity of legal systems.

In the chapter that follows, numerous international organizations will be mentioned by way of example. However, because, among international organizations, the European Union has developed into perhaps the most fully developed and legally potent among them, it will receive more frequent mention than others.

11.1 The structure and legal status of international organizations

Whatever the political or economic impetus for their formation may have been, international organizations invariably come into being through international legal acts of one kind or another – typically directly by treaty or international convention between states, or by an act of another international organization that is itself the product of a treaty or international convention between states. That being the case, comparative law will have been present at the organization's birth. The architects of the international instrument that gave rise to the international organization will have negotiated and drafted that instrument, bringing or attempting to bring to bear on that occasion legal notions – institutions, principles, and ideas – redolent of the legal systems in which they have been trained and have operated.

The Treaty Establishing the European Community, entered into initially by six European states, was the product of precisely such an international deliberative process.[1] As it happens, all six were continental European states that had developed in the civil law tradition (five of them sharing the French civil law tradition and a single one – the then West Germany – following the Germanist civil law tradition). Accordingly, divergences in legal tradition among the founding states were muted as compared with those found among international organizations having a wider and more legally diverse membership. The dominance among the six of French legal tradition, French legal institutions, and even the French language came to

---

[1] Treaty Establishing the European Economic Community, 25 March 1957, 298 UNTS 11.

be reflected in the shape and workings of the European Communities' own basic institutions. A pervasive understanding of French law through the lens of comparative law smoothed the way for the acceptance of the French model for this new multi-national organization.

11.2 International organizations and their immediate legal environment

All international organizations are centred in a geographic location, and the law of that place is obviously critical for many purposes. For example, when persons or entities located in other jurisdictions do business with such an organization, they must take due account of the legal regime under which the organization was created and operates. For these persons and entities, comparative law is an essential tool. The case of antitrust litigation in the United States against the Organization of the Petroleum Exporting Countries (OPEC) provides a perfect illustration. American plaintiffs bringing an antitrust action against OPEC in a US court for price-fixing of oil discovered that in order to serve process validly on OPEC, even under US procedural law, it was necessary to serve process in a fashion that was legal in OPEC's place of incorporation, namely Austria. Because Austrian law immunized OPEC from service of process, service in the US action could not be validly performed, and the lawsuit for that reason alone failed.[2]

In this particular respect, it is true, international organizations are no different from any foreign entities. The moment that the functioning of any party – public or private – transcends national borders, multiple bodies of law potentially enter into play. When a transaction involves an international organization, both it and the parties that deal with it find themselves essentially within the domain of private international law (or conflict of laws).

The moment private international law is engaged, so, too, is comparative law. The powerful dependence of private international law on the discipline of comparative law is well established and documented elsewhere in this volume. Suffice it here to say that any transaction involving actors from, or interests of, multiple legal orders generates questions about the applicable law, about the reach of national courts in disputes arising out of that transaction, and about the legal weight and effect in one jurisdiction of

---

[2] *Prewitt Enterprises* v. *OPEC*, 353 F 3d 916 (2003).

decisions rendered in another. Comparative law is the discipline that informs all decision-making processes in private international law.

To revert to the European Union example, consider the lawsuit initiated by the European Commission in a US court against a number of cigarette manufacturers for illegal smuggling of tobacco products into the EU and avoidance of member state taxation.[3] The EU had, among other things, to understand the unusual statute – the Racketeering Influenced and Corrupt Organizations Act (RICO)[4] – under which the action could be brought. It had also to determine whether the institution of litigation on a contingent fee basis and in pursuit of treble damages, as provided for by RICO, could be sufficiently squared with European legal practices and principles to go forward. And it had to determine whether such an action which, if successful, would yield a judgment measured in part by the member states' lost taxes, could be sufficiently likened to a suit by one state to collect taxes in the courts of another state, as ostensibly prohibited by the so-called 'revenue rule'. For its part, the US court had, among other things, to determine whether the Commission had 'constitutional' authority within the EU system to bring such an action and whether, since revenues are collected by the member states rather than the EU itself, the EU suffered injury in fact and thus earned standing within the meaning of that term in the US litigation system.

11.3 Norm production by international organizations

Comparative law perhaps enters most meaningfully into play in the workings of international organizations when those organizations are engaged in prescriptive activity – that is to say, law-making or other modes of norm production. The extent and depth to which an organization delves into comparative law depends therefore on the level and intensity of its engagement in prescriptive work, which in turn depends on the organization's mission.

The notion of law-making in the context of international organizations must be understood very broadly. Relatively few international organizations have recognized authority to enact prescriptive measures that are automatically legally binding within the legal orders of the participating states. UNIDROIT's Principles of International Commercial Contracts, for

---

[3] *European Community* v. *RJR Nabisco*, 424 F 3d 175 (2005).
[4] Racketeer Influenced and Corrupt Organizations Act, 18 USC §§1961–8.

example, lack immediate legal effect. More often, such measures have a somewhat less direct effect within national legal orders. They may be incorporated by reference by national legislators or regulators. They may be enforced by arbitrators in the absence of a designated applicable law. They may be treated as a kind of 'safe harbour' in the sense that any product or service meeting the standards set by those measures will be deemed to satisfy national requirements. They may constitute 'soft law', in every sense of the word, meaning that they may simply be used as benchmarks for assessing the adequacy of national measures, or voluntarily complied with by private actors, or incorporated by reference in private agreements.[5]

Let us take a classic standard-setting organization, such as the Food and Agriculture Organization (FAO). Its mission is to establish standards of food safety. Those standards are not immediately applicable, in a binding sense, to countries around the world. But they operate as important benchmarks. Countries may adopt FAO standards as domestic law, enforcing them as such. They may declare that food products meeting FAO standards shall be automatically deemed to meet the domestic food safety standards that otherwise exist within that jurisdiction.

Take the further exotic example of the conservation of whale species. How many whales may be taken in any given period? Are there any species of whale that, for reasons of biodiversity, may not be taken? Is there a point in time in the life of a whale before which the killing of whales is prohibited? Are there humanitarian limits on the methods by which whales may be killed? Participating states have law and policy on these matters, and the differences among them must somehow be bridged if universally agreed-on norms are to emerge.

In the deliberations within international organizations that result in the adoption of norms, policy differences will invariably occupy centre stage. Depending on the subject, the outcomes may be in great part science-driven and/or value-driven. But to the extent that policy differences of any nature are embedded in existing legal norms and traditions within the participating states, comparative law becomes once again a tool of choice in the gauging of commonalities and differences that is critical to the harmonization process. The standards that are set within an international organization like the FAO – or any number of others such as the International Civil Aviation Organization

---

[5] See J. Alvarez, *International Organizations as Law-Makers* (New York: Oxford University Press, 2005), 217–44.

(ICAO) or the World Intellectual Property Organization (WIPO) – are or should be set in consideration of the laws that already exist in the participating jurisdictions. International harmonization of law is a subject in itself.

A question of particular interest in this regard is where standards will ultimately end up being set when participating states enter into discussions with disparate domestic law and policy on the subject. Many different scenarios are possible. Producers of norms within international organizations may settle for what might be called a least common regulatory denominator, because they want the widest possible participation among states. Alternatively, they may aspire to the standard of the state entering the deliberations with the highest existing domestic standards, although the ability to achieve that will depend on the relative power among the states and the voting formula. Then, too, some sort of middle ground or compromise may be reached. Unless and to the extent that the charter of the organization designates one of these as the standard-setting measure, the organization will, through the operation of its internal decision-making rules, set the bar where its members and its leadership see fit to do so.

The essential point is that norm production by international organizations for any of the above purposes entails the establishment of substantive standards on the subject at hand that are ultimately agreeable as a legal and policy matter to the membership, or a sufficient fraction of the membership, of the organization. It is impossible to generalize as to how differences in law and policy among the membership of an international organization are bridged in order to arrive at a set of standards agreeable to all. The outcome may depend on the voting system within the organization. In an entity like the European Union, which has a well-defined legislative process, with weighted voting and a requirement of a mathematical qualified majority rather than unanimity for the passage of legislation, it is the particular line-up of states on any given legislative proposal that will determine the level of protection that the measure will ultimately end up establishing. In a great many other settings, the organization will act prescriptively only by consensus among its members.

11.4 International organizations as sponsors of treaties and draft legislation

Within the field of law as such, one of the most prominent international organization activities that takes place is treaty-making. This sort of activity is distinctive because it does not merely produce policy standards of the sort described in the previous section, but produces fully fledged legal texts which have the force of law that national attitudes towards international treaties allow. The Hague Conference on Private International Law (which has produced an impressive number of private international law treaties) and the Council of Europe (which produced the European Convention on Human Rights) typify such bodies.

The legal weight carried by the treaties resulting from this process within domestic law will vary with the national legal orders. The treaties may present themselves and be received as self-executing once signed and ratified, or they may require statutory transposition at the national level before becoming effective, and thus become effective only when and to the extent that they are transposed.

Sometimes, what emerges from international organization activity of this sort is not, and was perhaps never meant to be, a treaty at all. The organization may content itself with producing what aims to be nothing more than a model statute that states may or may not adopt, with or without modification, but nevertheless an instrument that, to the extent adopted, greatly enhances the international harmonization of law. The UNCITRAL Model Law of International Commercial Arbitration is an excellent example. Alternatively, the organization may content itself with producing a comprehensive statement or restatement of the law that is neither treaty nor model law, but a kind of 'soft law' that may be incorporated by reference in contracts, may be reverted to by international arbitrators who are not bound to apply a particular national law, or serve as an inspiration to national legislatures. The UNIDROIT Principles of International Commercial Contracts fall within this category.

Of all the scenarios depicted in this chapter, treaty-making is the one to which comparative law has the most obvious contribution to make and perhaps the most to accomplish. For what is a treaty or model law other than an instrument intended to become formally a part of the legal fabric of the state? Each participating state will have in mind a whole series of questions that have to do with the interface between the new instrument and what already exists within the national legal order. How drastically will the instrument affect existing law? To what extent will it upset legitimate private party expectations? To what extent will it task existing institutions with responsibilities for which they are not currently equipped? To what extent will it prove to be incongruous, even if not flatly contradictory, with other parts of the national legal order, so that the legal order's very coherence is imperilled? The task of comparative law is absolutely central to law development and law-reform exercises of this sort, precisely because the resulting product must somehow 'mesh' with what the national legal system is and is otherwise likely to become.

11.5 International organizations and legal method

If all international organizations have a mission of one kind or another, they also have procedures through which that mission is undertaken and accomplished. To one extent or another, the modus operandi of an international organization has a legal dimension.[6]

In the previous section, I addressed comparative law's contribution to the setting of standards. International organizations may thus have a legislative procedure of sorts. The World Trade Organization most certainly does. Here, I wish only to point out that even an international organization that plays a purely monitoring and information-gathering role follows procedures for the performance of those functions that constitute for them a kind of 'procedural law'.

Here, too, the function of comparative law must be to examine the procedural norms that prevail at the national and sub-national level within states with a view to determining the criteria by which the effectiveness, the accuracy, the cost, and the fairness of procedures may be judged. All states that participate in the work of the organization, or may come to do so, have an interest in ensuring that the organization follows procedures that do not deviate substantially from national standards for effective, accurate, affordable, and fair decision-making.

Regardless of how conscious they may be of this fact, the architects of international organizations engage in comparative procedural law as they establish the procedural requirements through which the organization will carry out its work. On some occasions the choice of a procedural model may be the result of a deliberative process by which a conscious and inevitably comparative-law-informed decision is made concerning procedural ground

---

[6] A.-M. Slaughter, A. S. Tulumello, and S. Wood. 'International Law and International Relations Theory: A New Generation of Interdisciplinary Scholarship', (1998) 92 *American Journal of International Law* 370 ('[I]nstitutionalized cooperation has taken an increasingly "legalized," "judicialized," or constitutional form').

rules. On other occasions the choice may appear to have been imposed by the state or states that dominated the decision to establish the organization in the first place, or whose legal tradition preponderated among the states that participated in the organization's establishment.

Predictably, in an international organization like the European Union that has its own executive branch (the Commission), its own legislature (the European Parliament and in effect the Council of Ministers), and now upwards of a score of specialized administrative agencies, procedures abound. Consciously or unconsciously, comparative law will have had its influence. A salient example concerns the structure of the relationship between the courts of the union and those of the member states. The treaty drafters most certainly canvassed the domestic systems of both the member states and non-member states (particularly federal states like the United States) in crafting a judicial architecture. They eventually opted for a structure that echoes the system of preliminary references and preliminary rulings that Austria, Germany, and Italy had put in place years earlier for purposes of delineating the relationship between their 'ordinary' and their constitutional courts.

For a legal audience there is no better example of an international organization arena in which these considerations occupy centre stage than an international court or tribunal. Whether the body is adjudicating human rights violations, war claims, border disputes, or trade disputes, it will be judged in large measure by the quality in all these respects of the procedures by which it operates. International tribunals are discussed immediately below.

11.6 International organizations and their courts

The architects of international organizations rarely endow them with judicial or quasi-judicial organs. But they sometimes do. The tribunal thereby created may be somewhat ancillary to the organization's more overtly political and regulatory organs. This can be said of the European Union. For all its importance, the European Court of Justice (ECJ) is not the operations centre of the European Union. Increasingly and in other domains (international human rights, for example), however, international tribunals are, for all practical purposes, the international organization itself.

Differences in adjudicatory styles are among the most widely noted in the comparative law literature. Decisions as to how these differences are to be bridged are sometimes made in the instrument that set up the tribunal. More often, the tribunal will issue at the outset a set of procedural rules. On some matters, how the tribunal operates will be decided over time and in practice.

I would include among the areas of procedural difference such structural issues as the selection of judges, norms of judicial independence, and the role of public prosecutors. Another central set of considerations has, of course, to do with adjudicatory process, which covers a vast area including the adversarial–inquisitorial divide, rules of evidence, the relative predominance of written and oral interventions, the use of amicus curiae briefs, transparency of files and proceedings, testimonial privileges, burdens and standards of proof, avenues of rehearing or appeal, and, indeed, judicial remedies generally. Even the finished product – the judgment – will have features that are not accidental. A formal or informal decision will be made about the form judgments should take, their prolixity or terseness, and the admissibility of concurring and dissenting opinions.

Within the European Union, the form of judgments of the ECJ still reflects the dominance of continental civil law style. While French judicial practice – particularly the practice of the French administrative courts – exerted a preponderant influence over the workings of the court, the French model was not slavishly followed. Moreover, the advent of common law countries into the EU has brought with it some less than dramatic changes in legal method.

The ECJ has developed a good number of substantive legal principles by engaging in a comparative law analysis of the member states' legal orders.[7] It has a variety of methods for 'taking the pulse' of national legal systems and ultimately finding a balancing point.[8] On matters as diverse as the tort liability of the European institutions and the protection of fundamental rights of EU nationals, the ECJ has searched for general principles of law held in common by the member states.[9] While the ECJ remains committed to the idea of formulating EU law through commonly accepted principles, complete consensus among the member states can by no means always be found. Sometimes the ECJ establishes EU law by embracing a legal principle shared by the majority of member states. In the case of *Brasserie de Pêcheur*

---

[7] K. Lenaerts, 'Interlocking Legal Orders in the European Union and Comparative Law', (2003) 52 *International and Comparative Law Quarterly* 873.

[8] Ibid., 906.

[9] See *Van Gend en Loos*, Case 26/62 [1963] ECR 1; *Austl. Mining and Smelting Ltd.* v. *Commission*, Case 155/79 [1982] ECR 1575.

and *Factortame*, regarding member state liability for violating EU law, the Court overcame the opposition of a minority of member states.[10] On other occasions, as when the ECJ finds much more divergence than consensus, it may devise an 'autonomous Community solution'.[11] Regardless of the degree of difference among member state laws, the controlling interest of the ECJ is to find 'the best solution in the "middle-line" which should enjoy credibility and acceptability in the member states and which will ensure the effectiveness of [EU] law'.[12] The ECJ can only accomplish this objective by conducting an appropriate comparative law examination of the relevant features of the member states' legal orders in the light of the EU's own objectives.

11.7 Comparative law and constraints on international organization behaviour

International organizations operate on a 'supranational' level – not in the sense that they are legally superior to national legal systems, but in the sense that they simply transcend them. To what legal order, then, are these organizations legally responsible? Of course, an international organization likely depends on national institutions to implement or enforce whatever policies it may have established or decisions it may have rendered, and is to that extent responsible to them. But there has emerged a strong consensus that, precisely because they escape hierarchical control by any national legal system, international organizations must also be made subject to a supranational normative legal order. That legal order can be nothing other than international law, which is a body of law consisting not only of treaty law (including the very treaty by which the organization may have come into being), but also customary international law and general principles of law.

This is not the place to enter into the difficult questions of the processes and standards in accordance with which customary international law and general principles of law come to be created. Such is the domain of public international law, as understood generally and by different states. The fact remains that, to the extent that international law consists of these

---

[10] *Brasserie de Pêcheur* and *Factortame*, Cases C-46/93 and 48/93 [1996] ECR I-1029.
[11] *Netherlands* v. *Reed*, Case 59/85 [1986] ECR 1283.
[12] Lenaerts, 'Interlocking Legal Orders', 906.

two additional sources – namely customary international law and general principles of law – its ascertainment is and can only be the product of comparative legal inquiry.

By definition, '[c]ustomary international law results from a general and consistent practice of states followed by them from a sense of legal obligation.'[13] In order for a practice of states to become a rule of customary international law, states must not only follow the practice, but do so out of a sense of legal obligation. According to the US Restatement (Third) of Foreign Relations Law, '[g]eneral principles common to the major legal systems [of the world], even if not incorporated or reflected in customary law or international agreement, may be invoked as supplementary rules of international law where appropriate.'[14] They play a particularly salient role in the workings of international organizations, as evidenced by the following description:

> General principles common to systems of national law may be resorted to as an independent source of law. That source of law may be important when there has not been practice by states sufficient to give the particular principle status as customary law and the principle has not been legislated by general international agreement.
>
> General principles are a secondary source of international law, resorted to for developing international law interstitially in special circumstances. For example, the passage of time as a defence to an international claim by a state on behalf of a national may not have had sufficient application in practice to be accepted as a rule of customary law. Nonetheless, it may be invoked as a rule of international law, at least in claims based on injury to persons, because it is a general principle common to the major legal systems of the world and is not inappropriate for international claims. Other rules that have been drawn from general principles include rules relating to the administration of justice, such as the rule that no one may be judge in his own cause; res judicata; and rules of fair procedure generally. General principles may also provide 'rules of reason' of a general character, such as acquiescence and estoppel, the principle that rights must not be abused, and the obligation to repair a wrong. International practice may sometimes convert such a principle into a rule of customary law.[15]

To the extent that international organizations act in accordance with international law having sources such as these, they necessarily operate in a profoundly comparative-law-oriented environment. As is well known and practically definitional, neither customary international law nor general

---

[13] Restatement (Third) of the Foreign Relations Law of the United States, §102(2).
[14] Ibid., §102(4).   [15] Ibid., §102(4), Comment l.

principles of law can be ascertained without a comparative inquiry into the laws and practices of multiple legal orders.

11.8 Conclusion

International organizations are created through law, are situated within a legal system, operate through legal procedures, produce legal norms and decisions of various kinds, and are themselves subject to legal constraints. The multi-national nature of international organizations means that differences between the national laws and legal practices of participating states must be mediated and a legal ground staked out that is both acceptable to the states and consonant with the organizations' distinctive missions. None of the determinations associated with these aspects of international organization life and activity can properly be made without recourse to comparative law.

Further reading

On European integration
C. Harlow, 'Voices of Difference in a Plural Community', (2002) 50 *American Journal of Comparative Law* 339

O. Lando, 'The Contribution of Comparative Law to Law Reform by International Organizations', (1977) 25 *American Journal of Comparative Law* 4

P. W. Schroth and A. D. Boston, 'International Constitutional Law and Anti-corruption Measures in the European Union Accession Negotiations: Romania in Comparative Perspective', (2005) 52 *American Journal of Comparative Law* 625

P. Stone, *EU Private International Law: Harmonization of Law* (Cheltenham: Edward Elgar, 2006)

W. Van Gerven, 'Bridging the Unbridgeable: Community and National Tort Laws after *Francovich* and *Brasserie*', (1996) 45 *International and Comparative Law Quarterly* 3

D. R. Verway, *The European Community, The European Union, and the International Law of Treaties: A Comparative Legal Analysis of the Community and Union's External Treaty-Making Practice* (The Hague: TMC Asser, 2004)

On international criminal tribunals
M. Findlay, 'Synthesis in Trial Procedures? The Experience of International Criminal Tribunals', (2001) 50 *International and Comparative Law Quarterly* 26

J. Meernik, 'Victor's Justice or the Law? Judging and Punishing at the International Criminal Tribunal for the Former Yugoslavia', (2003) 47 *Journal of Conflict Resolution* 2

On international organizations generally

C. F. Amerasinghe, *Principles of the Institutional Law of International Organizations* (Cambridge University Press, 2005)

P. De Cruz, *Comparative Law in a Changing World* (New York: Routledge, 1999)

J. Friedrich, 'Legal Challenges of Nonbinding Instruments: The Case of the FAO Code of Conduct for Responsible Fisheries', (2008) 9 *German Law Journal* 1539

J. Friedrich and E. J. Lohse, 'Revisiting the Junctures of International and Domestic Administration in Times of New Forms of Governance: Modes of Implementing Standards for Sustainable Development and their Legitimacy Challenges, (2008) 2 *European Journal of Legal Studies* 1

J. W. Head, 'Supranational Law: How the Move toward Multilateral Solutions Is Changing the Character of "International" Law', (1994) 42 *University of Kansas Legal Review* 605

A. Stone, 'What Is a Supranational Constitution? An Essay in International Relations Theory', (1994) 56 *Review of Politics* 3

Part III

Comparative law in the flux of civilizations

The East Asian legal tradition 12

Teemu Ruskola

12.1 Introduction

It has been observed that it is foolish, even dangerous, to attempt to provide
a summary description of a topic as vast as the East Asian legal tradition.[1]
I shall nevertheless proceed with such an attempt, with the important
qualification that what follows is the description of *an* East Asian legal
tradition – namely, what I call the classical legal tradition of East Asia, or by
way of analogy, a kind of East Asian *ius gentium*. Although it is a historically significant tradition, by no means does it exhaust the entire East
Asian legal universe. To suggest so would, indeed, be foolish.

Yet the very notion of an East Asian legal tradition itself – whether
characterized as singular or plural – requires some further methodological
observations. First, just what does the term 'East Asia' encompass? Second,
what do we mean by a 'legal tradition'? The answer to neither question is
obvious. After addressing these preliminary considerations, I shall turn to
developing the broad outlines of a classical East Asian legal tradition.

12.2 Locating East Asia

Historically, the eastern end of the Eurasian landmass has known a variety
of systems of legal ordering. On the one hand, it is obvious that it is

I am indebted to several individuals for their insights: William Alford, Mauro Bussani, Albert
Chen, Donald Clarke, Jerome Cohen, Benjamin Elman, David Eng, James Feinerman, Chaihark
Hahm, John Haley, Stanley Lubman, and Ugo Mattei. Needless to say, I alone am responsible
for all errors of interpretation and fact.

[1] J. V. Feinerman, 'Introduction to Asian Legal Systems', in R. A. Danner and M.-L. Bernal
(eds.), *Introduction to Foreign Legal Systems* (New York: Oceana, 1994), 95. Patrick Glenn
offers a definition for an even larger 'Asian legal tradition', which he characterizes as a
'tradition of persuasion'. H. P. Glenn, *Legal Traditions of the World: Sustainable Diversity in
Law*, 3rd edn (Oxford and New York: Oxford University Press, 2007), 303–43.

impossible to identify a single, all-encompassing, homogeneous East Asian legal tradition that has endured over time. On the other hand, it is not unjustified that this volume should have a chapter with just that title. Whether or not there is a stable historical or geographical referent that corresponds to the term, the East Asian legal tradition clearly exists as an object of knowledge: volumes have been written on it. (It is also occasionally referred to as the 'Far Eastern legal tradition' – an outdated term that gratuitously privileges Europe as a global standard of propinquity.)

The term 'East Asia' is best understood as a geocultural and geopolitical notion. In common usage, it refers primarily to China, Japan, and South Korea. East Asia in turn is conventionally distinguished from South East Asia and South Asia. Yet even the most cursory look at a map reveals that according to a strictly geographic definition the entire northern half of East Asia consists of Russia. Nevertheless, ordinarily Russia is hardly regarded as an East Asian civilization. The contemporary notion of a culturally delimited East Asia is in part the legacy of a Cold War designation of politically salient 'areas' of study: in 1958, the United States Congress legislated such areas into existence through Title VI of the National Defense Education Act. Each designated area was to be studied (with government support) by a particular group of area studies specialists; one of these areas was East Asia. At the same time, as an object of study East Asia is of course indebted to earlier formations of knowledge as well, developed by previous generations of missionaries, adventurers, traders, Sinologists, and Orientalists of various sorts.[2]

What we today refer to as East Asia is perhaps most usefully described, in historic terms, as the sphere of influence of Chinese culture, or what Alexander Woodside calls an 'East Asian classical civilization'.[3] (Even while using the term 'East Asia', it is pertinent to remember that the category 'Asia' is itself a European concept that has historically meant nothing to the putative 'Asians' who lived there.) Both Japan and the Koreas are certainly included within this definition, in addition to China, which anchors this cultural sphere. Although this cultural definition

---

[2] For an excellent critical assessment of the potential and limits of the area studies model, see W. van Schendel, 'Geographies of Knowing, Geographies of Ignorance: Jumping Scale in Southeast Asia', (2002) 20 *Environment and Planning D: Society and Space* 647.

[3] A. B. Woodside, *Vietnam and the Chinese Model: A Comparative Study of Nguyen and Ch'ing Civil Government in the First Half of the Nineteenth Century* (Cambridge, MA: Harvard University Press, 1988), 7.

excludes the vast East Asian portion of Russia, it includes Vietnam, for example, even though geographically Vietnam is typically categorized as part of South East Asia. For present purposes, then, I use the term 'East Asian legal tradition' to refer to legal traditions on the eastern end of the Eurasian landmass that were influenced, to some considerable degree, by the classical Chinese legal tradition – notably, China, Japan, Korea, and Vietnam.[4]

It is important to emphasize that this area – if we so choose to call it – is indeed a primarily cultural and social entity. The area-studies model of the world ordinarily assumes that where one area ends another one begins, and, further, that each area is an internally coherent unit. In fact, such assumptions are rarely justified, and certainly not with regard to East Asia. The spread of Chinese political and cultural influence has been uneven and discontinuous, both in space and in time. Moreover, today the hegemony of classical Chinese culture in East Asia has been replaced largely by a Western cultural and political hegemony – evidenced most dramatically by China's own political rejection in the twentieth century of its Confucian heritage.[5]

In recognition of this historical fact and to keep the subject matter reasonably manageable, this chapter focuses only on the 'classical' aspects of East Asian law. Two important limitations follow. First, I shall not address the increasingly divergent contemporary Western legal forms that have been superimposed on the classical foundation. The resulting new legal formations are obviously of great interest, but they no longer constitute a unified East Asian legal tradition (as I argue in the last section of this chapter). Second, what follows is not a description of the Chinese,

---

[4] It is important to note that elements of this classical legal tradition were also appropriated, to various degrees, by 'non-classical' civilizations of East Asia, including 'barbarians' who turned to the Chinese dynastic model. In effect, as Herbert Franke observes, historically many 'tribal chieftains' in the Chinese periphery 'tried to set up their rulers as Chinese emperors (*huangdi*), and some succeeded in doing so'. H. Franke, 'The Role of the State as a Structural Element in Polyethnic Societies', in S. R. Schram (ed.), *Foundations and Limits of State Power in China* (London: School of Oriental and African Studies, 1987), 87.

[5] As Paul Cohen, for example, has noted, it is risky to divide Chinese history into 'traditional' and 'modern' periods, given that the latter term is usually privileged insofar it refers to 'the period of significant contact with the modern West'. P. A. Cohen, *Discovering History in China: American Historical Writing on the Recent Chinese Past* (New York: Columbia University Press, 1985), 58. In this chapter, I use the term 'classical' more often than 'traditional'. However, even when I refer to 'traditional China', I wish simply to denote a certain historical period, without implying a particular teleological view of history that necessarily ends in 'modernity'.

Japanese, Korean, and Vietnamese legal orders as such, but only an analysis of some of their historic commonalities that collectively constitute the classical legal tradition of East Asia. A full appreciation of these constituent units of the region as separate legal orders would require outlining their significant differences as well as their similarities. Self-evidently, none of the legal orders addressed here – including that of China itself – was reducible to the classical tradition alone.

12.3 Defining law

For the study of comparative law, it is a fact of utmost significance that the notion of law we use is itself of Western origin. This is not to say that it has a singular and fixed meaning even in the West. It is to say that it should be used only with great self-consciousness, precisely because its meaning seems so self-evident. Not only is our entire vocabulary of politics essentially of Greek and Roman origin – beginning with such basic terms as 'democracy' and 'republic' – but the notion of a conceptually distinct realm of 'politics' is itself a culturally specific concept.[6]

Most notably, it is exceedingly difficult for us to conceive of politics without the notion of rights. Consider the following definition in the *International Encyclopedia of Social and Behavioral Sciences*: '"Politics" is a category of human activities concerned with the determination and enforcement of rules governing the assignment of rights and duties to variously classified members of an organization such as the state.'[7] In fact, for most of its history most of the world has not thought of politics in terms of rights. Yet it is hardly purely coincidental that the encyclopaedia author above associates rights with the state. The state is not simply one organization among others, as the entry innocently suggests: in terms of our contemporary political understanding, legal membership in a state is the very condition of having rights in the first place.[8]

---

[6] See generally J. Gernet, 'Introduction', in S. R. Schram (ed.), *Foundations and Limits of State Power in China* (London: School of Oriental and African Studies, 1987), xv.

[7] H. Fukui, 'East Asian Studies: Politics', in N. J. Smelser and P. B. Baltes (eds.), *International Encyclopedia of Social and Behavioral Sciences* (Amsterdam and New York: Elsevier, 2001), 3971.

[8] As Hannah Arendt observes succinctly, citizenship is 'the right to have rights'. H. Arendt, *The Origins of Totalitarianism* (New York: Harcourt, 1973 [1951]), 296. Despite the increasing

While we can discern a historically identifiable East Asian legal tradition of statehood, that tradition was in many ways different from that which developed in Europe. Most notably, membership in a polity was not conceptualized in terms of rights, nor did the state distinguish adjudication from other kinds of administration. Hence the question, whatever system of governance obtained in East Asia, was it 'law'? Ultimately, this must be matter of definition and choice of translation, as there is no correct, final answer to it. The question is nevertheless urgent because the dominance of the Western legal tradition is not merely political but ultimately epistemological. Those who study Europe and its institutions are typically not viewed as being engaged in a set of particular, local studies, as are area studies specialists. In the end, Europe is not just an 'area': it is the home of the disciplines. Hence the study of European law, politics, and philosophy (for example) is silently conflated with the study of law, politics, and philosophy as such. Emblematic of this tendency, there is a long tradition of Western scholarship on East Asia that tends to associate the latter, negatively, with a relative *absence* of law[9] – or, as two contemporary comparatists put it, with 'a dim view of law'.[10]

Hoping to avoid the tendency to view 'real' law in Weberian terms as a system of formal-rational rules – something that Europe has and East Asia seemingly lacks – I use the more expansive term 'legal tradition', rather than simply 'law'.[11] As John Henry Merryman explicates the notion of a legal tradition, it refers not to legal rules on specific legal subjects but to the culturally conditioned attitudes that underlie those rules and, even more broadly, to ideas about the role of law in the organization of the polity and in society, and even in inter-state relations.[12] It is evident that one component of the classical East Asian civilization was a shared conceptual vocabulary of politics and statehood.

institutionalization of human rights after the Second World War, the discourse of rights is still dominated overwhelmingly by states.

[9] I analyse this phenomenon extensively in T. Ruskola, 'Legal Orientalism', (2002) 101 *Michigan Law Review* 179.

[10] K. Zweigert and H. Kötz, *Introduction to Comparative Law*, trans. T. Weir, 3rd rev. edn (Oxford: Clarendon; NewYork: Oxford University Press, 1998), 287.

[11] This is not to concede that the Chinese legal system, for example, did not have both 'formal' and 'rational' rules. See, e.g., T. Metzger, *The Internal Organization of Ch'ing Bureaucracy: Legal, Normative, and Communication Aspects* (Cambridge, MA: Harvard University Press, 1973).

[12] J. H. Merryman, *The Civil Law Tradition: An Introduction to the Legal Systems of Western Europe and Latin America*, 2nd edn (Palo Alto: Stanford University Press, 1985), 2.

Below, I analyse the classical East Asian legal tradition as a language of normative ordering and a widely shared structure of political imagination that gave rise to a kind of far-flung 'Confucian commonwealth' in East Asia.[13]

12.4 Chinese legal traditions

What, then, are some of the hallmarks of the classical Chinese legal tradition that in turn influenced other legal traditions in East Asia? The simplest and most common answer is to characterize Chinese law with the simple epithet 'Confucian'. This characterization is typically shorthand for features such as an emphasis on family hierarchy, community, respect for authority, mediation, and harsh penalties. These features represent no doubt real aspects of the classical Chinese legal tradition, but to reduce the entire tradition to them is overstated and superficial. Perhaps most importantly, it is inaccurate and misleading to treat Confucianism as synonymous with Chinese culture *tout court*.[14] Of the five elements listed above, the first four are at least arguably Confucian, but the emphasis on penalties is decidedly not. Rather, this emphasis can be traced to a competing political tradition, Legalism.

Much of traditional Chinese political thought is predicated on the opposition between two different instruments of social control: *li*, or moral suasion by ritual, associated with Confucians, and *fa*, or coercion by law, favoured by the so-called Legalist thinkers.[15] In the idealistic view of the early Confucian thinkers, human nature is good (or at least capable of becoming good), so that all that is needed is a government of superior

---

[13] Woodside, *Vietnam and the Chinese Model*, ii.

[14] It is important to note that the word 'Confucianism' itself is a Western coinage invented by Jesuit missionaries. See generally L. Jensen, *Manufacturing Confucianism: Chinese Traditions and Universal Civilization* (Durham, NC: Duke University Press, 1997). The Chinese term *rujia* is more accurately translated as 'the tradition of the literati', rather than 'Confucianism'. In any event, the range of ideas, ideologies, and dynasties that have travelled under the banner of Confucianism is so impossibly wide that it defies historical generalization. In this chapter, I use the generic term 'Confucianism' to refer to the state ideology perpetuated by the imperial civil service examination system. This ideology was related to, yet distinct from, the philosophical Confucianisms in which it originated.

[15] For a classic exposition of the *li–fa* dichotomy, see B. Schwartz, 'On Attitudes toward Law in China', in J. A. Cohen (ed.), *The Criminal Process in the People's Republic of China 1949– 1963: An Introduction* (Cambridge, MA: Harvard University Press, 1968), 62.

men whose moral influence will transform those below through the functioning of *li*. Legalist thinkers, on the other hand, dismissed all appeals to virtue as naïve, and insisted that the average person operates on a crude pleasure–pain principle and therefore can be controlled only by severe penalties prescribed in unambiguous draconian laws.

China was first unified as a single state in 221 BCE. In governing his realm, Qin Shi Huangdi – the First Emperor – followed a harsh version of the Legalist model, which included uniform laws with heavy penalties (along with the standardization of taxation, coinage, script, and weights and measures). Ever since, law has been associated with an oppressive state. When the First Emperor was overthrown in 206 BCE, subsequent dynasties denounced Legalism as a political theory, and turned to Confucianism to legitimize their rule. However, upon gaining political patronage, even Confucian ideologues found rule by the sheer force of superior virtue inadequate, and they too resorted to law as an instrument of social control. Put simply, the penal sanctions of *fa* were recruited to enforce the Confucian morality embodied in the *li*. The moral code became *mutatis mutandis* the penal code. This process has been characterized as the 'Confucianization of law',[16] although it might just as well be described as the 'legalization of Confucianism'. In any event, the ensuing legal tradition cannot be described adequately as either simply Confucian or Legalist; the end result is an amalgam of (at least) two competing major traditions.

Before describing these traditions further, it is important to emphasize the peculiar nature of the paradigmatic Western legal subject: the singular individual. It is an axiom of modern Western legal thought that all rights and duties must be held by a person. Law's persons are essentially Cartesian subjects of reason, who create obligations among themselves by exercising their individual wills. In establishing their rights and in their pursuit of justice, these persons are represented by a class of professionals: lawyers. As William Jones puts it trenchantly, '[t]hese "persons" are no longer human beings, but the central abstractions or figures of the legal system'.[17] Ultimately, the need to ground all rights in personhood has generated the fiction of so-called legal persons as well, such as corporations, and even

---

[16] The characterization belongs to T. Ch'ü, *Law and Society in Traditional China* (Paris: Mouton, 1961), 267–79.

[17] W. C. Jones, 'Introduction', in *The Great Qing Code*, trans. W. C. Jones (Oxford University Press, 1994), 5.

states, who are indeed 'international legal persons' in their relations with each other.

In contrast, the Confucian political and cosmological view privileges a person's connectedness to others – especially to kin – rather than his disconnectedness and separation from others. Therefore it is kinship, not radical individuality, that provides the preferred model for political, social, and economic relations. The emperor, for example, was conceptualized as a kind of paterfamilias writ large, while district magistrates were popularly known as *fumuguan*, or 'father-and-mother officials'. Evidently the Confucian notion of kinship is just as much an idealized abstraction, a political and legal metaphor, as is the notion of the Western individual person. For instance, traditional Chinese economic enterprises preferred to organize themselves both socially and legally in the guise of the family, although the kinship that bound them together was often no less fictive than the personhood of a Western corporation.[18]

Ever since Confucianism was first adopted as a state orthodoxy in the Han dynasty (206 BCE–220 CE), it received the backing of a strong, coercive state. Indeed, a centralized bureaucratic state – structured around the so-called Six Boards, or six central ministries – emerged in China centuries before its European equivalent. Its officials were selected primarily on the basis of merit, in statewide examinations based on Confucian classics. From the Song dynasty (960–1279 CE) onward, Neo-Confucian interpretations of the classics by master Zhu Xi (1130–1200 CE) became the standard of political orthodoxy in these civil service examinations (which continued until 1906).

Each dynasty promulgated its own code as one of its foundational acts. The main features of subsequent codes were already present in the classic Tang Code (first promulgated in 624 CE, with subsequent revisions), which was used as a model in Korea, Japan, and Vietnam as well.[19] The dynastic codes were primarily concerned with the smooth administration of the empire and the maintenance of peace. Hence they contained a great deal of what we would today characterize as constitutional and administrative law. Much of the remainder can be classified as family law and criminal law, with carefully defined penalties that were graduated according to the social status of both

---

[18] See T. Ruskola, 'Conceptualizing Corporations and Kinship: Comparative Law and Development Theory in a Chinese Perspective', (2000) 52 *Stanford Law Review* 1599.

[19] See W. Johnson (trans.), *The Tang Code: Volume One: General Principles* (Princeton University Press, 1979).

the criminal and the victim. Although the codes have indeed been characterized as primarily penal, private property and contracts were also protected by the state. However, the basis for doing so was largely customary rather than statutory. In fact, while the imperial state's reach was extensive, it was not necessarily deep. Despite popular clichés about 'oriental despotism', much local regulation was left to extended families, through clan rules, and to associations of merchants, through guild (*hang*) regulations.

12.5 Decentring Sinocentrism

The above is obviously a highly selective description. However, it is important to be aware that even the 'Chinese' legal tradition to which it refers did not govern all of what today is China. Notably, 'China' is not even China's own name for itself. The historic Chinese term 'Zhongguo' means, literally, the 'central state' – often rendered into English rather more romantically as the Middle Kingdom. The territorial reach of that state has varied greatly over time. (Approximately two-thirds of the territory of the People's Republic of China today consists of 'minority' areas, such as Tibet and Xinjiang.)

Importantly, the classical Chinese conception of political space was not that of a modern nation state, namely exclusive territorial jurisdiction. Modern territorial jurisdiction entails a conception of political space as empty and homogeneous: each state's law governs every square inch of its territory equally, and each state represents a separate but homologous unit. Although it is risky to pin down a single, authoritative view of traditional Chinese political space, there is a long Confucian tradition which Western scholars have dubbed Sinocentrism. From the orthodox Confucian perspective, the classical Chinese state represented civilization as such, and its power radiated in concentric squares from an imperial centre where its strength was at its maximum, out towards increasingly 'barbaric' peripheries where its cultural and political force (which were seen as indissociable) gradually declined. At least in theory, outsiders were always welcome to join the charmed Central State as long as they accepted the superiority of its civilization and became properly acculturated. Ultimately, however, there was only one true sovereign: the Son of Heaven, or the Chinese emperor. He generously recognized lesser neighbouring rulers as long as they acknowledged his ritual and cosmological superiority, most evidently by sending envoys to pay tribute.

Needless to say, this was an idealized and self-congratulatory worldview. Although the mythic Confucian geography had a certain, albeit limited, historic basis, the so-called tributary system that is said to have been its core was in fact far from systematic, nor was it the sole institution for extending Chinese sovereignty from the imperial centre. Nevertheless, it has enjoyed considerable currency in Western scholarship, which has used it to construct an analytic framework characterized as 'the Chinese world order'.[20]

In fact, as new Qing history has shown, for all its Confucian orthodoxy the imperial state was capable of remarkable ideological and legal pluralism. Perhaps most notably, outside their conventional self-representations, Qing emperors presented themselves to Tibetans as Buddhist *cakravartins* ('wheel-turning kings'). An extensive repertoire of multi-ethnic ruling strategies, ranging from Confucianism to shamanism, allowed multiple forms of law and sovereignty to be encompassed within the empire, as its reach came to include numerous minority (i.e. non-Han Chinese) groups who embraced different political and legal traditions altogether – not only Buddhist Tibetans in the south-west but also various indigenous peoples in southern borderlands, Mongols and Turkic Uighurs in Central Asia, and so on.

In short, just as the notion of a single, coherent East Asian region is inaccurate, it is equally misleading to reduce China to a single legal tradition. Although it is conventionally depicted as a monolithic and static entity, the imperial state had multiple competing conceptions of political space and time, of which Confucianized law was only one articulation, albeit an ideologically privileged one.

12.6 Delocalizing China

Spatially, rather than thinking of the classical East Asian civilization as a solid, monochrome surface on a map, it may be more useful and accurate to think of it as a cultural archipelago in continental space, or perhaps a kind of cultural network.[21] Indeed, although the status of classical Chinese civilization was undoubtedly hegemonic in cultural East Asia, the capacity

---

[20] See, for example, J. K. Fairbank (ed.), *The Chinese World Order: Traditional China's Foreign Relations* (Cambridge, MA: Harvard University Press, 1968).
[21] For different models of cultural space, see van Schendel, 'Geographies of Knowing'. For the notion of a cultural archipelago, see M. W. Lewis and K. E. Wigen, *The Myth of Continents: A Critique of Metageography* (Berkeley: University of California Press, 1997), 142.

of the Chinese state to exert direct domination over its neighbours was necessarily limited. At various times, Korea, Vietnam, and Japan all did send envoys to China, where they were received as paying tribute to the superiority of Chinese civilization. The extent and the political and/or economic motivation of these contacts are highly contested. Their cultural significance, however, is immense, as the envoys and their entourages took home with them an increasing familiarity with Chinese institutions. The Chinese tradition provided quite literally the language of statecraft for these three civilizations: not only did Korea, Japan, and Vietnam adopt the centralized Chinese state as a model to be appropriated, they all also borrowed the Chinese script and the political vocabulary to which the script gave expression.[22]

Although it is difficult to underestimate the significance of Chinese key terms in the political epistemology of major East Asian civilizations (much as it is difficult to underestimate the significance of Greek and Roman terms in the West), those terms inevitably became indigenized in different ways, in varying degrees, and at uneven speeds. Remarkably, Sinocentrism was not necessarily even tethered to Chinese soil, but could and did travel. Ultimately, the imperial state's superiority was premised on a claim to civilizational supremacy, rather than simple geography; the putative Middle Kingdom just happened to be where civilization flourished in its most perfected form. However, as neighbouring states adopted the Chinese script and various Chinese institutions, increasingly they came to adopt the very worldview that had given birth to them. For example, many states that sent tributary envoys to China also recruited their own tributaries on the Chinese model, thus creating their own scaled-down, hybridized replicas of a 'Chinese world order', with themselves at the centre. Following the fall of the Ming in China in 1644 CE, the Chosŏn dynasty of Korea, for example, insisted that it was the true repository of civilization, as China was being taken over by ethnic Manchus who ultimately established the last imperial dynasty, the Qing. Similarly, Confucianized elites in Vietnam and Japan also insisted at various times that they were the true inheritors of Chinese civilization.

---

[22] Eventually, Korea developed an alphabetic system of writing and Japan a syllabary, but Chinese characters continue to play an important role in both scripts (especially in Japan). Under French colonial pressure, Vietnam ultimately switched from Chinese characters to the Roman alphabet.

12.7 Elements of an East Asian *ius gentium*

The remainder of this chapter outlines some key features of the legal traditions of Korea, Japan, and Vietnam insofar as they formed part of a larger East Asian classical civilization. It bears repeating that none of those traditions can be reduced simply to their classical component. The classical Chinese language of statecraft was one idiom among many others that originated locally as well as translocally (such as Buddhism, most influentially). Moreover, its dissemination was a dynamic one of continuous translation and negotiation, rather than of unilateral influence by 'superior' Chinese institutions.

Although the notion of a Chinese world order is misleading insofar as it is presented as a complete and accurate reflection of all political organization in East Asia, it did provide a shared language of interstate relations and a set of discursive criteria for legitimate political action. In this regard, it can be usefully thought of as a kind of transnational East Asian legal order, a Confucian *ius gentium* that provided a normative standard of civilization for political recognition, a set of constitutional norms for a properly administered polity, and guidelines for interactions among states. The analogy to the European tradition of *ius gentium* is hardly definitive, but it is instructive. Both traditions claimed universality, while each in fact reflected a distinctive set of imperial norms – Roman and Chinese. Much as the *ius gentium* of the Roman legal world was subsequently reinterpreted, glossed, and re-glossed by European jurists, thus laying the foundation for a modern law of nations, the classic works of Chinese antiquity came to constitute a transnational textual community which informed the enactment and interpretation of legal regimes across political boundaries in East Asia. Perhaps most notably, the *Zhouli* – 'rituals of Zhou' – a classical Chinese text purporting to describe the administrative structure of the ancient state of Zhou – became a constitutional document of sorts that was drawn on for diverse purposes in China, Korea, Japan, Vietnam, and elsewhere, over the course of some two millennia.[23]

---

[23] While the comparison with *ius gentium* is meant to be suggestive only, it is notable that ideas of an analogous 'East Asian common law' have been invoked by others as well, with definitions of varying precision. See, e.g., C. Choi, *Law and Justice in Korea: South and North* (Seoul: Seoul National University Press, 2005), 126–8, 261–2; C. Ma, 'Dongya fazhi zhixu de juxian yu chaoyue weidu', (2003) *Zhongguo Faxue* 183; and Z. Zang, 'Cong Zhonghua faxi dao Dongya fa', (2007) *Nanjing Daxue Xuebao* 118. Benjamin Elman's

12.7.1 Classical legal institutions in Korea

If the so-called tributary system was the ultimate institutionalized expression of an idealized Sinocentric world order, Korea was undoubtedly China's most exemplary tributary. Without resistance, Korean rulers positioned themselves as mere kings (*wang*) vis-à-vis the one and only emperor (*huangdi*) of China. The dominant outside influence in early Korean society was Buddhism, but as early as 788 CE the kingdom of Silla (57 BCE–935 CE) set up a civil service examination system based on the model of the contemporaneous Tang dynasty (618–907 CE) in China. With increasing numbers of Korean students spending time in China, Chinese influence increased throughout the Koryŏ dynasty (918–1392 CE).

Yet it was not until the establishment of the long-lived last dynasty, the Chosŏn (1392–1910 CE), that Korea became a 'moral polity in the Confucian sense', to borrow Martina Deuchler's phrase.[24] After the Chinese Ming Code was translated in 1395, it eventually came to enjoy a quasi-constitutional status.[25] In fact, Korea became in many ways even more Confucian than China, at least in its own view. As noted above, with the 1644 CE fall of the Ming and the establishment of the Qing by 'barbaric' Manchus from the north, Chosŏn Korea came to see itself as the true successor to Confucian civilization – to the point where it even referred to itself as a 'little China' (literally, a 'little Central State').

Buddhism, which had enjoyed a semi-official status earlier, became an object of state oppression as the Chosŏn adopted from China an almost literal interpretation of Zhu Xi's Neo-Confucian orthodoxy. Most notably,

---

superbly edited volumes provide an extensive elaboration of the transnational reach and diversity of the Confucian tradition and its various historical transformations. See B. Elman, H. Ooms, and J. Duncan (eds.), *Rethinking Confucianism: Past and Present in China, Japan, Korea, and Vietnam* (Los Angeles: UCLA Asia Institute, 2002); and B. Elman and M. Kern (eds.), *Statecraft and Classical Learning: The Rituals of Zhou in East Asian History* (Leiden: Brill, 2009). For an argument about the specifically legal nature of some of the Confucian classics, see D. Schaberg, 'The *Zhouli* as Constitutional Text', in Elman and Kern, *Statecraft and Classical Learning*, 33. Janet Ainsworth makes an important argument on the continuing relevance of the classical tradition in understanding the contemporary legal world as well. See J. E. Ainsworth, 'Interpreting Sacred Texts: Preliminary Reflections on Constitutional Discourse in China', (1992) 43 *Hastings Law Journal* 273.

[24] M. Deuchler, *The Confucian Transformation of Korea: A Study of Society and Ideology* (Cambridge, MA: Council on East Asian Studies, 1992), 89.

[25] See generally W. Shaw, 'Traditional Korean Law and Its Relation to China', in J. A. Cohen, R. Randle Edwards, and F.-M. Chang Chen (eds.), *Essays on China's Legal Tradition* (Princeton University Press, 1981), 302.

Zhu Xi called for a strictly patrilineal lineage kinship system as the basis of social and political order. While it was rhetorically easy to adopt Chinese legal vocabulary, it was not easy to render it meaningful in Korea's very different social world, with historically flexible notions of kinship, a matrilineal orientation, and a relatively high social status for women. Nevertheless, in order to rationalize Korean social organization on the basis of Zhu Xi's model, the Chosŏn embarked on an ambitious programme of social legislation, aimed most of all at modifying marriage customs and instituting primogeniture, in recognition of the ritual significance of the eldest son and in order to abolish a historic tradition of inheritance rights of younger brothers as well as daughters. (Paradoxically, Chinese law was in practice less faithful to such idealized notions of Confucian kinship, which in any event were a relatively late development in the Song; shared inheritance among sons remained the legal norm in China, its ritual impropriety notwithstanding.)

The Koryŏ and Chosŏn states modelled themselves on China administratively as well. Given their smaller scale and the more homogeneous nature of Korean society, it was easier for them to achieve centralization and Confucian orthodoxy than for China itself. Yet by no means were the Korean state and society simply second-order reflections of a Chinese model. The Neo-Confucian orthodoxy that both China and Korea claimed to embody did not in fact describe *any* historical polity, Chinese or otherwise. Instead, it drew its principles from an idealized, mythic past. This gave Chosŏn Korea as good a claim to representing 'true' Confucianism as contemporary China: *both* differed in significant ways from the prototypes of classical Chinese antiquity on which Zhu Xi and other Neo-Confucians based their theories.[26]

The end result, in sum, was a distinctly Korean interpretation of the Confucian legal tradition. Perhaps most notably, Chosŏn society remained semi-aristocratic in its political constitution, despite its formal adoption of an examination system based on Confucian merit. Moreover, the influence of Confucian social legislation did not reach the population evenly: it was far greater among the ruling *yangban* class, while the lives of other segments of society continued to be informed largely by Buddhism and shamanism.

---

[26] Deuchler, *Confucian Transformation of Korea*, 287.

12.7.2 Classical legal institutions in Japan

Japan's place within an East Asian *ius gentium* is more ambiguous than Korea's. There is no question, however, that when it established a unified state for the first time in the seventh and eighth centuries CE, Japan, too, quite self-consciously copied the main formal features of the Chinese bureaucratic state. The first Chinese influences arrived in Japan via Korea. Prince Shōtoku decreed the adoption of the Chinese calendar and Chinese script, among other things, and in 604 CE he issued a so-called Seventeen Article Constitution which integrated indigenous political philosophy with transplanted Buddhist and Confucian principles of imperial rule. Shōtoku and his successors sent numerous missions to Tang China to study its institutions. The Taika Reform Edict of 646 CE entailed another set of administrative and legal reforms based on the Chinese model of a centralized monarchy. These reforms were followed in 701 CE by the establishment of a system of written laws (*ritsuryō*) modelled on the Tang Code.[27] In a combination of Chinese imperial ideology and native Shintoism, the Japanese emperor – or *tennō*, itself a Sino-Japanese term – was constituted as part of an unbroken line of divine descent from the sun goddess Amaterasu.

Formally, this period of intensive imitation of Tang-dynasty China left an enduring legacy. Substantively, its influence should not be exaggerated. Masaji Chiba, for example, insists that the resulting legal order is best understood not as 'indigenized Chinese law' but as a kind of indigenous law that was 'based on transplanted Chinese law but almost completely modified by Japanese culture'.[28] Moreover, two centuries later the central imperial bureaucracy had lost much of its jurisdiction to local custom and private power-holders. With the emergence of military government under the shogunate at the end of the twelfth century, the emperor's role was reduced further. A Confucian bureaucracy never replaced aristocratic elites, and over time Confucian ethics gave way to a *samurai* ethos. As John Haley observes, 'the great legal reforms of the country's earliest history remained in place', but they were 'narrowed in application and supplemented by warrior edicts to near oblivion'.[29]

---

[27] Inoue Mitsusada dates an early version of a *ritsuryō* code to 668 CE. M. Inoue, 'The *Ritsuryō* System in Japan', (1977) 33 *Acta Asiatica* 83, 100.

[28] M. Chiba, 'Japan', in Poh-ling Tan (ed.), *Asian Legal System: Law, Society and Pluralism in East Asia* (Sydney: Butterworths, 1997), 82, 98.

[29] J. Haley, *The Spirit of Japanese Law* (Athens, GA: University of Georgia Press, 1998), 8.

With its brazen attack on Korea in 1592 CE and its further (unrealized) designs even on China itself, Japan challenged the very foundations of the Sinocentric world order. The newly unified Japan did not have formal relations – tributary or otherwise – with the Chinese empire thereafter and it continued to reject squarely Chinese imperial claims to supremacy. Nevertheless, Neo-Confucianism constituted the dominant political philosophy even in Tokugawa (1603–1868) Japan. Indeed, there was even a new 'mini-reception' of Chinese law, based not so much on substantive borrowing as on the adoption of Chinese legal methods: many of the *daimyo* – rulers of the 265 feudal domains beyond the shogun's central control – relied on newly translated Chinese legal literature and its jurisprudential methods as they codified the local custom of their domains. Paradoxically, for Tokugawa Confucians the fact that decentralized Japan bore little resemblance to the centralized bureaucratic Chinese state was a virtue, not a failing; it only proved Japan's greater fidelity to the 'true' classical ideal, namely, the feudal multi-state order that had obtained in China *before* its imperial unification.[30] Although Japanese Confucians thus rejected the Neo-Confucian orthodoxy of late imperial China, they, too – like their Korean counterparts – ultimately claimed to be the true custodians of the classical civilization, especially as they bore witness to China's descent into 'barbarism' under the Qing.[31]

12.7.3 Classical legal institutions in Vietnam

Despite its common classification as part of South East Asia, for at least two thousand years Vietnam was culturally within the sphere of the East Asian classical civilization. For a millennium (111 BCE to 939 CE), northern Vietnam was under the control of the Chinese empire, but even during the ensuing period of self-rule Vietnam, like Korea and Japan, adopted several of the basic structures of Chinese central bureaucratic institutions and sent tributary envoys to China. Like their Japanese counterparts, Vietnamese officials adopted an interpretation of Confucianism that was in some ways even more fundamentalist than that of the Chinese bureaucracy.

---

[30] D. F. Henderson, 'Chinese Studies on Eighteenth-Century Tokugawa Codes', in J. A. Cohen, R. Randle Edwards, and F.-M. Chang Chen (eds.), *Essays on China's Legal Tradition* (Princeton University Press, 1981), 270, 282.

[31] On Japan's relationship to Confucianism see, e.g., H. Harootunian, 'The Functions of China in Tokugawa Thought', in A. Iriye (ed.), *The Chinese and the Japanese: Essays in Political and Cultural Interactions* (Princeton University Press, 1980), 9.

That is, they, too, made literal-minded appeals to the political ideals of China's pre-imperial antiquity, with its celebration of small states over large ones. A preference for smallness obviously suited Vietnam well, as it sought to overcome the problems of scale inherent in an effort to transpose the legal and administrative structure of a vast empire on to a much smaller polity that existed in the midst of the multipolar and enormously complex political universe of South East Asia.

The Vietnamese court, too, found itself adopting key aspects of the Chinese *Weltanschauung* along with Chinese legal and political institutions. Unlike Korean monarchs, who were satisfied with calling themselves kings, Vietnamese rulers took on the grandiloquent Sino-Vietnamese title of emperor, *hoàng-đế* (derived directly from the Chinese *huangdi*, in contrast to the more hybridized Japanese *tennō*), and they, too, set up their own miniaturized tributary systems, with lesser South East Asian rulers journeying to pay homage in the Vietnamese capital. However, for purposes of tribute missions to China even Vietnamese rulers still used the more modest title of king, thus recognizing the unique legal and cosmological status of the Chinese emperor.

Despite their eagerness to embrace Chinese institutions, Vietnamese officials made numerous adaptations in the face of distinct social and cultural conditions. Although Vietnam adopted the examination system, this did not result in a generally meritocratic system of recruitment on the Chinese model. Equally notably, the examination curriculum included not only Confucian but also Buddhist and Daoist elements. Such syncretism notwithstanding, the Lê Code (in effect from 1428 to 1788 CE) seemed to exemplify the formal triumph of Vietnamese Confucianism. The Code was derived at least nominally from the Chinese Tang Code, which by then had already served as a model in several parts of East Asia. Yet only about 200 of a total of more than 700 articles were in fact based on the Chinese model. As compared with the Tang Code, the Lê Code entailed greater statutory (in contrast to Chinese customary) protection of real property and other private interests. It also accorded greater personal and property rights to women. Moreover, due to Buddhist influence, the Chinese system of penalties was ameliorated in various ways. Effectively, the code – like the Vietnamese examination system – combined Confucian, Buddhist, and other elements.[32]

---

[32] N. H. Nguyen, T. Van Tai, and T. Van Liem, *The Lê Code: Law in Traditional Vietnam: A Comparative Sino-Vietnamese Study with Historical Juridical Analysis and Annotations* (Athens, OH: Ohio University Press, 1987).

The last Vietnamese dynasty, the Nguyễn (1802–1945), also proclaimed its own codification, the Gia Long Code, in 1812. The Gia Long Code sought to embrace Chinese precedents as faithfully as possible. It was modelled on the contemporary Qing Code, rather than the Tang Code, and unlike the Lê Code it was an almost exact replica of its Chinese counterpart. Paradoxically, the Nguyễn were motivated by a sense that the more closely Vietnam could approximate Chinese political and legal forms, the less China could claim authority over it and the better it would be able to preserve its autonomy. Indeed, in 1805 the Gia Long emperor, too, referred to his state as the 'Middle Kingdom'. Evidently, a term that had conventionally referred to China no longer had a single geographic referent but had become a phrase that could be used 'to refer to any kingdom, founded upon the principles of Chinese classics, which felt itself surrounded by unread barbarians'.[33]

This, then, is a brief tour of the legal tradition that formed a key part of a larger East Asian classical civilization. In the end, the metaphorical Middle Kingdom was wherever classical civilization flourished in its most authentic form. Although this civilization was identified with China as its point of origin, the China to which it referred existed as much in political imagination as in history. In his critique of 'the idea of China', Andrew March insists that there is 'no cultural or historical entity that can rationally be subsumed under this single term'.[34] In one sense, March is absolutely right. In another sense, the observation misses the point, as far as the classical civilization of East Asia is concerned. European classical antiquity, too, was reborn above all as an idea, as it was rediscovered in the Renaissance and re-imagined by its modern heirs, yet it was an idea with concrete cultural and political effects. The *ius gentium* of the Roman empire that provided the foundation for a transnational European legal order was evidently one of those effects. In the case of the East Asian classical civilization, too, what mattered ultimately was not China as a historical entity but the idea of a Middle Kingdom. As the above survey suggests, rather than a precise blueprint, China's classical legal tradition provided a common language of politics and a shared vocabulary of statecraft which were interpreted and institutionalized in unique ways in different parts of East Asia.

---

[33] Woodside, *Vietnam and the Chinese Model*, 18–19.
[34] A. March, *The Idea of China: Myth and Theory in Geographic Thought* (New York: Praeger, 1974), 23.

12.8 End of an East Asian legal tradition

This chapter's treatment of an East Asian legal tradition is a historic one, and purposely so. Whatever aspects of the classical legal tradition have survived, over the course of the past two centuries or more of colonialism and semi-colonialism that tradition has lost its most important currency: its cultural hegemony. Without a doubt, many aspects of traditional legal ordering continue to play socially important roles in East Asia, yet those aspects tend to survive outside systems of formal law. At the same time, although it is alive in various social contexts, the Confucian tradition no longer has a superior claim to political legitimacy. Unquestionably Confucian values continue to enjoy enormous popularity in many arenas of life (most notably family and education). However, insofar as the political organization of the state is concerned, in the contemporary era of globalization cultural and intellectual hegemony has quite clearly passed to the Western legal tradition and to the ideal of rule of law it represents – in self-conscious contrast to the Confucian ideal of the rule of virtuous men.[35]

Even if the classical East Asian legal tradition has lost its ideological supremacy, has a new East Asian tradition emerged to take its place? It is possible to argue so. Some have hypothesized that state-led developmental capitalism is a new defining feature in the East Asian legal world.[36] Others postulate an 'East Asian law region' whose legal cultures are 'non-legalistic' and 'non-litigious'.[37] These hypotheses are defensible, but ultimately unpersuasive. Although a preference for state-led development is surely a real phenomenon, this preference is far from unique to East Asia and is in fact shared globally by a number of newly industrialized countries.[38] And as to characterizing East Asian law in terms of its 'non-legalistic' nature, this

---

[35] I elaborate on the construction of this contrast in T. Ruskola, 'Law without Law, or Is "Chinese Law" an Oxymoron?', (2003) 11 *William and Mary Bill of Rights Journal* 655.

[36] K. Jayasuriya (ed.), *Law, Capitalism and Power in Asia: The Rule of Law and Legal Institutions* (London and New York: Routledge, 1999), 2.

[37] N. Yasuda, 'The Evolution of the East Asian Law Region', in K. Kroeschell and A. Cordes (eds.), *Vom nationalen zum transnationalen Recht* (Heidelberg: C. F. Müller, 1995), 279.

[38] Moreover, if we include North Korea in the analysis it is debatable whether this mode of development is capitalist or socialist – even if we choose to disregard the fact that the People's Republic of China also still officially professes socialism.

seems an unduly negative definition, too easily reminiscent of orientalist critiques of the lawlessness of unindividuated Asiatic masses.[39]

At the same time, the tradition of Western law that has conquered East Asia politically has been accompanied by the establishment of radically divergent economic and political systems. Hence, in today's East Asia we find legal orders based on civil law, socialist law, and common law (in the case of Hong Kong). Although the classical East Asian tradition was far from unitary, the contemporary political and ideological fragmentation seems even greater and the commonalities even fewer.

To be sure, even the many divergent contemporary forms of law do in fact share a common foundation in European political epistemology and its valorization of the nation state as the primary form of political membership. It may indeed be said that the ultimate significance of the arrival of the Western legal tradition (for lack of a more precise term) in East Asia is that today it is the primary source of the language and vocabulary of politics and governance, in much the same way as the classical East Asian legal tradition was earlier. Even in socialist China, workers are increasingly framing their claims in terms of rights,[40] and, of course, the Chinese state itself has reconceptualized its sovereignty in accordance with the norms of (Western) international law.

However, even if the arrival of Western law is creating a new rights consciousness in East Asia, along with new political and legal subjectivities, by definition the Western language of rights is not unique to East Asia – even if it is necessarily interpreted locally, as all law is. This is not an argument either in favour of or against the globalization of the Western legal tradition. It is simply a statement about the decline of an identifiable East Asian tradition of legal discourse that once claimed hegemony within its cultural sphere.

---

[39] It is noteworthy that in the latest edition of their *Introduction to Comparative Law*, even Zweigert and Kötz abandon their earlier category of a 'Far Eastern Legal Family', in recognition of the fact that – even comparing only two countries – 'the law of the People's Republic of China and that of Japan are fundamentally different'. When scholars as methodologically conservative as Zweigert and Kötz give up the notion of a presently identifiable East Asian legal tradition (or 'Far Eastern Legal Family', in their parlance), there seems to be little doubt that it is time to let go of the notion as a category of contemporary comparative analysis. See Zweigert and Kötz, *Introduction to Comparative Law*, 287.

[40] See, e.g., C. K. Lee, *Against the Law: Labor Protests in China's Rust Belt and Sun Belt* (Berkeley: University of California Press, 2007).

Further reading

W. Alford, 'Of Arsenic and Old Laws: Looking Anew at Criminal Justice in Imperial China', (1984) 72 *California Law Review* 1180

D. Bodde and C. Morris, *Law in Imperial China* (Cambridge, MA: Harvard University Press, 1962)

A. H. Y. Chen, *An Introduction to the Legal System of the People's Republic of China*, 3rd edn (Singapore: Butterworths Asia, 2004).

L. Cheng, A. Rosett, and M. Woo (eds.), *East Asian Law: Universal Norms and Local Cultures* (New York: Routledge, 2002)

B. D. Chun et al., *Traditional Korean Legal Attitudes* (Berkeley: Institute of East Asian Studies, 1981)

D. H. Foote (ed.), *Law in Japan: A Turning Point* (Seattle: University of Washington Press, 2007)

J. Gillespie and A. H. Y. Chen (eds.), *Legal Reforms in China and Vietnam: A Comparison of Asian Communist Regimes* (London and New York: Routledge, 2010)

T. Ginsburg (ed.), *Legal Reform in Korea* (New York: RoutledgeCurzon, 2004)

C. Hahm, 'Ritual and Constitutionalism: Disputing the Ruler's Legitimacy in a Confucian Polity', (2009) 57 *American Journal of Comparative Law* 135

P. Hahm, *The Korean Political Tradition and Law* (Seoul: Royal Asiatic Society Korea Branch, 1967)

S. Lubman, *Bird in a Cage: Legal Reform in China After Mao* (Palo Alto: Stanford University Press, 1999)

B. McKnight (ed.), *Law and the State in Traditional East Asia: Six Studies on the Sources of East Asian Law* (Honolulu: University of Hawaii Press, 1987)

A. von Mehren (ed.), *Law in Japan: The Legal Order in a Changing Society* (Cambridge, MA: Harvard University Press, 1963)

R. Peerenboom, *China's Long March toward Rule of Law* (Cambridge University Press, 2002)

M. J. Ramseyer and M. Nakazato, *Japanese Law* (University of Chicago Press, 1999)

W. Shaw, *Legal Norms in a Confucian State* (Berkeley: Center for Korean Studies, 1981)

D.-K. Yoon (ed.), *Law and Democracy in South Korea* (Masanhappo-gu: Kyungnam University, 2010)

I. Yu, *Law and Society in Seventeenth and Eighteenth Century Vietnam* (Seoul: Asiatic Research Center, Korea University, 1990)

13 The Jewish legal tradition

J. David Bleich and Arthur J. Jacobson

13.1 The structure and sources of law in the Jewish tradition

Judaism is fundamentally a religion of law, a law that governs every facet of the human condition. Jewish tradition maintains that the Torah – the first five books of the Bible that include the Written Law transmitted by Moses at Mount Sinai as well as the Oral Law accompanying it – contains not merely a set of laws, but also canons of interpretation and principles according to which conflicts among the rules of law may be resolved. Maimonides, the preeminent early medieval philosopher and expounder of the Torah, records the doctrine that the Torah will not be altered, either in its entirety or in part, as one of the Thirteen Principles of Faith. The divine nature of the Torah renders it immutable and hence not subject to amendment or modification.

Although the Torah itself is immutable, the Sages of the Talmud[1] teach that the interpretation of its laws and regulations is entirely within the province of human intellect. The Torah is divine, but '*lo ba-shamayim hi*'– 'it is not in the heavens' (Deuteronomy 30:12); it is to be interpreted and applied by man. A remarkable corollary to the principle of the immutability of the Torah is the principle that, following the revelation at Sinai, no further heavenly clarification of doubt or resolution of ambiguity is possible. Clarification and elucidation are themselves forms of change. Since there can be no new revelation, a prophet who claims the ability to resolve disputed legal points by virtue of his prophetic power stands convicted by his own mouth of being a false prophet.

Once revealed, the Torah does not remain in the heavens. God charges man with interpreting the text, resolving doubts, and applying the provisions of the Torah's laws to novel situations. The Gemara, *Bava Meẓi'a* 59b,[2]

---

[1] See *infra* note 2.

[2] The Gemara contains the second layer of rabbinic commentary on the Torah. The first layer, the Mishnah, edited by Rabbi Judah the Prince around 200 CE, is essentially a restatement of Jewish law as expounded by his predecessors and colleagues – the *Tanna'im*. The second

vividly illustrates the principle of *lo ba-shamayim hi* in a dispute between Rabbi Eliezer and the Sages regarding a point of ritual law. R. Eliezer refused to accede to the view of the majority of his rabbinic colleagues. He successfully invoked a number of heavenly signs in support of his position. He caused the course of nature to change; he worked miracles, and even summoned a heavenly voice. But the Sages correctly failed to be impressed: The interpretation of Halakhah – the corpus of Jewish law – has been entrusted to the human intellect and, accordingly, human intellect must proceed in its own dispassionate way, uninfluenced and unprejudiced by supernatural phenomena.

Even more dramatic is the narrative recorded in *Bava Meẓi'a* 86a. Here we are told of a controversy between the Heavenly Academy and God Himself with regard to a case of possible ritual defilement. The Almighty ruled that there was no cause for ritual defilement, while the Heavenly Academy ruled that there was. The Gemara records that the matter was left for final adjudication to Rabbah bar Naḥmani, 'who is singular [in his proficiency] in such matters'. Certainly God did not need to be instructed in His Law by mortal man. The Gemara teaches that the Law was designed to be understood, interpreted, and transmitted by man. Accordingly, man's understanding of Torah must prevail. Man's interpretation is not only inherent in the content of revelation but is the one which God Himself wills to prevail.

Moreover, Jewish teaching recognizes that two conflicting conclusions may, at times, be derived from identical sources by different scholars. Which is correct? Both are correct! 'These and those are the words of the living God', declare the Sages of the Talmud (*Gittin* 6b). If two conflicting conclusions may be derived from the same corpus of law, then both must be inherent in that corpus. In the realm of theory both are correct, both Torah. In practice, however, one must be able to derive a definitive halakhic ruling (*psak halakhah*); there must be a means of deciding between the conflicting views, lest legal anarchy result. To this end Halakhah, as a legal system, includes canons of judicial decision-making. The canons produce decisions

layer, the Gemara, is a record of discussions in the rabbinic academies that focused on the Mishnah as the primary text. The Sages of the academies during that period were known as *Amora'im*. Together, the Mishnah and the Gemara constitute the Talmud. The Talmud is divided into six orders and each order is divided into tractates. Each tractate contains portions of Mishnah, where a portion of Mishnah is followed by the part of Gemara commenting on it. *Bava Meẓi'a* ('Middle Gate') is the second of three tractates in the Talmud devoted to matters of civil jurisprudence.

that have absolute binding authority. Nonetheless, rejection of a view in practice does not nullify its theoretical validity. On the contrary, insofar as the study and pursuit of the Torah is concerned, such a view has undiminished importance. In the eyes of God both have precisely equal validity. Definitive *psak halakhah* is a matter of practical necessity, not a reflection on transcendental truth.

The existence of conflicting, yet valid, conclusions should not give rise to the impression that subjective considerations or volitional inclinations may ever be allowed consciously to influence scholarly opinion. Torah study requires, first and foremost, intellectual honesty. Bet Hillel, a school of contributors to the Mishnah hailed for their permissive rulings, did not purposely adopt a policy of permissiveness, and Bet Shammai, a rival school known for their restrictive rulings, a policy of stringency; Bet Hillel did not set out to be easy-going and Bet Shammai to be hard and unbudging. Each reported sincerely held convictions, conclusions reached in as detached and dispassionate a manner as possible. Neither permitted the conscious intrusion of motives other than the correct formulation of the law. It is a travesty of the halakhic process to begin with a conclusion apart from the law and then attempt to justify it by means of halakhic dialectic. Neither Hillel nor Shammai nor any of their spiritual heirs engaged in sophistry in order to justify previously held points of view. The dialectic of halakhic reasoning has always been conducted in the spirit of '*yikov ha-din et ha-har*' – 'let the law bore through the mountain'. The law must be determined on its own merit and let the chips fall where they may.

'These and those are the words of the living God' is a dictum applicable only when fundamental prerequisites have been met. The corpus of Halakhah must be mastered in its entirety and accepted in its entirety as the content of divine revelation. Canons of interpretation, which are an integral part of the Torah, must be applied in an objective manner. Then, and only then, are the conclusions the 'words of the living God'. Then, and only then, may it be assumed that from the time of the giving of the Torah these conclusions were destined. It is conceivable that two different individuals of equal intelligence and erudition, both equally sincere, may reach antithetical conclusions. Since the Torah was given by God and disparate human intellects were created by God, the inference is inescapable: it was part of the divine scheme that scholars reach both conclusions. Since both conclusions are derived from accepted premises and both are defended by cogent halakhic argumentation, it follows that both are legitimate expressions of Halakhah and hence both are equally valid. Of insights attained in this manner the Sages have taught, 'Even that which a conscientious student will one day teach in the presence of his master was already told to Moses at Sinai' (Palestinian Talmud, *Pe'ah* 2:4).

Of course, the development of correctly formulated decisions governing matters of practice is of singular importance. The methodology by which some opinions are accepted and others excluded from application in practice constitutes a highly complex aspect of Halakhah. Halakhic decisions are not a matter of arbitrary choice. Decision-making is also bound by rules of procedure.

The verse 'Judges and officers shall you make for yourself in all your gates' (Deuteronomy 16:18) bestows autonomous authority on the rabbinic judges in each locale. They are empowered to promulgate their views within their jurisdiction. The local populace may accept their teaching with confidence. Thus in the city in which R. Eliezer was the chief halakhic decisor the populace chopped trees, built a fire, and boiled water on the Sabbath in preparation for a circumcision,[3] while in a neighbouring town such actions constituted a capital offence. R. Eliezer's opinion to the effect that Sabbath restrictions are suspended not only for circumcision itself but even for preparation of the necessary accoutrements of this rite was authoritative in his jurisdiction. The contradictory opinion of his colleagues was binding in their jurisdictions. Only on a decision of the supreme halakhic authority, the Bet Din ha-Gadol, the Great Court or Sanhedrin sitting in Jerusalem, did one of the views become binding on all Israel.

A rabbinic authority may issue decisions in accordance with his own views when such views are not in conflict with a position already binding on the community of Israel as a whole. He may rely on his own opinion only if he has attained the requisite degree of Torah scholarship and erudition and if the conclusion is genuinely arrived at on the basis of his own study and analysis. It goes without saying that his decisions are authoritative only if his personal piety and religious probity are beyond question.

---

[3] Halakhah requires circumcision of a male child eight days after birth, even on the Sabbath. Rabbi Eliezer maintained that the requirement that a circumcision be performed eight days after birth entails that not only excision of the foreskin but also preparatory acts such as chopping trees, building a fire and boiling water, also be performed on the Sabbath. The Sages regarded such preparatory acts as forbidden even when failure to perform them would entail postponement of the circumcision.

Frequently, however, the rabbinic decisor is lacking in comprehensive scholarship or has not formulated a strongly held opinion. In such cases, he must decide in accordance with one of a number of views expressed by his predecessors or colleagues. The ability to formulate definitive *psak*, or rulings in matters of Halakhah, is the product of highly specialized skills. It is in choosing between conflicting precedents and opinions that the expertise of the decisor becomes apparent. The decisor may not arbitrarily seize on an individual opinion or a solitary source in preference to the weight of halakhic precedent or consensus. He may not be swayed by the consideration that the resultant decision be popular or expedient or simply by the fact that it appeals to his own predilection. He must carefully weigh opinions and decisions, assigning weight not merely on the basis of sheer number but also on the relative stature of the scholars who hold the opinions, and must at the same time assess the complexities and importance of any number of component factors.

Technological advances and changing social institutions have raised issues that could not have been confronted by decisors of preceding generations. Yet, although the Torah is eternal and unchanging, one may plumb its depths for answers to questions that would have been imponderable in earlier ages. Indeed, different scholars may advance differing answers to such questions and each position may be well founded in authentic halakhic teaching.

This, too, reflects a fundamental principle of Jewish law and was recognized by the Sages. *Midrash Shoḥer Tov* (a medieval collection of rabbinic dicta arranged as a commentary on the book of Psalms) 12:4 reports:

Rabbi Yan'ai declared, 'The words of the Torah were not given in final form (*ḥatukhin*). Rather, with regard to every single matter that the Holy One, blessed be He, told Moses, He enunciated forty-nine considerations [to render it] pure and forty-nine considerations [to render it] impure. Moses exclaimed before Him, "Sovereign of the Universe, when shall we arrive at a clarification of Halakhah?" God said to him, "According to the majority shall you decide" (Exodus 23:2). If those who declare it impure are more numerous, it is impure; if those who declare it pure are more numerous, it is pure.'

Clearly, the 'matters' to which the Midrash refers are not those presented to Moses unequivocally in the corpus of either the Written or the Oral Law. They are, then, matters that force human intelligence to seek answers by grappling with principles and precedents firmly established within the system of Halakhah. Halakhah thus constitutes a dynamic and ongoing process.

13.2 Jewish law in the Diaspora and in the state of Israel

Jewish law has survived and continued to govern observant Jews, not only in ritual matters, but also in commercial, financial, and interpersonal affairs in their host countries throughout their exile. In large part that phenomenon is attributable to Judaism's recognition of an obligation to remain self-governing by establishing an autonomous judiciary and an accompanying prohibition against recourse to secular courts for adjudication of disputes between members of the Jewish community.

'Judges and court officers shall you place unto yourself in all your gates' (Deuteronomy 16:18) is cited by numerous early authorities as establishing an obligation to institute courts, or Batei Din, in every locale. Maimonides, in his restatement of Jewish law, *Mishneh Torah, Hilkhot Sanhedrin* 1:2, explicitly rules that the commandment is binding, not only in the Land of Israel, but in the Diaspora as well. The sole distinction between the Land of Israel and the Diaspora with regard to the ambit of this commandment is that the obligation to establish Batei Din in each district in addition to Batei Din in each city is limited to the Land of Israel, while the obligation to establish Batei Din in each city is binding in the Diaspora as well.

Jewish law provides that in the absence of a communally appointed court that has the authority to compel appearance before it, in the event of a justiciable dispute, each litigant may nominate one member of the Bet Din and that the two judges designated in this manner are empowered to choose a third member of the tribunal. That procedure is known as '*zabla* (*zeh borer lo eḥad ve-zeh borer lo eḥad*)' – 'this litigant chooses one [judge] and that litigant chooses one [judge])'. Since, subsequent to the destruction of the Temple, rabbinic courts have not been authorized to impose penal sanctions, to what purpose is there an ongoing obligation to establish a standing court? The essential distinction between a communally established Bet Din and an ad hoc tribunal selected by the litigants is that an ad hoc court derives its authority from the consent of the litigants whereas an established Bet Din has the right to summon any person subject to its jurisdiction and to compel his appearance. The distinction is roughly parallel to that between an agreement to be bound by the decision of an arbitration panel and submission to the jurisdiction of a court. Establishment of a judiciary having the authority in Jewish law to assert jurisdiction and to enforce judgments constitutes the essence of the commandment.

Historically Jewish communities in Europe were organized on the basis of the *kehillah* (organized autonomous community) system. In every town, village, and hamlet the Jewish community designated individuals to administer communal institutions and to provide for the spiritual and temporal needs of the inhabitants. A rabbinic scholar was designated to serve as chief rabbi of the city and was usually assisted by *dayyanim* who served as associate judges. Their primary responsibility was to rule on matters of religious law relating both to individual observance and to the community as a whole and to sit as a court to adjudicate any financial or interpersonal disputes. With a court in place, a litigant could neither plead that he preferred to appear before the court of a neighbouring city nor demand the right to designate a judge of his own choice. In many communities it was customary for all householders to affix their signatures to the formal *ketav rabbanut*, or rabbinic contract, presented to a newly appointed rabbi and specifically designating him as the presiding judge of the local rabbinic court or Bet Din. The practice was instituted so that no person could refuse to obey a summons issued by the communal rabbi on the ground that he did not recognize the rabbi's judicial authority. Thus was the commandment 'Judges and court officers shall you place unto yourself' fulfilled.

Not so in our age. The *kehillah* system has not been replicated in most Western countries. Rabbis are engaged by individual congregations rather than by the community at large. Membership of a synagogue does not *ipso facto* imply binding acceptance of the authority of the synagogue's rabbi, no matter how qualified he may be in adjudicating matters of Jewish law. The result is that no rabbi enjoys the authority to compel a litigant to appear before him and to accept his judicial authority. Batei Din established by rabbinic organizations or by a group of neighbourhood or regional pulpit rabbis, rather than by the community as a whole, enjoy no greater authority. To be sure, a plaintiff dare not sue in a secular court and a defendant may not simply ignore the summons of a Bet Din, but any litigant may insist on his right not to appear before the court that has summoned him and to insist on a Bet Din designated by the parties. Since in such countries no Bet Din can compel appearance, Jewish communities in those countries are in violation of the commandment 'Judges and court officers shall you set unto yourself'.

The absence of formally established Batei Din in most Western countries has given rise to the phenomenon of otherwise scrupulously observant Jews having recourse to civil courts for resolution of disputes involving other members of the Jewish community. Such action entails serious violations of Jewish law.

A pre-eminent early-nineteenth-century scholar, Rabbi Akiva Eger, in a gloss appended to *Shulḥan Arukh, Ḥoshen Mishpat* 26:1, cites R. Simon ben Zemaḥ Duran (1361–1444), *Tashbaẓ*, II, no. 190, in declaring that acceptance of any monetary award of a secular court in excess of that which would have been awarded by a Bet Din in accordance with Jewish law constitutes an act of theft. The same authority rules that one who accepts such funds is disqualified under Jewish law from serving as a witness. Indeed, *Tashbaẓ* comments that 'this matter is so simple that it need not be recorded'.

More fundamental is the transgression involved in the very act of petitioning a civil court for redress. The standard translation of Exodus 21:1 is 'And these are the ordinances [*mishpatim*] which you shall set before them' – that is, before the children of Israel. Talmudic exegesis endows this passage with an entirely different meaning.

The Hebrew term '*mishpatim*' is a multivalent term and, depending on the context, can connote either 'ordinances' or 'lawsuits'. The Gemara, *Gittin* 88b, assigns the second meaning to this term in commenting '"And these are the lawsuits which you shall place before them" – but not before non-Jewish courts.' The conventional translation of the biblical text renders the entire passage simply as an introduction to the lengthy list of ordinances that follow. Rabbinic tradition understands the passage as referring to litigation that may be brought on the basis of those statutes and as expressly commanding that such suits be brought before *them*, namely the judges designated for that purpose by Moses. The verse thus refers to the judges whose appointment is recorded in a preceding scriptural section, Exodus 18:13–26.

The rationale underlying this prohibition is incorporated in a sixteenth-century codification of Jewish law by R. Joseph Karo, the *Shulḥan Arukh, Ḥoshen Mishpat* 26:1, in the words, 'And whosoever comes before [non-Jewish courts] for judgment is a wicked person and it is as if he has blasphemed and lifted a hand against the Torah of our teacher Moses, may he rest in peace.' Every student of Rashi's commentary on the Pentateuch is familiar with his depiction of such a person as one who 'profanes the Divine Name and ascribes honour to the name of idols'.

Halakhic sources recorded in *Ḥoshen Mishpat* 26:1 make it clear that the nature or provenance of the legal code administered by civil courts is irrelevant. Recourse to such a forum is prohibited even if the law that is applied is in no way associated with an idolatrous cult, and is forbidden even if the secular law applicable to the suit is identical to Jewish law in every respect. The essence of the transgression lies in rejection of the Law of Moses in favour of some other legal system; recourse to a civil forum is tantamount to a declaration by the litigant that he is amenable to allowing an alien code of law to supersede the law of the Torah. Such conduct constitutes renunciation of the Law of Moses.

Fundamentally, idolatry is renunciation of God and His Torah. Hence recourse to civil courts, even when the law administered by such courts is not derived from idolatrous cults, does not involve a novel prohibition but constitutes a form of idolatry – that is, the heresy of denying the applicability of the Law of Moses to adjudication of the dispute. Thus the prohibition against supplanting the Law of the Torah by another legal code is subsumed under the prohibition against idolatry. Little wonder, then, that historically in Jewish circles suing a fellow Jew in a secular court was regarded as an act of ignominy.

Apart from the religious imperative, a major factor in preserving Jewish law as a vibrant force in Jewish life is the fact that during the medieval period Jews constituted an *imperium in imperio* throughout Europe. Among the prerogatives of this 'nation within a nation' was judicial autonomy. A close comparison in the modern age is the status of Indian tribes in the United States, which enjoy a limited degree of self-governance and judicial autonomy. In some jurisdictions, particularly in the Iberian peninsula, autonomy extended even to criminal matters. In most jurisdictions the authority of the courts established by the Jewish community was limited to matters of civil jurisprudence and family law, while secular authorities reserved jurisdiction in criminal matters to the state. In all jurisdictions matters of marriage and divorce were adjudicated by ecclesiastic courts, as was the case with other religious groups. The authority of religious courts in matters of marriage and divorce changed rapidly in the period following the French Revolution. It persisted in Russia until the overthrow of the Czar in 1917. Since the Russian Orthodox Church did not permit divorce, dissolving a marriage was a privilege enjoyed only by Jews and Muslims.

The exclusive authority of rabbinic courts with regard to marriage and divorce persists even today in the state of Israel. It persists not because Israel is a Jewish country, but because of an accident of history. Prior to the demise of the Ottoman Empire after the defeat of Germany and its allies in the First World War, Palestine was ruled by Turkey. The *millet* system, which accorded all recognized religious communities autonomy in such matters, was in effect throughout the Ottoman Empire, including Palestine. The British retained the *millet* system during the Mandate. In 1948 one of the first acts of the nascent state of Israel was to ratify all existing laws as the law of the state unless and until modified by the Knesset, the Israeli parliament. Israel's political system, including its system of proportional representation and the proliferation of small parties that render coalition governments a necessity, has ensured maintenance of the status quo in this area.

13.3 The position of Jewish law regarding its relationship to other systems of law

Jewish law, which understands itself to be the product of divine revelation rather than a social or political arrangement, is transnational. The principle of comity is not indigenous to Jewish law. Hence there is no inherent reason why, even in the Diaspora, it should recognize the binding nature of other systems of law. Of course, there may be pragmatic reasons for its adherents to do so, not the least of which are fear of punishment and gratitude for refuge.

Nevertheless, the Talmudic dictum '*dina de-malkhuta dina*' – 'the law of the land is the law' (*Gittin* 10b; *Bava Kamma* 113a; *Bava Batra* 54 b; and *Nedarim* 28a) – has gained wide currency and is almost as widely misunderstood. The principle itself is hardly self-evident and its validity requires justification. Medieval scholars proposed a wide range of theories, each of which serves to define and limit the ambit of the rule. The theories range from the relatively simple explanation that the principle reflects a rabbinic enactment promulgated for pragmatic reasons but having the status of a rabbinic, as distinct from a biblical, law to the notion that title to all real property is vested in the monarch, who may legitimately demand rent in the form of taxes in return for the right of domicile and impose other restrictions on use of his land as a condition of tenancy.

There is unanimity of opinion that '*dina de-malkhuta dina*' does not confer authority on the sovereign to compel violation of any provision of religious law. For example, the sovereign may not require compulsory voting and demand that Jewish nationals desecrate the Sabbath in marking their ballots. In fact, Jewish law would say that he dare not interfere in any manner with the free exercise of religion. Nor may a Jew justify violation of a tenet of Judaism on the plea that he is bound by Jewish law itself to obey the law of the land. Whether the threat of incarceration or a heavy financial penalty is sufficient to justify breach of any particular Jewish law is a different issue; resolution of that issue depends on the nature of the infraction and the severity of the punishment rather than on enshrinement of 'the law of the land' as an overarching principle of Jewish law.

Nor does Jewish law abdicate its authority in interpersonal matters, such as commerce and finance, having no bearing on social welfare. Thus, for example, it is Jewish law rather than the law of the state that Jewish law regards as governing the interpretation and enforcement of contracts. Nevertheless, in most areas of commercial law individuals may order their affairs as they please. Jewish law presumes that people intend to conduct their affairs in accordance with prevailing custom or trade practice. The provisions of *Hoshen Mishpat*, the section of the *Shulhan Arukh* devoted to matters of commerce and finance, are, in effect, the default rules to be applied in the absence of express stipulation or established custom. As a result, the law of the land may well become normative in such matters, not because Jewish law endows the state with legislative authority, but because the legislative norms have been commonly accepted and transformed into trade practice.

In the state of Israel – apart from matters of marriage and divorce, which remain within the authority of rabbinic courts – the law is an amalgam of Ottoman law, the law of the British Mandate and legislation enacted by the Knesset. Early in its history the state of Israel adopted the rule that, absent legislation by the Knesset, any precedent, even those dating to the days of the Ottoman Empire and of the British Mandate, governs adjudication of matters brought before Israeli courts. In the absence of either statute or precedent within the state of Israel or its antecedent political entities, any decision of any English court, even the most obscure, was regarded as binding precedent. More recently, in the Foundations of Law Act of 1980, the Knesset adopted a rule stating that in the absence of legislation, precedent in Israeli law or analogy that might be drawn to existing law, any doubtful question should be adjudicated in accordance with 'principles of liberty, justice, equity and peace of the heritage of Israel'. The motives for adopting that law – known as the *hok ha-lakuna*, 'the law of the gap' – were purely chauvinist. 'Heritage of Israel' is not a circumlocution to be equated with 'Jewish law'. Indeed, 'heritage of Israel' is a vague and amorphous notion that can be taken to mean what any judge wishes it to mean. In effect, it permits a court that finds no applicable law or precedent in Israeli law to develop its own notions of equity, justice, and fairness and simply to declare that its conclusions are consistent with the spirit of Jewish tradition.

Outside the state of Israel rabbinic courts do not have compulsory jurisdiction in any area of law. Judaism nevertheless requires its adherents to submit any dispute to a rabbinic court for adjudication. However, under appropriate circumstances the Bet Din will grant leave for recourse to a civil court if one of the parties refuses to appear before a Bet Din. Even under such circumstances, recovery is limited to that which would have been awarded by a Bet Din.

The United States and other Western countries accord the hearing conducted by a Bet Din the status of an arbitration proceeding. The decision of a Bet Din will be treated as an arbitral award enforceable in a court of common jurisdiction. However, enforcement of such a decision in the United States is dependent on conformity with rules regulating arbitration as spelled out in the statutes of the various jurisdictions or, in the alternative, in a form of common law arbitration. A signed submission to arbitrate before the Bet Din is required and the submission must specify the nature of the dispute submitted to arbitration. As arbitrators, members of a Bet Din must comply with any other provisions of applicable statutes. They must also conform to due process requirements, including according litigants the opportunity to be represented by counsel. In matters governed by contract, appearance before a Bet Din may be assured by inserting a clause requiring that all disputes be submitted to a Bet Din for arbitration.

Judaism recognizes the 613 Commandments of the Sinaitic Code to be binding only on its adherents. Judaism, however, also posits a corpus of law it regards as universally binding on humanity. These laws are known as the Seven Commandments of the Sons of Noah or as the Noaḥide Code.

God commanded the first six of those commandments to Adam: forbidding idolatry, blasphemy, homicide, sexual licentiousness (including incest, adultery, and pederasty), and theft, with an additional commandment, *dinin*, which will be discussed presently. God revealed the seventh commandment, the prohibition against eating a limb torn from a living animal, to Noah on his emergence from the Ark. Judaism teaches that non-Jews who accept and observe the Noaḥide Code deserve reward and merit eternal life.

The Seven Commandments are not regarded as universally binding as a priori principles discoverable by the light of reason alone. They are regarded as binding on the basis of dogmatic revelation, a revelation that preceded God's covenant with the Jewish people that was established at Sinai. Maimonides declares that obedience to those commandments on the basis of moral sensitivity or reason does not assure immortality; non-Jews are expected to observe the commandments of the Noaḥide Code because they constitute the revealed law of God.

The nature of the commandment of *dinin* is the subject of significant controversy. Maimonides regards *dinin* as a commandment requiring non-Jews to establish judicial systems for the purpose of bringing violators of the six other commandments to justice. The term '*dinin*' literally means 'laws'. For Maimonides, the connotation of the term in this context is enforcement of 'laws' by punishing violations of the Noaḥide Code. Failure to bring perpe trators to justice is regarded by Maimonides as a capital crime, as is violation of the other commandments of the Noaḥide Code.

Maimonides understood the biblical narrative of the slaying of the inhabitants of Shechem (modern-day Nablus) by Simeon and Levi as the imposition of punishment for their violation of the commandment of *dinin*. The people of Shechem were not directly complicit in Ḥamor's abduction and rape of Dinah, Simeon's and Levi's sister. They were, however, fully aware of the incident, but made no attempt to punish Ḥamor. For failure to do so they, too, incurred the death penalty. Rape of an unmarried woman is not per se a capital crime in the Noaḥide Code. Maimonides, however, understands 'theft' as defined for the purpose of the Noaḥide Code as a very broad concept, encompassing, *inter alia*, kidnapping and rape.

In disagreement with Maimonides, Naḥmanides, a thirteenth-century biblical scholar and halakhic commentator, understands the concept of *dinin* more broadly. According to Naḥmanides, violation of *dinin* is not a capital offence. The commandment includes not only an obligation to establish a judiciary and to mete out punishment to malfeasors but also constitutes a broad exhortation to promulgate rules and regulations governing commerce, labour, interpersonal financial relations, and so on. The term '*dinin*' as understood by Naḥmanides means 'laws' in the literal sense.

The precise nature of the laws subsumed under Naḥmanides's definition of *dinin* is the subject of controversy among later authorities. Some main- tain that the laws in question are identical to the laws of commerce, repayment of debts and prompt payment of wages, fraud, and so on, that are present in the corpus of law incumbent on Jews. In effect, *dinin* is the incorporation by reference of Jewish financial and commercial law in its entirety into the Noaḥide Code. Maimonides would regard most, if not all, of the self-same rules to be subsumed under the rubric of 'theft'. Thus, other than with regard to the capital nature of failure to prosecute evildoers, the controversy is essentially a matter of nomenclature.

Other authorities define the 'laws' commanded by this provision of the Noaḥide Code in a far different manner. They regard *dinin* as requiring non-Jews to establish a legal system that will result in a well-ordered society but as granting non-Jewish society broad discretion with regard to the content of its laws. For example, non-Jews may legislate that, in the absence of an express agreement between the parties, the wages of a labourer must be paid on a daily, weekly, or monthly basis. They may legislatively adopt any expedient they deem to be beneficial to the welfare of society, but they must promulgate *some* rule lest the fabric of society unravel in the absence of legal norms. Whereas, according to Maimonides, Noaḥide courts must be proficient in Jewish law and apply its provisions to litigants who come before it, according to this interpretation they may legitimately apply the provisions of, for example, the Uniform Commercial Code or any other applicable civil statute.

13.4 The survival of Jewish law

The Noaḥide Code has not formally been recognized or accepted by any significant number of non-Jews, at least not subsequent to the period of the Second Temple (a period ending in the first century of the Common Era). The history of the Sinaitic covenant, which is the heritage of the Jewish people, is remarkably different.

A professor at a prominent Israeli law school relates that he was asked a rather incongruous question. On the last day of classes in a course on Roman law, a student soliciting information about the approaching final examination asked, 'Should we revise only the material in the textbook or should we study recent cases as well?' It is, of course, ludicrous to speak of 'recent cases' in conjunction with a system of law that, despite its continued and profound influence over other systems of law, has for many centuries not been sovereign in any jurisdiction.

A similar question, if asked in a class devoted to the study of Jewish law, would not have elicited a derisive response. Despite the fact that Jewish law was not the law of any sovereign jurisdiction from the time of the exile of the people of Israel from their ancestral homeland until its limited reinstatement in rabbinic courts in the state of Israel, Jewish law remains alive and healthy throughout the Diaspora. Barely a day goes by that does not bring with it publication of new opinions and responsa that expand and deepen our understanding of the immutable principles embodied in Halakhah while simultaneously bearing witness to the vitality and dynamism of Jewish law in confronting novel situations.

There is a well-known hasidic[4] tale that recounts that, on Passover eve, one of the hasidic masters announced that he would not begin the seder – the Passover ritual and repast – until a quantity of Turkish wool, Austrian tobacco, and oriental silk was brought to him. Within a short time everything that he requested was procured. Thereupon, he announced that one additional item was required: a crust of bread. His disciples were taken aback by this strange request, but they unquestioningly set out to fulfil their master's command. They scoured the town, but to no avail. They were forced to return empty-handed and crestfallen. The hasidic master listened in silence as they reported their lack of success. Then, with a smile enveloping his face, he raised his hands and exclaimed, 'Master of the Universe! The Russian Czar deploys thousands of guards to patrol his borders, employs countless numbers of police officers in order to enforce his edicts and administers a vast penal system to punish those who violate his laws. But look at the contraband that can be found within his borders! You, Master of the Universe, have no guards, no police and no prisons. Your only weapon is a brief phrase in the Torah, forbidding Jews to retain ḥameẓ [grain products other than unleavened bread] in their possession on the eve of Passover, but nevertheless not a bit of ḥameẓ can be found in the entire city!'

Indeed, the fact that Jewish law remains vibrant is testimony to the loyalty and devotion of the Jewish people. No other such comprehensive system of law has survived without the police power of the state to enforce adherence to its dictates.

---

[4] The hasidic movement arose in the eighteenth century, in part as a response to a perceived over-intellectualization of Judaism. Many folk tales arose in which the key figure was one of the leaders of the movement intent on demonstrating the worthiness of even an unlearned Jew.

Further reading

On Jewish law in general

The Mishnah: for an English translation see *The Mishnah: Translated from the Hebrew with Introduction and Brief Explanatory Notes by Herbert Danby* (Oxford: Clarendon, 1933)

The Talmud: a recent translation of the entire Talmud is *Talmud Bavli, The Gemara: The Classic Vilna Edition, with an Annotated, Interpretive Elucidation, as an aid to Talmud Study*, rev. and enlarged edn (New York: Mesorah Publications, 2001)

J. D. Bleich, *Contemporary Halakhic Problems*, 5 vols. (vols. 1–4: New York and Hoboken: Ktav Publishing House, 1977–95; vol. 5: Southfield: Targum, 2005)

On the rabbinic tradition

The Code of Maimonides (Mishneh Torah), 14 vols., Yale Judaica Series (New Haven: Yale University Press, 1980)

R. Joseph Karo, *Ḥoshen Mishpat*, trans. in 10 vols. by E. B. Quint as *A Restatement of Rabbinic Civil Law* (New York and Jerusalem: Gefen, 2007)

The Rashi Chumash: with the complete Metzudoth-Chazal Haftaroth, trans. S. Silverstein (Southfield, MI: Targum; Nanuet, NY: Feldheim, 1997)

On the Talmud generally

Zevi Hirsch Chajes, *The Student's Guide through the Talmud (Mevo ha-Talmud)*, trans. and ed. J. Shachter (New York: P. Feldheim, 1960)

On Jewish civil law

I. Herzog, *Main Institutions of Jewish Law*, 2 vols. (New York: Soncino Press, 1980)

On biomedical ethics

J. D. Bleich, *Bioethical Dilemmas: A Jewish Perspective* (Hoboken: Ktav Publishing House, 1989)

Bioethical Dilemmas Volume 2: A Jewish Perspective (Southfield, MI: Targum, 2006)

Judaism and Healing: Halakhic Perspectives (New York: Ktav, 1981)

I. Jakobovits, *Jewish Medical Ethics: A Comparative and Historical Study of the Jewish Religious Attitude to Medicine and its Practice* (New York: Bloch, 1975)

J. Preuss, *Biblical and Talmudic Medicine*, trans. and ed. F. Rosner (New York: Sanhedrin Press, 1978)

On business ethics

L. Jung and A. Levine, *Business Ethics in Jewish Law* (New York: Hebrew Publishing, 1987)

A. Levine, *Case Studies in Jewish Business Ethics* (Hoboken: Ktav, Yeshiva University Press, 2000)

Economic Public Policy and Jewish Law (Hoboken: Ktav, Yeshiva University Press, 1993)

Economics and Jewish Law (New York: Ktav, Yeshiva University, 1987)

Free Enterprise and Jewish Law: Aspects of Jewish Business Ethics (New York: Ktav, Yeshiva University, 1980)

Moral Issues of the Marketplace in Jewish Law (New York: Yashar Books, 2005)

The Islamic legal tradition 14

Khaled Abou El Fadl

14.1 Introduction

The Islamic legal system consists of legal institutions, determinations, and practices that span a period of over fourteen hundred years and arise from a wide variety of cultural and geographic contexts that are as diverse as Arabia, Egypt, Persia, Bukhara, Turkey, Nigeria, Mauritania, Mali, Indonesia, and India. Despite the contextual and historical contingencies that constitute the complex reality of Islamic law, rather paradoxically the Islamic legal legacy has been the subject of widespread and stubbornly persistent stereotypes and over-simplifications, and is highly contested and grossly under-studied at the same time. Whether espoused by Muslim or non-Muslim scholars, highly simplified assumptions about Islamic law, such as the belief that Islamic legal doctrine stopped developing in the fourth/tenth century, the presumed sacredness and immutability of the legal system, or the phenomenon of so-called Qadi justice, are, to a large extent, products of turbulent political histories that contested and transformed Islamic law (or what is commonly referred to as Shari'a) into a cultural and ideological symbol. As part of the legacies of colonialism and modernity, Islamic law was then transformed into a symbolic construct of highly contested issues such as legitimacy, authenticity, cultural autonomy, or traditionalism, and reactionism, or religious oppression. Intellectually, there is a continuing tendency to treat Shari'a law as if it holds the keys to unlocking the mysteries of the Muslim heart and mind or, alternatively, as if it is entirely irrelevant to the formation and dynamics of Muslim societies. In all cases, however, because of the disproportionately politicized context of the field, Islamic legal studies remains largely undeveloped, and the discipline is plagued by inadequate scholarship, especially in the field of comparative legal studies. It is important to stress the point because, for all the generalizations one often encounters in the secondary literature on Islamic law, the reality is that, considering the richness of the legal tradition, our knowledge of the institutions, mechanisms, and micro-dynamics, discourses, and determinations of Islamic law in various places and at various times is very limited.

14.2 The difference between Islamic law and Muslim law

Not all legal systems or rules followed by Muslims are part of the Islamic legal tradition, but, at the same time, the boundaries of Islamic law are far more contested and negotiable than any fundamentalist or essentialist approach may be willing to admit. Part of what makes this issue particularly challenging is that, inescapably, it involves judgments as to the legitimacy and authenticity of what is Islamic and what is not necessarily so. But, more critically, the differentiation cannot be intelligibly addressed unless one takes full account of the epistemology and philosophy of Islamic jurisprudence, or the rules of normativity, obligation, and authority, and the processes of inclusion and exclusion in Islamic legal practice and history. Although Islamic law grew out of the normative teachings of the Prophet Muhammad and his disciples, the first generations of Muslim jurists borrowed and integrated legal practices from several sources, including Persia, Mesopotamia, Egypt and other Roman provinces, Yemen and Arabia, and Jewish law. But, at the same time, many existing and actual customary or executive administrative practices prevalent in pre-modern Muslim societies and polities were not integrated or recognized as being part of, or even consistent with, Islamic law or Islamic normative values.

Distinguishing Islamic from Muslim law has only become more elusive and challenging in post-colonial modern-day Muslim societies. Most contemporary Muslim countries adopted either the French-based civil law system or some version of the British common law system, and limited the application of Islamic law to personal law matters, particularly in the fields of inheritance and family law. In addition, in response to domestic political pressure, several Muslim countries in the 1970s and 1980s attempted to Islamize their legal systems by amending commercial or criminal laws in order to make them more consistent with purported Islamic legal doctrine. The fact remains, however, that the nature of the connection or relationship of any of these purportedly Islamically based or Islamized laws to the Islamic legal tradition remains debatable. Islamic legal doctrine was grafted onto what structurally and institutionally, as well as epistemologically, were legal systems borrowed and transplanted from the West. In practically every Muslim country, the complex institutional structures and processes of the Islamic legal system, especially in the nineteenth century, were systematically dismantled and replaced not just by Western legal systems but, more importantly, by the legal cultures of a number of Western colonial powers.

14.3 The sources of Islamic law

It is important to distinguish the formal sources of law in the Islamic legal tradition from what are often called the practical sources of law. Formal sources of law are an ideological construct – they are the ultimate foundations invoked by jurists and judges as the basis of legal legitimacy and authority. The practical sources, however, are the actual premises and processes utilized in legal practice in the process of producing positive rules and commandments. In theory, the foundations of all law in Islamic jurisprudence are the following: the Qur'an, the Sunna (the tradition of the Prophet Muhammad and his companions), *qiyas* (analogical or deductive reasoning) and *'ijma* (consensus or the overall agreement of Muslim jurists). In contrast to mainstream Sunni Islam, Shi'i jurisprudence, and a minority of Sunni jurists, recognize reason, instead of *qiyas*, as a foundational source of law. These four are legitimating sources, but the practical sources of law include an array of conceptual tools that greatly expand the venues of the legal determination. For instance, practical sources include presumptions of continuity (*istishab*) and the imperative of following precedents (*taqlid*), legal rationalizations for breaking with precedent and *de novo* determinations (*ijtihad*), application of customary practices ('*urf* and '*adah*), judgments in equity, equitable relief, and necessity (*istislah, haja, darura*, etc.), and, in some cases, the pursuit or the protection of public interests or public policies (*masalih mursala* and *sadd al-thara'i' wa al-mafasid*). These and other practical jurisprudential sources were not employed as legal tropes in a lawless application of so-called Qadi justice. In fact, sophisticated conceptual frameworks were developed to regulate the application of the various jurisprudential tools employed in the process of legal determination. These conceptual frameworks were not only intended to distinguish legitimate and authoritative uses of legal tools, but, collectively, they were designed to bolster accountability, predictability, and the principle of the rule of law.

Being the ultimate sources of legitimacy, the formal sources of law do not play a solely symbolic role in Islamic jurisprudence. Many legal debates and determinations originated or were derived directly from the textual narrative of the Qur'an and Sunna. Nevertheless, it would be erroneous to assume, as many fundamentalists tend to do, that Islamic law is a literalist explication or enunciation of the text of the Qur'an and Sunna. Only very limited portions of the Qur'an can be said to contain specific positive legal commandments or prohibitions. Much of the Qur'anic discourse, however, does have compelling normative connotations that were extensively explored and debated in the classical juristic tradition.[1] Muslim scholars developed an extensive literature on Qur'anic exegesis and legal hermeneutics as well as a body of work (known as *ahkam al-Qur'an*) exploring the ethical and legal implications of the Qur'anic discourse. Moreover, there is a classical tradition of disputations and debates on what is known as the 'occasions of revelation' (*asbab al-nuzul*), which deals with the context or circumstances that surrounded the revelation of particular Qur'anic verses or chapters, and on the critical issue of abrogation (*naskh*), or which Qur'anic prescriptions and commandments, if any, were nullified or voided during the time of the Prophet.

Similar issues relating to historical context, abrogation, and hermeneutics are dealt with in the juristic treatment of the legacy of the Prophet and his companions and disciples. However, in contrast to the juristic discourses on the Qur'an, there are extensive classical debates on the historicity or authenticity of the hadith (oral traditions attributed to the Prophet) and the Sunna (historical narratives typically about the Prophet but also his companions). While Muslim jurists agreed that the authenticity of the Qur'an, as God's revealed word, is beyond any doubt, classical jurists recognized that many of the traditions attributed to the Prophet were apocryphal. In this context, however, Muslim jurists did not just focus on whether a particular report was authentic or a fabrication, but on the extent or degree of reliability and the attendant legal consequences. Importantly, Muslim jurists distinguished between the reliability and normativity of traditions. Even if a tradition proved to be authentic, this did not necessarily mean that it was normatively binding, because most jurists differentiated between the Prophet's sacred and temporal roles. Not everything the

---

[1] The classical juristic tradition is generally understood as Islamic jurisprudence from the seventh to seventeenth centuries CE.

Prophet said or did created normative obligations on Muslims. Part of the challenge for Muslim jurists was to ascertain when his statements and actions were intended to create a legal obligation or duty (*taklif*), and when they were not meant to have any normative weight.

14.4 The nature and purpose of Islamic law

As an essential point of departure, it is important to underscore that in jurisprudential theory the ultimate point of Shari'a is to serve the well-being or achieve the welfare of people (*tahqiq masalih al-'ibad*).[2] The word '*Shari'a*', which many very often erroneously equate with Islamic law, means 'the Way of God and the pathway of goodness', and the objective of Shari'a is not necessarily compliance with the commands of God for their own sake. Such compliance is a means to an end – the serving of the physical and spiritual welfare and well-being of people. Significantly, in Islamic legal theory, God communicates God's Way (the Shari'a) through what is known as the *dalil* (pl. *adillah*). '*Dalil*' means 'indicator', 'mark', 'guide', or 'evidence', and in Islamic legal theory it is the fundamental building block of the search for the divine will and guidance. The most obvious type of indicator is an authoritative text (sing. *nass Shar'i* or pl. *al-nusus al-Shar'iyya*), such as the Qur'an, but Muslim jurists also recognized that God's wisdom is manifested through a vast matrix of indicators found in God's physical and metaphysical creation. Hence, other than through texts, God's signs or indicators could manifest themselves through reason and rationality ('*aql* and *ra'y*), intuitions (*fitrah*), and human custom and practice ('*urf* and '*adah*).[3] Especially in early Islam, which of these could legitimately be counted as avenues to God's will, and to what extent, were hotly debated issues.

In Islamic jurisprudence, the diversity and complexity of the divine indicators are considered part of the functionality and suitability of Islamic law for all times and places. The fact that the indicators are not typically precise,

---

[2] Ṣ. Maḥmaṣānī, *Falsafat al-Tashrī' fī al-Islām: The Philosophy of Jurisprudence in Islam* (Leiden: Brill, 1961), 172–5; M. Abū Zahrah, *Uṣūl al-Fiqh* (Cairo: Dār al-Fikr al-'Arabī, n.d.), 291; M. Zayd, *al-Maṣlaḥah fī al-Tashrī' al-Islāmī wa Najm al-Dīn al-Ṭūfī*, 2nd edn (Cairo: Dār al-Fikr al-'Arabī, 1964), 22; Y. Ḥāmid al-'Ālim, *al-Maqāṣid al-'Āmmah li al-Sharī'ah al-Islāmiyyah* (Herndon, VA: International Institute of Islamic Thought, 1991), 80; M. b. 'Alī b. Muḥammad al-Shawkānī, *Ṭalab al-'Ilm wa Ṭabaqāt al-Muta'allimīn: Adab al-Ṭalab wa Muntahā al-Arab* (n.p.: Dār al-Arqām, 1981), 145–51.

[3] A more historical translation for 'text' would be '*matn*' or '*khiṭāb*'.

deterministic, or unidimensional allows jurists to read the indicators in the light of the demands of time and place. So, for example, it is often noted that one of the founding fathers of Islamic jurisprudence, al-Shafi'i (d. 204/820) had one set of legal opinions that he thought properly applied in what is now Iraq, but changed his positions and rulings when he moved to Egypt to account for the changed circumstances and social differences between the two regions.[4] The same idea is embodied in the Islamic legal maxim: 'It may not be denied that laws will change with the change of circumstances' (la yunkar taghayyur al-ahkam bi taghayyur al-zaman wa al-ahwal).[5]

One of the most important aspects of the epistemological paradigm on which Islamic jurisprudence was built was the presumption that in most matters the divine will is unattainable, and even if attainable, no person or institution has the authority to claim certitude in realizing this will. This is why the classical jurists rarely spoke in terms of legal certainties (yaqin and qat). Rather, as is apparent in the linguistic practices of the classical juristic culture, Muslim jurists for the most part spoke in terms of probabilities or in terms of the preponderance of evidence and belief (ghalabat al-zann). Muslim jurists emphasized that only God possesses perfect knowledge – human knowledge in legal matters is tentative or even speculative; it must rely on the weighing of competing factors and the assertion of judgment based on an assessment of the balance of evidence on any given matter. So, for example, Muslim jurists developed a rigorous field of analytical jurisprudence known as tarjih,[6] which dealt with the methodological principles according to which jurists would investigate, assign relative weight, and balance conflicting evidence in order to reach a preponderance of belief about potentially correct determinations.[7]

---

[4]   Maḥmaṣānī, Falsafat al-Tashrī', 59; B. Abū al-'Aynayn Badrān, Uṣūl al-Fiqh (Cairo: Dār al-Ma'ārif, 1965), 322; Ṣ. al-Ṣāliḥ, Ma'ālim al-Sharī'ah al-Islāmiyyah (Beirut: Dār al-'Ilm li al-Malāyīn, 1975), 46; M. Hashim Kamali, Principles of Islamic Jurisprudence, rev. edn (Cambridge: Islamic Texts Society, 1991), 285.

[5]   Maḥmaṣānī, Falsafat al-Tashrī', 200–2; A. b. Muḥammad al-Zarqā, Sharḥ al-Qawā'id al-Fiqhiyyah, 4th edn (Damascus: Dār al-Qalam, 1996), 227–9; C. R. Tyser, The Mejelle: Being an English Translation of Majallah-el-Ahkam-Adliya and a Complete Code on Islamic Civil Law (Lahore: Punjab Educational Press, 1967), 8.

[6]   In jurisprudential sources this field is known as 'ilm al-tarjīḥ' or 'ilm al-ta'ārud wa al-tarjīḥ' or 'ilm al-ta'dīl wa al-tarjīḥ' – 'the field of conflict and preponderance' or 'the field of balance and preponderance'.

[7]   B. G. Weiss, The Search for God's Law: Islamic Jurisprudence in the Writings of Sayf al-Dīn al-Āmidī (Salt Lake City: University of Utah Press, 1992), 734–8.

Contemporary fundamentalist and essentialistic orientations imagine Islamic law to be highly deterministic and casuistic, but this is in sharp contrast to the epistemology and institutions of the Islamic legal tradition that supported the existence of multiple equally orthodox and authoritative legal schools of thought, all of which are valid representations of the divine will. Indeed, the Islamic legal tradition was founded on a markedly pluralistic, discursive, and exploratory ethos that became the very heart of its distinctive character. According to classical legal reasoning, no one jurist, institution, or juristic tradition may have an exclusive claim over the divine truth, and hence the state does not have the authority to recognize the orthodoxy of one school of thought to the exclusion of all others.[8] While Shari'a is divine, *fiqh* (the human understanding of Shari'a) was recognized to be only potentially so, and it is the distinction between Shari'a and *fiqh* that fuelled and legitimated the practice of legal pluralism in Islamic history.

14.5 The difference between Shari'a and *fiqh*

The conceptual distinction between Shari'a and *fiqh* was the result of recognizing the limitations of human agency, and also a reflection of the Islamic dogma that perfection belongs only to God. While Shari'a was seen as an abstract ideal, every human effort at understanding or implementing this ideal was considered necessarily imperfect. In theory, Muslim jurists agreed that even if a jurist's determination is ultimately wrong, God will not hold such a jurist liable as long as he or she exerted due diligence in searching for the right answer. According to one group of legal theorists, those who are ultimately proven to be wrong will still be rewarded for their due diligence, but those who prove to be right will receive a greater reward. The alternative point of view, however, argued that on all matters of *fiqh* there is no single truth to be revealed by God in the hereafter. All positions held sincerely and reached after due diligence are in God's eyes correct. God rewards people in direct proportion to the exhaustiveness, diligence, and sincerity of their search for the divine will – sincerity of conviction, the

---

[8] J. al-Dīn 'Abd al-Raḥmān b. Abī Bakr al-Suyūṭī, *Ikhtilāf al-Madhāhib*, ed. 'Abd al-Qayyūm Muḥammad Shafī' al-Bastawī (Cairo: Dār al-I'tiṣām, AH 1404), 22–3; Y. Dutton, *The Origins of Islamic Law: The Qur'an, the Muwaṭṭa', and Madinan 'Amal* (Surrey: Curzon Press, 1999), 29; P. Crone and M. Hinds, *God's Caliph: Religious Authority in the First Centuries of Islam* (Cambridge University Press, 1986), 86.

search, and the process are in themselves the ultimate moral values. It is not that there is no objective truth – rather, according to this view, the truth adheres to the search.

This classical debate had an impact on the development of various doctrines and institutions in Islamic jurisprudence, the most important of which was negotiating the dynamics between Shari'a and *fiqh*. In the Islamic legal tradition, there is only one Shari'a (*Shari'at Allah*) but there are a number of competing schools of thought of *fiqh* (*madhahib fiqhiyya*). Although all jurists embraced the theological dogma that God's perfection cannot be reproduced or attained by human beings, this did not mean that they considered every aspect of Shari'a to be entirely unattainable or inaccessible until the hereafter. Some have suggested that Shari'a contains the foundational or constitutional principles and norms of the legal system. So, for instance, Shari'a imposes a duty (*taklif*) on Muslims to enjoin goodness and resist wrongfulness. There is little doubt that this duty is a part of Shari'a, but what it actually means and how to or who should implement it is part of *fiqh*. Nevertheless, the exact boundaries between Shari'a and *fiqh* were often contested and negotiable, and whether there is overlap between the two categories turned out to be challenging and at times ambiguous. Behind most of the jurisprudential conceptions of Shari'a was the basic idea that what cumulative generations of Muslims reasonably identified as fundamental to the Islamic religion (for instance, the five pillars of the Islamic faith: profession of faith (*shahada*), prayer (*salat*), fasting (*siyam*), almsgiving (*zakat*), and pilgrimage (*hajj*)) ought to be part of the unassailable Shari'a. As some have contended, this approach might have been important to the field of theology, but, in law, Shari'a could not be limited to inherited or popular ideas. Rather, Shari'a comprises the foundational or constitutional normative values that constitute the grundnorms of the Islamic legal system. For instance, the notion that the divine will cannot be represented by a single system of *fiqh*, and the celebration of diversity are themselves one of those foundational grundnorms. For example, it is firmly established in the Islamic legal tradition that Shari'a seeks to protect and promote five fundamental values: (1) life, (2) intellect, (3) reputation or dignity, (4) lineage or family, and (5) property. Furthermore, Muslim jurists overwhelmingly held that there are three basic levels of attainment or fulfilment of such values: necessities, needs, and luxuries. Under Shari'a law, legal imperatives increase in proportion to the level of demand for the attainment of each value. Thus when it comes to life, for example, the legal duty to secure a person's survival takes precedence over the obligation of guaranteeing human beings any basic needs that are above and beyond what is necessary for survival. Nevertheless, alongside these broad fundamental principles, historically, Muslim jurists developed specific positive commandments that were said to be necessary for the protection of the values mentioned above, such as, for instance, the laws punishing slander, which were said to be necessary for the protection of reputation or dignity, or the laws punishing fornication, which were said to be necessary for the protection of lineage and family. I shall discuss the *hudud* penalties further below, but for now it is important to emphasize that many of the positive legal determinations purportedly serving the five values were often declared to be a part of Shari'a, and not just *fiqh*, or were left in a rather ambiguous and contested status between Shari'a and *fiqh*. Claiming that a positive legal commandment is not a by-product of *fiqh* but is essentially part of Shari'a effectively endowed such a commandment with immunity and immutability. The boundaries between Shari'a and *fiqh* were negotiated in a variety of highly contextually contingent ways in the course of Islamic history, but the dynamics and processes of this history remain grossly understudied.

Purportedly, by the end of the tenth century CE, no fewer than one hundred schools of *fiqh* had emerged, but for a wide variety of reasons most of these schools ultimately failed to survive. The most striking characteristic about the legal schools that dominated the practice of law for more than three centuries after the death of the Prophet is their remarkable diversity and, in fact, one would be hard pressed to find any significant legal issue about which juristic disputations and discourses have not generated a large number of divergent opinions and conflicting determinations. Put differently, there did not seem to be many issues in Shari'a that were off-limits for the inquiries of *fiqh*.

Initially, what differentiated one school of law (*madhhab*) from another were methodological disagreements and not necessarily the actual determinations. Importantly, the founders of the schools of *fiqh*, and the early jurists in general, did not intend to generate binding legal precepts. Rather, acting more like law professors and legal scholars, they produced legal opinions and analysis, which became part of the available common law to be adopted by state-appointed judges in the light of regional customary practices. Legal scholars from the different schools of thought were often far more interested in hypotheticals that illustrated their analytical models and methodologies than in passing judgments on actual disputes. This is why *fiqh* studies did not speak in terms of positive legal duties or prohibitions but analysed legal issues in terms of five values: (1) neutral or permissible (*mubah/halal*), (2) obligatory (*fard/wajib*), (3) forbidden (*muharram*), (4) recommended (*mandub/mustahab*), and (5) reprehensible or disfavoured (*makruh*). Frequently, jurists wrote in probabilistic terms, saying, for example, 'what is more correct in our opinion', referring to the prevailing view within the jurist's school of thought (*al-murajjah 'indana*). The critical point is that the masters of *fiqh* understood that they were not making binding law but issuing opinions of persuasive authority. The difference between *fiqh* and positive law was akin to the distinction between *fatwa* and *hukm*. A *hukm* is a binding and enforceable legal determination, but a *fatwa* (responsa) is a legal opinion on a particular dispute, problem, or novel issue, which, by definition, enjoys only persuasive authority. Both *fiqh* and *fatawa* (sing. *fatwa*) become binding law only if adopted as such by a person as a matter of conscience or if adopted as enforceable law by a legitimate authority such as a state judge. In other words, *fiqh* and *fatwa* are normative legal proposals that are contingent on essential enabling acts or triggers: the conscientious acceptance of its mandatory authority by a Muslim practitioner or by an official adoption by a proper authority. Failure to appreciate this fundamental point about the construction and structure of the legal views expressed in *fiqh* works has led to a great deal of ill-informed and misguided scholarship regarding Islamic law.

One of the most entrenched myths about Islamic law is that the legal system ceased to develop or change from the tenth or eleventh centuries CE because, fearing diversity and fragmentation, the so-called 'doors of *ijtihad*' were declared to be forever closed. According to this claim, Muslim jurists were expected to imitate their predecessors (the practice of *taqlid*) without undertaking legal innovations (*ijtihad*). This myth seems to have emerged in the nineteenth century as a simplistic explanation of the purported stagnation of the Islamic legal system and as justification for the legal reforms of the time, which in reality amounted to little more than the importation of European legal systems.[9] More importantly, this myth persisted among contemporary scholars because of the paucity of studies on the micro-dynamics of Islamic law and because of the failure properly to understand some of the basic historical realities about the development of the Islamic legal system. For example, *taqlid* was not the instrument of legal

---

[9] W. B. Hallaq, *Shari'a: Theory, Practice, Transformations* (Cambridge University Press, 2009).

stagnation; it was an important functional instrument of the rule of law. In general, *taqlid* stabilized the law by requiring continuity in legal application, and by creating a legal presumption in favour of precedents unless a heightened standard of evidence justifying legal change is met. Indeed, many of the most important developments in Islamic law were accomplished by jurists centuries after the supposed doors of *ijtihad* were closed.

The essential point about the Islamic legal tradition, and especially the role of *fiqh*, is that the juristic method and the linguistic practices of cumulative communities of legal interpretation became not only the mechanism for legitimacy and authority, but also the actual source of law. As a community of guilded specialists with an elaborate system of insignia and rituals, in most cases structured around a system resembling the Inns of Court in England, the jurists played a critical role in upholding the rule of law and in mediating between the masses and rulers.[10] However, the primacy of the juristic method and the organized guilds representing the various schools of law, contrary to some stereotypical claims, did not mean that the application of Islamic law became completely streamlined or simply mechanical and formulaic. Within a single *madhhab*, it was common for various juristic temperaments and philosophical orientations to exist because the established schools of law became the common platforms where conservative or activist jurists had to pursue their legal agendas or objectives. Within a single established school of thought, there could be conservative, traditionalist, rationalist, or equity-oriented trends, but each of these orientations had to negotiate its particular approach within the demands of the juristic method of the *madhhab*. Fundamentally, whether a particular legal orientation emphasized the use of the text, reason, custom, equity, or public interest, these tools had to be justified, channelled, negotiated, and limited by the juristic method.[11] The point is not just that the juristic method became the prevalent mechanism for negotiating the tools and instruments of legal analysis, but, even more, the juristic method became Islamic law itself; it became the mechanism for negotiating not just the relationship between

---

[10] J. Makdisi, 'The Guilds of Law in Medieval Legal History: An Inquiry into the Origins of the Inns of Court', (1985–86) 34 *Cleveland State Law Review* 3.

[11] M. S. al-Būṭī, Ḍawābiṭ al-Maṣlaḥa fī al-Sharī'a al-Islāmiyya (n.p.: Mo'amu'sast al-Risālah, n.d.), 178–89; M. K. Masud, *Islamic Legal Philosophy: A Study of Abū Isḥāq al-Shāṭibī's Life and Thought* (New Delhi: International Islamic Publishers, 1989), 165, 174–5; W. B. Hallaq, *A History of Islamic Legal Theories: An Introduction to Sunnī Uṣūl al-Fiqh* (Cambridge University Press, 1997), 208.

Shari'a and *fiqh*, but between the realm of God and that of humans and, ultimately, between the sacred and the profane.

14.6 The sacred and the profane in Islamic law

The relationship between the sacred and the profane was negotiated in Islamic law through the ongoing historical dynamics demarcating the boundaries between Shari'a and *fiqh*. But, beyond this, there were several other conceptual categories and functional mechanisms through which sacred and temporal spaces were negotiated in Islamic law. Among these categories was the conceptual differentiation between *'ibadat* (laws dealing with matters of ritual) and *mu'amalat* (laws pertaining to human dealings and intercourses). In theory, all Islamic laws fall into one of these two categories: *'ibadat* are laws that regulate the relationship between God and humans, and *mu'amalat* are laws that regulate the relationship of humans with one another. As to issues falling under the category of *'ibadat*, there is a legal presumption in favour of literalism and for the rejection of any innovations or novel practices. However, in the case of *mu'amalat* the opposite presumption applies; innovations or creative determinations are favoured (*al-asl fi al-'ibadat al-'ittiba' wa al-asl fi al-mu'amalat al-'ibtida'*). The rationale behind this categorical division is that when it comes to space occupied exclusively by how people worship the Divine, there is a presumption against deference to human reason, material interests, and discretion. Conversely, in space occupied by what the jurists used to describe as the pragmatics of social interaction, there is a presumption in favour of the rational faculties and practical experiences of human beings. Underscoring the difference between *'ibadat* and *mu'amalat* was the fact that not only were the two identified as distinct and separate fields and specialties of law, but it was also quite possible to specialize and become an authority in one field but not the other (*fiqh al-'ibadat* or *fiqh al-mu'amalat*).

Beyond this clean categorical division, negotiating the extent to which a particular human act or form of conduct, whether it be public or private, primarily involved *'ibadat* or *mu'amalat* was not a simple and unequivocal issue. For instance, there were lengthy debates as to whether the prohibition of *zina* (fornication or adultery) or consumption of alcoholic substances falls under the category of *'ibadat* or *mu'amalat* or, alternatively, some mixture of both categories. Nevertheless, as in the case of the debates regarding the parameters of Shari'a and *fiqh*, although in principle there was a philosophical recognition that the spaces occupied by the sacred and profane require different treatments, in reality it was the juristic method that played the defining role in determining the function of text, precedent, and rational innovation in the treatment of legal questions. Ultimately, it was not the legal presumptions attaching to either category but the institutional and methodological processes of each legal school of thought that most influenced the way issues were analysed and determined.

Perhaps as a practical result of the epistemology of plural orthodoxy, in Islamic jurisprudence a court's judgment or finding was not equated with or considered the same as God's judgment. At a normative level, a court's judgment could not right a wrong or make wrong a right and it could not negate or replace the duties and responsibilities imposed by an individual's conscience. Jurists argued that individuals do have an obligation to obey court decisions as a matter of law and order, but judicial determinations do not reflect or mirror God's judgment. A classic example would be that of a litigant who, for instance, follows the Hanafi school of thought, and who is forced to submit to the jurisdiction of a Shafi'i court (see above for a general discussion of the differences among the juristic schools of thought). The Hanafi litigant would have to obey the judgment of the court not because it is correct but because a duly constituted court possesses legitimate positive authority (*sultat al-ilzam*). Not surprisingly, the proper balance between the duty of obedience to the public order and the duty to follow one's conscience, or school of thought, has been the subject of considerable jurisprudential debate.

Because of the reality of pluralist legal orthodoxy, in Islamic jurisprudence it is entirely conceivable even where Shari'a is the law of the land that an individual would legitimately feel torn between his duties towards the public order and those towards God. The legitimacy of the state and even the law were not absolute – both state and law performed a functional but necessary role. Beyond the fact that the state could not act as a proxy for God, legal determinations could not void the necessary role of personal beliefs or individual conscience because they did not replace the sovereignty of divine judgments.

14.7 The rights of God and the rights of humans

Perhaps the clearest articulation in Islamic jurisprudence of the distinctive spaces occupied by the sacred and profane is the categorical differentiation between the rights of God (*huquq Allah*) and rights of humans (*huquq al-'ibad*). Muslim jurists agreed that humans cannot benefit or harm God and so, unlike the rights owed to human beings, the rights of God do not involve any actual interests of God. Depending on the context, the word *huquq* (sing. *haqq*) referred to the province, jurisdiction, boundaries, or limits of God (*hudud Allah*). Interestingly, *huquq al-'ibad* did not refer to public or common rights but to the material interests and benefits belonging to each human being as an individual. The rights of God do not need a protector or vindicator because God is fully capable of redressing any transgressions committed against God's boundaries or commands. But, unlike God, human beings do need an agent empowered to defend them and redress any transgressions committed against their person or properties. Therefore the state is not simply empowered but is obligated to enforce the rights and obligations owed to people and may not legitimately ignore them or waive them. The state was precluded from enforcing the rights of God because the state was not God's representative and God had reserved these rights to God's exclusive jurisdiction and province.

Muslim jurists clearly recognized the exceptionality and exclusivity of the sacred space and even jealously guarded it from the encroachments of the profane. Ironically, however, it is in dealing with the issue of God's clear boundaries and limits that the jurists most famously collapsed the sacred and profane into a single space, at least in theory if not in application. In what is known as the *hudud* penalties, Muslim jurists asserted that there is a category of divinely ordained punishments that apply to violations committed against a class of mixed rights (*huquq mukhtalita*) which are shared by God and human beings. As a category, mixed rights involve issues where the material interests or well-being of people are involved but, at the same time, there is a discernible divine will staking a specific claim for the Divine over these issues. In the case of the divinely ordained *hudud* penalties, for reasons not necessarily known to human beings, God purportedly not only explicitly determined the punishable act and the exact penalty but also the exact process by which the crime is proven and the penalty is carried out. Although not all the *hudud* crimes were mentioned in the text of the Qur'an, a general juristic consensus was said to exist as to the divine origin of the penalties. In the classical tradition, fornication or adultery (*zina*), robbery (*sariqa*), consumption of alcohol, defamation (*qadhf*), and apostasy (*ridda*) were the violations most commonly included within the *hudud*. The real paradox of the *hudud* is that while in contemporary Islam they are often imagined to be the harbinger and flagship of Islamic law, in the classical tradition the *hudud* penalties were rarely applied precisely because of the space occupied by the Divine in defining and redressing the crime. On the one hand, by categorizing a crime under the *hudud*, the definition of the crime and the appropriate penalty became sanctified and immutable. But, on the other hand, by placing it within the category of *hudud*, the jurists effectively endowed the penalty with a largely symbolic role because the technical requirements and administrative costs of enforcing these sacred penalties were largely prohibitive. As with all matters involving the rights of God, as far as the state is concerned, it is imperative to tread cautiously lest in trying to uphold the bounds of God, whether through ignorance, arrogance, or incompetence, the state itself ends up committing an infraction against the Divine. The Prophet Muhammad's injunction, which was adapted into a legal maxim, commanded that any doubt must serve to suspend the application of the *hudud*. In addition to the presumption of innocence which applied to all criminal accusations, Muslim jurists often cited the injunction above in greatly circumscribing the application of the *hudud* penalties through a variety of doctrinal and procedural hurdles. In general, repentance, forgiveness, and doubt acted to prevent the application of the *hudud*. In dealing with the rights of God, it was always better to forgive than to punish; repentance of the defendant acted to suspend the *hudud*, and all doubt had to be construed in favour of vindicating the accused.

As far as the classical jurists were concerned, the *hudud*, like all matters implicating the rights of God, were better left to divine vindication in the hereafter. In most cases, instead of pursuing a *hudud* penalty, the state proved a lesser-included crime under a less demanding burden of proof, and applied lesser penalties, normally involving imprisonment, some form of corporal punishment, banishment, or a fine. Lesser penalties for non-*hudud* crimes, or lesser-included crimes, fell into two categories: *qisas* (talion, or punishment in kind of the offence, i.e. an eye for an eye) or *ta'zir* (penalties prescribed by the state for offences against public interest). *Qisas* was treated as a private recourse and right, where pardon or forgiveness was always preferable, but *ta'zir* were thoroughly profane punitive measures left to the authority and jurisdiction of the state and applied to protect the public through deterrence. Classical Muslim jurists enunciated various principles regulating and restricting the powers of the state over *ta'zir* punishments. Fundamentally, however, while *hudud* punishments were greatly circumscribed throughout Islamic history, what *ta'zir* punishments were applied and in what manner varied greatly from one time and place to another.

By circumscribing the enforcement of the rights of the Divine, the classical jurists of Islam constrained the power of the state to act as God's avenger. However, doctrinally the rights of God, as a concept, played an important normative and ethical role in the Shari'a dynamics taking place within Muslim societies. The rights of God symbolically represented the moral boundaries of appropriate social mores and values in the public space. This does not mean, as some contemporary reformists have claimed, that the rights of God are equivalent to or substantially the same as public interests or space. Normatively, the Shari'a is expected to pervade the private and public spaces by appealing to the private consciences of individuals and to societies as collectivities. But there is one way this could happen and that is through voluntary compliance. For the most part, Islamic jurisprudence invoked the compulsory powers of the state in order to enforce obligations or rights owed to people – not to God. Functionally, Islamic law was thought of not as a means of empowering the state to act on God's behalf but as setting limits to the powers of the state through the imposition of the rule of law. Therefore the greater legacy of the Islamic tradition deals with questions involving *mu'amalat* or social intercourses and dealings or the resolution of conflicts arising from competing claims and interests. Questions of social etiquette or proper public manners were not treated in books of jurisprudence but were relegated to the status of moralistic pamphlets (*kutub al-raqa'iq*) written often by religious preachers or sometimes by qualified jurists for the consumption of the laity.

14.8 Modernity and the deterioration of Islamic law

With the advent of the age of colonialism, the Islamic legal system was consistently replaced by legal systems imported from Western colonial states. The factors contributing to the deterioration and replacement of Islamic law are numerous, but primary among those factors was the pressure exerted by foreign powers for a system of concessions and special jurisdictions that served the economic and political interests of the colonizers and a parasitical native elite that derived and maintained its privileged status from the financial, military, and cultural institutions of colonial powers. Throughout the

Muslim world, this led to a protracted process by which colonial powers or, in the post-colonial age, local nationalistic governments consistently undermined the autonomy of, and eventually completely controlled, the traditional legal guilds, not only depriving them of any meaningful political role but also deconstructing their very legitimacy in Muslim societies. Perhaps more destructive to the Islamic legal system was the fact that the institutional replacement of Islamic law was accompanied by a process of cultural transformation that led to the deconstruction of the very epistemological foundations of Islamic jurisprudence. The cultural impact of colonialism on Muslim societies was, and continues to be, immeasurable.

Predictably, as the twentieth century came to a close and the twenty-first century began, the field of Islamic law suffered a crippling crisis of authority as Muslims struggled to rediscover the rules and criteria for defining the authoritative in modern Islamic law. The fact remains, however, that as a legal tradition Islamic law continues to carry considerable normative weight for millions of Muslims around the world, and also continues to influence, to one degree or another, the legal systems of a number of countries. The crisis of authority plaguing Islamic law today does not affect its relevance or importance. It does mean that Islamic law does not have effective means for regulating the reasonableness of the determinations generated on its behalf or attributed to it. In the contemporary age many voices speak in the name of Islamic law, and the problem is that some of these voices are quite unreasonable.

Further reading

K. Abou El Fadl, *And God Knows the Soldiers: The Authoritative and Authoritarian in Islamic Discourses* (Lanham, MD: University Press of America, 2001)

   The Great Theft: Wrestling Islam from the Extremists (San Francisco: HarperSanFrancisco, 2005)

   Speaking in God's Name: Islamic Law, Authority and Women (Oxford: Oneworld Publications, 2001)

P. Crone and M. Hinds, *God's Caliph: Religious Authority in the First Centuries of Islam* (Cambridge University Press, 1986)

Y. Dutton, *The Origins of Islamic Law: The Qur'an, the Muwaṭṭa', and Madinan 'Amal* (Surrey: Curzon Press, 1999)

W. B. Hallaq, *A History of Islamic Legal Theories: An Introduction to Sunnī Uṣūl al-Fiqh* (Cambridge University Press, 1997)

Shari'a: Theory, Practice, Transformations (Cambridge University Press, 2009)

M. H. Kamali, *Principles of Islamic Jurisprudence,* rev. edn (Cambridge: Islamic Texts Society, 1991)

J. Makdisi, 'The Guilds of Law in Medieval Legal History: An Inquiry into the Origins of the Inns of Court', (1985–6) 34 *Cleveland State Law Review* 3

M. K. Masud, *Islamic Legal Philosophy: A Study of Abū Isḥāq al-Shāṭibī's Life and Thought* (New Delhi: International Islamic Publishers, 1989)

B. G. Weiss, *The Search for God's Law: Islamic Jurisprudence in the Writings of Sayf al-Dīn al-Āmidī* (Salt Lake City: University of Utah Press, 1992)

The sub-Saharan legal tradition 15

Rodolfo Sacco

15.1 Introduction

The expression 'African law' refers to a legal family which is not comprehensive of the African continent as a whole. Northern Africa, namely where the Pharaonic, Persian, Alexandrine, Roman, and Ottoman empires ruled, has a history and legal framework with more in common with the Middle East and the Mediterranean area than with sub-Saharan Africa. South Africa, in turn, underwent an intense Europeanization process, which makes it different from other countries in the continent.

Africa as studied by the comparative lawyer is smaller than Africa measured by the geographer.

To present African law is not an easy task, since disparate realities characterized by contradictory elements coexist therein. Instead, to talk about single components of African law could be relatively easier. On one hand, authoritative law (both colonial and independent) is not very different from European law; it aims to oversee the administrative machine of governance, to manage credit instruments, and control trading companies. On the other hand, traditional law which continues to exist often regulates marriage and family institutions, land tenure regimes, the criminal law sector, and so on.

If it is true that written African law is not the whole of African law, it is also true that African traditional law is not the whole of African law.

In order to analyse African law it is necessary to restructure the meaning and features of all its elements and place them in their specific collocations in accordance with the general framework.

The elements to be considered here were either born in or brought to Africa at different times. However, the date of their appearance on the scene is approximately the same for all African countries. Consequently, it is

Rodolfo Sacco thanks Salvatore Mancuso, University of Cape Town, for his excellent assistance in translating and editing this chapter.

possible to consider African law as made out of superimposing layers, each one part of a complex reality.

The layers we are discussing are four.

The traditional stratum is the oldest. It embraces different legal sets which followed one another through the centuries without ever losing some fundamental and constant characteristics.

Chronologically speaking, the second layer is the religious stratum, mainly Islamic. It was first introduced in the Sahel through the Hillalian invasions (tenth and thirteenth centuries CE) and along the eastern coast of Africa by maritime colonization by Middle Eastern powers.

The third layer is the colonial era, developed from 1880 until 1960.

The epoch of independence, the fourth layer, can be divided into two phases. First (1960–80), Africa chased progress by imitating European models. Then the rediscovery of traditional values and rational choice among available models prevailed.

15.2 Traditional law

15.2.1 Characteristics

African traditional law – in its various manifestations – arose without professional lawyers, without the transmission of organized legal knowledge, and without legal terminology.

Anthropological methodology is needed to study and understand traditional Africa, both for practical research and conceptual organization. It is impossible to distinguish between the legal anthropologist and the 'Africanist' jurist interested in the investigation of the traditional layer. Moreover, cultural anthropology, even if not specifically legal cultural anthropology, contributed greatly to the study and understanding of African traditional law.

Given these preliminary remarks, it is important to draw attention to the mistake of confusing African traditional law with African law *tout court*. Traditional law is a layer and it is the oldest layer in the complex structure of African law. With the passing of time it has resisted the competition of subsequent layers, but sometimes paying the price of significant alterations, and only surviving to a limited extent.

African traditional law can itself be separated into numerous strata. For instance, the law of the Pygmies and San of the Kalahari Desert is far simpler than the law of other African peoples. The former lack collective activities and any kind of sovereign head (making it impossible to envisage any public law), there is no division of labour (which affects exchange regimes), the part played by supernatural powers is minor, and so on. The making of a more complex society required time and transition through important phases.

As already mentioned, political power initially tended to be uniformly distributed among all the members (adult men) of the society, alongside the authority granted to a chief *primus inter pares* in particular circumstances, or for limited purposes. At a given moment, the model of the sacral power of the king spread from Egypt all over Africa. However, a structural centralized power, based on the model of the Egyptian and Mesopotamian empires of the fourth century BCE, never came into being in traditional Africa. There were no fiscal system, no land register, no taxpayers' rolls (and no writing system), no permanent courts, no public works, no programmatic cult of the authority, no truth recognized and defended by a central power, no organized transmission of religious or laic knowledge, and so on.

African traditional law is linked to the sacred.

The sacred secures social and legal relationships. Supernatural sanctions can strike those who do not respect the rules. One of the fundamental qualities of a chief is the favour of the cosmic forces, which he flows to the society as a whole to make it prosper. Important decisions are suggested in dreams, and ancestors have important powers over both men and things (especially the earth). Relationships between living beings could be affected and compromised by magical practices that ill-intentioned persons carry out to the disadvantage of others. The law tries to intervene in this: the judge or arbitrator needs to know the facts, and magic enlightens and leads him to the truth.

African traditional rule is not issued by a political authority and is not written (African traditional society does not have a writing system); in general terms, the life of African traditional law does not involve writing. The judge's decisions, the embryonic transmission of legal knowledge, can do without writing. This consideration keeps the claim of orality as a characteristic of African traditional law.

More recently, it has been clarified that the term 'orality' is not accurate: the lack of the precise formulation and verbalization of African traditional rules is more important than the lack of missing written formulation. Law is practised, but its grammatical rules are not made explicit (in the same way, the rules of language and technologies are tacit in those cultures). In this regard, we have talked of 'mute law' (Sacco) or 'sign law' (Vanderlinden).

Reducing such rules for a sophisticated European language cannot be done without betraying the meanings. The automatic link between legal paradigm and legal effects, typical of European conceptualization, is absent in African traditional systems. There, a judgment is influenced by a number of elements extraneous to the fact (the qualities of the parties, need for a decision acceptable to both parties and third parties, and so on).

Despite the care and deep knowledge of the compilers, what has been said must be borne in mind when evaluating the collections of African customs which have been promoted and compiled during the colonization era.

15.2.2 Individuals and the family

According to African tradition, the subject entitled to a right is not always and exclusively the individual according to a general egalitarian rule. Rather, the status of the individual relies on his position in the group to which he belongs and the rank of his group in the society. Belonging to a group is the basis of individual rights and duties: a group member could be a victim of vengeance because of an offence committed by another member of the same group.

The human being is not the sole entity to have rights. Beside them, ancestors could have rights, as can supernatural entities and natural things such as plants. In particular, the earth is not only the object of rights, but is rather one of the parties in a legal relationship with the group and the individual.

Slavery was commonly practised in traditional Africa. Moreover, African society is usually stratified. While the aristocracy is at the top (in some cases conquerors), at the bottom are different castes (in some cases, shepherds) or sub-castes (typically, smiths and butchers).

The great importance attached to the fact of belonging to a group makes relationships within the group stable. The communitarian spirit of Africans is often admired by the Europeans as being counter to the aberrant individualism of industrial civilization typical of European society.

While the natural, and ubiquitous, group is based on the family, there are other structures: classification by age, which places people in groups according to their birthdate (and which are accessed as a result of often complex initiation ceremonies), and secret societies (those who followed African events in the 1950s remember the Mau-Mau of Kenya, fighting for independence of their country).

The family is of great importance in traditional life on the basis of kinship, and kinship systems can vary (there are eight hundred kinship systems in the world). In the formation of the family, marriage is essential. It can be monogamous or not, depending on the culture. The marriage tie is stable (although divorce and repudiation exist, they are limited by precautionary measures). The choice of the spouse is made, more often than not, by the families.

Among the reasons for marriage the creation of a sound bond between the families involved is pre-eminent. The Roman-style dowry (according to which it is the woman who brings money, goods, or estate to the marriage) is unknown in Africa. Instead, the suitor or his family pays the price agreed (generally quite high) to the family of the bride.

The choice of spouse is not completely free. First, as in other cultures, incest is avoided. Often marriage between cross cousins (children of brothers and sisters) is encouraged while that between parallel cousins (children of two brothers or two sisters) is discouraged. In the event of widowhood, the perpetuation of the tie between the two families is encouraged. The widower is entitled to marry the sister of his late wife and the widow is obliged to marry a member of the family of her late husband. While combating incest prevents excessive inbreeding, this is counterbalanced by a prohibition against marrying a woman to a man unrelated to the tribe.

In general terms, the child belongs by birth to a single family – which is different from Europe, where the kinship link is extended to the families of both the father and the mother. The family could be either patrilineal or matrilineal in descent. If kinship is based on the mother–child link, familial authority does not belong to the mother *tout court*; rather, it belongs to the closest adult man (usually the brother of the mother). Here and there the matrilineal link, relevant for certain aspects, is combined with the patrilineal link, relevant for other purposes. Occasionally, succession *mortis causa* works differently according to the nature of the goods at issue.

Once the wedding ceremony has been gone through, a couple can live where the family of either the husband or the wife resides, depending on the culture.

It can happen that the status of the firstborn is different from that of the other children.

15.2.3 Property

The traditional African property regime deserves special attention in an analysis of African law. African traditional society is a rural and peasant one, and people rely for subsistence on what the land can provide. The regime of land tenure is representative of African law, in that land is not subjected to an unlimited individual right of management, enjoyment, and exploitation. Land is endowed with sacral significance, and the relationship between human beings and the land takes root in and is protected by supernatural entities. This link is not generated by a single actor, but the connection involves the whole group and it is refined by the chief of the territory in question, who commands sacral powers. The chief works on the distribution of land among the subgroups or to individual households, and power over the land and its enjoyment by the group are harmoniously combined with individual powers and exploitation.

15.2.4 Exchange and conflict

European analysis is sceptical about the importance of the contract during the prehistoric age and before the systematic division of labour, which coincides with the birth of the city. This scepticism is well grounded as long as we consider the contract to be an agreement resulting from two declarations of intent (offer and acceptance). However, we should bear in mind that in 'primitive' societies an exchange is a fundamental act, even though it is not based on declarations of intent.

In simple societies, the individual who received something would then return something (this could be considered as a 'real contract' or, if someone prefers, as 'unjust enrichment'). If the individual has taken part in a co-operative action which was beneficial to the group, he will be given a quota of the benefits (e.g., after the collective hunt). The group member offers a gift to the chief (who may use it for collective needs as well) and the chief will take the donation into consideration when distributing the land by arranging preferential treatment for the altruistic man. The believer offers a sacrifice to the supernatural power, and counts on its protection of persons and goods.

Conflict is sometimes present in the relations within the same community or between different communities. Law deals with the sanction and the procedure that leads to sanction and reconciliation.

The most elementary form of protection is self-defence. Someone (Titus) commits a trespass (e.g., crosses the boundaries of someone else's land) and another person (Caius) takes a weapon and confronts him. If this form of protection does not work, the most basic consequence is the power of sanction recognized as accruing to the group as a whole, the instrument being vengeance by the aggrieved group member towards a member of the group held responsible. Retaliation is the most obvious form of vengeance (the principle of an eye for an eye), but there are types of multi-event vengeance. While in many cultures reconciliation excludes vengeance, in some others there must be reconciliation (e.g. a default payment specific to the kind of offence) and vengeance intervenes only to sanction the payment due.

Resort to arbitration is encouraged in preference to pacific reconciliation, and entrusted to an individual chosen by both parties or appointed by the authority at their request. In more complex societies, the authority appoints a judge on its own initiative or reserves the right to decide.

If the event that gave rise to conflict is not clear, it will be necessary to ascertain it. In very many cultures the sacred will help: supernatural indications will offer the judge the information required for the solution of the case.

15.3 The religious layer

15.3.1 Islam

Traditional Africa has its own flourishing and elaborate pre-religious supernatural (magic) practices, to which it refers for protection, success, security, and information on future and past events.

At a given moment, however, Muslim missionaries landed on the east coast of Africa. The monsoon facilitated voyages from Pakistan, Persia, and especially what is now Saudi Arabia towards the coast south-west of Cape Guardafui. The sultanate of Zanzibar was the most distinctly visible result of that religious expansion.

Soon afterwards, from the eleventh century, a dense wave of immigration (the Hillalian invasion) moved from Egypt to Morocco, then Senegal, and then from the west to the east, alongside the Sahel, immediately south of the Sahara desert. With time, Muslim empires were established in the Sahel, Ghana, Gambia, Mali, Kanem, and Songhai. Today, Islam is the predominant religion in Senegal, Gambia, Guinea, Mali, Niger, Nigeria, and Chad.

The first Muslims to arrive in Africa were not concerned with the law and compromised to a great extent with local traditions, to the point of tolerating sovereigns invested with authority based on kinship and magic powers. However, from the fourteenth to the eighteenth centuries a different, more rigorous, Islam took root in these areas. It consisted of brotherhoods of large numbers of believers, such as the Qaridiyya, Sanusiyya, Tijaniyya, and Muridiyya, inspired by men of faith and thought. These Sufic movements displayed an exceptional ability to attract followers. Their aim was to impose their organization on all previous social structures and to intervene strongly in all political issues: the legitimation of political power, the duties of rulers, holy war. This did not always and necessarily imply the implementation of the Shari'a.

African Islam is today fully Sunnite. Different schools – Hanif, Maliki, and Shafiite – divide the continent. However, the characteristic of African Islam is not the school itself (which is still important), but, rather, local peculiarities. It could happen that in a community (*giamia*) many members strictly follow a charismatic leader who exercises powers normally given to the state. A recently dead preacher can become an object of worship, later enlivened by miracles credited to him. The cult could become entwined with orthodox worship. It could happen that the 'ginn' (a kind of spiritual being, lacking the true vision and therefore inferior to angels) hides in a living being (such as an animal venerated by the pre-Islamic local culture) which is granted a special social standing.

Attention should be drawn to this African species of Islam. Despite its practical importance and its permanency in real African life, it has not been the object of thorough study. Even non-Muslim scholars focus only on official Islam, endowed with orthodoxy.

Islam has its own legal framework. However, Islam is compatible with any legitimation of political power (inherited, dynastic, or ethnically privileged, conquest, democracy) and even if it is accompanied by Shari'a – law revealed and wise, learnedly studied – it recognizes local customs of people who convert to the truth. Some branches of law are reserved to Shari'a (family and succession). It is nonetheless true that local traditions sometimes penetrate these areas as well, with no justifications either required or offered, (rarely) influencing the doctrine or (often) winning over daily praxis of the *qadi* (Islamic judge, who is not required to justify his decision and therefore has greater freedom of action).

15.3.2 Christianity

After the spread of Islam, during the colonial period (from the sixteenth century for Portuguese colonizers, the nineteenth century for the others), intense Christian missionary activity (Roman Catholic and Protestant) took place in Africa. Looking at legal rules specifically, Christian missionaries put forward claims only in the areas of marriage and filiation in addition to the recognition of the particular status of the clergy and its assets. In terms of general ideas, it found against slavery, then spoke up for the social and legal raising up of native peoples, and afterwards, in a third phase, entertained the idea of a distribution of resources between citizens of the colonizing state (who had to plan and to maintain order) and native people (who enjoyed their rights, protected within that order).

Traditional leaders needed a sound network of alliances by means of polygamous marriages. Thus Christianity harmed an important tool of traditional authority without having intended it. In general terms, Christianity undermined traditional power, widely based as it was on magic and the sacred.

15.4 The colonial layer

15.4.1 The colony

Around 1880, first the Portuguese and then the British, the French, the Spanish, the Germans, the Italians, and others seized almost the whole African continent, using their power for different purposes: to pour into Africa those who did not have sufficient resources in their native land; to monopolize part of local economic resources; to make use of harbours, thus controlling the sea and gaining access to other continents; and to benefit from a strategic geographic position. Those are referred to as peopling, commercial, or exploitation colonies. However, in that part of Africa in question, the migration of Europeans never caused a social Europeanization (unlike what happened in Canada and Australia), and the end of the colonization period put the destiny of African countries in the hands of the native peoples.

The development of African colonies gave birth to a legal doctrine drawn up with particular reference to the colonies. Unfortunately, this legal doctrine took no interest in the law existing in Africa prior to colonization, nor in the cohabitation of and the conflicts between this law and the law of the conqueror, nor in the changes that occurred in the native law due to the exposure to European law and the changes to which European law was subjected in its application in Africa. This legal doctrine was more concerned with the conceptual contrast between the state (and its boundaries and constitutive elements) and the colony; it was interested in the mechanism of the production of legal rules (from the colonizing state) to be applied in the colonies. 'Colonial law' developed on this basis lost any interests after decolonization. However, the analysis of the changes suffered by African law through colonization is of great interest, both from the point of view of the historical study of law and for the purpose of understanding African law of the twentieth century.

Obviously, colonization was regulated by international law. Moreover, agreements between European countries (such as the Berlin Conference of 1884–5) ordered the ways in which sovereignty could be acquired, delimited freedom of commerce, freedom of shipping on the main rivers, controlled the commitment to abolish slavery, and defined minimal standards of treatment of the native peoples.

International law and legal doctrine classified the different patterns of the colonies either strictly or broadly. Colonies in the strict meaning of the term were directly subject to the rule of the colonizing state (this was the most frequent occurrence), entrusted to an economic organization, or enjoyed partial autonomy. The colony *sensu lato* could be a protectorate or a territory under a mandate. When the international community entrusted a 'civilized country' with control over a territory considered not yet ready for independence, this was referred to as a mandate. The protectorate followed a similar legal pattern, based on an agreement between the controlling state and the country colony-to-be.

Colonizers axiomatically considered their culture to be superior to that of the colonized, and that they were for this reason entitled to educate the natives, with the aim of assimilating them. However, colonizers could also consider assimilation to be impossible, unnatural, or undesirable, either permanently or when the colonial link was first established. In the first case, when integration was considered as definitely unfeasible, the aim was to bring the law of the colonizing state to the colony and to subject colonial life in its entirety to the authority of the colonizing state. In the second case, however, the survival of local law, institutions, and authority was desirable (indirect rule). Political doctrine spoke out in favour of extreme positions: France strove for assimilation, while Britain's aim was indirect rule. Practice never tallied with theory, and the result was somewhere in the middle. Perhaps analysis should focus on the structural differences of different colonization experiences rather than relying on the antithesis of the assimilation and the indirect rule patterns. Indeed, operative decisions could be taken either in Africa or in

Europe; choices could be made by officials of the colonizing state, later settlers, or aboriginals; the level of paternalism shown by Europeans towards the indigenous peoples could differ colony by colony.

The British aimed for decentralization of power, entrusting authority to governors assisted by local counsellors or to local lords or emirs placed under British control. The creation of two coexistent pyramidal administrations, one controlled from the colonizing state, the other autochthonous, was incompatible with the access of native people to the administrative structures of power directly linked with the colonizing state.

15.4.2 Traditional and religious law during colonization

When Europeans settled in Africa they were prone to follow the law of minimum effort: they left in place previously functioning law and judicial organs, but did not let their own nationals abide by them (the double-path system).

Later, the nature of the administrative power pre-dating colonization started to clash with the new order. The former was based neither on the European, traditionally tripartite separation of powers, nor on any separation between the laic and the supernatural, and was in no condition to take charge of the new tasks assigned to the administrative authority by the colonial power. Moreover, the European of the colonial age was – and wanted to be – intolerant of slavery, which was widespread, and was willing to resort to force in order to halt it. Furthermore, he did not understand (and did not regret not understanding) the complex system of castes or degrees of aristocracy, or the different ranks of different ethnic groups, nor did he grasp the racial differences between Caucasoid descendants of Afro-Asiatic ancestors, Blacks and the Khoisan (including San and Khoi, once referred to as Bushmen and Hottentots respectively).

As time went by the European was forced to take some account of African pre-colonial rules, such as tribal vengeance, the impunity of a murderer following the payment of the blood price, and the inheritance of responsibility for public functions. Moreover, he was sceptical about the sacral or supernatural and wisdom-based sources of public powers or of foundations of private law rules (first of all, property). Thus, with time, colonial power was extended to African rules, subjecting them to criteria of 'natural justice', 'morality', 'public order', and definitely to the criterion of conformity to European principles.

Thus African customary law was attacked in three ways. If it was considered to be against European morality it was suppressed; aside from this, the colonial administration recruited judges of traditional law on the basis of criteria which excluded former judges from being recruited. The newly appointed judges ended up mangling the traditional settlement of disputes because of their inexperience. Often the judge knew traditional law only through European interpretations (sometimes compiled in official tables), all on the basis of an abstract legal paradigm, away from the consideration of varying and changeable circumstances (such as the nature of the parties or social data) which usually influenced judgments made in the African tradition.

Islamic law could resist better. Europeans avoided interfering in the sector of 'personal status' (family and successions *mortis causa*), which was jealously kept, and respected courts presided over by the *qadi*. The latter ended up expanding their jurisdiction to areas traditionally governed by custom.

15.4.3 European law and European colonial law in Africa

The measure of the penetration of Africa by the European model varied depending on the subject. The penetration was total where the colonial power did not encounter an autochthonous antagonist (at least a plausible one). Administrative and commercial laws (relating to companies and credit instruments) were immediately European; here, there was no uncertainty.

In other areas the law of the colonizing state was applicable without exception to Europeans and coexisted with native laws (both religious and traditional) which applied to the indigenes. However, new criteria were developed to ensure that Africans would submit, either freely or under compulsion, to rules laid down by the colonizing state.

The colonizing state elaborated a certain number of new colonial rules which were applicable in the colony only, being neither relevant nor appropriate for itself. The British imported recommended legal compilations originally drawn up for India (criminal law, procedural law, business law, property law, obligations, and so on) into their African colonies; the French introduced and promoted a code first relating to obligations and contract in Tunisia and Morocco. Other fields were less straightforward: ecclesiastical law was wayward *a priori* to Africa export. Major problems were faced when dealing with constitutional law.

European forms of power were also extended to Africa. Obviously the principle of self-determination was not extended to the colony, which could then have refused colonial power on that basis. In principle, laws were made by the colonizing state's parliament, but in practice they mostly came from the executive power. With time, in different colonies settlers and indigenous peoples could express their will through a vote in the parliament of the colonizing state, but were entitled to proportionately fewer votes. Elsewhere, a local parliament was created. It was not sovereign and was limited to later settlers. Later on, a way of giving a voice to native peoples was developed, without any use of electoral procedures (e.g. in Kenya and Rhodesia).

Fundamental differences set European constitutional laws both proclaimed and practised beside the constitutional law embraced in Africa. Colonizing states undermined African privileges based on affiliation to an ethnic group, on religion, or on social status, but introduced privileges for their own nationals.

Military power shaped the power of the unarmed official, while colonial administrative authority was used to revise the decisions of local indigenous courts (in order, for example, to avoid the legitimization of slavery, the taking of vengeance, or raiding attacks), actions which went against the principle of separation of powers. Power was concentrated in few hands, and during the colonial period for the most part no party political system existed.

Private law (relating to individuals and goods) also offers good examples of the form that European constitutional principles took in Africa.

Individual freedom was sometimes limited for political reasons. Once slavery was abolished, former slaves formed raiding groups for food, having no other means of surviving. In some cases, forced labour was imposed on the raiders, without this being openly acknowledged.

The Europeans transformed Africa by means of drainage. A system of concession was created to dodge full ownership in order to avoid proprietary claims over the drained areas.

15.4.4 Decolonization

After the Second World War, and especially during the 1960s, European countries gave up their colonies, either by a unilateral act, or after a local referendum, or by agreement negotiated between the colonizing state and the colony – in some cases following the intervention by the UN in the form of resolutions or acts of investigation.

According to public international law, independence was intended to take the form of the succession of the new state, and in principle general rules were applicable. Some waivers of sovereignty were introduced on the request of European countries and with the agreement of the new state. However, the question of their validity was often controversial.

Very important legal relationships have been created between new independent countries and former colonizers.

In 1958 France created La Communauté, aimed at perpetuating the link between France and its former African colonies. It not only exercises power through its structures, but also intervenes by means of agreements and conventions on monetary policies, wide technical assistance, the judiciary, and education. More recently, in 1993, the Organisation pour l'Harmonisation en Afrique du Droit des Affaires (OHADA) was created, establishing a commercial code, based on the European model, applicable in the former French colonies. A pyramidal judiciary system, again based on the European model (comprising judges who received ad hoc training) was also created under the umbrella of OHADA in order to enforce its rulings.

For its part, the European Union (at that time the European Communities, EC) connected with those former colonies of its members which constituted the African, Caribbean, and Pacific group of states (ACP) by means of the Yaoundé, Lomé, and Cotonou conventions. The conventions covered many areas, including (partial) freedom of exchange, technical assistance, and the funding of public works of economic and social significance.

15.5 The law of independence

At the moment of independence the new African states could choose to fashion themselves according to the models brought by the European colonizers or their own traditional models, or to find an eclectic solution.

They refused to go back to slavery (an exception being Mauritania) or to caste and lineage systems; they confirmed the importance of education and the spread of sanitation. The enormous growth in population (due to the sanitation revolution dating back to the colonial period) compelled the new states to deal with an efficient and dynamic economy, different from the traditional one. A simple step back to the past was not an option.

It was not even thinkable that new African states identical to European states be created, because of difference in their starting points, in terms of language and their own history and culture.

The vernacular languages spoken in sub-Saharan Africa number around a thousand. What each state has lacked is a language that, through prestige or other factors, could become the common language of all its citizens. The written language continues – today, as at the moment of independence – to be the language of the former colonizer. After independence was achieved, the spread of education and knowledge generally of the foreign language encouraged its use. The linguistic coupling of the ethnic and European languages is also enriched across many territories by the presence of Arabic as a religious language and of commercial languages (particularly Kiswahili, then Sangho, Lingala, and so on). The law is often expressed in the European language of the colonizer, which continues not to be understood by part of the population.

Given these conditions, teaching in the universities is mainly offered in European languages, and a true national literature is missing. European technical assistance sponsors foreign teachers. Thus education ends up being connected to a European context in different ways which are not necessarily obvious. It is important that this is borne in mind, especially in the area of law.

15.5.1 The birth of the African state

The African state is not a national state.

National identity is given by language, and each small linguistic community cannot undertake the tasks attributed to the state. When Africans finally became the owners of their own destiny, they accepted the boundaries inherited from colonization, together with the principle of their immutability.

At the moment of independence, there were often in the new states kings or lords granted traditional powers, and lords who endorsed colonial domination. Their powers were grounded in traditions only recently compromised by the colonial regime (such as in Zanzibar and Uganda). Independence wiped them away.

Before leaving Africa, Europe opened the doors of its universities to the people of its colonies, while African officials were given more and more important roles in public administration. With independence, administrative offices became ministries and Oxford or Paris graduates became ministers in anglophone and francophone Africa.

At the same time, the constitutions, already written thanks to the collaboration of colonial civil servants or African laureates in Europe, entered into force.

Based on the European model, they did not consider at all the multi-ethnic, multilinguistic, and pluralistic features of the indigenous societies. And the Africans themselves did not intervene to ask for a more realistic constitution, closer to the feelings and the traditions of their countries. They did not intervene because the constitution was drawn up on the basis of European knowledge, and the Europeans did not think to elaborate or to experiment with a law acknowledging differences and specificities (*ius condendum*). They did not intervene because they feared and rejected the idea of moving back to tribalism, paid no regard to the small ethnic group, and ruled out the idea of putting at the centre of the discussion an unwritten language spoken by very few; at the same time they offered no new theories or ad hoc doctrine. Particularism ran up against what could be defined as political excommunication, and conformity was secured by criminal law penalties.

The system of legal sources of law was affected by this. Law which was not written was mistrusted – as traditional, particularistic, tribal – and because customary and spontaneous law both general and tribal did not exist as such, written, authoritative law was favoured. In order to make law African lawmakers resorted to foreign law and for inspiration from already existing laws they looked to European law.

15. 5.2 Independence and European law

Independent Africa perpetuated the administrative law of the colonial period. Sound alternatives did not exist and still do not exist today.

African countries do not apply ecclesiastic rules; neither did the colonizer. Independence did not create the need for new rules.

Some states have declared themselves to be an 'Islamic republic' immediately following independence or subsequently. This element makes a state party to a wider and indivisible community (umma), but it did not affect the particular rules of administrative law. The rules that an independent state lays down for its nationals – civil law, criminal law, and corresponding procedural laws – deserve particular attention. The citizens of African states, and together with them their legislators, see in traditional law support for tribalism which the new state aims to eradicate; they see colonial rule, which imposed on them respect for traditional law, as labelling them as backward and as a tool for discrimination; they hurry to rid themselves of it.

European codes, codes which emulated European codes, and codes which would have liked to turn to tradition but were filtered through European cultures, played their part in this process.

Economic law was victim of the backlash of the political situation. Economic concerns belonging to Europeans were expropriated, causing the departure of Europeans from African countries and economic stagnation. In turn this led the state to take charge of fundamental economic activities and initiatives.

15.5.3 Independence and Islamic law

Independence caused backlashes against the authority of Shari'a that are not easy to evaluate. Colonial power reluctantly favoured it; since it loved to express itself in writing, and in some places, finding out that the language of religion was Arabic, thought that administrative texts and judicial decisions written in Arabic would be better understood. While the European administration wanted to respect the African reality, it gave greater credit to the *qadi* than to the tribal magician and undermined the competence of the latter by augmenting the power of the former. Independence could have crystallized these conquests of Islamic law. In general terms, secular codifications available for all the citizens and codifications compiled with the clear aim of interpreting Islamic law influenced and undermined Shari'a in different areas (e.g., polygamy, the consensus of the bride for the successful celebration of the marriage).

15.5.4 Independence and traditional law

As the application of European law became more general with independence, so traditional law withdrew; this is self-evident.

Here and there, attempts to revive old beliefs have been crushed. For example, soon after independence, Félix Houphouët-Boigny, the first president of Côte d'Ivoire, prohibited a syncretic cult of veneration of his person.

However, it has to be highlighted that law officially promulgated and proclaimed by the authorities must not be considered as being the only law acting in African countries. For a long time legal sciences have known the term 'submerged law', which is not publicized, memorized, or celebrated, nevertheless is operative, respected, and binding.

In Africa, official law works in the city, in the educated and Europeanized circles. However, it does not reach the bush, or the slums which surround the big city. Official law is not easy to get to know and it does not correspond with applied law; both official and applied laws are extraneous to the feelings and the culture of many African people still loyal to their past. Given this situation, any gap is filled by the ancient law.

15.5.5 Independence and the socialist option

African states started to gain independence from the 1960s, and since then have been able to choose the political system they favour. From the 1960s to the 1990s, they saw in the former colonizing countries political choices flourishing that had been inspired by economic and market freedom. However, elsewhere, they saw different patterns developing, inspired by Marxism-Leninism. Those paths proceeded through the three phases of (i) the abolition of the exploitation of people's lives by others, (ii) socialism (that is the collectivization of means of production) and communism yet-to-be (which would have come along with goods distribution according to the needs of the citizens).

The Marxist-Leninist option seduced many African countries at that time (Mali, Benin, Sudan, Republic of the Congo, Mozambique, and Angola). The choice was made by a political party or by alternative forces – that is, the military. This choice was followed by the dissolution of parties other than the one in power, or the reorganization of a single party designed to manage power. The party was supported by mass organizations of young people, women, workers, and paramilitary groups. A constitution was adopted and a national assembly was created, on which sat a strong leader, the head of state, the leader of the party, and the military.

The socialist revolution worked on the basis of a liberal and egalitarian spirit in the areas of individual rights and family law (at the expense of the Shari'a, where deemed necessary). In the economic sector factories were nationalized, co-operative societies were pushed forward and the land was brought under state control. Criminal law became extremely strict.

After the fall of the communist regime in the Soviet Union the communist option also became inapplicable in Africa.

15.6 African constitutionalism

15.6.1 African law and political power

The principle of the primacy of the constitution is not embedded in African states in the same way as it has been perceived by the Europeans for the last two centuries. Political power was usually acquired by means of force, especially during the last century. The coup was carried out by means of the creation of a totalitarian power managed by a single party. This led to a situation whereby constitutions were rapidly succeeding one another.

An ancient and deep-rooted African way of thinking emphasizes the importance of consultation and of reaching collective and unanimous decisions, but excludes the possibility that someone who does not agree is bound by the will of the others. The fundamental rule of democracy is not enhanced by this idea. However, the Africans do not go against the majority unless they have some serious reasons for doing so.

This conception, which held sway in all Africa during the last century and is still present today, gives rise to a series of consequences.

If the majority does not have legitimacy, the existence of opposition parties in itself delegitimizes the government. But then again, because the ruling party is often representative of the majority ethnic group or the most thriving brotherhood, the multiparty system does not imply any alternation and for those who represent the minority change will always be a hopeless prospect. The ideological basis of a party is not strong; the party only acts as a mediator of the citizens in terms of the benefits they wish to obtain from the state (jobs, concessions, and so on). In these conditions, a single party system could seem to be the least unjust solution. This is why there are procedures by which the majority party absorbs smaller parties or promotes the institution of unitarian national fronts. Often the law itself establishes which parties can participate in elections.

Europeans believe that the quality of their system relies on the separation of powers. In Africa those with political power are not willing to be controlled by the judiciary.

A fundamental European rule allows the unarmed authority (the head of state, the parliament) to impose its decisions on those who are armed. In African states this does not work automatically as in Europe. History has seen charismatic African men, able, even unarmed, to impose themselves to the military, such as Senghor, Nyerere, Kenyatta, Lumumba, Mobuto. But in the system of legitimization of power as it works in Africa, unarmed power is not the rule.

Especially during the last century, the military often took power through a coup d'état. Many scholars have closely studied the phenomenon and reached the following conclusions. Who takes power has at their disposal the resources of the state – public posts, military force, and administrative concessions – and through this it reinforces the link with its supporters. When the resources are gone those with power lose their strength and cannot survive against a new rival. The seizure of power can also be based on ethnic rivalry within the group in power. Thus it could arise because the military dislikes the government's political strategy or because their privileges are undermined by politicians.

A fundamental characteristic of constitutional law as applied in Africa is the huge power reserved to the head of state. The observer could be reminded of the traditional divine right of kings, perhaps still present in involuntary African political thought.

Also, African administrative life pays tribute to local historic peculiarities. Comparative lawyers understand that in francophone Africa the administrative legal system is the French one, while it is British in anglophone Africa. But the issue is different. In Europe feudal ties established the principle of the loyalty of the laic lord to the king and of the ecclesiastical official to the Church. Hence the spirit of loyalty could extend over the laic and democratic state. However, in Africa loyalty is inherent in the tribal community and is not shown with the same efficacy towards the entity embodied in the state. Administrative organs and judges look at their roles as being awarded on a personal base. Their positions may lead to licit enrichment.

15.7 The last chapter of African law

15.7.1 Traditional law

Islamic law, Christian beliefs, colonial rule, the powerful prestige of the European model have together devastated traditional African law. They have destroyed traditional institutions that no one wishes to revive (e.g. slavery), but by the same token have destroyed traditional institutions that should have survived.

What, then, of the value of African written law as inspired by European model?

We can outline two different scenarios. Let us imagine a society where the university teaches, the language is well learnt and understood, and the law is written in a universally known language, and this makes the judges able to apply the law and lead a cultural movement which coheres with the law and polemic against the tradition it meant to defeat. Let us now change the scenario and think about a society where the law is based on a foreign model and printed in a foreign language hard for the majority of the population to understand, and the judge, who is not university trained, is required to impose this law (that he does not know) on citizens who are determined to follow a different rule. Africa is not fully represented by either two scenarios.

Those in power will not witness legal affairs in silence. Power requires the unity of the country against tribal fragmentation. It has learnt the importance of environmental protection. It desires economic growth.

Thus criminal law punishes scarifications and tattoos which represent tribal labels (punishes both their creator and the person whose body is marked) and by destroying the symbol undermines the tribal tie.

Here come the laws – strengthened by international conventions and UN initiatives – that for the purpose of environmental protection limit the hunt. But the practice of the hunt accompanied the generational change-over, defined military rank, and shaped affiliation to a particular social class; the collective hunt reflected the complementarity of clans and dynastic groups. Hunting trophies marked occasions with a special, social, sacred meaning (e.g. judgments). It is not possible to regulate the hunt in a restrictive way and leave it to shape the life of the group according to the new rhythms. The London Convention of 1933 regulating the hunt entered into force in French Western Africa in 1948, and was followed by the Ivorian law of 4 August 1966. In 1974, the authorities had to disarm the citizens in order to make the rule effective in Côte d'Ivoire. Hence the initiation of the youth into adulthood, the selection of chiefs, the importance of extended family, the difference between economic tasks of men (hunting) and women (agriculture) all lapsed. Of the two significant aspects of the hunt – social and economic – only the economic survived; its social meaning vanished.

In Africa social rank was often conveyed by a specific occupation. The shepherd was considered noble and would have lost his nobility if he started working the land. Fishermen could be a sub-caste. However, the pressure from the centre of power destroyed this balance.

This does not mean that tradition died or is dying because of adverse criticism. Following the enthusiasm after independence for European models, either legal-functional or Marxist, a new idea emerged. This consisted in putting African authenticity at the centre of attention. Accurate analysis by both African and European jurists highlights that traditional Africa is neither dead nor vanished. In the public offices of the capital city the law inspired by European models is made operative thanks to knowledgeable employees, trained in universities. But Africa does not entirely consist of offices in capital cities. There is a spontaneous trend towards rediscovering the community and possibly linking the community and the law, legal particularism, and its sources – both local and customary sources.

From a positive law perspective, various phenomena follow this new path. The law is stepping back and leaving room for customary practice – and, even more meaningfully, leaving room for traditional procedures with traditional judges and investigation tools (in some cases based on magic). The law welcomes contents that are close to traditions (this is in relation to the reimposition of the death penalty). The judge interprets the law inspired by European model according to his own local culture. People empty the rule of meaning through its non-implementation (for instance, it could happen that civil status is completely ignored).

It could also happen that customary practices well protected by traditional justice maintain their force or are taken back into the sunlight, without meeting any counter force, even though they have no legal basis.

15.7.2 The family

Family law is the branch where differences between African law and Western law are greatest. In this sector, traditional European and Muslim models and new customs entwine. New native law sprang up from the remains of thousand-year-old practices no longer authorized and arose at the edges of the cities where various ethnic groups and tribes mingle.

According to African tradition the extended family has always been of great importance. It was up to the family to create alliances through the marriages of its members, fully respecting prohibitions and pre-emptions. The family collected the price corresponding to the approval of the marriage (dowry, or bride price). The effects of such compensation were intended to last even after the death of the husband: because of it the children belonged to the family of the late husband.

Today, the brother of the late husband can no longer assert in court his claim to marry the widow, and the authority of the head of the family that previously extended over family members is no longer officially recognized. However, the family still influences the choice of the spouse and negotiates the amount of the dowry, decides the occupation of the younger members, and passes friendships and enmities. The law fights against the dowry and in particular the excessive amounts involved.

Polygamy is a traditional practice throughout Africa. While it was once a privilege of the most powerful, today the practice is more widely spread. The state knows that it is unable to prohibit it by law, but rules against this custom.

The rules about patrimonial relationships between the spouses give the measures of the changes in African traditions. The traditional system allocated the fruits of the wife's labour to her husband's family (this was the original reason for the dowry). The spread of women's paid labour, more than colonial rule itself, undermined this practice. The trend to put together the salaries of the spouses and their incomes led to the regime of shared ownership of revenues and community of acquisitions. Oddly enough, European distinctions between primary and secondary regimes (i.e. the economic regime enjoyed by wives as opposed to that enjoyed by concubines) did not spread to independent francophone western Africa. Nevertheless, the community property regime hardly fitted, and was hardly applied to, polygamous marriages.

Hierarchies within the African family – the authority of the elder over the younger, the father over the family, the man over the woman – appears to be in crisis, as they are generally declared by the law to be wrong.

15.7.3 Property

While there is no uniform regime of land tenure throughout today's Africa, the same problems arise and the same solutions are reached. Everywhere the starting point is ownership by the group – the village, the tribe, or the extended family. On this basis individual exploitation of the land is allocated, more or less freely (and more often than not for a certain period or under certain conditions), as long as the allocation is by the 'chief of the land', with the duty of farming and taking care of the holding. The relationship between the group and the land is conveyed by the sacred and the sacred also intervenes in the individual allocations.

The individual to whom the land is allocated has no interest in improving a limited, temporary holding, and cannot mortgage it because of the limited title of ownership. Thus traditional African land tenure is to all intents and purposes a mortmain and lacking in any kind of dynamism.

At first colonial rule and then the authorities of the independent states tried to counteract the exclusion of land from any form of dynamic economic exploitation by means of registration or valorization of the land.

Registration (a record-keeping process in some form) implies an absolute property right, in Napoleonic style. This option is offered to the individual who exploits the land according to traditional practices; either it is imposed as a condition on which his already existing claim can be upheld in the courts, or it is a consequence of the expropriation and redistribution of land not hitherto exploited.

To register land in Africa has not been an easy task. It is hindered by complex and costly procedures, ignorance of the law, and the lack of any link being made between formal requirements of the cadastral registry and the feelings of the people towards their land.

The productivity of the land was an important factor both under colonial rule and then as expressed by the law on independence. For this reason, both systems operated in two stages: first, the expropriation of unproductive land and then its allocation (in many cases after drainage) to whoever undertook to exploit it most effectively.

In many states, expropriated lands are often huge districts, named national estates, while the exponents of traditional property-holding systems strongly resist registration and expropriation.

In Africa different types of property coexist, evolve, alternate, and conflict. There is no 'African property', but there is an African situation related to rights in property.

15.7.4 International law and Africa

Africa is a poor continent; the European expropriation of resources causing a fall in the productivity of African enterprises. There is a need to foster a fresh form of intervention (both entrepreneurial and financial), with African contractors able to participate more advantageously in global commerce and to express fully their managerial capacities. The heterogeneous set of norms governing this issue were referred to as 'aid law', then 'law of economic independence', then 'the new international economic order', and finally 'development law'.

Development law derives in part from international law and its practices (regarding business, financial aids, technical assistance), in part from the legislation of individual African states (regarding foreign investments and the transmission of technology or know-how), and in part from bilateral agreements between the developing country and a foreign power.

International law is based on the principle of equality among states, but makes concessions to developing countries: for example, it allows the expropriation of European property without indemnity by such countries. However, assistance to a needy country has (at least three) blind spots. First, the country has easier access to credit, of which it takes advantage, at the same time accumulating a burden of debt that is unaffordable. Second, the country offering assistance does so imposing stringent conditions favourable to itself. Finally, while assistance is widely available in times of general prosperity, it tends to run out when poor African countries are in greatest need.

National legislation often allows free export to a foreign trader up to a legal limit and then the return of the capital invested to the country of origin at the end of the cycle.

International agreements regulate and safeguard African countries through foreign technical assistance, which basically extends the presence of technical, sanitary, and cultural personnel and teachers which had already been developed during the colonial era. This implied mutual acculturation and concealed the dependence of African countries, which would be counteracted today, in principle, by assigning the various assistance roles to personnel from different countries.

15.7.5 Systemic characteristics of African law

Sub-Saharan African systems, tossed around by indigenous traditions, the advent of Islam, colonial rule, and contradictory political and politico-economic trends, adopt different legal solutions in every area. In some places a parliament functions, elsewhere a dictatorship is in place; here the family is atomistic and monogamous, there it is extended and polygamous; in some places land holding is individualistic and based on registration, in others it is based on concessions and, not far from there, land belongs to the group; in one place the law could be codified and its form of justice the only one, while in a nearby area tradition is accepted.

The contradictions exposed here are not yet deep-rooted and the situation could be reversed. Sometimes proclaimed law cohabits with a submerged law which prospers outside urban centres. But there are some regulatory schemes seen as 'typically African', because they are characterized by the frequency and degree of compliance with traditional African marks. This is true, for instance, when referring to the great concentration of power in the hands of the head of state, any control of such power being avoided; in most cases the head of state personally dispenses both remit of the military and the authority of the most powerful party.

A second recurring characteristic is the superiority of military over civil power which is expressed in various ways: the military leader is at the same time the head of state or government; the military supports as a figurehead head of state a non-military individual; or the military is confined to barracks but is ready to intervene when it considers that its rules are not observed.

Political power is both de facto and de iure superior to judicial power. Political parties can be reduced to a single party, as a way of pledging the moral unity of the country and of proclaiming the fight against tribalism and particularism. Equally, it is possible for two or three parties to be authorized. On the other hand, political freedom could notionally seem to be wider, but the life of political parties is regulated by a centralized power.

The central power does not manage the economy, but intervenes in it. The ability to nationalize land and to redistribute it by concessions is a power of primary importance.

The comparative lawyer notes five typical characteristics that were founded on tradition and have been strengthened with colonial rule. The military boasted its importance; the chief of colonial administration obeyed the colonizing state which was not visible in Africa, and indeed appeared as an absolute power; the administrative power controlled autochthonous courts and their judgments; political parties were not in place and dissidents were looked on with suspicion; and the colonizing state wanted the bush to become productive so that it nationalized it, drained it, and offered concessions.

Africa possesses some common fundamental features, and African law is made up of two components.

On the one hand, European law (in principle aimed at safeguarding the individual's civil rights and liberties), Muslim law (once freed of chauvinism and fundamentalism), and traditional law (once freed from oppressive and anachronistic rules) together build a set of rules of natural law (natural because inspired by impartiality), accepted by the consciousness of the whole world. On the other hand, there is a political law, based on emergency interventions and aimed at the maintaining of power. Political law controls constitutional life, the practice of concessions, and resorts to unwritten, criminal law which is severe and terrible, supported by arbitrary practice and assigned to politicized judges. Some traditional ideas, some practices during colonial rule, and – during its spread – the Marxist-Leninist revolutionary model offered material support to such absolutist law.

Further reading

African law in general and its systemic characteristics

M. Alliot, *Institutions privées africaines et malgaches, 2 vols.* (Paris: Laboratoire d'anthrop. Jurid., 1971)

A. N. Allott, *Judicial and Legal Systems in Africa,* 2nd edn (London: Butterworths, 1970)

A. Badara Fall, *Il diritto africano ha una sua collocazione nel diritto comparato?* trans. M. Carducci (Lecce: Pensa Ed., 2007)

G. Conaca (ed.), *Dynamiques et finalités des droits africains* (Paris: Economica, 1980)

D. Darbon and J. Du Bois De Gaudusson (eds.), *La création du droit en Afrique* (Paris: Karthala, 1997)

P. F. Gonidec (ed.), *Encyclopédie juridique de l'Afrique,* 10 vols. (Abidjan, Dakar, and Lomè: Nouvelles Editions Africaines, 1982)

M. Guadagni, *Il modello pluralista* (Turin: Giappichelli, 1996)

C. Ntampaka, *Introduction aux systèmes juridiques africains* (Namur: Presses Universitaires de Namur, 2005)

J. Poirier (ed.), *Etudes de droit africain et de droit malgache* (Paris: Cujas Editions, 1965)

F. Remotti, *Temi di antropologia giuridica* (Turin: Giappichelli, 1982)

N. Rouland, *Anthropologie juridique* (Paris: Presses Universitaires de France, 1988)

R. Sacco, *Il diritto africano* (Turin: Utet, 1995)

Le droit africain (Paris: Dalloz, 2009)

J. Vanderlinden, *Les systèmes juridiques africains* (Paris: Presses Universitaires de France, 1983)

'Africa', in *Digesto IV*, Sez. civ., I, 187 (Turin: Utet, 1987)

Anthropologie juridique (Paris: Dalloz, 1996)

African traditional law in general

A. N. Allott and G. R. Woodman (eds.), *People Law and State Law: The Bellagio Papers* (Dordrecht: Foris, 1985)

CNRS (ed.), *Sacralité, pouvoir et droit en Afrique* (Paris: CNRS, 1979)

T. O. Elias, *The Nature of African Customary Law*, 3rd edn (Manchester University Press, 1972)

M. Fortes and E. E. Evans-Pritchard (eds.), *African Political Systems* (London: Oxford University Press, 1940)

H. S. Maine, *Ancient Law* (London: John Murray, 1861)

J. Poirier (ed.), *La rédaction des coutumes dans le passé et dans le présent* (Brussels: Bruylant, 1962)

Traditional family law

C. Levi Strauss, *Les structures élémentaires de la parenté* (Paris: Presses Universitaires de France, 1949)

A. R. Radcliffe-Brown and D. Forder (eds.), *African Systems of Kinship and Marriage* (London: Oxford University Press, 1950)

Traditional land law

J. N. Hazard (ed.), *Le droit de la terre en Afrique au sud du Sahara* (Paris: Maisonneuse & Larose, 1971)

E. Le Bris, E. Le Roy, and F. Leimdorfer, *Enjeux fonciers en Afrique noire* (Paris: Karthala, 1982)

E. Le Bris, E. Le Roy, P. Mathieu, *L'appropriation de la terre en Afrique Noire* (Paris: Karthala, 1991)

E. and E. Le Roy, *Espaces disputés en Afrique noir* (Paris: Karthala, 1986)

R. Verdier and A. Rochegude (eds.), *Systems fonciers à la ville et au village* (Paris: L'Harmattan, 1986)

Traditional exchange and conflict law

M. Gluckman (ed.), *Ideas and Procedures in African Customary Law* (London: Oxford University Press, 1969)

The Allocation of Responsibility (Manchester University Press, 1972)

R. Verdier (ed.), *La vengeance*, 4 vols. (Paris: Cujas Editions, 1980–4)

The religious layer

J. N. D. Anderson, *Islamic Law in Africa* (London: Taylor & Francis, 1955)
C. Coulon, *Les musulmans et le pouvoir en Afrique noire* (Paris: Karthala, 1983)
H. Kuper and L. Kuper (eds.) *African Law: Adaptation and Development* (Berkeley and Los Angeles: MW Books, 1965)
F. Remotti, *Centri, capitali, città* (Turin: Giappichelli, 1984)

The colonial layer

E. Antonelli, *Manuel de législation coloniale* (Paris: Larose, 1926)
E. Cucinotta, *Diritto coloniale italiano*, 3rd edn (Rome: Foro Italiano, 1938)
P. Dareste, *Traité de droit colonial* (Paris: Robaudy, 1921)
M. Doucet and J. Vanderlinden (eds.), *La réception des systèmes juridiques: implantation et destin* (Brussels: Bruylant, 1994)
A. Girault, *Principes de colonisation et de législation coloniale*, 6th edn (Paris: L. Larose & L. Tenin, 1935)

Independent Africa

J. Buchmann, *L'Afrique noir indépendante* (Paris: R. Pichon & R. Durand-Auzias, 1962)
M. Guadagni (ed.), *Legal Scholarship in Africa* (Trento: Universitá di Trento, 1989)
G. A. Koussigan, *Quelle est ma loi? Tradition et modernisme dans le droit privé de la famille en Afrique noire francophone* (Paris: A. Pedone, 1974)
M. Pedamon, *Legal Education in Africa South of the Sahara* (Brussels: Bruylant, 1979)
J. Vanderlinden, *L'enseignement du droit en Afrique* (Addis Ababa: Université Haile Selassié I, Faculté de Droit, 1969)

The socialist option

M. Guadagni (ed.), *La scelta 'socialista' in Etiopia, Somalia e Tanzania* (Trieste: CLUET, 1979)
S. A. Hanna and G. H. Gardner, *Arab Socialism: A Documentary Survey* (Leiden: Brill, 1969)
R. R. A. Ul'janovskij, *Nekapitalisticeskij 'put? Razvitija stran Afriki* (Moscow: Nauka, 1967)

African constitutionalism

B. Asso, *Le chef d'état africain* (Paris: Albatros, 1976)
P. F. Gonidec, *Les systèmes politiques africains*, 2nd edn (Paris, 1978)

P. F. Gonidec and A. Bockel, *L'État africain*, 2nd edn (Paris: LGDJ, 1984)

M. Kamt, *Pouvoir et droit in Afrique noir* (Paris: LGDJ, 1987)

B. O. Nwabueze, *Constitutionalism in Emergent States* (London: C. Hurst, 1973)

J. Owona, *Droit constitutionnel et régimes politiques africains* (Paris: Berger-Levrault, 1985)

Military power in Africa

G. Calchi Novati, *Le rivoluzioni nell'Africa Nera* (Milan: dall'Oglio, 1967)

G. M. Carter (ed.), *African One-Party States* (Ithaca, NY: Cornell University Press, 1962)

B. Ewondo, *Les coups d'état militaires* (Paris: Quoi de nouveau?, 1971)

W. F. Gutteridge, *The Military in African Politics* (London: Methuen, 1969)

L. Hamon, *Le rôle extramilitaire de l'armée dans le Tiers Monde* (Paris: Presses Universitaires de France, 1966)

M. Janowitz, *The Military in the Political Development of New States* (Chicago University Press, 1964)

A. Mahiou, *L'avènement du parti unique en Afrique noire* (Paris: LGDJ, 1969)

M. L. Martin, *La militarisation des systèmes politiques africains (1960–1972)* (Sherbrooke, Québec: Naaman, 1976)

R. S. Morgenthau, *Le multipartisme en Afrique de l'Ouest francophone jusqu'aux indépendances: la période nationaliste* (Paris: L'Harmattan, 1998)

J. P. Pabanel, *Les coups d'état militaires en Afrique noire* (Paris: L'Harmattan, 1984)

The traditional layer in the twenty-first century

J. N. D. Anderson (ed.), *Family Law in Asia and Africa* (London: G. Allen & Unwin, 1968)

M. Bussani, 'Tort Law and Development: Insights into the Case of Ethiopia and Eritrea', (1996) 40 *Journal of African Law* 43

J. Fenrich, P. Galizzi, and T. Higgins, *The Future of African Customary Law* (Cambridge University Press, 2011)

G. A. Kouassigan, *Quelle est ma loi? Tradition et modernisme dans le droit privé de la famille en Afrique noire francophone* (Paris: A. Pedone, 1974)

E. Le Roy, *Les africains et l'institution de la justice* (Paris: Dalloz, 2004)

K. M'Baye, *Le droit de la famille en Afrique noir à Madagascar* (Paris: G.-P. Maisonneuve et Larose, 1968)

E. Rau, *Le juge et le sorcier* (Paris: Robert Laffont, 1976)

A. Retel Lauretin, *Sorcellerie et ordalies. L'épreuve du poison en Afrique noire* (Paris: Anthropos, 1974)

Land regimes in the twenty-first century

L. Castellani, *La difesa delle risorse naturali nel diritto dei paesi africani* (Milan: Giuffrè, 2003)

V. Gasse, *Les régimes fonciers africains et malgaches* (Paris: LGDJ, 1971)

A. Germano (ed.), *Strutture fondiarie e credito per lo sviluppo agricolo in Africa nera* (Milan: Giuffrè, 1989)

E. Le Bris, E. Le Roy, and P. Mathieu, *L'appropriation de la terre en Afrique Noire* (Paris: Karthala, 1991)

E. and E. Le Roy, *Espaces disputés en Afrique noir* (Paris: Karthala, 1986)

P. E. Ofori, *Land in Africa: Its Administration, Law, Tenure and Use. A Select Bibliography* (Nendeln: KTO Press, 1978)

Development law

M. Bennouna, *Droit international du développement* (Paris: Berger Levrault, 1985)

M. Flory, *Droit international du développement* (Paris: Presses Universitaires de France, 1977)

F. Luchaire, *L'aide aux pays sous-développés* (Paris: Presses Universitaires de France, 1966)

S. Mancuso, *Diritto commerciale africano* (Naples: Edizioni Scientifiche Italiane, 2009)

A. Pellet, *Le droit international du développement* (Paris: Presses Universitaires de France, 1978)

F. G. Snyder and P. Slinn, *International Law of Development: Comparative Perspectives* (Abingdon: Professional Books, 1987)

16 The Latin American and Caribbean legal traditions
Repositioning Latin America and the Caribbean on the contemporary maps of comparative law

Diego López-Medina

16.1 The contemporary limits of Latin America and the Caribbean as a legal space

The states and jurisdictions south of the Rio Bravo (alternatively known as the 'Rio Grande' in the United States) form a very large historical, cultural, economic, and geographic region usually known as 'Latin America'. Geographically speaking, these states encompass, with some exceptions that culturally belong to 'Anglo-America', the south-western corner of North America where a territorially diminished Mexico serves as regional borderline with the United States; most of the Central American isthmus and South America; and, finally, some island states and island colonies that sit within the waters of the Caribbean basin. By 2005, around 543 million people lived in this area of the world.[1] It has recently become fashionable to say that the next decade, even the next century, will belong to Latin America. For pundits on the left the region stands as the remaining chance in the world for true pluralism, alternative democratic experiments, and sustainable development;[2] with almost equal enthusiasm, businessmen and economic analysts on the right see in the region an expanding middle class that, with its entry into consumerism, will fuel global markets.[3]

Due to demographic and economic pressures, however, around 30 million Latin Americans have migrated towards the economically central regions

---

[1] According to the Earth Institute at Columbia University, http://sedac.ciesin.columbia.edu/gpw/index.jsp.

[2] Ó. Guardiola-Rivera, *What if Latin America Ruled the World? How the South Will Take the North Into the 22nd Century* (London: Bloomsbury, 2010).

[3] Thus the opinion of the president of the Inter-American Development Bank, Luis Alberto Moreno, in an interview published by *El Tiempo*, Bogotá, 17 January 2011: 'This is Latin America's decade', www.eltiempo.com/economia/internacional/ARTICULO-WEB-NEW_NOTA_INTERIOR-8786694.html.

of the world (mainly to the United States and western Europe).[4] In their backpacks and suitcases they have not taken with them their laws as have, for example, immigrants of Muslim persuasion. In their new milieus, Latin Americans have had to learn the trappings and requirements of what many take to be a more demanding and rigorous rule of law than the one they used to know in their homelands: many of them turn into disempowered 'illegal aliens', for example, who stick almost neurotically to the legal speed limit for fear that, if caught, they will not only be issued with a ticket but perhaps also deported. In situations of disempowerment and cultural disorientation, then, compliance with the law (i.e., how to become the all-important 'law-abiding person' or better, perhaps, the 'authority-obeying' individual of US culture) demands pervasive attention to detail and even to appearance.[5] For a Latin American living in the First World, the concept of 'jaywalking' becomes legally and culturally meaningful for the first time. On the other hand, the political empowerment of 'citizenship' generates familiarity, even some capacity to defy the state in the face of legal threats: the meaning and construction of 'speeding' or 'jaywalking' are better known (and perhaps better dealt with in case of non-compliance) by the citizen than by the illegal immigrant. In an infamous statement, a New York oligarch reportedly announced, undaunted by prosecution, that 'only the little people pay taxes'.[6] Illegal aliens are usually counted among the little people.

The states, laws, and institutions of Latin America were slowly and unevenly formed under the influences of the different colonial administrations that were established throughout the sixteenth, seventeenth and eighteenth centuries. Quite early the Treaty of Tordesillas of 1494 purported to divide the 'new' continent between the Spanish and Portuguese crowns that, as a consequence, became the dominant territorial powers of the region. Today it is difficult to deny that when people all over the world refer to Latin America they are implicitly talking about Hispanic and/or Luso America: taken together they form what we might call, more precisely, 'Iberian America'.

---

[4] 'El costado multimillonario de la inmigración latinoamericana', *El Clarín*, Buenos Aires, 30 September 2007, www.clarin.com/diario/2007/09/30/elmundo/i-02215.htm.

[5] See the controversy about the deportation policy and practices enforced in the town of Irving, Texas: 'Irving Mayor Defends Increased Deportations', *Dallas Morning News*, 21 September 2007, www.dallasnews.com/sharedcontent/dws/dn/latestnews/stories/092207dnmetirving.367bf3e.html); 'Texas Mayor Caught in Deportation Furor', *New York Times*, 4 April 2009, www.nytimes.com/2009/04/05/us/05immig.html.

[6] 'Helmsley's Dog Gets $12 Million in Will', Associated Press, 29 August 2007, www.washingtonpost.com/wp-dyn/content/article/2007/08/29/AR2007082900491.html

The expression 'Latin America', however, was originally coined in the nineteenth century by intellectuals who were poised to counter the evil and overpowering influence of 'Saxon America': in a 1856 poem written by José-María Torres[7] describing the cultural and political opposition between the Latin and the Saxon Americas, the United States is depicted as having rejected the natural political brotherhood that had united it since the revolutionary wars with the South American republics,[8] projecting only 'egotism, thirst for gold and hypocritical piety'. The poet reminiscences bitterly about what are still historical milestones of evil intervention in the region: the invasion of northern Mexico by the United States[9] and the infamous manoeuvres of

---

[7] José Maria Torres-Caicedo, 'Las dos Américas', *El Correo de Ultramar*, Paris, 15 February 1857.

[8] This proximity between the two Americas was strongly felt, for example, among the first generation of *criollos* who fought for independence from Spain between 1808 and 1815. The Philadelphia Constitution was a beacon of ordered liberty. In a preface to its first translation and publication in the *Nuevo Reino de Granada* in 1812, Miguel de Pombo was ecstatic: 'The Constitution of the United States is a form of government which is essentially good: she has caused the happiness of our brothers in the North; and will do so the same with ours if we imitate her virtues and adopt her principles'. Later, in that same piece: 'Washington and Franklyn would happily live among us if we adopted the precious treasure of the Constitution of the North' (author's translations). M. de Pombo, 'Discurso sobre los principios y ventajas del sistema federativo', in de Pombo, *La propuesta federal*, ed. V. Azuero (Bogotá: Universidad Nacional de Colombia, 2010). A similar fervour for the Philadelphia experiment was being displayed in Santiago by the first ideologues of national Chilean consolidation. Camilo Henríquez, in *La Aurora de Chile*, stated (referring to the United States), 'We all love the Constitution that has made its Nation the refuge of liberty and of all harassed humankind'. C. Henríquez, 'Datos históricos sobre Estados Unidos', 2nd part, in La Aurora de Chile, no. 13, 7 May 1812 (author's translation). J. Pinto Vallejos, 'El pueblo soberano? Modelo estadounidense y ficción democratica en los álbores de la República de Chile', in F. Purcell and A. Riquelme (eds.), *Ampliando miradas: Chile y su historia en un tiempo global* (Santiago: Universidad Católica de Chile, 2009), 73–94.

[9] From 1846 to 1848 the United States invaded Mexico in order to expand its territories beyond the border of Texas. Originally a colony of Spain and a region of Mexico, and later an independent republic, Texas officially became part of the United States in 1846. To consolidate its presence further in the south-west, the United States annexed the territories of Alta California and New Mexico. During the war, US forces advanced well into the Mexican heartland, occupying the territories of New Mexico, Alta California, Baja California, Coahuila, Veracruz, Puebla, and even Mexico City. The war came to an end with the Treaty of Guadalupe Hidalgo, which recognized the independence of Texas, established the international border at the Rio Grande, or Rio Bravo and completed the annexation through the fiction of a 'sale' of the territories of Alta California and New Mexico to the United States in exchange for $15,000,000. Mexicans of today do not completely forget the old affront. In the laundry list of US interventions in the region, it appears alongside several episodes in Cuba, the Dominican Republic, and, of course, Puerto Rico. Stories of covert intervention do exist in the history of most countries of Central America, the Caribbean, and, perhaps less overtly, in the larger nations of South America. These interventions remain alive in political

Walker in Honduras[10] to control one of the dismissively christened 'banana republics'. In the light of those events, the poet concluded that 'the race of the Latin America / in front has the Saxon race,/ mortal enemy that already threatens/ to destroy its freedom'. But this imagined 'Latin' America was, in reality, a reference to the old concept of 'Latinity' to which the powerful France of the day laid claim. According to intellectual historians, the 'Latin America' of the nineteenth century was, in reality, a geopolitical and intellectual artifact that sought to affirm the leadership of France among the southern countries of Europe and their former overseas colonies. And, certainly, one of the things that South Americans sought to acquire from the French civilizing experience was the social construction of *legalité* as paradigm for its own legal and political infrastructure.

In the same poem of 1856 this aspiration appears clearly: 'the rule of law [gobiernos de derecho] will reign/ slave to the Law, the citizen/ perfect sovereign of his own acts/ Reason will rule his actions'. This original purpose of the label 'Latin' America, however, has practically disappeared in contemporary use: the modern 'Latin America' refers almost exclusively to the Iberian America south of the Rio Grande, excluding thus the project of Torres and other Francophiles of like mind. The Latin American connection with France, however, has remained to this day on the maps of comparative law that are still current in the discipline.[11] In those maps people still firmly depict Latin America as part of the so-called 'civil law' family. In this dominant rendition, then, 'Latin America' is certainly an autonomous geographic 'place' that, nonetheless, 'belongs' genetically to a network of legal structures: the so-called 'civil law'. More precisely, it belongs to the cluster of legal institutions

memory and use through well-known works of literature: thus, for example, the almost incendiary collection of short stories by Guatemalan Nobel-laureate Miguel Ángel Asturias under the title 'Week-end in Guatemala', or the play 'I Took Panama', reminiscing about the loss of Panama in 1903 at the hands of US interests, by the Colombian writer Jorge Alí Triana.

[10] In that same laundry list of US affronts to Latin American patriotism nobody ranks higher than US filibuster William Walker. Walker initiated various campaigns with privately financed armies to invade Nicaragua and Honduras. In Nicaragua he even managed to be elected as president of the country in 1856. After many comings and goings, Walker was executed by the Honduran army in 1860.

[11] It appears, of course, in the traditional comparative textbooks that purport to give a genetic sense of the legal families. More recently, the same idea reappears in the literature that discusses the importance of 'legal origins' to the levels of economic prosperity in different parts of the world. The French affiliation of Latin America, in this case, becomes a liability, for it impedes the growth of dynamic financial markets. This argument appears in R. La Porta, F. Lopez-de-Silanes, A. Shleifer, and R. W. Vishny, 'Law and Finance', (1998) 106 *Journal of Political Economy* 1113.

and rules that sprang into being after the French Revolution and its very long shadow of influence over the local legal imagination during the nineteenth and the first half of the twentieth centuries. On traditional and current maps of comparative law, then, 'Latin American law' ends up being the basic legal structure of the Iberian republics of the Americas that replicates the general direction, style, methodology, and ideology of the post-revolutionary law of republican France.

Besides the participation of Spain, Portugal, and France, there are other exporters of law that have created durable channels and ties of influence with the region: the metropolises of England and Holland, of course, remain central to the understanding of the modern law of their colonies or former colonies (under the many legal forms that the latter relation may take). Their participation in a political and economic community of the Caribbean is well known; therein, at least, these other powers balance out and even outdo the Spanish cultural, economic, and political presence. On terra firma, on the other hand, the non-Iberian presence is quite marginal, close to invisible; for example, the Guatemalan official map does not, to this day, accept the strange presence of Belize[12] or 'British Honduras' as it is still called in Guatemala, in an effort to avoid its international recognition; likewise, the three Guyanas, west of Venezuela, seem to be territories[13] from a whole different continent with little political or cultural contact with the rest of South America. Ask a South American where Suriname is located and you will probably receive a blank stare as an answer. These examples of political exclusion and difference are important for understanding how law works at the regional level.

[12] Belize is a Central American country bordering Mexico and Guatemala. The first European conquerors who came to these territories were the Spanish in the sixteenth century. But, unlike the rest of Central America, Belize fell early under British influence. The history, in very broad brushstrokes, goes like this: Spanish authorities did not clearly mark (or govern, for that matter) the southern boundary of the Yucatán peninsula, allowing English pirates to seek refuge on the coast of this territory. English woodcutters and their slaves populated the coast in the seventeenth century. However, it was only in 1798 that a British colony was formally established when the British defeated the Spanish in the battle of St. George's Caye; in 1840 it was given the name 'British Honduras'. Guatemala signed a treaty with England for the devolution of these lands which became ineffective, however, when Belize achieved political independence. While Guatemala certainly recognized Belize's independence in 1993, official maps and public discourse inside the country still show clear signs of unhealed wounds.

[13] Two of them, Suriname and Guyana, are in fact sovereign states with their own conflicted history of neocolonialism. French Guiana, on the other hand, is still a colonial territory, tellingly known in French as a *département d'outre-mer*.

The cultural and linguistic distance between the Iberian and non-Iberian colonies is quite important from a legal point of view: there is no common Latin American and Caribbean legal tradition despite the geographical proximity. The former Spanish colonies in the Caribbean (Cuba, the Dominican Republic, and even Puerto Rico[14]) take part in a common legal dialogue with continental Iberian America and, moreover, with continental Europe; they base their legal origin and culture on a common bedrock of Spanish and also, much more importantly, broader European influences. An important part of the official ideology of the newly independent states of Latin America was to abandon the colonial law of Castile and to embrace, in its place, liberal, enlightened, and progressive European law, usually from France, Germany, Italy or, notice the irony, from the liberalized Spain of the second half of the nineteenth century. Spanish law at this time, in turn, was more indebted to liberal European institutions than to medieval Castilian law. Modern law in Latin America, therefore, remained somewhat connected to Spain, but rather to the new Spain that was rejecting its own traditional laws, costumes, and systems of governance to become a modern and liberal state.

By contrast, the English Caribbean followed quite closely the institutional and legal imprint of the common law, with no significant proximity to Iberian America. Furthermore, the English Caribbean followed a Burkean understanding of institutional history, denying any significant break in the law between the pre-colonial and the independent periods, between *old* and *new* law. Finally, the French and Dutch Caribbean, mostly still under colonial rule, developed the law directly with and through their metropolises, although republican France (starting with the public law of its own revolution) claims to be, through widespread ideological influence, the *modern* formative force behind all Latin American law and institutions. French political liberalism is still the main component of the remnants of Latin American legal Francophilia.

These boundaries of intellectual influence work quite surprisingly: just think of the immense amount of cultural and legal dialogue that there is, to this day, between the Dominican Republic and Cuba (despite a huge ideological schism of many years); meanwhile, and despite sharing the same

---

[14] The Puerto Rican adaptation of the US adversarial system of criminal procedure was chosen, by the US government, as a model to be followed in its quest to get many Latin American countries to reform their systems of criminal procedure in a wave of reforms that has spanned the region in the wake of the security challenges caused by drug trafficking and other forms of organized transnational crime in the region.

basic legal codes from the nineteenth century (well, sharing the same island!), there is no significant legal exchange between the neighbouring Dominican Republic and Haiti: when asked about it, a Dominican lawyer will describe her own legal system as structurally 'French', but, no, never, 'Haitian'!

These impressionistic views are not offered in judgement on the dignity or worth of any of these countries: they give, however, a good mental map of how lawyers imagine and think of their regional neighbourhood. These schematic maps express clear, if implicit, regional hierarchies: Latin American law (meaning, again, the Hispanic and Portuguese traditions) is imperial within its own domain (but weak and subordinated on the global map). The non-Hispanic Caribbean functions as an internal periphery in political and legal terms. This is, of course, a legal and political map coloured by chauvinism and ignorance, as this piece is written by a Colombian legal scholar. The map, then, cannot be real. Rather, and this is its only use, it is a snapshot of generalized perceptions in the minds of Latin American lawyers. The work of describing a Latin American and Caribbean legal tradition is, perforce, almost impossible. One could attempt the enterprise and even enlist the political arguments why these two vastly divergent legal traditions should be harmonized, but the final result would be mostly prescriptive, with little descriptive worth.

One could say, for example, that Latin America and the Caribbean have enough political and commercial convergences to largely justify the construction of harmonized or even uniform legal and institutional structures – for example, a common Inter-American Court of Human Rights where the basic dignity and fundamental rights of the American citizens are enshrined and protected; or a common commercial organization (CARICOM) that would strengthen commercial exchange between and the economic growth of Caribbean countries. But within these organizations the legal traditions of Iberian and non-Iberian countries really function more as an obstacle to the rapprochement of the serious interests being negotiated or considered there.

An example might be useful: the author of this chapter had the privilege of serving as an ad hoc judge of the Inter-American Court of Human Rights, sitting next to the recently appointed Jamaican judge. Making sense together of the proceedings was extremely stimulating for the both of us: however, our common background and interest in human rights was not strong enough to overcome the marked differences in juridical style which the Jamaican judge immediately recognized in this heavily 'Latin American' environment. Please remember, to start with, that the Court sits in San José,

Costa Rica. I tried to serve, to the best of my abilities, as a comparative interpreter of what was going on: the cultural meaning and purpose of a 'hearing', of 'evidence', of 'judging', of 'legal interpretation', of 'fundamental right', of 'indemnity', of 'wrong', and a long etcetera was split between background assumptions coming from my 'European continental law' and her 'common law' background (in the Jamaican judge's categorization), whatever the meaning these placeholders could carry. We quickly surmised that there were 'functional' similarities between our understanding of what a 'hearing' was and what it served for; but this well-intended functional cosmopolitanism was not enough to reduce the technical and ideological schisms that the two traditions formed, again and again, in this high-pressured environment. Our common commitment to human rights discourse and practice was not as potent as the ideological force of our 'background' traditions. I think this is a good description of what happens most of the time when Iberian and non-Iberian lawyers talk about the law in concrete situations. Interactions (institutional, commercial, etc., etc.) between Iberian lawyers are much more frequent and they rest on shared assumptions about the law; contacts between Iberian and, for example, English Caribbean lawyers are less frequent and they go on despite a marked sense of legal and cultural difference.

The same cultural distance is not quite apparent in dialogues between the Hispanic and Brazilian legal cultures, despite evident linguistic differences. Brazilians and Hispanic American lawyers do share a rather common map of legal influences, institutions, and ideologies. Their conversations, at a certain *abstract* level, show a common ground in history, in legal theory, in bibliographical references, and in institutional and political values and commitments. These common transnational, regional references are the *space* within which one can talk about a 'Latin American' legal tradition. This space, however, does not come from pre-Columbian or colonial times. In fact, it was explicitly structured with the purpose of *excluding* the disturbing presence of traditional indigenous and colonial laws. Only recently some reconstructive projects of the 'indigenous legal tradition' have reappeared that intend to salvage, at least at a highly abstract constitutional level, the impact of non-European, pre-Columbian laws and political values as tokens, for now, of multiculturalism.[15] These projects, however, do not bear much

[15] R. Yrigoyen, *Pautas de Coordinación entre el Derecho Indígena y el Derecho Estatal* (Guatemala: Fundación Myrna Mack, 1999). The best example in this direction comes from

promise of impacting everyday law and transactions. Some Latin American legal historians have also argued extensively in favour of a view of law that recognizes the influence that Castilian and Portuguese colonial law and practice continue to have, at some deep level, on the modern law of the region. Whatever the merits of this historical interpretation, however, it remains extremely marginal in the ideology of lawyers.[16] The truth seems to be, on the contrary, twofold: first, that Latin Americans of the nineteenth century distanced themselves from Spanish and Portuguese law to give priority to the powerhouses of European Law, mainly France, Germany, and Italy, with some minor attention being paid to the modern law of Belgium, Spain,

the Bolivian Constitution of 2009, whose preamble is worth citing in part: 'From time immemorial mountains rose, rivers flowed and lakes formed. Our Amazonia, our Chaco, our high plateaux were covered with plants and flowers. We populated this sacred Mother Earth with different faces, and we understood the plurality of all things and our diversity as individuals and as cultures. We thus created our peoples, and never knew racism until we were subjected to it during the terrible times of colonialism. We, the Bolivian people, of plural composition, from the depths of its history, inspired by past struggles, in the indigenous anticolonial rising, in the independence, in the popular struggles of liberation, in the manifestations of indigenous, social, and union organizations, in the conflicts over water, in the struggle for land and territory, and in the memory of our martyrs, constitute a new State' (author's translation).

[16] Several concrete examples may be used to illustrate this general tendency (indeed, an inbred prejudice) of the legal historian to heighten the influence of the laws and institutions of pre-independent Latin America: in the first place, the local civil law is said, as in Europe, to come straight from Roman law. Latin American universities and scholars, however, never fully participated in the creation and transformation of the European *ius commune*. Despite efforts to see the national civil law as an extension of the European *ius commune* (e.g. in L. Muñoz, *Derecho romano comparado con el derecho colombiano* (Bogotá: Temis, 2007)), it is a fact that there remains a political and academic gap between the two traditions. Latin Americans had a late and insecure start within the Roman law tradition; at about the time for the *criollos* to construct the national laws of the independent republics (*derechos patrios*), the project of codification and legal positivism and statism had completely undermined the Romanist project of legality. Roman law was indeed widely taught in a scholarly manner, but Latin America never ranked high in the scholarly network that produced the swansong of that tradition in the nineteenth century. See F. Betancourt, *La recepción del derecho romano en Colombia (saec. XVII)* (Seville: Universidad de Sevilla, 2007). In another disciplinary area, Professor Malagón has tried to prove that the central concepts of administrative law do not come from French influences and doctrines, as is widely believed. Instead, according to Malagón, they still come directly from Spanish colonial administrative practice. The thesis thus impugns the idea of massive French transplants of administrative law. The evidence offered, although interesting, remains elusive and subtle. The legal remnants of the past, said to be decisive in contemporary law, end up in the margins of the working doctrines of the present, and rather as institutional ghosts coming out of the 'legal unconscious'. M. Malagón, *Vivir en policía: una contralectura de los orígenes del derecho administrativo colombiano* (Bogotá: Universidad Externado, 2007).

and Portugal. Second, whenever influence came from Spain or Portugal in the late nineteenth century it was through the liberal codes and rules that these countries were fashioning to modernize and liberalize their own late-medieval legal traditions.

The contemporary 'Latin American' tradition was forged during the nineteenth century, when a renewed 'European legal space' was created, of course, in the old Continent. In the same nineteenth century, the law and institutions of the new Latin American republics linked themselves to this web of juridical books, doctrines, ideologies, and histories to form, in time, what we might call the 'Euro-Latin American legal space'. This is not simply the same European *ius commune* created by Romanistic culture in the thirteenth century. While it may be easier for Europeans to see a historical continuity between the 'Roman Law tradition' and the formation of the European legal science and space of the nineteenth century,[17] that way of looking at things makes less sense for Latin Americans. The European *ius commune* that spanned the thirteenth to the eighteenth centuries was not extensively used in Latin America: legal contact, since the 'discovery', was established only spasmodically if it ever really occurred; local customary practices remained central to communities that were hardly reached and poorly tended by the colonial institutions of law and adjudication; the practicalities of government in the Americas demanded direct action through royal law and executive command, not the application of the scholarly tradition of Roman law; therefore the Spanish metropolis relied mainly on national laws and institutions and, furthermore, in a specialized body of rules, the *derecho indiano*, which was in itself exceptional vis-à-vis the ordinary law of Castile. Finally, the *ius commune* was a scholarly tradition that was not amply received or used in everyday law due to obvious shortcomings and lack of investment in the academic or administrative networks of *ultramar*.

French and German scholars began in the second half of the nineteenth century to form a common space for the production and sharing of legal science, ideas, and institutions. For them, back in Europe, this legal space was a re-creation of the supranational construction of the *ius commune* that

---

[17] As presented, for example, in a long and distinguished tradition of scholarship: P. Stein, *Roman Law in European History* (Cambridge University Press, 1999); J. H. Merryman, *The Civil Law Tradition: An Introduction to the Legal Systems of Western Europe and Latin America* (Palo Alto: Stanford University Press, 1969); G. Wesenberg and G. Wesener, *Historia del derecho privado modern en Alemania y Europa* (Valladolid: Lex Nova, 1998).

had occurred since the latter Middle Ages. It was a 'modern' *ius commune* as it was in fact called. For Latin Americans, on the other hand, this was probably the first instance when they could participate in a highly cosmopolitan and supranational idea of law, but for more practical and urgent purposes. Non-European jurists (in Latin America, but also elsewhere) began to participate also in this open space: in 1898, Luis Claro Solar, the foremost Chilean jurist of the turn of the century, was able to make a list of the leading countries of this transnational space, as witnessed from the remote southern town of Santiago (now turned into a veritable 'global city'[18]): Germany, France, and Belgium. He wrote, perhaps for the first time, a treatise on the Chilean Civil Code that made extensive use of comparative materials from these European countries.[19] Foreign doctrine became quite prestigious and widely used: when reading these books, there seems to be a seamless web of doctrine between the *Précis* of Baudry-Lacantinerie[20] in Paris and Claro's *Explicaciones*. Looking with attention at these developments, Latin American legal reformers and scholars voluntarily threw themselves into this intellectual web of transnational doctrine with the purpose of building up and consolidating their own national legal systems. Nation-building demanded legal institutions, but the respite during which to implement them came only half a century later, after the drums of war had definitely ceased in the region. Theirs was a target of opportunity: in charge, as they were, of the establishment and strengthening of the legal institutions of the young republics of America, they saw in this pool of legal science the materials, tools, and resources (a veritable legal quarry) that might be deployed in their own endeavours. This Euro-Latin American space was being consolidated by the end of the nineteenth century; it was stable and clearly dominant during the twentieth; and, finally, it is still powerful, but not without challenges, in the dynamic map of the law of our times.

To conceptualize with some level of precision this networked space, it is perhaps advisable to use the expression 'Euro-Latin American legal space'. With this expression we try to capture the formation of European legal science from the point of view of Latin American legal elites who partook of that project, used their resources in the creation of the legal infrastructure of their own countries and, at the end, had to endure the strictures and

---

[18] S. Sassen, *The Global City* (Princeton University Press, 2001).

[19] L. Claro Solar, *Explicaciones de Derecho Civil chileno y comparado* (Santiago: Establecimiento Poligráfico Roma, 1898).

[20] G. Baudry-Lacantinerie, *Précis de Droit Civil*, 3 vols. (Paris: Larose, 1882–4).

hierarchies that the network imposed on them. We must also direct our attention to the derivative network of dialogue that in time was formed in Latin America: there is to this day a regional dialogue of legal science with very active local influences and transplants in which, for example, the original French *cassation*, to this day, has been interpreted and understood in El Salvador through the doctrine and case law expounded by the Colombian Supreme Court. In time, and this is fundamental to notice, the derivative regional dialogue became much more fluid and dynamic than the original exchanges with liberal European law. The amount of material that circulates inside Latin America is huge and, in many examples, constitutes the autonomous reworking and retooling of concepts original to the European space: think, for example, of the amazing importance for contemporary constitutional law of the concept of 'Estado Social de Derecho' that is genetically linked to the political idea of the German 'Sozialrechtsstaat', but which has also been transformed to serve new and important uses endogenous to Latin America. With it, Latin Americans have massively reshaped their political and constitutional rhetoric, have enhanced the role of fundamental social rights in adjudication and have reshuffled, not necessarily for the better, the redistribution of social entitlements in contexts of dire scarcity.

For the comparative lawyer of today, then, it is necessary to explain the structure, the channels, and the functions of this Euro-Latin American legal space, a story that in general has remained absent from the standard recounting of the so-called 'civil law tradition'. The 'civil law tradition', as it has usually been constructed,[21] is a misleading concept on several counts relating to Latin America: the civil law tradition tells the history of European legal science and of its influence, and this is, at a certain level, irreproachable. But this rendition obscures the precise ways in which the dialogue of the law happens at a regional level, obscures the fact that this regional dialogue is not marginal but, rather, central, that it certainly goes on with chunks and pieces of European legal *science*, but that these chunks and pieces have been widely transformed by many other legal influences and local political purposes; and, finally, it obscures the fact that all of this interaction, borrowing, and common influence happens, not

---

[21] In the disciplinary textbooks, for example, of R. David, *Major Legal Systems of the World Today: An Introduction to the Comparative Study of the Law* (London: Stevens, 1985); K. Zweigert and H. Kötz, *Introduction to Comparative Law*, trans. T. Weir, 3rd rev. edn (Oxford: Clarendon; New York: Oxford University Press, 1998).

in the reconstructed Latin of antiquity (after all, the supposed lingua franca of the civil law), but in the modern Spanish (and Portuguese) of today.

Finally, what might be the purpose of studying this *espacio jurídico euro-latinoamericano* in an introduction to regional comparative law? As with almost all other endeavours in general comparative law, the purpose of these introductory macro-comparisons is powerful but limited: the description of the *espacio jurídico euro-latinoamericano* will give readers a sense of the background legal conversations that local Latin American lawyers have when they interact in transnational spaces in the conduct of both public and private businesses. It is as if we were peeking at the preliminary and perfunctory chit-chat that creates recognition and accreditation between lawyers of different countries when they share common disciplinary stories about the law. This background knowledge feels like an abstract common language: powerful enough to distinguish between insiders or outsiders (certainly a *gringo* lawyer is an outsider), but not powerful enough to draft the contract or the lawsuit in all its technical legal detail. This is why, for example, an Argentinean lawyer in a US-based law firm can coordinate the due diligence for projects all over Latin America. She can speak the regional language. But each jurisdiction has its own national dialect that cannot be wholly cracked open through background knowledge extracted from the *espacio.* Linguistic structures will continually provide arguments to limit and circumscribe the local force of the dialect; and vice versa. The *espacio,* however, will not teach you to speak the dialect convincingly. This description, perhaps, could also work to explain the dialogue between an English and a US lawyer or between Muslim scholars in Africa staring at each other across the divide between the Shāfiʿī and the Mālikī *madhhabs* or schools. It would be interesting to make comparisons of how strong these languages remain within each tradition. I shall hazard a bold and purely speculative assessment based on personal experience: I would say that the language of the *espacio euro-latinoamericano* exerts today a stronger disciplining and harmonizing force than can the 'common law' in an Atlantic conversation between US and English legal workers; it even exerts a stronger force than the 'civil law' familiarity between, say, a Honduran and a French lawyer today. However, I would not be able to say how it feels, from an internal point of view, in a conversation between Muslim jurists.

But this Euro-Latin American space has also been impacted by other influences, mainly the slow, reluctant, but now powerful, invasion of US law and, more importantly, jurisprudence. Although the region has been culturally Americanized throughout the twentieth century, many claimed that this process was neither possible nor desirable in the law, where genetic affiliation to Europe had created some sort of niche of immunity. This, of course, is not true: the global weight of the United States has created forces that pull, in Latin America and elsewhere, towards that legal model. Although the subject would necessitate a volume in itself, the Americanization of Latin American law can be told in broad-brush outline: first, the incandescence of French prestige started to lose its brightness, while mistrust of the Saxon America faded in memory as the twentieth century began to unfold. Another writer, Marco Fidel Suárez, foretold in his 1925 'Dreams of Luciano Pulgar' the ascendant role of the United States: 'It is time for the Americanization, as we, progressive citizens, call the impulse coming from America, that is, the United States, which will transform this island'.[22] For intellectuals at the dawn of the twentieth century, the US experience was of great interest: more administration, more business, less politics, less ideology; the US experience was depicted by many as the real doorway to practical economic modernity out and away from that thick and highly volatile political modernity that French ideology had brought into the region as an escape from the irreducible confrontation between political liberalism and Catholic conservatism that had stifled the growth of these forsaken countries.

The second fundamental element was that, at some point during the thirties, the United States began to see that it could actually export its law and, in consequence, began aggressively to do so. New statutory and regulatory law, mainly regarding banks and finance, were demanded by many Latin American countries. The regulations were, in turn, easily translatable to the general doctrines of obligations or administrative law that constituted the scientific core of the European legal tradition. The American statutes created 'obligations' or defined 'banking contracts' or demanded 'administrative acts' or granted 'jurisdiction'. All these notions were interpreted and applied with the thicker theories and conceptual ways of thinking that the Euro-Latin space had already formed. Latin doctrine and case law already had well-formed theories of obligations, contracts, administrative acts, or jurisdiction that were used, in turn, to interpret systematically new regulatory ideas coming from the United States. These general theories spoke the

---

[22] M. Fidel Suárez, *Sueños de Luciano Pulgar* (Bogotá: Minerva, 1940) (author's translation).

European legal language, but with clear local accents and dialects:[23] upon them, furthermore, one could lay down many regulatory or policy strategies brought from other 'families' of the law. In this way, Latin America soon proved that the apparently irreducible distance that existed between the common and the civil law families was not real. Rapprochement was possible, but in particular fields and without bringing to the table the harder, culturally embedded differences that exist in the core, structural doctrines of 'obligation', 'contract', 'administrative act', or judicial structure and ideology. When Édouard Lambert[24] declared in Egypt, throwing his arms in the air in despair, that the French and the English could not establish a real legal dialogue of mutual adaptation and accommodation, he was not taking into account the more modest Latin American path to 'Americanization': the transplant of American statutory law into civil general structures, not the creation, overly ambitious to this day, of common basic doctrines of private law. This modest path was, in fact, the real point of contact that the common law and civil law traditions began to have in the region. The strategy was not, at the end, that modest: it served to Americanize local law at growing speed and in very many different areas. Today, in a deeper and riskier gamble, Latin America has taken up the adversarial trial system to try to fix its own problems with expanding criminality. The change has not yet impacted the general theory of process, much less the general theory of crime. On the contrary, the general theories of process and crime still serve the purpose of understanding the adversarial system, thus creating a strange mixture of Euro-Latin concepts and American practices. These changes, nonetheless, have brought new expectations to the field of criminal procedure with its attendant importance in the political life of Latin American countries.

Later US law has become something more than simply a repository of statutory ideas and quick fixes: pushed to a brutal generalization, one could say that US law and jurisprudence represent today, in Latin America, the general idea according to which law is a purposeful instrument of governance

[23] It is extremely common for European jurists to notice misunderstandings of general theories as they are applied in Latin America. They can also be understood as useful 'transformations'. The first attitude demands repentance and submission to orthodoxy; the second discusses the consequences of the adaptation. D. López-Medina, *Teoría impura del derecho: la transformación de la cultura jurídica latinoamericana* (Bogotá: Legis, 2004).

[24] É. Lambert, *Conception générale, définition, méthode et histoire du droit comparé. Le droit comparé et l'enseignement du droit. Congrès Internationale de Droit Comparé, tenù á Paris du 31 Juillet au 4 Août 1900. Procès verbaux des séances et documents*, vol. 1 (Paris: LGDJ, 1905), 26–61.

that implements policy in the areas that it regulates. US legal science is the place from which Latin America extracts the bits and pieces of 'policy analysis' that seem to counter and balance the 'doctrinal and conceptual analysis' that stems from the classical European tradition. This is the continuous message of contemporary American jurisprudence, under the guise of either economic analysis or critical legal studies. Even a neo-conceptualist like Ronald Dworkin has been read in like fashion: his books show a heightened sensibility for the role that policy analysis plays in legal thinking, at least when compared with French legalism or European conceptualism.

16.2 The place of Latin America in the hierarchies of comparative law

I shall finish with some remarks about the politics of comparative law: the language spoken in the Euro–Latin American legal space ranks low in the hierarchies of traditional comparative law. There are at least two main reasons for this: in first place, it is usually supposed that Latin American law is merely an 'affiliated' legal family that depends heavily on European law, mainly of the so-called French variety. The master architect of legal families, René David, described Latin America in the following terms:

The laws of the twenty nations of Latin America belong, with no argument, to the Western legal system, and particularly to the French group of that system. The conception of the world that they purport to actualize is typically that of western Europe. Found in them is the same adhesion to the principles of Christian morality, liberal democracy and the capitalist structure of society. In all those states, besides, one can find Codes that are very similar, both in content and form, to the European Codes, and particularly the French as far as private law is concerned ... The similarity is so great that one can state with complete certainty: the best way that a jurist has of becoming familiar with the bulk of the laws of Latin America is, without doubt, by resorting to extracting from Europe, and especially from France, the knowledge of the general principles that dominate in all those legal systems and the methods that allow one to study and to understand them.[25]

The language spoken, according to David, seems to be French. He might accept that there are local dialects, but the general language is unmistakably

[25] R. David, *Tratado de derecho civil comparado. Introducción al estudio de los derechos extranjeros y al método comparativo* (Madrid: Editorial Revista de Derecho Privado, 1953), 251–2 (author's translation).

French. For David, then, Latin American not only has a *droit franchophile*, but a veritable *droit francophone*. My thesis in this chapter will be to say that the *espacio jurídico euro-latinoamericano* indeed has had at some point strong ties with France; but, on the other hand, it is not particularly helpful to say or believe, without more specification, that Latin American law is today a legal or political extension of *francophonie*. This belief gives excessive weight to the influence of the French codification and its attached principle of *legalité*. French jurists know this quite clearly, for they understand that the cultural projects of *francophonie* and *francophilie* apply to their former colonies in Africa in a sense that has probably never been the case in Latin America. David perhaps misrepresented and exaggerated the type of tie that linked French and Latin American law. Latin America has undoubtedly participated in the European space, but the borrowed doctrines and laws have been heavily appropriated and reinterpreted for multiple different purposes. Latin America is not part of the civil law family anymore, if such conceptual abstraction still holds any validity; and certainly it is not part of the *francophilie*.

However, the real, structural point that remains in David's conception is political: Latin American countries possess affiliated and secondary laws, the deployment and use of which are less successful and credible. Highly legalistic as Latin Americans are, the rule of law in Latin America remains of poor quality, their apprehension of doctrine incomplete and parasitic, and the real efficacy of their institutions marginal and discriminatory. In comparative law exchanges, then, little attention is paid to the development and recent state of Latin American law. Their proposals, in political settings, suffer from lack of respect and power; academically, likewise, the comparative interest in Latin American law remains marginal. Legal Latin Americanists suffer from an acute case of the 'Cinderella complex' within a discipline that has its own deep-seated issues of self-esteem. In the light of these doubts, can we offer some final arguments to try to reposition Latin American law in the context of the contemporary maps of comparative law?

First of all, the *espacio jurídico latinoamericano* has become quite polycentric. There is no single site of legal production that has a marked leadership in the region. Latin Americans have always been curious and adventurous in the broad markets of comparative law: they confer prestige and status to the legal doctrines and forms of many states and regions. They have used, by direct or indirect import, the laws of many European states (such as France, Spain, Portugal, Germany, Italy, and Belgium); they now also take advice on different matters from ideas, institutions, or doctrines from the United States and other so-called 'common law' traditions, really taking their cue not from the 'common law' part but rather from modern statutory and regulatory law whenever it seems feasible for internal needs and purposes; they have paid heed to the legal innovations and political projects proposed by multilateral agencies in the context of, for example, protecting human rights or foreign investment; finally, and most importantly, Latin Americans have an increasingly active circulation of legal ideas and experiences among themselves. Latin American legal culture and behaviour has been certainly an open, receptive, docile, and, at times, almost submissive social enterprise. Each characterization is partially true, but each suggests a different appreciation of the phenomenon.

Second, I want to argue that the secondary position, esteem, and respectability of Latin America in comparative studies is in itself a political artifact, a long-term prejudice that is easily reiterated but seldom and inefficaciously criticized. Witness, for example, the laws and institutions of Aruba and their positioning in the strategic maps of comparative law: in a famous recent case, the *Holloway* case, the pressure exerted on Aruban authorities to find those behind the disappearance of a young American woman moved them to seek active support from Dutch criminal investigators. This was a move to counter the widespread idea, at least put forward in the US press, that local institutions of criminal investigation were inept at best, if not outright corrupt. Aruba was being depicted as a tourist paradise, but mired in institutional corruption.[26] This may or may not be a fact, of course. The important point is that Latin and Caribbean legal systems are routinely perceived as such. This perception, in turn, seems to be embedded in the way in which the discipline of comparative law perceives and positions the region in its maps. That perception, of course, is not innocent: it certainly strengthens the position of whoever advances the criticism by undermining the credibility of local institutions and opening ways for legal or other types of intervention. Thus it is common to believe, with or without evidence, that there is some sort of deficiency in the quality of the law and legal institutions of Latin America and the Caribbean.

The criticism that other nations violate the 'rule of law' is, in many instances, a remark that some can throw at others as a consequence of their superior geopolitical power or as a projection of the confidence that one's

---

[26] D. Holloway, R. S. Good, and L. Garrison, *Aruba: The Tragic Untold Story of Natalee Holloway and Corruption in Paradise* (Nashville: Thomas Nelson, 2006).

own legal system functions better or more efficiently than the other's. Geopolitical power, then, is part of the hierarchy of comparative law that position and, to some extent, prefigure quite negatively the expectations that many hold about the workings of law in Latin America and the Caribbean. The archetypical depiction of this sense of legal superiority (and the resentment that it generates in Latin America) is shown in structural prejudices that surface, from time to time, in the world's press: thus the presence of Dutch authority was sought by the Aruban authorities to give support and credence to the local investigation in the Holloway case; it was certainly more difficult to criticize the legal institutions and proceedings of a 'First World' country. A credible 'rule of law' was replacing the unstable and fragile 'unrule of law' of Aruba.[27] But the affront to local pride did not pass unheeded: Aruban journals reported that on 5 July 2005 some islanders demanded 'respect [for] our Dutch law' in the face of protracted accusations of inefficacy and corruption by the Holloway family and the governor of the state of Alabama, where the family resided.[28]

Similar accusations have been made in many other cases. The Brazilian legal system was seen as incapable of offering criminal due process to American pilots charged with criminal offences after a mid-air collision in 2006.[29] The Colombian criminal and prison system was depicted by the

[27] C. J. Williams, 'As Missing Teen Case Cools, Aruba Turns Against Family', *Seattle Times*, 9 June 2007, http://seattletimes.nwsource.com/html/nationworld/2003741183_aruba09.html.

[28] Holloway's mother retracted her opinion of the Aruban legal system and accepted that it worked according to well-known juridical principles: 'I would like to apologize to the Aruban people and to the Aruban authorities if I or my family offended you in any way. I realize that the Aruban legal system abides by the presumption of innocence and I want to reassure everyone that I do respect the Aruban legal system.' CNN.com, 'Missing Teen's Mom Apologizes for Comments: Statement "Fueled by Despair"', http://edition.cnn.com/2005/LAW/07/08/missing.aruba/.

[29] On 8 December 2009, two US pilots of a private jet were charged in Brazil for causing a mid-air collision that killed 154 people. The pilots were detained in Brazil after the small jet they were flying collided with a Gol Airlines Boeing 737–800 at 37,000 ft over the Amazon jungle on 29 September 2006. Despite sustaining damage, the private aircraft was landed safely at a military air base. Brazilian federal police charged the pilots with 'endangering air safety'. The Brazilian investigation found out that the private jet's transponder was switched off at the time of the collision. The American investigation, on the other hand, faulted the Brazilian air control system. The criminal case of negligence continues in Brazil against the two US pilots. O Globo, 'Mais duas testimunhas devem depor sobre acidente com voo 1907 da Gol, http://oglobo.globo.com/cidades/mat/2010/08/17/mais-duas-testemunhas-devem-depor-sobre-acidente-com-voo-1907-da-gol-917413627.asp.

European Court of Human Rights as incapable of receiving in extradition an Israeli citizen sentenced to jail for training paramilitaries in the 1980s without violating his fundamental human rights under the European Charter; in the Court's decision, the main evidence for this mistrust was a press statement by Vice-President Francisco Santos, in which he wished that the so-called trainer of the right-wing paramilitary militia would 'rot in jail'.[30] The remark was intended to showcase before the international community of Human Rights the will of the Colombian government to put a stop to their violation. The strategy, however, backfired miserably for his statement was interpreted in Strasbourg not as zeal to combat the far right paramilitary, but rather as disregard for the rule of law that would imperil the life and integrity of an Israeli citizen. Finally, in an example that shows quite explicitly the symbolic effect of asymmetrical perceptions about the 'rule of law' in the world maps of comparative law, the US television show *Dateline* broadcast an exposé under the title 'Enemies at the Gate', in which an undercover journalist, by using a 'broker' with corrupt 'high-level contacts', was able to obtain legitimate Peruvian and Venezuelan passports that would pose serious threats to the US immigration system if used by terrorists or other dangerous individuals. The contacts in Lima also offered to provide the undercover journalist with a legitimate visa to enter the United States. Why not, then, try and get this as well? At this point, however, the journalist's zeal was diminished in the light of legal concerns: 'Because the situation raised concerns about a potential threat to US national security, NBC News approached US government officials in several agencies.

The US government, on the other hand, refused a petition by the families of the victims to withdraw flying licences of the pilots. O Globo, 'Governo dos EUA nega pedido de cassaçao de brevê de pilotos emvolvidos em accidente da Gol', 5 May 2010, http://oglobo. globo.com/cidades/mat/2010/05/05/governo-dos-eua-nega-pedido-de-cassacao-de-breve-de-pilotos-envolvidos-em-acidente-da-gol-916505568.asp. The confrontation between jurisdictions continues.

[30] European Court of Human Rights, *Klein v. Russia*, 1 April 2010. According to the Court (Para. 54), 'Furthermore, turning to the applicant's personal situation, the Court observes that the applicant fears that he would be singled out as a target of ill-treatment when in Colombia because Vice-President Santos reportedly stated that the applicant should "rot in jail". It considers that, regrettably, it is unable to assess fully the nature of the statement and the connotations it might have had in the original language, i.e. Spanish, since the applicant has not indicated the source of the information concerning the statement in question. However, it appears that the statement expressing the wish of a high-ranking executive official to have a convicted prisoner "rot in jail" may be regarded as an indication that the person in question runs a serious risk of being subjected to ill-treatment while in detention.'

Officials said that if [the journalist] were to file the visa application under a false identity, even for a news story intended to expose weaknesses in the system, it would violate US law.'[31] Needless to say, the irregular acquisition of passports was also a violation of Peruvian law. By this fallacious construct the Peruvian system looks corrupt while the American is saved, at the last minute, not by its efficacy (which remained to be tested), but by corporate risk aversion.

This embedded prejudice is not only projected on to Latin America; it is a way of characterizing other legal systems in order to generate not a description of their functioning but rather a valuation of their merit. It is not a general and unbiased macro-comparison of the 'spirit' of Latin American law: it is the beginning, already, of public and private negotiations in which compromise clauses or New York jurisdiction is required (and is many times imposed) in the light of the perceived judicial inefficiency of Argentina; it is the inducement to apply universal criminal jurisdiction by Italian, Spanish and Dutch judges in Peru, Guatemala, and Suriname; it is the prejudice that allows many to think that reports about positive Latin American law count only as anthropological information, not as alternatives in the urgent issues of today's law. This strategy, this comparative positioning in the maps of law, is naturally and frequently used against African countries: when a Spanish air crew was detained in N'Djamena in November 2007 for trafficking children out of Chad to be adopted in France under the auspices of the French charity l'Arche de Zoé, alarmed Spanish and French public opinion (and their governments) focused on the dire conditions of the prison system, not on the crime itself. (Despite the group's claim that the children were orphans from Darfur who were being taken to be fostered in France, most of the children were found to be Chadian, and to have at least one living parent or guardian.) The Chadian legal system was criticized as being incapable of trying the Europeans; if punishment were to be meted out, it would have to be functionally adapted to European laws and, of course, executed there.[32] This criticism missed its mark: it undervalued the substantive legal interests of Chad's law and government. A Chadian minister had to come before the press to announce that 'not everything is allowed in our country', referring

---

[31] Richard Greenberg, Adam Ciralsky, and Stone Phillips, 'Enemies at the Gate', www.msnbc.msn.com/id/22419963/.

[32] 'París pedirá a Chad el traslado de los miembros de El Arca de Zoé', *La Vanguardia*, Madrid, 27 December 2007, www.lavanguardia.es/lv24h/20071227/53421060886.html

to the fact that the children had to be legally adopted, not just physically removed, even if out of saintly concern.[33]

This disciplining mechanism is also applied to First World countries, but not in the structural manner that is embedded in the maps of comparative law for Latin America or Africa. The Chadian prison of the Arche de Zoé case is known by locals as 'Guantánamo'.[34] The known failures and imperfections of US law and institutions, however, are presented case by case against a backdrop of general systemic confidence. However, self-confidence is hard to come by in Latin America; the price for gaining trust is higher and must be paid by offering concessions and advantages, despite the goals and purposes of internal law: that self-doubting attitude has been somewhat internalized by Latin Americans to the point that many believe that foreign law is, in fact, some sort of super law that performs the functions that it is supposed to carry out very well. In those fabled institutions of the 'First World', the law is applied impartially and rigorously by serious and unpolluted 'law enforcement' agents: the difference from institutions at home is so stark that it is not only quantitative but almost qualitative. In real rule-of-law countries no impunity seems to exist. The immigrants know it: speed limits do function in the United States, but not in Colombia. What they do not know is that the forcefulness of the law is related to their social, political, and legal position, not by a miraculous eye of God that actually catches every single violation of the law in the United States, but not in Latin America. If they were respected citizens, in fact, they would find a milder, more negotiable law, a more flexible and docile instrument, not the peremptory rules that they take to be the staple of truly functioning legal systems. With more rights, in fact, they would find that the rule of law would be somewhat murkier, more amenable to their own capacity to negotiate it and change it, just as it happens, well, at home! Could it be, paradoxically, that contrary to standard accounts the legal systems in Latin America and the Caribbean are reasonably functional, or at least as generally functional as those of the 'First World'? This could be

[33] 'La gente cree que en África está todo permitido', *El País*, Madrid, 31 October 2007, www.elpais.com/articulo/internacional/gente/cree/Africa/todo/permitido/elpepiint/20071031elpepiint_2/Tes
[34] 'El Guantánamo de Yamena, la mejor opción posible', *El País*, Madrid, 4 November 2007, www.elpais.com/articulo/internacional/Guantanamo/Yamena/mejor/opcion/posible/elpepuint/20071104elpepiint_5/Tes

investigated by comparatists only if they shed the inbred prejudices that still lurk in their maps. I would say that Latin American legal culture precisely demands this!

Further reading

Some new theories on Latin America and its place in comparative law

D. Bonilla (ed.), *Teoría del Derecho y Trasplantes Jurídicos* (Bogotá: Universidad de los Andes/Siglo del Hombre Editores, 2009)

J. Esquirol, 'Alejandro Álvarez's Latin American Law: A Question of Identity', (2006) 19 *Leiden Journal of International Law* 931

'At the Head of the Legal Family: René David', in A. Riles (ed.), *Re-thinking the Masters of Comparative Law* (Oxford and Portland: Hart, 2001), 212

'Continuing Fictions of Latin American Law', (2003) 55 *Florida Law Review* 31

'The Failed Law of Latin America', (2008) 56 *American Journal of Comparative Law* 75

'The Fictions of Latin American Law', 1997 *Utah Law Review* 425

'Where Is Latin America Headed? A Critique of the Sociolegal Approach to Latin America', (2003) 9 *Beyond Law* 115

'Writing the Law of Latin America', (2009) 40 *George Washington International Law Review* 693

D. López-Medina, *Teoría impura del derecho: la transformación de la conciencia jurídica latinoamericana* (Bogotá: Legis, 2004) (Translation of a Ph.D. dissertation under the title 'Comparative Jurisprudence: Reception and Misreading of Transnational Legal Theory in Latin America', Harvard Law School, 2001 – on file with the author)

U. Mattei and L. Nader, *Plunder: When the Rule of Law is Illegal* (Oxford: Wiley-Blackwell, 2008)

P. G. Monateri, 'Black Gaius: A Quest for the Multicultural Origins of the "Western Legal Tradition"', (2000) 51 *Hastings Law Journal* 479

D. Rodrik, *One Economics, Many Recipes: Globalization, Institutions, and Economic Growth* (Princeton University Press, 2007)

T. Ruskola, 'Legal Orientalism', (2002) 101 *Michigan Law Review* 179

General introductions to the law in Latin America

J. Kleinheisterkamp, 'Development of Comparative Law in Latin America', in M. Reimann and R. Zimmermann (eds.), *The Oxford Handbook of Comparative Law* (Oxford University Press, 2006), 261

M. C. Mirow, *Latin American Law: A History of Private Law and Institutions in Spanish America* (Austin: University of Texas Press, 2004)

R. D. Rabinovich-Berkman, *Principios generales del derecho latinoamericano* (Buenos Aires: Astrea, 2006)

Legal transplants, normative cascades, and circulation of models

I. Flores, 'El lecho de Procrustes: Hacia una jurisprudencia comparada e integrada', (2008) 60 *Boletín Comparado de Derecho Comparado* 273

A. Guzmán Brito, *La codificación civil en Iberoamérica. Siglos XIX y XX* (Santiago: Editorial Jurídica de Chile, 2000)

L. Hammergren, *Envisioning Reform: Improving Judicial Performance in Latin America* (Pittsburgh: Penn State University, 2007)

D. Kennedy, 'Three Globalizations of Law and Legal Thought (1850–2000)', in D. Trubek and A. Santos (eds.), *The New Law and Economic Development: A Critical Appraisal* (Cambridge University Press, 2006)

M. Lánger, 'Revolution in Latin American Criminal Procedure: Diffusion of Legal Ideas from the Periphery', (2007) 55 *American Journal of Comparative Law* 617

D. López-Medina, *El derecho de los jueces en América Latina: historia, usos y técnicas* (San Salvador: USAID, 2011)

M. Mirow, 'Marbury in Mexico: Judicial Review's Precocious Southern Migration', (2007) 35 *Hastings Constitutional Law Quarterly* 41

J. Nolan, Jr, *Legal Accents, Legal Borrowings: The International Problem-Solving Court Movement* (Princeton University Press, 2009)

Á. Oquendo, 'The Solitude of Latin America: The Struggle for Rights South of the Border', (2008) 43 *Texas International Law Journal* 185

'Upping the Ante: Collective Litigation in Latin America', (2009) 47 *Columbia Journal of Transnational Law* 248

M. A. Orenstein, *Privatizing Pensions: The Transnational Campaign for Social Security Reform* (Princeton University Press, 2008)

Á. Santos, 'Three Transnational Discourses of Labor Law in Domestic Reforms', (2010) 32 *University of Pennsylvania Journal of International Law* 123

S. Zamora, 'The Americanization of Mexican Law: Non-trade Issues in the North American Free Trade Agreement', (1993) 24 *Law and Politics in International Business* 391

17 Mixed legal systems

Vernon Valentine Palmer

17.1 Introduction

The notion of mixed legal systems is essentially a modern idea that increasingly shapes discussions about the nature of the world's legal systems. A mere fifty years ago, mixed systems were treated as legal aberrations and were scarcely discussed. The focus was on a coherent ordering of *les grands systèmes*, and no space was found in taxonomies for composites and hybrids. Under the influence of 'mixed jurisdiction' studies and legal pluralism, however, there is growing awareness that mixed systems, whether restrictively or expansively defined, are a widespread and recurrent reality. They have recurred too often and have endured too long to be regarded as accidents and anomalies. A recent study[1] maintains that ninety-one legal systems may be categorized as 'civil law', and forty-two are 'common law'. However a higher number – ninety-four – are listed as 'mixed' systems. The study arranged these mixtures into ten subcategories, under such rubrics as 'Common law and Muslim law', 'Civil law and customary law', 'Muslim law and customary law', and 'Common law and civil law'. It is thus apparent that all the traditions discussed in the earlier chapters of this *Companion* – the Western, East Asian, Jewish, Islamic and sub-Saharan – have provided the legal material from which this vast array of hybrids was created.[2] (See the appendix to this chapter for the legal systems listed.)

An important difference of opinion, however, exists over the proper meaning and constituent elements of a mixed system. Scholars in the 'mixed jurisdiction' tradition, who follow the footsteps of early British comparatists (see section 17.2 below), tend to restrict its scope to a single kind of hybrid where the most comparative research has been done – mixtures of common

---

[1] N. Mariani and G. Fuentes, *World Legal Systems/Les systèmes juridiques dans le monde* (Montreal: Wilson & Lafleur, 2000).
[2] Ibid.

law and civil law.[3] In that perspective the number of mixed systems in the field shrinks to fewer than twenty around the world.[4] However, many scholars under the influence of legal pluralism (including the comparatists who conducted the Ottawa study just mentioned) use a more expansive, factually oriented definition that enlarges the field and has no obvious limits.

In this chapter we shall be concerned with understanding the origins, implications, and insights of these two theories of mixed systems. Since the idea 'mixed jurisdiction' had historical priority, we may turn to it first.

17.2 The mixed jurisdiction conception – origins

At the turn of the twentieth century many jurists tended to think in bipolar terms: on the one hand the empire of common law and on the other the empire of civil law. At that time, the classical mixed jurisdictions were simply strange and puzzling legal phenomena. They had no name and they belonged nowhere. Within a span of fifty or sixty years, however, a group of British comparatists took a great interest in studying these systems. They were responsible for the discovery and promotion of a new type of legal system. The leading figures were F. P. Walton, R. W. Lee, M. S. Amos, F. H. Lawson, and T. B. Smith.[5] Their special contribution – novel at the time – was to show that these jurisdictions straddled or combined the two worlds and did not exactly adhere to either one or the other. This new idea, says Reid, was 'the product of a failure of classification'.[6]

As early as around 1900, Walton, an Oxford-trained Scotsman who was then dean of the law faculty at McGill in Quebec, began writing of the existence of these hybrids. In his earliest article, Walton compared Quebec to Louisiana and Scotland, and observed that these jurisdictions 'occupy a position midway between the Common law and the Civil law'.[7] He argued

---

[3] T. B. Smith, *International Encyclopedia of Comparative Law, vol. 6, Property and Trust* (Leiden: Brill, 1974); V. V. Palmer, *Mixed Jurisdictions Worldwide: The Third Legal Family*, 2nd edn (Cambridge University Press, 2012).

[4] J. du Plessis, 'Comparative Law and the Study of Mixed Legal Systems', in M. Reimann and R. Zimmermann (eds.), *The Oxford Handbook of Comparative Law* (Oxford University Press, 2006), 477.

[5] K. Reid, 'The Idea of Mixed Legal Systems', (2003) 78 *Tulane Law Review* 5; V. V. Palmer, 'Two Rival Theories of Mixed Legal Systems', (2008) 3 *Journal of Comparative Law* 7.

[6] Reid, 'Idea of Mixed Legal Systems'.

[7] F. P. Walton, 'The Civil Law and the Common Law in Canada', (1899) 11 *Juridical Review* 282.

that Scotland could no longer be considered a civil law country, although it may have once been, for it had accepted (or had been forced to accept) English mercantile law, the doctrine of *stare decisis*, and a mass of English legislation made applicable to Scotland. Quebec seemed to be in much the same position. Its civil code was French law, but it displayed a strong tendency to accept the doctrine of *stare decisis*, its mercantile law and rules of procedure were generally English, and the Quebec courts embodied all the institutional powers of a common law court. These counterthrusts to the codified civil law in Quebec made for 'a peculiar and separate system'.[8]

Robert Warden Lee expanded the investigation well beyond the parameters treated by Walton and was the first to launch the expression 'mixed jurisdictions'. Previously a magistrate in Ceylon, where he acquired a life-long interest in Roman-Dutch law, Lee succeeded Walton in the deanship at McGill. He published in 1915 an article entitled 'The Civil Law and the Common Law – A World Survey'.[9] Here Lee attached a primitive hand-drawn map of the world.[10] Lee's purpose was to give a survey of the points of interaction between the civil and the common law worlds. His map was the first graphic to visualize the *dispersed fields* of this interaction. The legend to the map indicated that the territories marked with horizontal stripes (as opposed to dark areas for common law, and dotted areas for civil law countries) were 'mixed jurisdictions'. These were Quebec, Louisiana, British Guiana, Scotland, South Africa, Egypt-Sudan, Ceylon, and the Philippines. His aim was to assess how the civil law was faring against the 'ceaseless intrusions' of the common law. 'For more than a century past', he wrote, 'the Civil Law has been on the defensive. It is the Common Law that has been the active aggressor. I shall speak principally of the struggle between the two systems in some of the British Colonies. But the same tendencies, I believe, may be detected in other Civil Law jurisdictions, such as the State of Louisiana and the Philippines.'[11] Thus Lee treated the mixed jurisdictions as the battlegrounds and theatres of a far-flung contest. Every example he used seemed to show assimilation, capitulation, or resistance within the mixed jurisdictions.[12] The words 'mixed

---

[8] F. P. Walton, 'The Legal System of Quebec', (1913) 13 *Colorado Law Review* 223–5.

[9] R. Warden Lee, 'The Civil Law and the Common Law – A World Survey', (1915) 14 *Michigan Law Review* 89.

[10] Reid, 'Idea of Mixed Legal Systems'.   [11] R. Warden Lee, 'Civil Law', 94.

[12] Lee employed a wealth of examples from each jurisdiction in a systematic review of five areas of private law (ibid., 94) – persons, property, obligations (contract and delict),

jurisdiction', however, appeared but once in the article, in the legend of his map, and not elsewhere in the text. To this day it is unclear where Lee obtained this peculiar expression or why he was reluctant to use it directly. It has been speculated[13] that the most likely inspiration was provided by the international mixed courts tribunal in Egypt, which was sometimes described as 'the mixed jurisdiction'. Whatever the case, the conception gained a foothold, at least with the British comparatists, and has been kept to this day.

Interestingly, although Egypt is no longer regarded as a 'mixed jurisdiction' in their sense of the term,[14] it was a rendezvous point for the personalities involved in promoting the mixed jurisdictions. Walton left Quebec for Cairo and joined a third English comparatist already there, Sir Maurice Sheldon Amos. Amos was deeply involved in Egypt's complicated French/Islamic/British legal system. Fluent in Arabic and French, he served on the Egyptian Court of Appeal, later became director of the Khedival School of Law (Walton was his successor), and later still became judicial adviser (essentially minister of justice) to the Egyptian government. A close association with Walton bore fruit in a notable book – Amos and Walton's *Introduction to French Law*. In 1936 Amos published an article in the *Harvard Law Review* that surveyed all British possessions in which common law and the civil law were combined. It was again a panoramic account of the mixed jurisdictions, although the term was not used.[15]

These cosmopolitan scholars, their feet at times diversely planted in Montreal, Edinburgh, Cairo, and Colombo, led the pre-campaign for wider recognition of these interesting systems. Another influential figure in the campaign was F. H. Lawson at Oxford. Lawson, who was T. B. Smith's mentor, had a deep knowledge of Scots law and saw value in the study of mixed systems. In his inaugural address in the chair of comparative law at Oxford, he called attention to 'a most interesting group of laws which, because they display the influence of English law on a body of doctrine already profoundly Romanized, stand between the common and the civil

---

successions, and procedure. Egypt is mentioned only once, in passing, and no example is taken from its law.

[13] Palmer, 'Two Rival Theories'.

[14] Due to subsequent legal and political changes. See V. V. Palmer, 'Quebec and Her Sisters in the Third Legal Family', (2009) 54 *McGill Law Journal* 321.

[15] M. S. Amos, 'The Common Law and the Civil Law in the British Commonwealth of Nations', (1936–7) 50 *Harvard Law Review* 273, 1249.

law systems'.[16] He remarked in conclusion, 'I have spoken at length about these hybrid laws because I regard them as peculiarly favourable fields for comparative work in an English university.'[17]

Beginning in the 1960s T. B. Smith wrote a great deal on the subject of mixed jurisdictions,[18] and mounted an extensive international campaign on their behalf. He made extended visits to Louisiana, South Africa, and Quebec, and invited foreign colleagues back to Edinburgh on teaching visits. Smith popularized the term 'mixed jurisdictions' and employed it in the restricted sense of systems in which common law and civil law elements in the private law interacted and vied for supremacy. At first he carefully placed the term in quotation marks, and for literary variation he occasionally substituted the words 'mixed system', but this did not change the countries to which he was referring. In 1963 he introduced the term into the title of an essay for the first time and in the essay he ventured a fairly weak definition. He deemed a mixed jurisdiction to be 'basically a civilian system that had been under pressure from the Anglo-American common law and has in part been overlaid by that rival system of jurisprudence'.[19]

Within a few years scholars from Quebec, Louisiana, and Scotland followed his lead and adopted this definition. It became part of the basic grammar of comparative law when Smith published his entry 'Mixed jurisdictions' in the *International Encyclopedia of Comparative Law*.[20] Here he declared,

The 'mixed' or 'hybrid' jurisdictions with which this subchapter is concerned are those in which CIVIL LAW and COMMON LAW doctrines have been received and indeed contend for supremacy. Other hybrid systems where, for example, customary law or religious law coexists with western type law are not considered.

Smith had in mind certain practical aims, and he conducted cross-comparative studies of the mixed jurisdictions in order to strengthen and preserve their civilian character. He noted that 'lawyers in these systems have hitherto tended to work in isolation, and to forget that "neighbours in

---

[16] F. H. Lawson, 'The Field of Comparative Law', (1949) 61 *Juridical Review* 16, 26.
[17] Ibid., 29.
[18] See, e.g., T. B. Smith, *Studies Critical and Comparative* (Edinburgh: W. Green & Son, 1962).
[19] T. B. Smith, 'The Preservation of the Civilian Tradition in "Mixed Jurisdictions"', in A. N. Yiannopoulos (ed.), *Civil Law in the Modern World* (Baton Rouge: Louisiana State University Press, 1965), 4.
[20] Smith, *Property and Trust*.

law" are not necessarily those closest geographically'. He conceived of a boundless neighbourhood with shared characteristics based on common problems, methods, sources, and similar histories.

Later research has confirmed his view that there is an identity or inner relationship to the cluster of 'common law/civil law' systems. In what has been called a 'novel epistemic move',[21] Palmer refers to them as a 'third legal family'.[22] 'Family', of course, is not used in the biological sense, nor does a 'third' family imply that there are no others beyond. It is rather to indicate for didactic purposes that the classical mixed systems have impressive unity despite the indisputable diversity of peoples, cultures, languages, climates, religions, economies, and indigenous laws existing among them. Indeed, it is the background presence of these highly diverse settings which makes legal unity all the more remarkable and impressive.[23] Their entire historical evolution displays the same broad tendencies. At first (Israel being an exception) a civil law shaped by the reception of Roman and canon laws was implanted. A tide of common law influence later ensued, and a neo-civilian reaction to that influence occurred in the twentieth century. As we study their infrastructure we see the reasons for similar problems and patterns of development. (1) In all these systems civil law rules and principles are filtered through Anglo-American institutions. The civilian substance of the law is thus often insensibly modified by judges who are more than neutral conduits. (2) Judicial decisions are given strong precedential value whether the civil law is codified or not. In three systems, court decisions are accepted as an official source of law second only to legislation. (3) Civil procedure is adversarial and Anglo-American. The common law emphasis on remedies leaves a visible imprint on substantive civil law. (4) Common law makes incursions into the civil law sphere follow typical paths and patterns, penetrating the most porous points of entry, such as the law of delict, while leaving resistant institutions such as property law relatively unaffected. (5) Commercial law is transformed and replaced by Anglo-American commercial law, because of pressure to conform to the norms of the dominant economy.

Today, mixed jurisdiction studies are flourishing. Recent years have seen three large-scale historical and comparative works under the editorship of

---

[21] J. Husa, 'Legal Families', in J. Smits (ed.), *Elgar Encyclopedia of Comparative Law* (Cheltenham: Edward Elgar, 2006), 382.
[22] Palmer, *Mixed Jurisdictions Worldwide.*   [23] Ibid.

Reid, Visser, and Zimmermann which explore the connections between South Africa and Scotland.[24] A comparative survey and analysis of seven systems appeared in 2001,[25] and a new international organization to support further research was founded in 2002.[26] The papers of three Worldwide Congresses (New Orleans 2002, Edinburgh 2007, Jerusalem 2011) have added to the growing literature.[27] The first comparison of Louisiana and Scots private law appeared in 2009.[28] As Jacques du Plessis has well said, the movement that was once a one-man band led by T. B. Smith has now become an entire orchestra.

Yet the mixed jurisdictions still represent a circumscribed field designated by a label with a historically acquired meaning. The label resonates with comparative lawyers today (certainly those in the Anglo-American wing), but it has not been well understood by a wider community. Indeed, it has been readily confused with, even partly absorbed by, the wider theory advanced by comparatists, legal anthropologists, and pluralists. To the broader pluralist conception we now turn.

17.3 The pluralist conception

Perhaps a more liberal conception of the mixed legal system necessarily follows from pluralism's broader pursuit of legal phenomena, as when attention is turned not only to customary law, tribal law, and religious law recognized by the state, but also to the unrecognized and unofficial laws which escape state control and constitute the living law.[29] Pluralism's

---

[24] See R. Zimmermann and P. Visser, *Southern Cross* (Oxford: Clarendon, 1996); R. Zimmermann, *History of Private Law in Scotland*, 2 vols. (Oxford University Press, 2000); and R. Zimmermann, P. Visser, and K. Reid (eds.), *Mixed Legal Systems in Comparative Perspective* (Oxford University Press, 2004).

[25] Palmer, *Mixed Jurisdictions Worldwide*.

[26] The World Society of Mixed Jurisdiction Jurists. See website at www.mixedjurisdiction. org.

[27] See 'First Worldwide Congress', (2002) 78 *Tulane Law Review* 1–501. The papers of the Second Worldwide Congress are found online in the Electronic Journal of Comparative Law (2008).

[28] V. V. Palmer and E. Reid (eds.), *Mixed Jurisdictions Compared: Private Law in Louisiana and Scotland* (Edinburgh University Press, 2009).

[29] The distinction for G. J. van Niekerk, 'Legal Pluralism', in J. C. Bekker, C. Rautenbach, and N. M. I. Goolam (eds.), *Introduction to Legal Pluralism in South Africa*, 2nd edn (Durban: LexisNexis South Africa, 2007), 5–14, lies in the difference between 'state' pluralism and 'deep' pluralism.

focus is often on colonial, neo-colonial, and post-colonial societies in Africa and Asia where various personal laws coexist and interact with Western law as continuing effects of legal history.[30] It may be the Hindu, the Muslim, Jewish or African customary laws which govern different communities within the same territory and necessitate the use of inter-personal conflict rules to determine which personal law applies to whom. There are, of course, differences between the notion of 'personal law' and 'private law'.[31] For the purposes of this discussion personal law may be regarded as a subset of private law, a restricted list of topics (perhaps the most culturally significant legal areas) within the larger area of private law.[32] In this sense personal law may signify an ethnic enclave or niche in the midst of official law.[33] Personal law and private law are therefore intertwined, and it is necessary to grasp the cultural connection in order to understand the characteristic structure of the mixed systems.

According to the pluralist conception any interaction of laws of a different type or source – indigenous with exogenous, religious with customary, Western with non-Western – is sufficient to constitute a mixed legal system.[34] This not only transcends the conventional taxonomies of comparative law, but suggests the logical starting point for the reform of those classifications.[35] At bottom all systems may be described as diversified blends with unlimited possible recombinations: chthonic laws, religious laws (Jewish, Hindu, Islamic, or canon law), law merchant, natural law, Roman civil law, common law, and so forth. It is not difficult to discover five or six layers of exogenous elements in any single private law system one cares to examine. Zimmermann has pointed out that

---

[30] M. B. Hooker, *Legal Pluralism: An Introduction to Colonial and Neo-Colonial Laws* (Oxford University Press, 1975).

[31] In some systems the term 'personal law' may not be recognized as such. For example, it was unknown to classical Islamic jurists and did not gain currency until near the turn of the twentieth century. J. Nasir, *The Islamic Law of Personal Status*, 2nd edn (Leiden: Brill, 1990).

[32] For example, the topics of Jewish personal law recognized in India relate only to successions and marriage and divorce, whereas although Hindu personal laws in India have a somewhat broader coverage (successions, marriage and divorce, guardianship, adoption, joint family and partition, and religious institutions) they by no means fill the field of private law. The topics of Muslim personal law in India have similar scope. C. Rautenbach, 'Phenomenon of Personal Laws in India: Some Lessons for South Africa', (2006) 39 *Comparative and International Law Journal of Southern Africa* 244.

[33] See W. Menski, *Comparative Law in a Global Context*, 2nd edn (Cambridge University Press, 2006), 243.

[34] Hooker, *Legal Pluralism.*   [35] Palmer, 'Two Rival Theories'.

All our national private laws in Europe today can be described as mixed legal systems. None of them has remained 'pure' in its development since the Middle Ages. They all constitute a mixture of many different elements: Roman Law, indigenous customary law, canon law, mercantile custom and Natural Law theory, to name the most important ones in the history of the law of obligations.[36]

Of course, ancient systems could hardly have been 'pure' either. Both in its construction and collapse, the Roman empire absorbed the personal laws of foreign peoples under its domination, and Roman law was transformed in the process.[37]

Today mention of mixed systems is increasingly in vogue in European discussions. It is now not uncommon to hear that English common law has become a 'mixed' system[38] and, for that matter, that the European Union is a mixed supranational system.[39] These characterizations suggest that *mixité* is becoming an alternative way of describing the effects of legal harmonization on member states and Europe itself. English law has absorbed close to twenty EC directives affecting the area of traditional private law, and English judges have at times used continental reasoning, including the principles of proportionality and legitimate expectation, the distinction between private law and public law, the use of teleological and purposive reasoning, and the concept of good faith.[40] In that light the

---

[36] R. Zimmermann, *Roman Law, Contemporary Law, European Law* (Oxford University Press, 2001), 159.

[37] V. V. Palmer, 'Mixed Systems . . . and the Myth of Pure Laws', (2007) 67 *Louisiana Law Review* 1205.

[38] See T. H. Bingham, 'There Is a World Elsewhere: The Changing Perspectives of English Law', (1992) 41 *International and Comparative Law Quarterly* 513; J. E. Levitsky, 'The Europeanisation of British Legal Style', (1994) 42 *American Journal of Comparative Law* 347; X. Lewis, 'A Common Law Fortress under Attack: Is English Law Being Europeanized?', (1995) 2 *Columbia Journal of European Law* 1.

[39] Thus H. Kötz, 'The Value of Mixed Jurisdictions', (2003) 78 *Tulane Law Review* 435, 439 ('It may sound a bit premature and starry-eyed, but I will say it nonetheless: let us hope that the gradual establishment of a European law as a mixed jurisdiction will allow us to combine the best of both worlds').

[40] Bingham, 'There is a World Elsewhere', 522–4; J. E. Levitsky, 'The Europeanisation of the British Legal Style', (1994) 42 *American Journal of Comparative Law* 347; D. Nestorovska, 'Influences of Roman Law and Civil Law on the Common Law', (2005) 1 *Hanse Law Review* 79; M. Attew, 'Teleological Interpretation and Land Law', (1995) 58 *Modern Law Review* 696. The incorporation in 2000 of the European Convention on Human Rights, thus effectively providing a written bill of rights for Britain, is another continental influence of major importance. A. W. Brian Simpson, *Human Rights and the End of Empire: Britain and the Genesis of the European Convention* (Oxford University Press, 2001).

common law's *mixité* may refer to transformations at a deeper level and by a process different from what the language of transplants can convincingly describe.

17.4 Intersecting points

The overall effects of the pluralist conception on mixed jurisdiction studies are not entirely clear at this time, but there are important intersecting points.

First, the pluralist approach to hybrids provides an important corrective against selective, perhaps Eurocentric, accounts of comparative law. Although pluralism generally lacks a comparative dimension, it tends to bring forward all the legal elements in a social field, especially elements that might be omitted or downplayed in investigations conducted strictly in terms of common law and civil law interaction. Quebec, for example, has eleven distinct nations of aboriginal peoples within its borders. The laws of these nations have been called Canada's and Quebec's 'third legal tradition'.[41] The vast territory of Nunavik, the homeland of the Inuit, comprises about one-third of Quebec's territory. Yet research and reference to these laws, although they undoubtedly constitute part of the Quebec legal system, are exceedingly rare in the legal literature.[42] The same research gap exists in the other mixed jurisdictions and it may be preventing us from obtaining a holistic understanding of them.

Second, pluralism's focus upon personal laws touches on the *raison d'être* of these hybrids – namely the internal cultural struggle to preserve or maintain personal law. The creation of a mixed system, historically speaking, has often taken place when a people has lost its political sovereignty, yet has somehow preserved the right to continue living in accordance with its personal or private laws. Whether this was originally the Coutume de Paris implanted in Quebec, or the Roman-Dutch law brought with the

---

[41] A. Grenon, L. Bélanger-Hardy (eds.) *Elements of Quebec Civil Law: A Comparison with the Common Law of Canada* (Toronto: Carswell, 2008), 13–14, n. 29.

[42] The exceptions again prove the rule: see A. Lajoie, J. M. Brisson, S. Normand, and A. Bissonnette, *Le statut juridique des peuples autochtones au Quebec et le pluralisme* (Cowansville: Yvon Blais, 1996); H. P. Glenn, *Legal Traditions of the World* (New York: Oxford University Press, 2000); Law Commission of Canada (ed.), *Indigenous Legal Traditions* (Vancouver: University of British Columbia Press, 2007).

settlers to South Africa or the African custom of the indigenous population is only a difference in detail, for in each case the same cultural imperative was in play. The 'struggle' may be better documented in the case of the European settlers, but it lay behind complex pluralism in other parts of the world as well. Rarely has any people willingly given up its own personal law or voluntarily accepted someone else's. In South Africa, when the Cape fell into British hands, the Roman-Dutch law was the personal/private law of the Dutch settlers, and retention was allowed. At the same time and in the same territory African custom was retained as the personal law of various South African peoples. This pattern has replayed many times in history and not, it seems, because an international law norm so required (as has often been supposed),[43] but rather on account of cultural tenacity on the one hand and political calculation on the other. Esmein correctly observed many years ago that the policy of allowing a subjugated people to retain their personal law is often not a matter of choice but a kind of necessity imposed on the conqueror:

> There is in effect a necessity which is imposed on the conqueror, *of allowing their laws to be conquered*, every time that a conquest brings together two races too different in the degree and form of the civilization. This is what is done in our time in great measure by the French in Algeria, by the English and the French in India and in Indo-China.[44]

For similar reasons British policy in southern Africa was 'no more than a frank acceptance of the fact that colonial administrations were in no position to force their subjects to comply with Roman-Dutch law'.[45]

Third, pluralism's message that we live in a predominantly mixed and plural world may change some of the pejorative views and prejudices about mixed jurisdictions. It is now clearly a solecism to speak of them as historical accidents[46] or marginal cases, as 'odd men out' in a binary civil

---

[43] Palmer, *Mixed Jurisdictions Worldwide*.

[44] A. Esmein, *Cours élémentaire d'histoire du droit français* (Sirey: Paris, 1950), 50–1 (emphasis added, author's translation).

[45] T. W. Bennett, 'The Conflict of Laws', in J. C. Bekker, C. Rautenbach, and N. M. I. Goolam (eds.), *Introduction to Legal Pluralism in South Africa*, 2nd edn (Durban: LexisNexis South Africa, 2007), 17.

[46] Glenn compares them to anomalies in the world of science where complex structures may represent 'frozen accidents'. H. P. Glenn, 'Quebec: Mixité and Monism', in E. Örücü, E. Attwooll, and A. S. Coyle (eds.), *Studies in Legal Systems: Mixed and Mixing* (The Hague: Kluwer, 1996), 2, 14.

law/common law world. They can hardly be pariahs and paradigms at the same time. Some future classification scheme should accept their centrality as its point of departure.[47] The thought that 'pure' legal systems are somehow privileged, that some mixtures are superior to others, or that the 'utility' of mixed systems may be judged by the incidental lessons or insights they may have for their parents are also some ideas we may need to discard. It is frequently remarked that mixed jurisdictions such as Scotland and Louisiana are 'laboratories of comparative law' and that others might benefit from studying their experiences or their practices. In reality all systems are laboratories of comparative law and any system's experience could be of some value for others.

Appendix

From N. Mariani and G. Fuentes, *Les systèmes juridiques dans le monde/ World Legal Systems* (Montreal: Wilson & Lafleur, 2000), 16–17.

Mixed legal systems

The term 'mixed', which we have arbitrarily chosen over other terms such as 'hybrid' or 'composite', should not be construed restrictively, as certain authors have done. Thus this category includes political entities where two or more systems apply cumulatively or interactively, but also entities where there is a juxtaposition of systems as a result of more or less clearly defined fields of application.

Mixed systems of civil law and common law
Botswana
Cyprus
Guyana
Louisiana (United States)
Malta

---

[47] Palmer, 'Mixed Systems ...'. Esin Örücü shares the view that all legal systems are overlaps and mixes to varying degrees and thus their mixed nature should be the starting point of comparative classification. E. Örücü, 'Family Trees for Legal Systems: Towards a Contemporary Approach', in M. van Hoecke (ed.), *Epistemology and Methodology of Comparative Law* (Oxford and Portland: Hart, 2004), 363.

Mauritius
Namibia
Philippines
Puerto Rico (unincorporated US territory)
Quebec (Canada)
Saint Lucia
Scotland (United Kingdom)
Seychelles
South Africa
Thailand

Mixed systems of civil law and customary law

Burkina Faso
Burundi
Chad
China
Congo, Democratic Republic of (Congo Kinshasa)
Congo, Republic of (Congo Brazzaville)
Côte d'Ivoire
Equatorial Guinea
Ethiopia
Gabon
Guinea
Guinea Bissau
Japan
Korea, North
Korea, South
Madagascar
Mongolia
Mozambique
Niger
Rwanda
São Tomé & Príncipe
Senegal
Swaziland
Taiwan
Togo

Mixed systems of civil law and Muslim law

Algeria
Comoros
Egypt
Iraq
Kuwait
Lebanon
Libya
Mauritania
Morocco
Syria
Tunisia

Mixed systems of civil law, Muslim law, and customary law

Djibouti
Eritrea
Indonesia

Mixed systems of civil law, common law, and customary law

Cameroon
Lesotho
Sri Lanka
Vanuatu
Zimbabwe

Mixed systems of common law and Muslim law

Bahrain
Bangladesh
Oman
Pakistan
Qatar
Singapore
Sudan
United Arab Emirates

Mixed systems of common law and customary law

Bhutan
Hong Kong (China)

Malawi
Micronesia, Federated States
Myanmar
Nepal
Sierra Leone
Solomon Islands
Tanzania
Uganda
Western Samoa
Zambia

Mixed systems of common law, Muslim law, and customary law
Brunei
Gambia
India
Kenya
Malaysia
Nigeria

Mixed systems of common law, Muslim law, and civil law
Iran
Jordan
Saudi Arabia
Somalia
Yemen

Mixed systems of Talmudic law, civil law, and common law
Israel

Further reading

T. W. Bennett, 'Comparative Law and African Customary Law', in M. Reimann and
    R. Zimmermann (eds.), *Oxford Handbook of Comparative Law* (Oxford
    University Press, 2006), 641
M. Chiba, *Legal Cultures in Human Society* (Tokyo: Shinzansha International, 2002)
J. Griffith, 'What Is Legal Pluralism?', (1986) 24 *Journal of Legal Pluralism and
    Unofficial Law* 1

H. Kotz, 'The Value of Mixed Legal Systems', (2003) 78 *Tulane Law Review* 435

H. MacQueen, 'Looking Forward to a Mixed Future: A Response to Professor Yiannopoulos', (2003) 78 *Tulane Law Review* 411

W. Menski, *Comparative Law in a Global Context*, 2nd edn (Cambridge University Press, 2006)

E. Örücü, 'Family Trees for Legal Systems: Towards a Contemporary Approach', in M. van Hoecke (ed.), *Epistemology and Methodology of Comparative Law* (Oxford and Portland: Hart, 2004), 373

E. Örücü, E. Attwool, and S. Coyle (eds.), *Studies in Legal Systems: Mixed and Mixing* (Kluwer: The Hague, 1996)

V. V. Palmer, *Louisiana: Microcosm of a Mixed Jurisdiction* (Durham, NC: Carolina Academic Press, 1999)

'Mixed Systems . . . and the Myth of Pure Laws', (2007) 67 *Louisiana Law Review* 1205

'Quebec and her Sisters in the Third Legal Family', (2009) 52 *McGill Law Journal* 321

C. Picker, 'International Law's Mixed Heritage: A Common/Civil Law Jurisdiction', (2008) 41 *Vanderbilt Journal of Transnational Law* 1083

C. Rautenback, 'Phenomenon of Personal Laws in India: Some Lessons for South Africa', (2006) 39 *Comparative and International Law Journal of Southern Africa* 244

E. Reid and D. L. Carey Miller, *A Mixed Legal System in Transition: TB Smith and the Progress of Scots Law* (Edinburgh University Press, 2005)

Lord Rodger of Earlsferry, '"Say Not the Struggle Naught Availeth": The Costs and Benefits of Mixed Legal Systems', (2003) 78 *Tulane Law Review* 419

T. B. Smith, 'The Preservation of the Civilian Tradition in "Mixed Jurisdictions"', in A. N. Yiannopoulos (ed.), *Civil Law in the Modern World* (Baton Rouge: Louisiana State University Press, 1965), 4

W. Tetley, 'Nationalism in a Mixed Jurisdiction and the Importance of Language (South Africa, Israel, and Quebec/Canada)', (2003) 78 *Tulane Law Review* 175

R. Zimmermann, D. Visser, and K. Reid (eds.), *Mixed Legal Systems in Comparative Perspective* (Oxford University Press, 2004)

18 Democracy and the Western legal tradition

Mauro Bussani

18.1 Introduction

The availability of democracy is usually presented as a prerequisite for any evaluation, be it political, economic, or legal, of any country, and as an imperative to pursue (with or without Western help) for all societies that do not enjoy it.

Here it cannot be discussed how political scientists define democracy and the bases for those definitions, nor can it be debated whether the 'just' is inherent in notions of democracy.[1] What is evident in the global arena, however, is that besides those who consider the non-democratic societies to be pathological, there are those who view our democracies as local expressions of a particular culture and those who, for given places and ages, discuss the merits of different forms of government, including those of an autocratic or epistocratic nature.[2] Nowadays the latter views recur in particular in and about east Asian and Islamic societies.[3] It is difficult to challenge any of these perspectives without being dogmatic and in a way that respects the cultural differences of the 'others'. Yet one can start by noting two points. First, entrusting power to a wise or an autocratic elite presupposes agreement about the 'wisdom' and the qualities of these elites, which, in turn, requires a

---

[1] A useful synthesis of this wide-ranging debate can be found in the contributions collected in K. Dowding, R. E. Goodin, and C. Pateman (eds.), *Justice and Democracy* (Cambridge University Press, 2004).

[2] See, among others, D. M. Estlund, 'Why Not Epistocracy?', in N. Reshotko (ed.), *Desire, Identity and Existence: Essays in Honor of T. M. Penner* (Kelowna, B.C.: Academic Printing & Publishing, 2003), 53; D. M. Estlund, *Democratic Authority: A Philosophical Framework* (Princeton and Oxford: Princeton University Press, 2008); A. Olbrecht, 'Long Live the Philosopher-King?', (2006) 1 *Rerum Causae* 37; S. S. Wolin, *Democracy Incorporated: Managed Democracy and the Specter of Inverted Totalitarianism* (Princeton and Oxford: Princeton University Press, 2008), 159 ff.; as well as J.-P. Benoit and L. A. Kornhauser, 'Only a Dictatorship is Efficient or Neutral', New York University Law and Economics Working Papers 85 (2006).

[3] For the debate and for further, essential, references, see M. Bussani, *Il Diritto dell'Occidente: Geopolitica delle regole globali* (Turin: Einaudi, 2010), 149 ff., 185 ff.

social body generally sharing homogeneous values. These are requirements that one cannot take for granted for the long term, particularly today, in the majority of known societies. Second, in non-democratic forms of government, there are no guarantees of the rulers' culture and preferences remaining in step with the changing needs of the society. The lack of adaptation to societal needs, on the one hand, does not deter authoritarian shifts aimed at imposing the ruler's views on the social body, and, on the other hand, makes it certain that its inner flexibility and receptiveness to change make democracy preferable 'over time'.[4] This ought to be considered as crucial, and also biologically inevitable, if each generation, and each of us, accepts that it answers to the next and subsequent generations like a tenant to the landlord.

But the above is just a part of the argument, even for our purposes. The desirability of democracy is one thing; its internal structure is another. A fully developed discussion of non-democratic systems, and the Western aspiration to transform them, must take into account the basic elements of our democratic societies, and the very threads from which the fabric of our democracy is woven. Doing so will unveil arguments that go in an opposite direction to that pursued by both the detractors of democracy and those who believe that democracy is an easily exportable commodity. This requires us, however, to draw on the reservoir of knowledge made available by comparative law and to investigate the grounds on which mainstream arguments thrive today. This requirement is critical, even though it is usually met through analyses which are (attractive, but from our perspective) relevant only to a certain extent.

18.2 Law and democracy

Let us start by asking about the foundations, or, better, the prerequisites, which – from a legal point of view – have made it possible to establish and to develop our democracies.

---

[4] See also G. Sartori, *The Theory of Democracy Revisited* (Chatham, NJ: Chatham House Publishers, Inc., 1987), 77 f.; A. Dixit, G. M. Grossman, and F. Gul, 'The Dynamics of Political Compromise', (2000) 108 *Journal of Political Economy* 531. On the temporal dimension of political and cultural preferences, see *e multis* D. Acemoglu and H. A. Robinson, *Economic Origins of Dictatorship and Democracy* (Cambridge and New York: Cambridge University Press, 2006), 23 ff.; M. H. Halperin, J. T. Siegle, and M. M. Weinstein, *The Democracy Advantage* (New York and London: Routledge, 2010), esp. 13 ff.

It would be naive to indulge in the idea that democracy is only located on the level of the (changeable) constitutional forms. Evidence of the limited relevance, within our specific analysis, of any discussion of the centrality of constitutional frameworks, may come straightforwardly from the comparison with Islamic countries – that is, a kind of society criticized by Westerners for their lack of democracy. In the West, as well as in the Islamic world, there is invariably a level of 'constitutional' legality which is higher than the will of each single parliament or government. When these bodies, in Islamic societies as well as in the West, issue any law, they do so in their capacity as organs bound by 'superior' laws, principles, and values, those embedded, respectively, in our constitutions and in the Shari'a. The crucial point is represented by the content and, even more, by the way in which the superior constitutional structure operates, which in the West is the way(s) we know, and 'there' is given by the complex interaction between the Shari'a and the state-posited law, the siyāsa. This is why much more than just their mere existence, or their written provisions, makes our constitutions not just a 'sacred' text, but an instrument for political battles transferred to legal grounds and then disputed or disputable before the (secular) courts.[5]

Going back to our question, an intuitive answer invokes the models for the selection of the rulers. This answer is incontestable, but it is not sufficient in itself: the ways in which rulers are selected are quite variable, and may overlap with those in force in non-democratic societies. This is why one has to turn to more consistent legal foundations. The search for the latter brings to the surface the great principles of equality and of freedom of expression. But in addition to, and earlier than, these principles, history has assigned a prominent role to the (bundle of phenomena which in the long run have produced) free accessibility to, and effective protection of, property rights, which have proved to be a reservoir of duties, of rights, and, especially, of communicative resources. These resources, over time – and with the

---

[5] Further, it is easy to understand the dialectic relationship which exists – in the West as well as in the Islamic countries – between civilization and legal tradition: the 'secular' legal tradition is a fundamental pillar of our civilization, as much as the Koranic tradition is for the Islamic countries. In other words, within both traditions we can observe: (1) a one-to-one correspondence between the values of civilization and the values of the law; (2) the main role in the development of those values played by the jurist – a layman in the West, a religious figure in the Islamic countries – as the maker and the messenger of that complex of rules which make up the historical and current ground of the different societies. See below, subsections 18.3 and 18.4, and A. Quraishi, 'Interpreting the Qur'an and the Constitution: Similarities in the Use of Text, Tradition, and Reason in Islamic and American Jurisprudence', (2006) 28 *Cardozo Law Review* 67 ff.

recurring risks of abuses, at the expense of non-owners or small-owners – have been able to direct to the individual, and then radiate from her, values and claims which ended up shaping the individual's legal subjectivity towards other members of society, as well as towards the public powers themselves. In fact, it is not by chance that the protection of property rights has historically been tied to the idea according to which the rights belong to the individual as such, and not because of her membership of a family, a tribe, or a religious, ethnic, or political group. The recognition that rights and duties belong to the individual is further connected with the principle that responsibility is personal, and not to be ascribed to a group. And the latter principle is mirrored by the acknowledgement of the intangibility of the private sphere of each individual, whose protection, in turn, developed along the lines of that afforded to property rights.[6]

As to the question about the prerequisites of democracy, a second answer is closely linked to the above. Looking at the way in which it is understood in the West, democracy reveals itself as a complex of rights and duties. Legal systems, as implemented by the law-applying institutions, guarantee that these rights and duties are respected on a day-to-day basis, both by individuals and by public institutions. It is the latter guarantee which is a fundamental feature of our democracies. In particular, the very fact that public institutions, too, have become (over time) subject to the control of the law enables the democratic circle to open and close around individual persons. In order to discover, evaluate, and develop their own preferences, and make their own political choices, individuals need the 'communicative' resources which, in our societies, are provided by the common awareness that every person is able effectively to defend his or her rights against anybody.[7]

18.3 Specialism and secularism (popes and kings, millers and fullers)

Another essential clue to the understanding of 'our' democracies is that the Western mindset assigns to justice and the law an autonomous space,

[6] A. Gambaro and R. Sacco, *Sistemi giuridici comparati*, 2nd edn (Turin: Utet, 2002), 58.
[7] J. Habermas, *Zwischen Naturalismus und Religion* (Frankfurt am Main: Suhrkamp, 2005), 30 ff., 47 ff., 327 ff.; A. Sen, *The Argumentative Indian* (London: Penguin, 2005), 12 ff.; K. Dowding, 'Are Democratic and Just Institutions the Same?', in K. Dowding, R. E. Goodin, and C. Pateman (eds.), *Justice and Democracy* (Cambridge University Press, 2004), 25 ff., also for further essential references.

beyond the areas of the purely political, the purely moral, or the purely religious. An autonomy which has over the time shown a parallel dynamism on both sides of the Channel,[8] experiencing cyclical restrictions and erosions, but which has always entrusted history with the role of ridiculing any attempt at its definitive suppression. Justice and law, in turn, are not meant as metaphysical perspectives, or conceptual nomenclatures, written texts, prisons, and taxes, but as widespread mentality, deep-rooted tradition, a daily vision of what legality is, and by whom and in which ways it is to be administered.[9]

This social and cultural framework is another fundamental prerequisite among those with which history entrusted us, for each of our democracies. Unequivocally, from the twelfth century, one can grasp the autonomy[10] of the legal space in a bi-univocal correspondence with the widespread conviction that the administration of the law must be assigned to a class not of theologians or ideologists, but of technocrats – the jurists. These are professionals who carry out their activities on the basis of a specialist knowledge, which is cultivated by the professionals themselves, and perceived by lay persons as independent from the incumbent ruler, be they a politician, a king, or a religious leader. Legal culture's specialism and secularism, acting together as a filter to the will of God and king, have represented the fertile ground able to receive, grow and spread over all our societies, when history has made it possible, the seeds of liberty and of equality – as prerogatives that belong to the individual and not to any other power, and that are best protected not by the sovereign or the Church, but by the law.

---

[8] H. J. Berman, *Law and Revolution: The Formation of Western Legal Tradition* (Cambridge, MA: Harvard University Press, 1983), 273 ff., 434 ff.

[9] 'Individually, almost none of these factors was unique to the West. The combination of them was, however, and this is what gave the West its distinctive quality.' S. P. Huntington, *The Clash of Civilization and the Remaking of the World Order* (New York: Simon & Schuster, 1996), 72. See also U. Mattei, 'Why the Wind Changed: Intellectual Leadership in Western Law', (1994) 42 *American Journal of Comparative Law* 195.

[10] A notion which, clearly, 'does not mean neutrality of the law nor its subtraction from the theater of history: in a very human reality like the legal one neutral areas are indeed, if not unthinkable, at least extremely limited. Autonomy is therefore a relative notion . . . and it means only that the law is not the expression of this or of that regime or of the forces which refer to it.' P. Grossi, *L'ordine giuridico medievale* (Bari and Rome: Laterza, 1995), 51 (author's translation). On the alternating fortunes, and the different configurations, that that autonomy met with over the centuries, see, e.g., Berman, *Law and Revolution*, 49 ff.; R. C. van Caenegem, *An Historical Introduction to Western Constitutional Law* (Cambridge University Press, 1995), 34 ff.

None of the above results would have been possible if the forces which guided the evolutions of our history, including economic history, had not needed the law as we know it, and had not promoted its development.[11] Nor would it have been possible if another motor of our civilization, Western Christianity, had not supported, since the time of Pope Gregory VII[12] (with some lapses to be sure), the evangelic rule which encourages respect towards Caesar.[13] But all these circumstances would not have been sufficient had the legal technocracy not been able to shape claims and duties independently from the crown and the cloth. The legal technocracy acted as an effective 'insulating' device with respect to the pressures of political and religious powers. This contributed to building and spreading that frame of mind, that baggage of cultural reflexes, which over time allowed Magna Carta, the Golden Bull of King Andrew II,[14] King Podiebrad,[15] and, later, the Illuminists, British parliamentarians, Madison and Co. (and all other efforts to minimize the impact on our societies of the arbitrariness of rulers), to make legitimacy prevail over sovereignty of any nature.

Specialism and professionalism are also significant in another way. They have become organizational factors of Western legal systems, which happened from 'the bottom' as well as from 'the top' of our societies. First, because the day-to-day perception of what is technically 'lawful' slowly soaked up the concept of what is abstractly 'just' – as was already the case for the millers of Potsdam and, before, for the artisans of Figeac, the fullers of Ghent and all the other initiators of the proto-union struggles of the

---

[11] For an in-depth analysis of the complex relationship between establishing 'clear and strong' property rights and promoting economic development, see David Kennedy, 'Some Caution about Property Rights as a Recipe for Economic Development', (2010) 1 *Accounting, Economics, and Law* 1, available at www.bepress.com/ael/vol1/iss1/3.

[12] Berman, *Law and Revolution, passim,* esp. 87 ff. (and note 1 p. 574 ff.), 94 ff.; J. Le Goff, *The Birth of Europe,* trans. J. Lloyd (Malden, MA: Blackwell, 2005), 60 f., 67 f.

[13] On the demarcation line between Christianity on the one hand, and Islam and Judaism on the other, to be founded on the incorporation by the former of the differences between 'sacred' and 'secular', see, e.g., J. Neusner and T. Sonn, *Comparing Religions through Law: Judaism and Islam* (London and New York: Routledge, 1999), 2 ff.

[14] For the original text of 1222, and for the revised one, of 1231, see H. Marczali, *Enchiridion Fontium Historiae Hungarorum* (Budapest: Athenaeum, 1901), 104 ff., 134 ff.; see also J. M. Bak, G. Bónis, and J. R. Sweeney (eds.) (with the collaboration of L. S. Domonkos), *Decreta regni mediaevalis Hungariae/The Laws of the Medieval Kingdom of Hungary, Vol. 1 (1000–1301),* 2nd edn (Idyllwild, CA: Charles Schlacks Jr, 1999), 32 ff. and (for the English translation) 95 ff. See also Berman, *Law and Revolution,* 294, 515.

[15] See the visionary, warning and fascinating *Tractatus* (1464), now in J.-P. Faye (ed.), *L'Europe une* (Paris: Gallimard, 1992), 52 f.

1200s and 1300s.[16] Second, because on the one hand, specialized legal knowledge became indispensable for describing the legal system, and, on the other, the very functioning of the legal system depended on the work and the culture of the secular jurists – not of the politicians or the ministers of religion.

This latter perspective also accounts for the variety of institutional structures, categories, and nomenclatures one can find in Western societies themselves. Suffice it to think of the distances between monarchies and republics; between systems which are markedly free-market oriented and those which aim at 'social market' models; between common law countries and those whose tradition is 'romanistic' or 'civilian'. Paradoxically, all these differences are possible precisely because in the Western tradition the autonomy of the legal dimension from fleeting political choices has affirmed itself as a fundamental and widespread value. Thus the law's autonomous evolution has been able to continue irrespective of the similarities and the divergences which history brought to our societies, our political institutions, and our economies.[17]

18.4 Law between 'purity' and totalitarianisms

At the basis of our interpretation of the relationships between democracy and the law there is thus a sort of circularity between individual rights and freedom, secularism and professionalism, and communicative resources and widespread mindsets.

Nobody can fail to acknowledge (as has already been pointed out) that each of the results we are talking about is both the seed and the fruit of a combination of economic, religious, and social factors. Nor can one overlook the fact that the above account fits closely the evolution of private law – which plays the role of effective and authentic connective tissue of the fundamental relationships 'with' goods, and 'between' the individuals.[18] In matters such as administrative or constitutional law the influence of political factors can certainly be much more important. However, it is worth stressing that the law is – everywhere – the social infrastructure of public

---

[16] Le Goff, *Birth of Europe*, 166 ff.
[17] Gambaro and Sacco, *Sistemi giuridici comparati*, 65.
[18] See also (2008) 56 *American Journal of Comparative Law*, Special Symposium Issue, 'Beyond the State: Rethinking Private Law' (N. Jansen and R. Michaels guest eds.).

and private conduits; that in our democracies the law is also the fundamental ground for the exercise of power; and therefore that, in the West, the
ruler in office can be legitimately chosen, and function, only according to
the law. Thus it is this technical and cultural framework that sets the
background for any discussion of the 'political' dimension of the law.

The above also explains how misleading – in our perspective – the positivistic debate (this too, *et pour cause*, an all-Western debate) about the
abstract 'purity' of the law having its own purpose in itself turns out to be.
Purity arguments, on the one hand, deny the obvious – the law is positioned
everywhere in a dynamically working one-to-one relationship with the
civilization to whose shaping it contributes and of which it is an expression.
On the other hand, and consequently, these arguments also prove to be
incapable of realizing how often the law is enmeshed in sets of values,
whose aims are only apparently neutral.[19] These could be 'natural', moral,
or religious values[20] (for the transcendentalism of which the most evident
problem – on top of the fact that these same values can already be expressed
differently when crossing a border – is, even in the West, the rate of sharing
in societies whose members are less and less ready to gather the wide gamut
of their life choices under a compact vision of transcendences[21]). Or they
could be the values which sustain a 'customary' law, whose pace of development allows at best keeping the status quo. This is why those who remind us
that the battle of values in any society is also fought on the field of the law are
not mistaken; nor are they wrong when they insist that legal systems in their

---

[19] Besides the classic reference to H. Kelsen, *Reine Rechtslehre*, 2nd edn (Vienna: Verlag Franz
    Deuticke, 1960), esp. 200 ff., see B. Z. Tamanaha, *Law as a Means to an End: Threat to the
    Rule of Law* (New York: Cambridge University Press, 2006), 5 ff., 61 ff., 75, also for the
    discussion of the stance taken on this point by a large group of protagonists of the political
    and legal debate, ranging from F. Engels to F. Cohen, from O. W. Holmes to R. von Jhering
    (from the English translation of whose *Der Zweck im Recht* (Boston: The Boston Book
    Company, 1913) Tamanaha took the title).

[20] See *e multis* E. J. Weinrib, 'Legal Formalism: On the Immanent Rationality of Law', (1988) 97
    Yale Law Journal 949 (for the taking root of the legal phenomenon in the paradigm of
    the 'classical' natural law); J. Finnis, *Natural Law and Natural Rights* (Oxford: Clarendon,
    1980), 65–103 (the reference to natural law is the one in the Catholic version of Thomas
    Aquinas); M. S. Moore, *Educating Oneself in Public: Critical Essays in Jurisprudence*
    (Oxford University Press, 2000), 295 ff. (the reference is to 'moral realism'); J. Gordley,
    'The State's Private Law and Legal Academia', (2008) 56 *American Journal of Comparative
    Law* 639, esp. 643 f., 647 f. (for the interaction between natural law and legal positivism).

[21] See e.g. C. Schmitt, 'Die Tyrannei der Werte', in *Säkularisation und Utopie. Ebracher
    Studien. Ernst Forsthoff Zum 65. Geburtstag* (Stuttgart: W. Kohlhammer Verlag, 1967
    [1960]), 37 ff.

generality are 'contested sites of meaning, where dominant ideas and values provide the framework for contestation and for advancing alternative understandings and practices'.[22] But what change, across time and places – and it is a critical fact – are the different legal cultures widespread in societies. What changes is the capacity of the jurists, secular or otherwise, to contribute to, or resist, the twists and turns imposed on the rules by those who govern the society. In the West, unlike anywhere else, this capacity was consolidated through the means of a secular technocracy, becoming the main characteristic of the relationships between power and the individual, and constituting a firm support for the role that the law has been able to play so durably in our societies.

Among the many possible examples, there is one which is particularly worth mentioning here. Without the autonomy of the law, as interpreted above, it becomes difficult to explain the resilience of the legal tradition, and of the widespread *mentalité* underpinning it, to the rise of European totalitarian regimes, a resilience which until now has signalled a reliable promise to overcome any autocratic episode: a sort of biotic serum against the totalitarianism[23] which Western law, on its own, of course, lacks the means to prevent, but has so far had the strength to relegate to history quite quickly. It is by these means that we can understand the relative ease with which democracy earned its place in Italy and in Germany after the Second

---

[22] R. Sieder and J. Witchell, 'Advancing Indigenous Claims through the Law: Reflections on the Guatemalan Peace Process', in J. K. Cowan, M.-B. Dembour, and R. A. Wilson (eds.), *Culture and Rights: Anthropological Perspectives* (Cambridge University Press, 2001), 203; and, more generally, J. M. Maravall, 'The Rule of Law as a Political Weapon', in J. M. Maravall and A. Przeworski (eds.), *Democracy and the Rule of Law* (Cambridge University Press, 2003), 261 ff. See also, showing how the statement quoted in the text applies to what happens (and happened) everyday and everywhere, M. J. Horwitz, *Transformation of American Law, 1780–1860* (Cambridge, MA: Harvard University Press, 1979), 1 ff.; L. Friedman, *History of American Law*, 2nd edn (New York: Touchstone, 1985); H. Jacob, 'Introduction', in H. Jacob, E. Blankenburg, H. M. Kritzer, D. M. Provine, and J. Sanders, *Courts, Law and Politics* (New Haven and London: Yale University Press, 1996), 6 ff.; as well as J. Djoli, 'Le constitutionnalisme africain: entre l'officiel et le réel ... et les mythes. Etat de lieux', in C. Kuyu (ed.), *A la recherche du droit africain du XXIe siècle* (Paris: Connaissances et Savoirs, 2005), 175 ff.

[23] As is confirmed, e.g. in eastern Europe, by the reunion of today's law with the Romanistic tradition typical of those systems up to the emergence of the communist regimes (G. Ajani, *Diritto dell'Europa orientale* (Turin: Utet, 1996), 33–162), but also from the substantially untouched force of the German Civil Code, dated 1896, before and after the Nazi period, and that of the Spanish Civil Code, dated 1889, before and after the Franco regime, as well as by the technical continuity between the Italian Civil Code of 1865 and the 'fascist' one of 1942, still in force.

World War. It is for these same reasons that associating, without an analysis such as this one, the Italian or the German experiences[24] and the Iraqi or Afghan course towards democracy appears to be an argument much more inclined to the grotesque, than to any possible opportunism.

Wherever democracy prevailed, it did so after a demanding and costly struggle, whose winners did not simply aim – as too often happens around the world today – to level the legal ground for the adoption of market devices.[25] But this victory could not have been won had the battlefield not been cleared of the political and religious transcendentalism, and had the legal tradition we mentioned, its techno-structure, and its professionals not been available. These winning conditions must be emphasized as the most reliable indicator of what the West is, as compared to what it is not, and as the key difference between those places where democracy could take root within a reasonable time, and those where the road to it risks leading into a cul-de-sac, or to rather long and bumpy detours.

Further reading

F. Ahmed, 'Shari'a, Custom, and Statutory Law: Comparing State Approaches to Islamic Jurisprudence, Tribal Autonomy, and Legal Development in Afghanistan and Pakistan', (2007) 7(1) *Global Jurist*

Th. T. Ankersen and Th. Ruppero, 'Tierra y Libertad: The Social Function Doctrine and Land Reform in Latin America', (2006) 19 *Tulane Environmental Law Journal 69*

T. Awaji, 'Les japonais et le droit', in Société de Législation Comparée (ed.), *Etudes de droit japonais* (Paris: Société de législation comparée, 1989), 9

Z. Barany and R. G. Moser (eds.), *Is Democracy Exportable?* (Cambridge University Press, 2009)

D. A. Bell, *East meets West: Human Rights and Democracy in East Asia* (Princeton University Press, 2000)

A. Bellenger, 'La conscience du droit chez les Japonais' (1993) 45 *Revue internationale de droit comparé* 660

P. N. Bhagwati, 'Religion and Secularism under the Indian Constitution', in R. D. Baird (ed.), *Religion and Law in Independent India*, 2nd edn (New Delhi: Manohar, 2005)

[24] E.g., C. Gearty, *Can Human Rights Survive? The Hamlyn Lectures 2005* (Cambridge University Press, 2006), 78; but see also (with reference to Germany and Japan) United States Department of State, *The Future of Iraq Project*, 13 vols., 2001–3, National Security Archive Electronic Briefing Book No. 198, www.gwu.edu, *Overview*, 11.

[25] See also M. Bussani, *Il diritto dell'Occidente: Geopolitica delle regole globali* (Turin: Einaudi, 2010), 52 ff., 185 ff., 205 ff.

D. Bodde, 'Authority and Law in Ancient China', (1954) 17 *Journal of American Oriental Society* 54

M. Bussani, *Il Diritto dell'Occidente: Geopolitica delle regole globali* (Turin: Einaudi, 2010)

T.-J. Cheng and D. A. Brown (eds.), *Religious Organizations and Democratization: Case Studies from Contemporary Asia* (Armonk, NY, and London: M. E. Sharpe, 2006)

M. Chiba (ed.), *Asian Indigenous Law in Interaction with Received Law* (London: KPI, 1986)

W. Th. de Bary, 'Some Common Tendencies in Neo-Confucianism', in D. S. Nivison and A. F. Wright (eds.), *Confucianism in Action* (Palo Alto: Stanford University Press, 1959), 25

J. D. M. Derrett, *Religion, Law and State in India* (London: Faber, 1986)

H. de Soto, *The Mystery of Capital. Why Capitalism Triumphs in the West and Fails Everywhere Else* (New York: Basic Books, 2000)

G. P. Fedotov, *The Russian Religious Mind*, 2 vols. (Cambridge, MA: Harvard University Press, 1946–66)

F. Fukuyama, 'Confucianism and Democracy', (1995) 6 *Journal of Democracy* 20

D J. Galligan and M. Kurkchiyan, *Law and Informal Practices: The Post-Communist Experience* (Oxford and New York: Oxford University Press, 2003)

C. Hahm, 'Ritual and Constitutionalism: Disputing the Ruler's Legitimacy in a Confucian Polity', (2009) 57 *American Journal of Comparative law* 135

W. B. Hallaq, *The Origins and Evolutions of Islamic Law* (Cambridge University Press, 2005)

S. Hoch, *Serfdom and Social Control in Russia* (University of Chicago Press, 1986)

G. J. Jacobsohn, *The Wheel of Law: India's Secularism in Comparative Constitutional Context* (Princeton University Press, 2003)

C. Jauffret-Spinosi, 'Le code civil russe et la famille des droits romanistes', (2009) 61 *Revue international de droit comparé* 507

G. C. Kozlowski, 'When the "Way" Becomes the "Law": Modern States and the Transformations of Halakhah and Sharī'a', in W. M. Brinner and S. D. Ricks (eds.), *Studies in Islamic and Judaic Traditions*, vol. 2 (Atlanta: Scholars Press, 1989), 97

T. Kuran, 'The Rule of Law in Islamic Thought and Practice: A Historical Perspective', in J. J. Heckman, R. L. Nelson, and L. Cabatingan (eds.), *Global Perspectives on the Rule of Law* (London and New York: Routledge, 2010), 71

C. Kuyu (ed.), *A la recherche du droit africain du XXIe siècle* (Paris: Connaissances et Savoirs, 2005)

J. P. LeDonne, *Absolutism and Ruling Class: The Formation of the Russian Political Order, 1700–1825* (New York: Oxford University Press, 1991)

E. Le Roy, 'La généralisation de la propriété privée de la terre, une fausse "bonne solution" pour l'Afrique noire', (2006) (H.S.) *Juridicités, Cahiers d'anthropologie du droit* 93

X.-Y. Li-Kotovtchikhine, 'Le pragmatisme juridique dans la Chine post-Mao', (2009) 61 *Revue international de droit comparé* 715

T. Lindsey, 'Indonesia: Devaluing Asian Values Rewriting Rule of Law', in R. Peerenboom (ed.), *Asian Discourses of Rule of Law* (London and New York: Routledge-Curzon, 2004)

V. Lobachev and V. Pravotorov, *A Millennium of Russian Orthodoxy* (Moscow: Novosti Press, 1988)

T. Lubin, D. R. Davis, and J. K. Krishnan (eds.), *Hinduism and Law: An Introduction* (Cambridge University Press, 2010)

T. McDaniel, *Autocracy, Capitalism, and Revolution in Russia* (Berkeley and London: University of California Press, 1988)

W. Menski, *Comparative Law in a Global Context: The Legal Systems of Asia and Africa*, 2nd edn (Cambridge University Press, 2006)

Hindu Law: Beyond Tradition and Modernity (New Delhi: Oxford University Press 2003)

R. Míguez Núñez, 'Las Oscilaciones de la Propiedad Colectiva en las Constituciones Andinas', (2008) 8 (1) *Global Jurist*

M. C. Mirow, 'Origins of the Social Function of Property in Chile', (2011) 80 *Fordham Law Review* 1183

W. J. Mommsen and J. A. de Moor (eds.), *European Expansion and Law: The Encounter of European and Indigenous Law in 19th- and 20th-Century Africa and Asia* (London: Berg, 1992)

R. Peerenboom, *China Modernizes: Threat to the West or Model for the Rest?* (Oxford University Press, 2007)

China's Long March toward the Rule of Law (Cambridge University Press, 2002)

R. Pipes, *Russia under the Old Regime* (Harmondsworth: Penguin, 1977)

U. Procaccia, *Russian Culture, Property Rights and the Market Economy* (Cambridge University Press, 2007)

R. L. Prosterman, 'Land Reform in Latin America: How to Have a Revolution without a Revolution', (1966–7) 42 *Washington Law Review* 189

L. W. Pye, *Asian Power and Politics* (Cambridge, MA: Belknap, 1985)

S. Rajagopalan, 'Secularism in India: Accepted Principle, Contentious Interpretation', in W. Safran (ed.), *The Secular and the Sacred, Nation, Religion and Politics* (London and Portland: Frank Cass, 2003), 241

M. V. Rajeev Gowda and E. Sridharan, 'Parties and the Party System, 1947–2006', in S. Ganguly, L. J. Diamond, and M. F. Plattner (eds.), *The State of India's Democracy* (Baltimore: Johns Hopkins University Press, 2007), 3

L. Rocher, 'Hindu Conceptions of Law', (1978) 29 *Hastings Law Journal* 1283

K. Rokumoto, 'Law and Culture in Transition', (2001) 49 *American Journal of Comparative Law* 545

L. J. Rolfes, Jr, 'The Struggle for Private Land Rights in Russia', (1996) 1 *Economic Reform Today* 10

S. Runciman, *The Orthodox Churches and the Secular State* (Auckland: Oxford University Press, 1971)

J. Sanders, 'Courts and Law in Japan', in H. Jacob, E. Blankenburg, H. M. Kritzer,
    D. M. Provine and J. Sanders (eds.), *Courts, Law and Politics* (New Haven: Yale
    University Press, 1996), 315

A. Sen, *The Argumentative Indian* (Harmondsworth: Penguin, 2005)

T. Shanin, *Russia as a Developing Society*, vol. 1 (London: Macmillan, 1985)

T. Shanin (ed.), *Peasants and Peasant Societies*, 2nd edn (Oxford: Basil Blackwell,
    1987)

A. Walicki, *Legal Philosophies of Russian Liberalism* (Oxford: Clarendon, 1987)

Index

judicial review 153–154, 155
legal profession 216–218
political aspects of legal tradition 271, 272
prosecutor incentives 65
Jewish law
Diaspora 283–287
Hebrew as legal language 102–103
Israeli State 283–287
Judaism and 278–283
and other legal systems 287–291
political aspects 286–287, 288–289
sources 278–283
structure 278–283
survival 291–292
judgments
preclusive effect 226–230
judicial review *see* administrative law
judiciary
'career' and 'recognition' types 64
incentives 64–65
macro level economic analysis 64–65
selection 64–65
selection of judges 215
jurisprudence
connection of comparative law and
philosophy 28

Korea, South *see also* East Asian legal
tradition
Chinese influence 258–259, 266–267
civil procedure 211–212
freedom of information 167
judicial review 153–154, 155
political aspects of legal tradition
269–270

labour law *see* employment law
language *see* legal language
Latin
transition to national languages 91–92
as universal legal language 89–90
Latin American legal tradition
and anthropology 364–365
Brazilian and Hispanic legal dialogue
351–353
civil procedure 211–212
competition law 63
constitutional law and positivist theory
44–45
economic aspects 344–345, 348,
356–359
Inter American Court of Human Rights
350–351

judicial review 153–154
as legal family 359–366
legal language 359–360
as 'legal space' 344–359
legal transplants 354–355, 358, 367
political aspects
British influence 348
comparative law generally 359–366
criminal procedure 358–359
development of legal tradition 354–356
Dutch influence 348
French influence 346–347, 349
Italian influence 345, 353, 361, 364
migration from Latin America 344–345
political convergence 350, 351–353
political mapping 350
US influence 346–347, 356–358
law
definition of 260–262
'Law and Economics' *see* economics
lawmaking
macro level economic analysis 71
law of nations (*ius gentium*) *see* private
international law; public
international law
lawyers *see* legal profession
Lebanon
judicial review 153–154
legal anthropology *see* anthropology
legal education
macro level economic analysis 66
legal families
Africa 313 *see also* Sub-Saharan legal
tradition
civil law *see* civil law
common law *see* common law
economic analysis 71–72
and economic growth, macro level analysis
67–68
groupings 211–212
Latin America 347–348, 359–366 *see also*
Latin American legal tradition
and legal transplants 70
Middle East *see* Islamic law; Jewish law
mixed legal systems 373
Socialist 37
legal history
clash with comparative law 24–25
and comparative law 13–14, 21–22,
22–25, 31
methodology 24
object of 24
pluralism and 374–375